EXECUTIVE POLICYMAKING

EXECUTIVE POLICYMAKING

The Role of the OMB in the Presidency

Edited by
MEENA BOSE
ANDREW RUDALEVIGE

BROOKINGS INSTITUTION PRESS
Washington, D.C.

Copyright © 2020
THE BROOKINGS INSTITUTION
1775 Massachusetts Avenue, N.W.
Washington, D.C. 20036
www.brookings.edu

All rights reserved. No part of this publication may be reproduced or transmitted in any form or by any means without permission in writing from the Brookings Institution Press.

The Brookings Institution is a private nonprofit organization devoted to research, education, and publication on important issues of domestic and foreign policy. Its principal purpose is to bring the highest quality independent research and analysis to bear on current and emerging policy problems. Interpretations or conclusions in Brookings publications should be understood to be solely those of the authors.

Library of Congress Control Number: 2020943087
ISBN 9780815737957 (pbk)
ISBN 9780815737964 (ebook)

9 8 7 6 5 4 3 2 1

Typeset in Sabon

Composition by Elliott Beard

Contents

Foreword   vii
THE HONORABLE JACOB J. LEW

Acknowledgments   ix

Introduction   xiii
Challenges and Opportunities for OMB Leadership
in U.S. Policymaking Today
THE HONORABLE JACOB J. LEW

ONE   Understanding OMB's Role in Presidential Policymaking   1
MEENA BOSE

PART I
OMB AND THE BUDGET PROCESS

TWO   OMB, the Presidency, and the Federal Budget   11
JAMES P. PFIFFNER

THREE   The Office of Management and Budget   41
and the Congressional Budget Process
The View from Capitol Hill
MOLLY E. REYNOLDS

FOUR   The President's Budget Powers in the Trump Era   69
ELOISE PASACHOFF

PART II
CENTRAL CLEARANCE

FIVE   OMB's Role Inside the White House   101
MARTHA B. COVEN

SIX	Projects Worth the Price *OMB and the Central Clearance of Legislation and Executive Orders* ANDREW RUDALEVIGE	117
SEVEN	Learning from Failure *A "Failure CV" for the Office of Information and Regulatory Affairs* RACHEL AUGUSTINE POTTER	145

PART III
OMB—MANAGING THE BUREAUCRACY (AND ITSELF)

EIGHT	OMB in Its Management Role *Evidence from Surveys of Federal Executives* DAVID E. LEWIS | MARK D. RICHARDSON | ERIC ROSENTHAL	175
NINE	State of the Agency *Internal Developments at OMB* GEOVETTE E. WASHINGTON | THOMAS E. HITTER	207
TEN	Guarding the Emperor's New Clothes *OMB, the Presidency, and the "Problem" of Neutral Competence in the Era of Trump* MATTHEW J. DICKINSON	233
ELEVEN	Conclusion *OMB and Presidential Transitions: Building a More Effective Government through a Transformed Office of Management and Budget* KRISTINE SIMMONS | PETER KAMOCSAI	265

Appendix BOB/OMB Directors 1921–2020	279
Contributors	281
Index	289

Foreword

The Office of Management and Budget (OMB) is a remarkable institution at the heart of executive branch policymaking. Whether developing the president's budget submission, advocating for administration priorities in budget negotiations, reviewing and analyzing proposed bills and regulations, or overseeing management processes, OMB is integral to the governing of our nation. OMB's cross-cutting responsibilities allow it to exercise outsize influence on the policymaking process, and it plays a key role in budgetary and regulatory decisions stretching across every function of government and sector of the economy, from entitlements and defense programs to education grants, nuclear safety, and automobile emissions.

For all of OMB's influence in shaping and executing policy priorities, it remains an intimate and low-profile institution, especially compared to other, larger Cabinet-level agencies. OMB's workforce is bound together by duty, pride in service, and deep and apolitical expertise. For decades, OMB's ethos of meticulous competence has safeguarded its government-wide reputation for insight and analysis and protected its seat at the table in vital national discussions.

I spent over seven years at OMB, including nearly four years as director under two presidents. In that time, and by engaging with OMB in subsequent roles, I developed a deep respect for the committed civil servants who carry out its mission across administrations, and I take pride in the years I participated in OMB's shaping and executing national priorities. Heavy workloads and tight schedules, coupled with the scope and importance of OMB's work, made for an intense experience, but I treasure my time there as some of the most rewarding years I spent in government. Further, I am grateful I had the opportunity to explore the full breadth of government programs and economic activity throughout our nation, with the support of an incredibly talented team. I often relied on what I learned at OMB in subsequent roles as White House Chief of Staff, Secretary of the Treasury, and Deputy Secretary of State.

OMB is rightly celebrated for the work it does by directing its considerable analytic capacity outward, but this volume represents a chance to reverse that perspective and turn the analytical lens inward. I hope the lessons contained in this volume will inform the next generation of civil servants and policy officials as they improve and continue OMB's essential mission.

—*The Honorable Jacob J. Lew*

Acknowledgments

The origin of this project, centered on the myriad responsibilities of the Office of Management and Budget (OMB) in executive policymaking, was Hofstra University's Conference on the George W. Bush Presidency in March 2015. That conference and the three edited volumes preserving its scholarship[*] inspired participants to wonder whether Hofstra might expand its focus on the presidency to include executive branch institutions. After all, as OMB nears its centenary (the agency was created as the Bureau of the Budget in 1921), we are overdue for an assessment of its evolving role in budget policy, executive branch management, and central clearance for legislative proposals, regulations, and executive orders. How OMB's long history of "neutral competence" survives and thrives in our presently polarized political landscape is of key concern to all who care about the efficient and effective management of our sprawling federal establishment. Which is to say, all of us. A symposium at Hofstra followed in April 2019, bringing together scholars and practitioners for

---

[*]Meena Bose, ed., *The George W. Bush Presidency, Volume I: The Constitution, Politics, and Policymaking* (Hauppauge, NY: Nova Science Publishers, 2016); Meena Bose and Richard Himelfarb, eds., *The George W. Bush Presidency, Volume II: Domestic Policy* (Hauppauge, NY: Nova Science Publishers, 2016); Meena Bose and Paul Fritz, eds., *The George W. Bush Presidency, Volume III: Foreign Policy* (Hauppauge, NY: Nova Science Publishers, 2016).

conversations regarding all of these functions and OMB's broader role in the federal establishment. The relevance of those conversations has only grown since—indeed, today's headlines place budget minutiae, in the form of the apportionment footnotes that governed release of the military aid appropriated for Ukraine in fiscal year 2019, at center stage of only the third presidential impeachment trial in American history.

Our first acknowledgement, then, must be to Hofstra University and its appreciation of the importance of scholarship on the American presidency and policymaking, and specifically, with deepest gratitude, to Hofstra trustee Peter S. Kalikow (class of 1965) for establishing the university's Peter S. Kalikow Chair in Presidential Studies in 2006, the Peter S. Kalikow Center for the Study of the American Presidency in 2007, and the Peter S. Kalikow School of Government, Public Policy and International Affairs in 2015. Mr. Kalikow inspires students and faculty alike with his dedication to advancing scholarly and public understanding of politics, policy, and public service. His continuing encouragement, counsel, and assistance in organizing events are instrumental in developing that understanding.

Many other offices and individuals at Hofstra were also indispensable to making the OMB symposium and this edited volume possible, including (but hardly limited to) the Board of Trustees; Hofstra Cultural Center; Office of University Relations; Hofstra University Museum; Hofstra University Library Special Collections; President Stuart Rabinowitz; Provost Herman A. Berliner; Dean of the Hofstra College of Liberal Arts and Sciences Benjamin Rifkin; the Kalikow Center Faculty Advisory Council; and the Political Science Department. We also thank Elizabeth McCormack, Dean of Academic Affairs at Bowdoin College as well as the college's Faculty Development Committee and Department of Government and Legal Studies, for additional support.

Bridging the worlds of academe and policymaking is no easy task, and the symposium participants—chapter authors and discussants both—illustrate in the pages that follow how constructive conversations that connect the two can be. We are very grateful to the scholars who took the time to expand our knowledge of OMB with new research at Hofstra's 2019 symposium and then revised their analyses for this volume. Thanks as well to the Partnership for Public Service, which adapted and updated portions of their excellent 2016 report *From Decisions to Results* to serve as the conclusion to this volume.

Special thanks go to Jacob "Jack" Lew, the only person to serve as OMB director in two separate administrations. Director Lew not only wrote the foreword to this volume but gave the symposium's keynote address and has allowed us to reproduce it here. His remarks stress the extraordinary career staff that serve OMB—and have done since its inception. Symposium participants bore direct witness to the expertise and professionalism of a small sample of that staff: deep thanks to Kathleen Peroff, Kathy Stack, and Boris Bershteyn for participating as symposium discussants and providing indispensable commentary and guidance on the research presented here.

We also want to thank a group of Budget Bureau and OMB alumni/ae and current staff who took part in a collective interview and whose hundreds of years of collective agency experience were hugely helpful to the authors. These include Barry Clendenin, Phil Dame, Susan Jacobs, Bernie Martin, Larry Matlack, Kathy Peroff, Alan Rhinesmith, Ken Ryder, Kathy Stack, and Mary Cassell. We additionally thank Jeffrey Weinberg from OMB for sharing his expertise and commentary in a roundtable with some of the symposium contributors at the 2019 Annual Meeting of the American Political Science Association and for his strong support of research into OMB over the years.

Finally, we thank Brookings Institution Press, notably Bill Finan for his keen interest in and support of this project from the outset, and Elliott Beard for designing such an engaging and thought-provoking cover. Special thanks also to Kathi Anderson, Fred Dews, Cecilia González, Steven Roman, and Robert Wicks for their painstaking work in producing and publicizing this book.

The absolute dedication of everyone who contributed directly or indirectly to this volume with informed, respectful analysis made this process not just informative but enjoyable: it served as a model for scholarly discourse. That fruitful intellectual collaboration underlies and informs the entire volume.

INTRODUCTION

Challenges and Opportunities for OMB Leadership in U.S. Policymaking Today

THE HONORABLE JACOB J. LEW

This volume will examine many aspects of the Office of Management and Budget's (OMB) broad role, from budget levels to review of regulations and legislation to management processes and statistical approaches. In this introduction, I offer a personal view from the "Gray Building," as the old Eisenhower Executive Office Building is known across Pennsylvania Avenue in the "Red Building"—or the New Executive Office Building—where most OMB career staff spend their days, and, too often, their nights as well. Looking at the audience today, I am pleased to see so many colleagues and friends who served in those two buildings.

OMB is unique in that it touches every function of government and every sector of the economy, which makes it central to the business of running the country. This role is well understood, even feared, in Wash-

---

*A slightly different version of this chapter was delivered as the keynote address to the "Prioritizing Presidential Policies: How Does OMB Influence Executive Policymaking?" Symposium held at the Peter S. Kalikow Center for the Study of the American Presidency, Peter S. Kalikow School of Government, Public Policy and International Affairs, Hofstra University, on April 11, 2019.

ington. Yet outside of government, that role is less familiar than it should be, so I applaud this effort to shed light on an important American institution.

OMB's influence flows from the authority to say yes or no within the executive branch to agency funding requests and proposed regulations, and from representing the president in negotiations with Congress. But this does not explain fully OMB's capacity to shape and execute policy, often at a level of intricate detail. OMB's more expansive role is earned, not delegated, and comes from deep respect for the agency as a source of information, skillful analysis, and insight.

Although housed within the Executive Office of the President, OMB's authoritative role is not shaped by political officials but by an extraordinary team of dedicated and talented career professionals who provide unvarnished analysis to support decisions by presidential appointees. Unlike so many White House offices that see their role as serving the current president, OMB defines itself as serving the presidency as well, which means protecting executive authorities for present and future administrations and making sure policy decisions are executed well.

Modern OMB got off to a rocky start. After the Bureau of the Budget became the Office of Management and Budget in 1970, the Nixon administration overreached, testing the limits of executive authority by refusing to spend appropriated funds. Congress responded by passing the Congressional Budget and Impoundment Control Act of 1974, creating the contemporary budget process and the Congressional Budget Office (CBO) so that, going forward, Congress would have an independent source of expert budget analysis and an ability to counter the singular role of OMB as an authoritative source of budget data and studies.

I will come back to the dangers of executive branch overreach, but by way of introduction I simply want to contrast the difference between the CBO and OMB, because it underscores the essential character of OMB.

While the CBO is exclusively an analytic agency with no policymaking responsibilities, OMB is an analytic agency that also plays a key role making and executing policy. This makes OMB central at every stage of the policy process, but also puts a premium on protecting OMB's reputation as a trusted source of facts and analysis, a reputation that enables OMB to often be the arbiter of fact.

This dual capability is a powerful combination. In the 1980s, as domestic policy advisor to House Speaker Thomas P. O'Neill Jr., I staffed many budget negotiations with OMB directors. I was struck that, in addition to deep familiarity with a broad range of issues, Dave Stockman always had thick binders filled with tabs on every item we would discuss, and as we hit one impasse after another, he would open the book and suggest alternatives to keep the conversation moving until we were able to reach an acceptable compromise. No one else in the room had a similar book with what seemed like infinite options. That book was not just a reference tool; it was a source of real power to shape outcomes.

I did not imagine then that I would be the bearer of those binders not once but as OMB director for two presidents, and that I would rely on many of the same career professionals to drive complex negotiations touching so many aspects of federal policy. Like Stockman, I gained broad familiarity with the many details of federal activities, but my ability to operate effectively was enhanced exponentially by the encyclopedic preparation contained in those notebooks and the many briefings associated with them. Whether health care, defense levels, income transfer, or any other programs, OMB has the ability, with a small footprint in each area, to draw on the agencies and their own expertise to cover the entire terrain of the federal government.

To be effective, OMB directors need the trust of the president. But to add real value for the president, they need to see across the landscape of all federal activities and make trade-offs to achieve the best possible outcomes to advance administration priorities. With expertise and strategic perspective across different policy areas, OMB has the tools to coordinate within the executive branch and work effectively with Congress. And not just at the level of OMB director, but down to program examiners who frequently have a major voice not just on funding decisions but also on questions of program design, implementation, and evaluation.

This is a long way of saying that OMB career staff are key to maintaining OMB's integrity as an analytic agency, and to balancing the dual functions of OMB's mission: policy analysis and policymaking.

The line between career staff and political appointees can be clearly articulated: career staff do the analysis and present options, often with recommendations, and political appointees make final policy decisions. But this line can be harder to discern as one delves into the intricate detail of technical decisions, which often do not rise to political appointees.

As many in this room know well, OMB career staff often hold strong views on the right path forward. But the measure of their impact is not simply whether their preferred position is followed but whether their analytic work informs the final decision. Career staff understand that every administration will have its own policy inclinations; the challenge is to make sure that whatever the political leanings of "policy officials," as political appointees are fondly called by the career staff, decisions are informed by the facts and the best analysis possible.

For policy officials, the challenge is to develop relationships of trust and respect with a career staff who only a day before may have worked for a political team with very different policy views. That comes more easily to some than others, but ultimately evolves out of necessity, and to be effective, the sooner that happens the better.

OMB directors give straightforward guidance on funding levels during annual budget reviews that walk agency by agency, and often line by line, through the details of the president's annual budget. My practice at the end was to do a final pass, asking, "What should I know now that we did not cover, so I will not be surprised later?"

But each day, examiners, branch chiefs, and deputy associate directors—all career staff—take actions on a myriad of issues, ranging from apportioning appropriated funds to approving how many staff positions can be filled at agencies, and providing a green or red light to proposed rules. No OMB director can pass judgment on each item. Program associate directors, the senior political appointees who sit between the career staff and the OMB director, oversee this process, and even they do not review each of the thousands of matters that come through OMB for approval.

In my experience, OMB staff work very hard to carry out policy guidance. Branch chiefs and deputy associate directors train every new analyst to understand how important it is for policy officials to provide policy direction, even if general guidance sometimes needs to be interpreted. Of course, budget examiners sometimes make choices that policy officials disagree with and occasionally actions are reversed, but these are unusual exceptions, and even more rarely are they willful.

Every OMB director has his or her own style. I know that, for better or worse, I had the reputation of wanting a great deal of detail, though I tried very hard not to micro-manage. For me, working directly with the full team was the best preparation for meetings and negotiations, where I would have the distinct advantage of more and better information. And nothing reflects serious consideration of staff work better than questions that show you absorbed a memo or a presentation and are probing to understand it fully. This Socratic process might lead to a simple decision to approve a staff recommendation, but also may reveal ambiguity or a need for further analysis. Even when a director manages at a higher level of detail, as some do, and more through senior and middle level staff, policymakers still need to receive the best possible information and analysis, and to provide at least outlines of guidance.

During my first tour, OMB had roughly 500 people, and there are fewer today. Whether 450 or 500, OMB punches above its weight, and as its numbers shrink, the responsibilities are only growing. When Congress looks to delegate assignments requiring analytic rigor and sound execution, it frequently turns to OMB, but rarely with additional resources, further stretching the institution and its career staff.

It is important to also recognize what OMB is not. Unlike many countries where revenue and spending both are in the Finance Ministry, since the Bureau of the Budget was moved from Treasury to the White House in 1939, we have divided these responsibilities. From the perspective of leading both institutions and knowing the workloads, the decision to separate the functions in our system is wise, but it creates a need for coordination.

Fiscal projections and fiscal policy require spending and revenue to come together in a single budget. And the scope of negotiations with Congress often entails trade-offs between tax and spending policy. Unlike Congress, where coordination can be challenging because of jurisdictional lines between independent committee chairs, all executive branch departments report to the same president, and typically negotiating teams are overseen by the White House chief of staff and include senior assistants to the president like the head of the National Economic Council. Some White House chiefs of staff, like Leon Panetta and myself, who were former OMB directors will engage in great detail. Others will play more of an oversight role. But in negotiations, OMB leadership typically keeps track of all the moving pieces and helps the president and chief of staff make the hardest trade-offs across policy areas.

In major budget negotiations in the 1980s, 1990s, and since, OMB, Treasury, and the White House were joined at the hip. This led to historic agreements like the Andrews Air Force Base negotiations in 1990 that produced the Budget Enforcement Act and the Balanced Budget Agreement in 1997. And sometimes success was to avoid disaster, like in 2012 when we were hours or days away from default.

I am particularly proud that many negotiations improved our fiscal position while protecting or expanding critical programs ranging from health care coverage to the Earned Income Tax Credit and ensuring sufficient room in annual appropriations for urgent priorities like education, research, and infrastructure. And even when negotiations fail to produce major positive outcomes, like 2012, which produced the Budget Control Act but not a grand bargain, OMB was still able to drive policy discussions to produce a menu of deficit reduction options capable of winning bipartisan support. Those options became building blocks in later years to avoid damaging cuts through sequestration—the actual product of the 2012 agreement to avoid default.

Administrations and congressional negotiators rarely get everything they want in a budget negotiation. The Reagan budget deals had more health care savings than congressional Democrats wanted, but also included White House concessions to expand Medicaid and the earned income tax credit (EITC). The Balanced Budget Act of 1997 cut the capital gains tax, a priority for Speaker Newt Gingrich, but also created the State Children's Health Insurance Program to extend health coverage to millions of children, a major priority for President Clinton. Each side achieved its highest priorities, and under President Clinton we balanced the budget and ran a surplus not once but three years in a row. Sadly, the idea of such compromise now feels quite distant, and I worry that the very idea seems to have become synonymous with being compromised.

The United States today faces multiple challenges. We are running massive and growing budget deficits during a period of economic growth, and we also face pressing challenges from inadequate infrastructure, a ticking clock on climate change, and income and wealth inequality that is harming our democracy. Solutions will require significant government action and investment, and policies must be workable and sustainable. When there is once again political will to make hard trade-offs, OMB will play a critical role.

There is no urgency to balance the budget immediately as we continue uninterrupted, if modest, growth ten years after the worst recession since the Great Depression. But it is a problem that we seem to have an appetite to spend at a rate between 20 to 23 percent of GDP but only to raise revenue at 16 or 17 percent of GDP. And it is not the moment to plow ahead and add enormous amounts of new debt.

This situation cannot go on forever, and it did not come about by accident. Since the 1980s, relentless attacks on government spending as wasteful have fueled the idea that government spending delivers little value. Ironically, one hears that some Americans do not believe the services they most value, like Social Security and Medicare, are even government spending. And for decades, tax cuts have been used to create fiscal pressure to shrink spending and "starve the beast."

In the current political climate, it is hard to find a strong base of support for a balanced fiscal approach on either side.

Republicans passed a tax cut that added trillions of dollars of deficits, and this was not the first or the second, but the third, time we slashed our revenue base on the false promise that tax cuts would pay big fiscal dividends. The current administration budget plans trillion-dollar annual deficits as far as the eye can see, but is short on long-term investments and would make dangerous cuts to Medicaid, Medicare, and domestic discretionary spending. It would be wrong to cut social programs to pay the bill for the most recent tax cut, and there is a need for new revenues to fill the gap.

It is encouraging that Democratic legislators and candidates are debating aspirational goals to deal with profoundly serious challenges. But some are calling for major new spending without a clear sense of whether it should be paid for, and if so, how. New economic theories will not erase the cost of servicing the debt, or the risk to our financial future if we simply abandon the notion that there is a limit to how much we can borrow and how much money we can print. Even in a low interest rate environment, our growing debt is likely to present challenges. In coming years, foreign demand for Treasuries may soften, particularly as countries like China see current account surpluses turn to deficits. And turning more heavily to U.S. domestic markets to finance our debt is likely to drive up borrowing costs. As interest rises as a percentage of our budget, there will be growing pressure to curtail spending, and we know from history that presents a special risk to the social safety net and domestic investments for a better economic future.

For anyone who believes, as I do, that government must address pressing national challenges—including income inequality, aging infrastructure, and climate change—maintaining a stable fiscal foundation should also be a priority. To me, this is the definition of a pragmatic progressive agenda. If we need to debate new revenue proposals to pay for the government we need, we should do so, a view I also held when I was OMB director and we balanced the budget while extending health care coverage to millions of kids and expanding tax credits for people working their way out of poverty.

Political pendulums swing in both directions, and when market or political conditions change, there is likely to be renewed concern about deficits. With a demographic reality that the baby boom is retiring, literally every day, fiscal pressures would be real even without the recent tax cuts, but the pace of the challenge has accelerated. And the prospect for bipartisan cooperation to address that challenge is strained by the recent tax cut. We need to start by filling at least some of the hole it created before we are likely to be able to find compromises to address longer-term trends.

As OMB looks to the future, there is much need for clear-headed analysis that falls squarely in OMB's wheelhouse.

First, we must prioritize investing scarce resources where investments will improve the lives of poor and middle-class Americans, while tackling critical gaps like infrastructure, apprenticeships, child care, and investments in sustainable energy. These policies would help millions achieve or maintain middle-class living standards, while building the physical and human capital we need for the future.

Second, we need to ensure the financial soundness of tremendously successful programs like Social Security, Medicare, and Medicaid. Too many people today worry these programs will not be there when they need them. While I might see more revenues in a solution and others may see more benefit reductions, surely it would be better not to wait for a moment of crisis to act, when it will be too late to avoid much more difficult solutions.

Third, new programs should be paid for, and we need a realistic and honest assessment of how much revenue is required for the government we want and need. There are many ideas about how to raise revenue while addressing income inequality, and my suggestion is to start by looking again at how we tax unearned income and, particularly, appreciated assets. If we are really concerned about income and wealth inequality, how can we allow substantial gains to escape taxation forever as their value steps up when passed from one generation to another without any tax?

We may also need to link new revenues with desired expenditures. For example, investments to repair, build, and reduce the environmental footprint of infrastructure could be funded by a carbon tax, or other measures that encourage more sustainable behavior. A menu of complementary options would help policymakers when they are ready to address these difficult issues.

Finally, policies must be administrable to be effective: technical details can be the difference between a real solution and a measure that wastes time, resources, and political capital—like a tax plan that inadvertently opens new loopholes or fails to produce the intended outcomes. Practical considerations are not a reason to think small, but they remind us to double down and get the details right.

Ultimately, the responsibility of leaders is to budget sustainably for a safer, healthier, and more equitable future, and we should settle for nothing less. I still believe what I said during my first term as OMB director, that budgets are not just books of numbers. They are a tapestry, the fabric, of what we believe. The numbers tell a story that is a self-portrait of who we are as a country.

Some of my reflections may not match the reality of Washington today, but it is critical that we maintain OMB's proud tradition and its careful internal balance as both the leading source of accurate information and analysis and the fulcrum of presidential policymaking. And as we learned from the response to impoundments in the 1970s, we need to be mindful that the price of overreaching in the use of broad executive authority, such as ill-founded emergency designations, can lead to a backlash that could erode the executive flexibility we will need to respond to real emergencies in the future.

OMB is a resilient and adaptable institution with a proud and strong culture. When the political winds blow even slightly toward compromise, I am confident that OMB will be ready to help pave the way for a return to more responsible and sustainable budgeting, and a more secure and prosperous path for the future of our country.

EXECUTIVE POLICYMAKING

ONE

Understanding OMB's Role in Presidential Policymaking

MEENA BOSE

This volume examines key areas of study about the Office of Management and Budget (OMB) and executive policymaking. Since its creation in 1921 as the Bureau of the Budget (BOB) (which was reorganized in 1970 to become OMB), the agency has been instrumental in developing the president's budget, thereby putting executive policy priorities into practice. OMB also is responsible for coordinating and clearing all communications from executive agencies with Congress, including draft legislation as well as executive orders, to ensure consistency with the White House agenda. It is the largest agency within the Executive Office of the President (EOP), and as former OMB Director Jacob J. Lew stated in his highly insightful April 2019 commentary at Hofstra, "OMB is unique in that it touches every function of government and every sector of the economy, which makes it central to the business of running the country."[1]

In the twenty-first century, annual U.S. budgets of more than $4 trillion and deficits nearing (or topping) $1 trillion illustrate OMB's widespread responsibilities. The agency works closely with the White House to determine how to allocate the discretionary spending that comprises about 30 percent of the annual budget (including both defense and nondefense spending). The Congressional Budget Act of 1974 created a roadmap for the White House and OMB, outlining how the budget process should operate. In recent years, though, polarization and party politics in Congress and between Congress and the White House have complicated the process, raising concerns about the government's attentiveness to the country's long-term economic health.[2]

Understanding how OMB operates institutionally and how it influences presidential policymaking is essential for determining how to address these national economic and political concerns. With a staff of just over 500 and an annual budget of about $93 million, OMB shapes the federal government through yearly budget development, central clearance of legislation and executive orders, and regulatory review. In addition to the OMB director, five other top administrators require presidential nomination and Senate confirmation, thereby linking the agency closely to both the executive and legislative branches. The OMB director reports directly to the president, indicating the office's importance for policymaking.[3] As one article notes, "The OMB Director is best known for his role in producing the annual Budget and his role trying to influence appropriations legislation that sets annual spending levels for the Government."[4] The White House works closely with the OMB director and staff to prepare annual budgets that Congress will approve, analyze the fiscal costs of proposed legislation, and determine immediate and long-term national priorities. Examining the evolution of OMB's mandate to meet these responsibilities will demonstrate its strengths and clarify its challenges in continuing to do so in the coming decades.

This volume is organized into three sections. The first section evaluates OMB's role in the federal budget process, examining perspectives from the White House and Capitol Hill, as well as how the budget process exercises control over federal agencies. The second section examines central clearance in OMB, from its role within White House agenda-setting to its review of legislation and executive orders (EO) to its role in regulatory review. The third section analyzes how OMB manages its internal bureaucracy, incorporating perspectives from within the agency as well as scholarly and other external assessments.

OMB AND THE BUDGET PROCESS

While OMB's responsibilities extend well beyond setting fiscal priorities, the agency's leadership in the annual budget process is perhaps its most visible role in policymaking. In chapter 2, Jim Pfiffner traces the evolution of BOB/OMB's central role in budget control and identifies key challenges the office faces today. Since OMB's creation, its influence over the federal budget has been linked to U.S. fiscal flexibility and opportunity. From the 1920s to the 1970s, the annual federal budget focused primarily on discretionary spending, which enabled OMB to work with departments and agencies to establish fiscal priorities and develop a coherent spending program. But since the 1980s, rising deficits, a ballooning national debt and increasing costs for mandatory spending on programs such as Social Security and Medicare have restricted funding opportunities. Increased party polarization has severely impeded bipartisan policymaking. As Pfiffner writes: "OMB could analyze the consequences of large entitlement programs, but could not, by itself, force bi-partisan agreement in Congress on a coherent fiscal policy." Still, Pfiffner finds that OMB's highly knowledgeable career professionals continue to navigate the budget process skillfully, applying their expertise to assist agencies in maintaining fiscal viability for key programs.

Molly Reynolds examines OMB's responsibilities in the annual budget cycle from the congressional perspective in chapter 3. The legislative and executive branches are constitutionally required to work together to enact budget legislation, but the creation of BOB in 1921 and the rise of the modern presidency in the 1930s gave the executive branch a primary role in agenda setting and in shaping legislation. Congress asserted its role in the process in 1974 with the Congressional Budget and Impoundment Control Act, which created standing budget committees in the House and Senate, as well as the Congressional Budget Office (CBO) to conduct research and provide information to both legislative chambers. Reynolds examines four topics: OMB's role in the broader congressional budget process; OMB's involvement in the past three decades in enforcing congressionally-imposed fiscal limitations; congressional efforts to influence OMB operations; and conflicts between Congress and OMB in recent years about the agency's role in providing budgetary information. The chapter concludes: "these partisan dynamics [in recent years] that have shaped the various interactions between the agency and

Congress are unlikely to abate, absent broader change in the American political system."

Executive-legislative budget negotiations determine the national government's policy priorities every year. In chapter 4, Eloise Pasachoff examines three stages of the president's budget process—preparation, execution, and the president's management agenda, which takes place as part of the budget process—discusses how the Trump administration has used these policy levers to advance priorities, and considers possibilities for procedural reforms. The Trump White House has employed or attempted to use several funding tools to control policy choices, from apportionment of appropriated funds to rescission and deferral of funds to transfer or reprogramming of funds. While procedural reforms could be enacted to restrict these actions, Pasachoff concludes: "the only realistic source of regular control over the presidential budget process lies with political actors in Congress, as bolstered by the public and other civic institutions." Instead, Pasachoff argues for increased transparency about executive budgetary actions, so Congress and the public are able to evaluate the consequences of funding decisions.

CENTRAL CLEARANCE

In addition to its foundational role in budgetary politics and policymaking, the OMB guides many other areas of policymaking for the White House as well. Martha Coven, who served in the Obama White House on the Domestic Policy Council and then as OMB Associate Director for Education, Income Maintenance, and Labor, explains how the White House staff and OMB can work together most productively to accomplish the president's policy objectives. Coven discusses how building trust between White House appointees and OMB's career staff takes time, especially at the start of a new administration, but that doing so is essential for "operationalizing the president's agenda throughout an administration." OMB's "problem-solving" expertise applies to budget issues and management, including procurement, information technology, legal issues, and regulatory processes. Coven demonstrates how White House staff and OMB work together to advance policy development through two case studies: the annual preparation of the state of the union address and executive mobilization for crisis response, using the example of natural disaster relief efforts.

Another way in which OMB operationalizes the president's agenda is through its review of legislation, enrolled bills, congressional testimony by executive branch officials, and executive orders. OMB's "central clearance" responsibilities were established when its BOB predecessor agency moved from the Treasury Department to the newly created EOP in 1939. In chapter 6, Andrew Rudalevige examines the evolution of central clearance for legislation and executive orders, finding that it provides a systematic review process to enact the president's policy program. While some appointees may, and will, try to bypass the review process and approach the president directly with policy proposals, Rudalevige shows how central clearance ensures numerous useful checkpoints that are difficult to ignore. As he writes, central clearance "is an early warning system. . . . This informational service helps agencies find out what their peers are up to—and to protect themselves against any self-aggrandizement those peers might attempt. This in turn helps OMB protect the president."

The creation of OMB's Office of Information and Regulatory Affairs (OIRA) in 1980 (replacing an office with comparable responsibilities) extended the agency's central clearance responsibilities to include regulatory review. Rachel Potter, in chapter 7, examines how OIRA has fared since then in reviewing agency rules (and, more recently, guidance documents), evaluating both successes and failures. Among the office's successes are keeping and expanding regulatory review functions, establishing core principles for such review, and managing transparency in its review process with the need to achieve policy goals. Given numerous conflicts about OIRA's jurisdiction over the years, Potter notes that "OIRA's foremost success lies in its very survival." But Potter also identifies weaknesses in OIRA's work, including failures to routinize Regulatory Impact Analyses (RIAs), systematically oversee guidance documents from executive agencies, standardize regulatory lookbacks, and increase staff capacity. Addressing these issues is necessary, Potter concludes, for OIRA to have "a more streamlined and effective regulatory review process, one that instills confidence among both agencies and the public."

OMB—MANAGING THE BUREAUCRACY (AND ITSELF)

As OMB's budgetary and central clearance responsibilities have expanded, so, too, have its management duties for overseeing activities of federal agencies. A comprehensive understanding of OMB's management role requires perspectives from federal executives inside the agency as well as in other agencies that work with OMB. In chapter 8, David E. Lewis, Mark D. Richardson, and Eric Rosenthal examine data from two surveys of federal executives, conducted in 2007 and 2014, to evaluate how OMB works with federal agencies. They find variations in OMB's influence over policymaking, depending on the type of agency. For political actors, OMB exercises strong influence over agency policy decisions, and it is highly important in interagency processes. But independent agencies and agencies that have differing policy views from the White House, or that have reputations for skilled workforces, tend to view OMB as less influential. Consequently, the authors conclude that "presidents would be well advised to take great care to select qualified appointees to run OMB and be attentive to its health and effectiveness." Furthermore, "for independent, highly skilled, and more ideological agencies," presidents should identify "carefully selected appointees to head those agencies rather than relying on centralized control."

A major challenge for OMB senior staff is meeting increasing responsibilities with limited resources. Geovette E. Washington and Thomas E. Hitter examine in chapter 9 how OMB's power and influence have grown even as its size has remained largely constant over the last few decades, and they evaluate the agency's current resources and needs. They find that even though both the White House and Congress have increased their expectations for OMB to work with agencies on internal management, the staffing for both the agency's "B side" (budget) and "M side" (management) "largely reflect[s] what was in place when the agency was originally organized under President Nixon's administration." As other chapters in the volume discuss, OMB oversees the preparation and publication of executive orders and proclamations, coordination and clearance of agency recommendations on legislation, and coordination and review of federal regulations. The authors recommend creation of a senior career-level position in OMB as well as strategic planning of the agency's "role and responsibilities," stating that these changes "will allow the agency to continue to deliver for each of its stakeholders in a way that also supports the health of the organization and those that serve within it."

OMB senior staff present additional important insights about the agency's responsibilities in the policymaking process. In chapter 10, Matthew J. Dickinson builds upon interviews conducted with more than two dozen current and former OMB employees to evaluate how the agency has changed since BOB's reorganization as the OMB in the Nixon administration. In particular, Dickinson examines whether political scientist Hugh Heclo's widely cited concern from the mid-1970s that OMB was experiencing a decline in what he termed "neutral competence" applies today. Dickinson finds that OMB employees are highly committed to providing the White House with professional expertise, regardless of the president's political party. At the same time, the White House expects OMB to assist with development and execution of the president's policy agenda, and that responsibility has implications for the agency's actions as well as for perceptions thereof. As Dickinson writes, after the Nixon administration's reorganization of the OMB, "presidential expectations became greater, time horizons for accomplishing them shorter, the political constraints more daunting, resources increasingly scarce and—not least—the budgetary, regulatory, and management tasks even more complex." Meeting these responsibilities while maintaining "neutral competence" is no easy task.

CONCLUSION

As OMB moves forward in the twenty-first century, certain agency reforms may promote more effective policymaking within the organization as well as in the federal government more broadly. In 2016, the nonprofit, nonpartisan Partnership for Public Service organization prepared a report that examined OMB's areas of responsibilities and recommended measures to improve the agency's effectiveness in achieving results that meet public needs.[5] For this edited volume, in chapter 11, the Partnership presents a special update of recommendations from its 2016 report. Consistent with several of the analyses presented in the volume, the Partnership discusses how changes in OMB's "organizational structure and processes" would improve the agency's ability "to ensure its directives have been adopted and that the priorities and goals outlined in the president's budget have been met." The conclusion also anticipates questions about transitions in a presidential election year, whether from one administration to another or from a first to second term, and explains how OMB can be employed to advance a president's agenda from the outset, working with the Cabinet and other agencies to plan strategically on how to enact top priorities.

As the conceptually coherent and empirically grounded analyses in the forthcoming chapters demonstrate, OMB is well positioned to serve as the engine of the president's policy agenda for many years to come. With additional external resources of funding and staff and internal efforts to strengthen budgetary, regulatory, and management processes, the agency may improve its ability to achieve an administration's priorities as well as its own long-term agency goals. The chapters in this volume demonstrate why those changes are needed in the twenty-first century and how they may be achieved.

Notes

1. Secretary Lew's commentary from April 11, 2019, is reprinted as the Introduction in this volume.

2. Center on Budget and Policy Priorities, "Policy Basics: Introduction to the Federal Budget Process," www.cbpp.org/research/policy-basics-introduction-to-the-federal-budget-process.

3. The White House Transition Project, 1997–2017, Report 2017-22, *The Office of Management and Budget: An Insider's Guide*, www.whitehousetransitionproject.org/wp-content/uploads/2016/10/WHTP2017_22_OMB_an_Insiders_Guide.pdf.

4. Jeffrey A. Weinberg, "The View from the Oval Office: Understanding the Legislative Presidency," *Journal of Legislative Studies* 24, no. 4 (2018), pp. 395–412.

5. Partnership for Public Service, "From Decisions to Results: Building a More Effective Government Through a Transformed Office of Management and Budget," October 2016, pp. 1–42, https://ourpublicservice.org/publications/from-decisions-to-results/.

PART I

OMB AND THE BUDGET PROCESS

TWO

OMB, the Presidency, and the Federal Budget

JAMES P. PFIFFNER

Since the creation of the executive budget in 1921, central control of executive branch spending has been at the core of presidential power, and the budget bureau has been the instrument of that power. From the Bureau of the Budget's (BOB) focus on budget control in its early decades to the economic mobilization for World War II to its response to the 1960s government activism, BOB was at the center of budget control.

After BOB's reincarnation as the Office of Management and Budget (OMB) in 1970, it has played an increasingly important role in defending the president's budget and policy priorities in Congress. Increased partisan polarization and the focus on deficits changed budgetary policymaking from a bottom-up process to top-down control, in which the politics of fiscal policy eclipsed the budget bureau's impact on federal budget outcomes.

For its first fifty years, when most of the federal budget comprised discretionary spending, BOB's influence over the federal budget was at its zenith. But as deficit spending grew out of control and the national debt approached 80 percent of GDP, OMB's impact on budget totals decreased. OMB could analyze the consequences of large entitlement programs but could not, by itself, force bipartisan agreement in Congress on a coherent fiscal policy.

Nevertheless, OMB's career professionals continued to be masters of the details of the programs and agencies of the executive branch. With OMB's political leadership paying more attention to contentious issues affecting fiscal policies, budget examiners have had as much or more influence over executive branch agencies as had those of BOB.

This chapter will present an overview of BOB's first half-century and the establishment of the executive budget; it will then turn to its second half-century, with the transformation from bottom-up budgeting to imperative control from the top, driven by increasing deficits. Finally, it will analyze the trends that have led to an unsustainable fiscal future: the disintegration of the regular budgetary order, continuing resolutions and government shutdowns, and the rise of mandatory spending.

THE FIRST FIFTY YEARS: PRESIDENTIAL CONTROL AND THE BUDGETARY PROCESS

From its humble creation in the Budget and Accounting Act of 1921, BOB grew to become the major staff arm of the presidency, with control over executive branch budgeting. During most of this period, there was a broad political consensus that balancing the federal budget was a priority. The major exception was financing World War II, but President Eisenhower returned to the focus on budget balance. Despite Kennedy and Johnson's Keynesian perspectives, the budget was balanced in fiscal year 1969. Whether it was the tight spending control of the 1920s and 1950s or the more expansive periods of the New Deal or the Great Society, BOB was central to presidential priorities.

1920s: Creating the Executive Budget and Spending Restraint

In the nineteenth century, the executive budget process consisted of a Book of Estimates collected in the Treasury Department and forwarded to Congress with no coordination or prioritization among the separate requests by the president. The lack of coordination was mirrored in Congress, where taxing and spending authority were distributed among a number of committees. The result was increased deficit spending, with the proliferation of rivers and harbors projects (pork barrel), which created stress on the federal budget. In the executive branch, funds were increasingly transferred among different accounts, and agencies often practiced "coercive deficiencies," presenting Congress with *faits accom-*

plis by spending more funds than were appropriated and forcing Congress to pay the bills.[1]

To remedy these problems, Congress passed the Budget and Accounting Act of 1921, which created the Bureau of the Budget in the Treasury Department (as well as the General Accounting Office).[2] The newly created BOB was empowered to "assemble, correlate, revise, reduce, or increase the estimates of the several departments or establishments."[3] Charles Dawes, its first director, promised that BOB would be "nonpartisan, nonpolitical, and impartial."[4] Dawes's immediate successors in the 1920s continued his emphasis on budget control, including imposing budget saving restrictions on BOB itself, down to the allocation of pencils and paper clips.[5] This self-imposed narrow perspective of BOB's role fit with its number of personnel of fewer than thirty, precluding it from taking a more expansive view of its role.[6]

1930–1950: Depression, WWII, and Budget Expansion

During the 1920s, when presidents wanted to constrain agency spending, BOB carried out its duties as an "agent of spending control," and initially President Franklin Roosevelt used BOB for reducing expenditures.[7] But with the deepening of the Great Depression, expenditures had to expand to finance New Deal agencies and their programs. FDR's shift to increased spending so alarmed his fiscally conservative BOB director Lewis Douglas that Douglas resigned in 1934.[8] During FDR's presidency, BOB gained more influence over the executive branch with central legislative clearance, which was expanded from merely budgetary issues to all legislative proposals to determine if they were "in accord with" the president's program.[9] The BOB also acquired apportionment control and was active in broader aspects of administrative management.[10]

The growth of government activities during the New Deal made it obvious that the presidency needed more administrative capacity to coordinate and lead the executive branch. In 1937, the President's Committee on Administrative Management (the Brownlow Committee) recommended the expansion of central executive resources, both personal and institutional. The committee declared, "The president needs help," and argued that the budget bureau was the right staff agency to provide institutional support.

In response to the recommendations of the Committee on Administrative Management, Congress passed the Reorganization Act of 1939, giving the president limited reorganization authority. With this flexibility, Roosevelt issued Executive Order 8248, establishing the Executive Office of the President, and he transferred BOB from Treasury to the new Executive Office of the President (EOP). Directors Harold Smith and James Webb led BOB during the 1940s, the only era of the budget bureau in which the management function was highly valued and powerful.[11] By 1945, BOB comprised 80 percent of total EOP staff.[12]

The impetus provided by the government's response to the Great Depression and World War II greatly expanded the role of BOB and increased its personnel from 156 in 1940 to 567 in 1945.[13] During World War II, BOB was the primary staff support for the president; in addition to its budget portfolio, it focused on the managerial dimensions of the war effort.

1950s and 1960s: Establishing the "Regular Order" of the Budgetary Process

After World War II, President Truman proposed an active policy agenda, and BOB had a monopoly on the data, expertise, and analysis of the operation of the executive branch. With a relatively small White House staff, Truman came to use BOB as a presidential staff agency, a role that would expand in the future.[14] Roosevelt and Truman distinguished between their personal staffs concerned with their partisan interests and the duties of BOB to the institution of the presidency.[15] Truman distinguished his policy needs from BOB's functions; as he said, "Give me your best professional analysis. I'll make the political judgment."[16]

After World War II, President Eisenhower, in contrast to President Truman, did not have an active policy agenda, and subordinated BOB's management functions to budget control. He was determined to use BOB as his instrument of spending control, and BOB delivered. The huge deficits of WWII, amounting to 20 to 30 percent of GDP, were brought down and the budget ran surpluses or small deficits through the 1950s.[17] In this era, the federal budget process became more predictable and the "regular order" of the mid-twentieth-century budgetary process was established.

Aaron Wildavsky characterized the regular budgetary process of the 1950s as "classical budgeting." Budgetary outcomes were marked by incrementalism, with agencies protecting their base budgets and focusing their efforts on the annual increments they hoped to gain from appropriations committees in Congress. Budgeting in this era was an iterative, bottom-up process conducted within an annual budget cycle. The BOB sent out budget guidance in the spring; agencies made their budget requests to departments in the summer, which forwarded them to BOB in the fall, which were then subjected to the director's review (with possible appeals to the president). The BOB then consolidated the president's budget proposal for the following fiscal year and submitted it to Congress early the next year.[18]

This program-driven executive branch budgeting fit well with the congressional budget process, and BOB staff coordinated with appropriations committee staffs on the Hill. The president's budget request was disaggregated and considered by appropriations committees in both Houses, then subjected to conference committee compromises. Richard Fenno, in *The Power of the Purse*, documented the appropriations committees' decisionmaking in the regular order from the late 1940s to the early 1960s, the classical era in the budgetary process.[19] During this era, most of the budget was "controllable" and went through the appropriations committees, and BOB's influence on the overall budget was considerable. Expenditures that were not controlled through appropriations consisted of "borrowing authority" or expenditures from trust funds, such as Social Security. These "entitlements" and "uncontrollables" were called "backdoor spending" and were a relatively minor portion of total spending, but they would overwhelm budget making in the second half of the twentieth century.

Presidents Kennedy and Johnson saw BOB as too hidebound by its traditional role of cutting budgets and did not consider it well suited to their activist policies of the New Frontier and Great Society.[20] They pushed BOB to more effectively support their creative agendas and began to centralize policymaking in the White House staff. This began the transition from bottom-up budgeting to an era of top-down budgeting, beginning as policy centralization in the White House and leading to the decline of the regular budgetary process and the domination of budgeting by deficits. Kennedy and Johnson also began to use Keynesian-inspired fiscal policy more consciously.

Presidents needed BOB because it had a monopoly on the technical information necessary to make informed budgetary decisions. The BOB's influence was based on the budget examiners' intimate familiarity with the programs and agencies they oversaw. The institutional staff of BOB grew from thirty in the 1930s to 156 in 1940; World War II pushed its numbers to 567 in 1945. At this time, BOB constituted 80 percent of the total EOP staff, but in 2019 it was 28 percent.[21] BOB directors became top-level advisors to presidents. As the size of the White House staff grew after 1970 and control of policymaking was centralized, they would be more closely integrated with presidents' political advisers. The role of political appointees became more important, and their numbers grew after the creation of OMB.

THE SECOND FIFTY YEARS: DEFICITS, POLARIZATION, AND BREAKDOWN OF THE REGULAR ORDER

When President Nixon created the Office of Management and Budget in 1970, he intended to make it more responsive to presidential priorities through an overlay of more political appointees. Nixon was successful, and in the 1980s David Stockman took OMB power to a new level by effectively harnessing OMB to implement President Reagan's budget priorities. Presidents George H. W. Bush and Bill Clinton both increased taxes and cut spending, leading to a string of four balanced budgets at the turn of the century. After that, deficit spending spurred by the Great Recession led to deficits of more than $1 trillion and a national debt approaching 80 percent of GDP.

1970s: Creation of OMB and the 1974 Budget Act

As a conservative (for that era) chief executive facing a Democratic Congress, President Nixon wanted tighter control of the executive branch, and he saw the budget bureau as a key to that control. Nixon's approach was to centralize policymaking in the White House at the expense of Cabinet secretaries, and to reorganize the budget bureau. Consequently, on July 1, 1970, Reorganization Plan No. 2 transformed BOB into the Office of Management and Budget. Nixon distinguished policymaking, a White House function, from administration: "The Domestic Council will be primarily concerned with *what* we do; the Office of Management and Budget will be primarily concerned with *how* we do it and *how well* we do it."[22] The reality, however, was that OMB would play an even more important role in presidential policymaking after 1970.

In previous years, the director and deputy directors had always been appointed by the president, though the deputy was most often elevated from the career ranks. To emphasize presidential control of policy, the new OMB director, George Shultz, was given an office in the West Wing of the White House. In addition, political control was pushed deeper into the budget bureau. Whereas in BOB, eight career program division heads reported directly to the director, in OMB the division heads reported to four new, politically appointed program associate directors (PADs).[23]

Members of Congress felt that, under Nixon, OMB was becoming too powerful, particularly because of Nixon's aggressive impoundment of funds.[24] A bipartisan committee report said OMB had become a "super department with enormous authority over all of the activities of the Federal Government. Its Director has become, in effect, a Deputy President who exercises vital Presidential powers."[25] Consequently, in 1974, Congress passed a law requiring the director and deputy director of OMB be confirmed by the Senate.

As part of its reaction to the "imperial presidencies" of Johnson and Nixon, Congress enacted a number of laws to constrain presidential power. The budgetary dimension of this reassertion of congressional prerogatives was the Congressional Budget and Impoundment Control Act of 1974. The act created a new congressional budget process that was intended to return the power of the purse to Congress. Deficits had been increasing, and there was no single place in Congress where the budget as a whole was considered in order to balance spending, taxing, and borrowing.

To remedy the lack of coherence, the 1974 Budget Act created budget committees in both Houses and a new budgetary process that would allow Congress to set national priorities and produce coherent fiscal policies. The new process called for the budget committees to report in the spring a concurrent resolution that would set totals for budget authority, outlays, and revenues, as well as the resulting surplus/deficit. After Congress agreed to these broad outlines, the authorizing and appropriating committees would make specific spending decisions.

Toward the end of the fiscal year (changed from July 1 to October 1), Congress could pass another concurrent resolution. If the aggregate of spending and taxing decisions would result in exceeding the totals in the concurrent resolution, Congress could pass a reconciliation bill that would force specific committees to revise previous decisions to report out totals that would bring them into accord with the concurrent resolution. Although originally intended to be a minor procedure at the end of a fiscal year, reconciliation has come to be used as an enforcement mechanism passed along with concurrent resolutions. When it is paired with an omnibus budget bill, it must be signed by the president and can, thus, be vetoed.

Nixon's aggressive use of executive power, the new budget process, and increasing deficits changed the way OMB was used by presidents. The presence of more political appointees—Carter added two new executive associate directors above the program associate directors—meant that OMB would be more active in pursuing presidential priorities on the Hill. This trend accelerated significantly in the Reagan administration. By the end of the Nixon presidency, OMB was criticized as being too politicized and responsive to the president's partisan and political needs to the neglect of its broader institutional duties.[26]

1980s: President Reagan and David Stockman

The electoral victory of Ronald Reagan gave him the opportunity to make drastic shifts in budget priorities. In the election year of 1980, Congressman David Stockman prepared a "Black Book" of potential budget cuts to agency programs that impressed Reagan so much that he appointed him director of OMB.[27] Stockman, only thirty-five years old, soon became one of the most visible budget directors and the architect of the Reagan administration's budget agenda.

Stockman mastered budget data and the congressional budget process; once he was confirmed, OMB worked overtime to revise completely President Carter's FY1982 budget proposal. Reagan and his top White House staff delegated broad authority to Stockman to make sense of the numbers and enforce their priorities.[28]

Reagan's FY1982 budget made significant cuts in domestic spending, primarily human resources programs, but defense spending was another matter. At the end of his administration, Carter had increased defense spending by 5 percent; not to be outdone, Reagan increased it by another 7 percent in real terms, resulting in the largest peacetime defense appropriations bill ever passed, totaling $199.7 billion. As a result, real growth in defense spending from 1980 to 1986 amounted to 10 percent per year.[29]

Although candidate Reagan and Republicans had long denounced deficit spending and the increasing public debt, President Reagan was willing to drop his aversion to budget deficits in favor of increased defense spending and his tax cut priorities. Reagan had adopted the "supply-side" argument that large tax cuts to those in upper tax brackets would pay for themselves by stimulating increased investment by businesses, which would, in turn, result in greater profits and, thus, tax revenues resulting in a balanced budget by 1984.[30]

Stockman later explained the supply-side approach as a "dangerous experiment of a few supply siders who had gotten the President's good ear."[31] Reagan's arguments for tax cuts and defense increases were bolstered by OMB's "rosy scenario" of unrealistically optimistic projections of economic growth, which Stockman characterized as "our cockeyed economic forecasts."[32]

The failure of the 1981 tax cuts to increase revenues forced Reagan in 1982 to adopt the largest peacetime tax increase in U.S. history.[33] But the tax increases in 1982 and 1983 were not able to replace the revenue lost to defense increases and tax cuts, and the budget deficit reached 5.9 percent of GDP in 1983. The result of Reagan's budget and taxing policies, with their accumulated deficits, was a tripling of the national debt between 1981 and 1989, increasing it from 25 percent to 40 percent of GDP (table 2-1).[34] Scholar Iwan Morgan concluded, "Had Reagan not demonstrated such boldness, determination, and skill in pursuit of his

TABLE 2-1. **Debt Increased from 25 Percent to 40 Percent of GDP in the 1980s**
Budget Deficits and Debt as % GDP

Year	Deficit as % GDP	Debt as % GDP
1980	2.6	25.5
1981	2.5	25.2
1982	3.9	27.9
1983	5.9	32.1
1984	4.7	33.1
1985	5.0	35.3
1986	4.9	38.4
1987	3.1	39.5
1988	3.0	39.8

Source: Congressional Budget Office, *The Budget and Economic Outlook: 2018–2028* (April 2018), Appendix E-1, p. 145.

agenda, the 1980s would not have gone down in history as an era of huge deficits."[35]

The Stockman era at OMB increased the centralization of presidential control of budgeting through top-down imposition of budget cuts in discretionary and mandatory spending. Defense of agency budgets on the Hill had, in the past, been done by agency heads, but Stockman replaced their agency-specific arguments with a top-down imperative that focused on the totals, not the component pieces.

During the 1980s, the shift from bottom-up to top-down budgeting was wrenching for career OMB staff. Barry Anderson, former assistant director for budget review, worked closely with Stockman and imposed the necessary cuts on agencies to meet broad deficit targets. He prided himself on creating "budget gimmicks" in pursuit of presidential goals, and consequently he was effective at thwarting budget gimmicks to maintain or increase spending on agency programs. According to Anderson, resistance to top-down budgeting decreased only as career OMB staff were replaced with new ones.[36]

During the Stockman era, the executive budget process and congressional decisions became more blended and intertwined, in contrast to the previous practice of handing off the president's budget proposal to Congress for its consideration and final decisions. Rapidly changing economic circumstances led to constant revisions in estimates and continual renegotiations with congressional committees. The budget process in Congress changed from a regular, annual process to a continual set of negotiations, with Stockman asking OMB staff "what if" questions and demanding quick turnarounds. The focus of OMB leadership shifted from individual programs and agencies to budget aggregates of total expenditures, deficits, discretionary expenditures, entitlements, tax revenues, etc.

Stockman effectively forced President Reagan's priorities through Congress. From his perspective, Congress was "reduced to the status of a ministerial arm of the White House. . . . The constitutional prerogatives of the legislative branch would have to be, in effect, suspended" to achieve "rubber stamp approval" of Reagan budget priorities.[37]

The Reagan era of the 1980s began the breakdown of the regular budgetary process, with record deficits, the use of accounting gimmicks, continual partisan bickering, and an unwillingness to face the structural problems that produced large deficits. President Reagan's political success in cutting taxes marked the change from traditional Republican fiscal conservatism to uncritically embracing tax cuts regardless of their fiscal consequences. The tax increases in 1982 and 1983 were, thereafter, forgotten as part of the Reagan legacy. Cutting taxes without "paying for them" with corresponding spending cuts were priorities of the George W. Bush and Trump administrations.

The continuation of large deficits during the Reagan administration led Congress to pass the Balanced Budget and Emergency Deficit Control Act of 1985, known as Gramm-Rudman-Hollings (GRH) in 1985 (revised in 1987). The purpose of GRH was to reduce the deficit by specific percentages each year until the deficit was eliminated. If the deficit targets were not met, discretionary spending was to be cut (sequestered) across the board automatically. The fixed deficit targets were unrealistic and were avoided by various gimmicks, for example, using unrealistic economic assumptions and shifting the accounting of spending from one fiscal year to another. When the state of the economy led to lower levels of revenue and, thus, required unacceptable automatic budget cuts, GRH was abandoned and replaced by the pay-as-you-go (PAYGO) procedures of the Budget Enforcement Act of 1990.[38]

1990s: Bush 41, Clinton, and Balanced Budgets

Under Presidents Bush (41) and Clinton, OMB's knowledge of agency programs continued to be crucial at the agency level, and both presidents decreased the number of OMB staff, despite new responsibilities for managerial functions.[39]

President Bush's first budget was based on optimistic economic assumptions and resulted in a projected deficit of more than $400 billion, 4 percent of GDP. As the economy slowed down, it became clear in 1990 that unless serious steps were taken the deficit would balloon unacceptably and a GRH sequester of enormous proportions would be required. OMB Director Richard Darman convinced Bush that, for the good of the country, he had to abandon his campaign promise of "no new taxes" and negotiate a deficit reduction package with Democrats in Congress. The agreement included tax increases, cuts in entitlements, and discretionary spending caps that reduced the deficit by about $500 billion over five years."[40]

The compromise in the fall of 1990 resulted in the Budget Enforcement Act, which repealed GRH and its sequestrations. The constraints in the act were intended to control spending and tax cuts rather than deficits, which were subject to economic fluctuations and emergencies. Spending caps were set on discretionary spending and PAYGO applied to mandatory spending and tax changes. That is, if new legislation increased spending, it had to be offset by decreases elsewhere or revenue had to be increased. Similarly, any tax cuts had to be offset by decreased spending or other revenue increases. The PAYGO requirements lasted until the expiration of the act in 2002. Bush's courageous deficit reduction package, despite denunciations from Republican conservatives, helped make possible the balanced budgets at the end of the 1990s.

Bill Clinton was elected in 1992 after campaigning for increased social spending, but after he was inaugurated, the deficit hawks among his economic advisors convinced him that a continuation of large deficits would hurt the economy and jeopardize the rest of his presidency. They convinced him to recommend tax increases and spending cuts amounting to about $500 billion over several years. Clinton's proposal, the Omnibus Budget and Reconciliation Act (OBRA) of 1993, was passed with no Republican votes and one-vote margins in the House (218 to 216), with Vice President Gore breaking a tie in the Senate.[41]

When Republicans took over Congress in 1995, they resolved to force the large cuts in entitlements and program eliminations they had promised in the "Contract for America."[42] They had decided to spare cuts to Social Security and defense spending, and called for large cuts in Medicare and Medicaid. In October, they passed the largest reconciliation bill passed to that time, including large cuts in health care and welfare programs, and the elimination of many agencies, including several cabinet departments. They also threatened to default on the national debt if Clinton did not go along with their cuts and sign the omnibus reconciliation bill.

Nevertheless, Clinton vetoed a continuing resolution, triggering a six-day shutdown of most of the government, involving 800,000 federal workers. A new continuing resolution was passed, and several appropriations bills were passed and signed. But the continuing resolution ran out on December 15, and 280,000 government workers were furloughed. Finally, presidential candidate Robert Dole announced to Republicans in Congress that "enough is enough" and Congress passed a continuing resolution on January 6 to end a twenty-one-day shutdown. Clinton and the Republicans finally came to agree on a budget that was calculated to eliminate the deficit within seven years. The booming economy of the 1990s and the deficit reduction packages of 1990 and 1993 led to balanced budgets from 1998 to 2001, the longest string of balanced budgets since the 1920s (table 2-2).

Both Bush and Clinton were hurt politically by their deficit reducing measures, but they were acts of political courage that enabled the government to produce balanced budgets at the turn of the century. Ironically, one of the issues in the presidential campaign of 2000 was about how to deal with the budget surpluses.

Bush 43, Obama, and the Great Recession

In what Irene Rubin termed "The Great Unraveling," policy choices in the early twenty-first century turned the four years of surplus from 1998 to 2001 into a pattern of deficit spending, which was greatly exacerbated by the Great Recession of 2008–2010.[43]

Despite winning the 2000 elections with fewer votes than Al Gore, President Bush claimed a mandate and won large tax cuts in 2001 and 2003. When some pointed out the increasing deficits and their danger in 2003, Vice President Cheney asserted that "Reagan proved that deficits don't matter. We won the mid-term elections, this is our due."[44] The reconciliation process, which was originally intended to enforce reductions in spending (and thus the deficit) was used by the Bush administration to force through its tax cuts, thus increasing the deficit.[45] In addition, the new Medicare Part D prescription drug benefits program and the wars in Afghanistan and Iraq added to the increasing deficits. The discipline

TABLE 2-2. **Four Years of Budget Surplus**
Budget Surplus and National Debt as % of GDP

Year	Surplus as % GDP	Debt as % GDP
1998	0.8	41.6
1999	1.3	38.2
2000	2.3	33.6
2001	1.2	31.4

Source: Congressional Budget Office, *The Budget and Economic Outlook: 2018–2028* (April 2018), Appendix E-1, p. 145.

provided by the 1990 Budget Enforcement Act (BEA), with its PAYGO provisions, lapsed after 2002 (table 2-3).

Top-down budgeting continued and was reinforced, with OMB focusing less on the specifics of program budgets and emphasizing budget aggregates, particularly under President Bush.[46] Presidents Clinton and Bush both made cuts in OMB staff, despite its responsibility for the National Performance Review under Clinton and the Program Assessment Rating Tool (PART) under Bush.

At the end of the Bush administration, failures in financial regulation, reckless borrowing and lending by financial institutions, and the subprime loan crisis led to the beginning of the Great Recession in 2008–2009. The Bush administration responded with a range of programs, including the Troubled Assets Relief Program (TARP, for which the Treasury was eventually reimbursed). When Barack Obama came to the presidency in 2009, he convinced Congress to pass the American Recovery and Reinvestment Act (ARRA), a huge stimulus program of tax cuts and spending increases, amounting to $787 billion. The combination of the stimulus package and decreased tax revenue resulted in record-high peacetime deficits of more than $1 trillion from 2009 to 2012 (7 to 10 percent of GDP).[47]

Huge deficits increased the national debt from 35.2 percent of GDP in 2007 to 70.4 percent in 2012. The United States was lucky that interest rates on U.S. borrowing did not increase significantly, because fiscal uncertainty in the rest of the world led investors to see the United States as a safe haven despite its economic and budgetary problems. The Great

TABLE 2-3. **The "Unraveling" of Budget Balance**
Budget Deficits and Debt as % GDP

Year	Deficit as % GDP	Debt as % GDP
2002	1.5	32.6
2003	3.3	34.5
2004	3.4	35.5
2005	2.5	35.6
2006	1.8	35.3
2007	1.1	35.2

Source: Congressional Budget Office, *The Budget and Economic Outlook: 2018–2028* (April 2018), Appendix E-1, p. 145.

Recession reduced federal revenues in FY2009 and FY2010 to 14.6 percent of GDP, as opposed to expenditures of 24.4 percent of GDP.[48]

To address the huge deficits created by the decrease in revenue and stimulus spending to recover from the Great Recession, in 2010 President Obama appointed the National Commission on Fiscal Responsibility and Reform (Simpson-Bowles) to propose a bipartisan compromise deficit reduction package.[49] The committee wrote a report, but too few committee members supported the final proposal of the cochairs, and it was rejected by Congress.

After Simpson-Bowles failed, President Obama made a proposal to House Speaker John Boehner for a $4 trillion deficit-reducing "Grand Bargain," which included cuts in Social Security and Medicare in exchange for tax increases. Obama would probably have been able to win support from congressional Democrats, but the Freedom Caucus of Republican conservatives in the House would not agree to the tax increases, and Boehner abandoned negotiations (table 2-4).

After the failure of Simpson-Bowles and the attempted Grand Bargain, Congress passed the Budget Control Act of 2011 (BCA), which raised the debt ceiling (after a downgrade of U.S. bonds by Standard and Poor from AAA to AA+) and created the Joint Select Committee on Deficit Reduction (Super Committee) to propose a deficit reduction plan.

As an incentive for the bipartisan committee to compromise, the law set up an unacceptable outcome if they failed to come to an agreement. The law provided that OMB had to reduce (sequester) funds annually across the board from discretionary domestic and defense spending. This

TABLE 2-4. **Record Deficits after the Great Recession**
Budget Deficits and Debt as % GDP

Year	Deficit as % GDP	Debt as % GDP
2008	3.1	39.3
2009	9.8	52.3
2010	8.7	60.9
2011	8.5	65.9
2012	6.8	70.4

Source: Congressional Budget Office, *The Budget and Economic Outlook: 2018–2028* (April 2018), Appendix E-1, p. 145.

approach to trimming budgets was considered so extreme in size and so irrational—for example, not choosing priorities—that it would force both sides to make compromises. When the two parties failed to agree, OMB ordered the budget cuts, causing disruptions in executive branch programs and agencies. The threat of sequester, which was designed to be a poison pill, became a reality that pleased no one. In subsequent years, from 2014 to 2019, the impact of sequestration was lessened, though not eliminated, by a series of compromises, totaling $439 billion, that lifted discretionary spending ceilings, somewhat reducing the disruption to programs caused by sequestration.[50]

The disruption to defense spending was considerably reduced by the exclusion of funds for Overseas Contingency Operations (OCO) from the caps on discretionary spending. The use of this type of supplemental appropriations for defense funding had been a common practice, amounting to about 2 percent of defense appropriations annually. But after 9/11, funding for the wars in Iraq and Afghanistan was paid through OCO appropriations, which amounted to 20 percent of Department of Defense (DOD) funding from 2001 to 2018, peaking at 28 percent of DOD budgets in 2007 and 2008. Because OCO funds were exempted from discretionary spending caps, funding for more routine operations could be protected by including them in OCO supplementals, and between 2006 and 2019 more than $50 billion in routine operations annually were included in OCO legislation.[51] From 2001 to 2020, total appropriations for OCO funding approached $2 trillion.[52]

Initial Trump Budgets

After the Budget Control Act of 2011, deficits declined until 2015, after which they began to climb again. During his campaign for the presidency, Donald Trump proclaimed, "We will balance the budget without making cuts in Social Security and Medicare."[53] But his actions belied his words, and even with a strong economy and low unemployment, he advocated a large, pro-cyclical tax cut.

The Republican Tax Cuts and Jobs Act (TCJA) of 2017 (PL 115-97) provided a short-run stimulus but led to significantly reduced projected federal revenues over the longer term.[54] When the huge projected deficits over ten years flowing from the tax cut were pointed out to Trump, he responded, "Yeah, but I won't be here."[55] Despite optimistic assumptions about economic growth and congressional decisions, President Trump's

TABLE 2-5. OMB Projections of Deficits

Year	Deficit $ Trillion	Deficit as % GDP	Debt as % GDP
2019	1.1	5.1	79.5
2020	1.1	4.9	80.7
2021	1.1	4.5	81.6
2022	1.0	4.2	82.1

Source: White House: The President's FY2020 Budget Request (2019), Summary Tables: S-1, p. 107; S-4, p. 110; S-5, p. 112.

FY2020 budget request projected continued deficits of more than $1 trillion (table 2-5). When asked why he did not mention the size of the deficit in his 2019 State of the Union address, his OMB director and acting White House chief of staff Mick Mulvaney replied, "nobody cares" about deficits.[56] In 2020, Trump responded to concerns about the growing national debt: "Who the hell cares about the budget? We're going to have a country."[57]

In 2018, the Congressional Budget Office (CBO) projected that the United States would continue to spend significantly more than the revenues it would bring in and that the national debt would be near 93 percent of GDP by 2029 and 150 percent by 2049.[58] The consensus among CBO, OMB, the Congressional Research Service (CRS), and the Government Accountability Office (GAO) was that current trends in deficit spending and accumulation of the national debt were unsustainable. Health costs were rising and would continue to increase, as would Social Security expenditures due to demographic shifts.[59] Even keeping the debt-to-GDP ratio at its relatively high 2019 level of 77 percent of GDP until 2047 would require cuts in the deficit (that is, tax increases and/or spending cuts) of $380 billion in each year, beginning in 2018. To achieve a debt-to-GDP ratio at the average of the previous fifty years would necessitate net savings of $620 billion annually.[60]

OMB as an Institution

In its most recent fifty years, as OMB leadership increased its influence with presidents, career staffers had less influence on overall administration policy. Nevertheless, they were masters of the details of government operations that often fall below the level of "political interest." Consequently, OMB career staffers continued to wield considerable control over their bailiwicks in the executive branch.[61] For instance, budget issues below the level of political visibility were often left to the discretion of OMB staff, and if there was a need to cut agency budgets, career staffers had significant discretion in how and where to make the cuts.[62]

The institutional staff of OMB peaked at 686 in 1975, and as the White House staff grew in size over subsequent decades, OMB staffing shrank to 480 in 2018 (the White House Office itself comprised 450 personnel).[63] In 2016, there were more than fifty political appointees, seven of them Senate confirmed.[64] Four recent presidents (Clinton, Bush 43, Obama, and Trump) highlighted the importance of OMB directors to their political fortunes by appointing their OMB directors subsequently to be their White House chiefs of staff.[65]

OMB has always had a reputation for how much work it extracts from its staff. The five Resource Management Offices, housing the traditional budget staff, from PADs to budget examiners, had only 235 FTE in 2016.[66] Its workload has only increased, because of the shrinkage of total staff and the functions added to its jurisdiction since 1970: Office of Federal Procurement Policy (OFPP) in 1974; Office of Information and Regulatory Affairs (OIRA) in 1980; Office of Federal Financial Management (OFFM) in 1990; and Office of E-Government & Information Technology and the Intellectual Property Enforcement Coordinator in 2002. Management functions, such as the Program Assessment Rating Tool (PART) of the Bush administration, also consumed much energy, though without significantly affecting budgetary decisions in Congress.[67]

DISINTEGRATION OF THE BUDGETARY PROCESS

Increasing polarization between the political parties has led to the disintegration of the traditional budgetary process. The continuing fissure is that Republicans favor cutting taxes and Democrats resist cuts to domestic programs, especially Social Security and Medicare. Political moderates (and realists) understand that deficits cannot be eliminated and the national debt reduced without some combination of increased taxes and programmatic cuts of these key uncontrollables. This section will explain the factors leading to the implosion of the budgetary process:

the breakdown of the regular order, increasing occurrence of continuing resolutions, and the rise of uncontrollable spending.

Collapse of the Regular Order

Between the 1974 passage of the Congressional Budget Act and 2015, Congress adopted a budget resolution by the mandated date (May 15, changed to April 15 in 1986) only six times.[68] The most recent year in which all appropriations bills were passed before the beginning of the fiscal year and signed by the president was 1996.[69]

As developed in the 1950s and 1960s, and fraying in the late 1970s, the regular order on appropriations involved the origin of appropriations bills in the House (from subcommittee to full committee to floor passage); then consideration in the Senate (from subcommittee to full committee to floor passage); then conference committee and final passage on the floors of both chambers. From 1975 to 2012, only 61 percent of regular appropriations bills were passed in the regular order.[70]

The regular order is sometimes still observed within the appropriations committees, which hold hearings and draft bills. But more often, there is a hybrid model in which continuing resolutions are passed and then spending bills are lumped together in omnibus or smaller "minibus" bills. Between 1986 and 2016, twenty-two separate omnibus laws were passed in nineteen different fiscal years, each covering some or all of the twelve (or thirteen) appropriations bills.[71] Omnibus legislation results in less transparency and time for deliberation, but it also allows both Democratic and Republican priorities to be packaged together, making it easier to get bills through both houses.[72]

While the House more often passed its bills before the beginning of the new fiscal year (88 percent), the Senate was often the sticking point. As the Senate became more individualistic, appropriations bills were increasingly filibustered or subjected to numerous amendments. As a result, the majority party in the Senate often combined appropriations bills into omnibus packages and brought them to the floor just before deadlines.

Peter Hanson has suggested some reforms that might ameliorate these problems: 1) limit filibusters on appropriations bills (though this has not solved the problems with executive branch appointments); 2) the Senate should not wait for House appropriations bills to pass before beginning Senate consideration; 3) allow limited earmarking to broaden coalitions;

and 4) reduce transparency by publicly reporting only total votes on bills, not by individual member, allowing members to make difficult compromises without public vilification by opponents.

Although restoring the regular order to the appropriations process would be salutary, regular appropriations now constitute an increasingly smaller portion of total spending, and reducing expenditures in discretionary spending will not significantly reduce the deficit or decrease the national debt.

Continuing Resolutions, Shutdowns, and the Debt Ceiling

Constitutionally, all agencies must be funded through appropriations bills passed by Congress; when it cannot agree on appropriations for one or all of the twelve appropriation bills, Congress must pass continuing resolutions (CRs) to keep agencies funded. These laws are stop-gap measures allowing the agencies to continue operating, generally at the previous year's levels. OMB strictly enforces the spending limits specified in the continuing resolutions, often a certain percentage of agencies' previous fiscal year appropriations; no new programs can be undertaken. Political polarization and the other factors just discussed have resulted in increasing use of CRs, which (along with sequestration) are extremely disruptive to executive branch operations.

Since passage of the 1974 Budget Act, all regular appropriations have been enacted before the beginning of the fiscal year only four times: 1977, 1989, 1995, and 1997. Since 1997, the average annual number of CRs enacted is six, their coverage averaging five months. In 2002, 2011, and 2013, some CRs lasted for the full year.[73] The continuing resolution passed in March 21, 2018, totaled $1.3 trillion and was 2,322 pages long.[74] Continuing resolutions and omnibus bills decrease budgetary transparency, disrupt federal agencies, and lead to less deliberative policy decisions. When continuing resolutions run out without an appropriation, governmental programs are further disrupted by government shutdowns.[75]

The Antideficiency Act (31 U.S.C. § 1341) prohibits government employees from obligating or spending funds that have not been appropriated. Thus, when the fiscal year begins without the passage of an appropriation or a continuing resolution, affected agencies must begin the shutdown process. Before the 1980s, there were occasional lapses in appropriations, but they did not stop agencies from carrying out their functions. During the 1980s, gaps in funding with no continuing resolution occasionally entailed the shutdown process for those agencies that had not been funded, though only for several days. During government shutdowns, the power of OMB is enhanced, since it must decide which programs and personnel are essential for the protection of life and property and, thus, must continue to operate during shutdowns.

In 1995, however, the lack of agreement on appropriations between Bill Clinton and the Republican Congress resulted in a shutdown that lasted twenty-one days (after a previous six-day shutdown), and in 2013 Republican attempts to stop parts of the Affordable Care Act resulted in a sixteen-day shutdown. In 2018–2019, when President Trump did not get sufficient funding for his promised "wall" along the border with Mexico, 800,000 federal workers were furloughed for thirty-five days.[76]

During shutdowns, those employees in affected agencies who are deemed by OMB to be essential for the protection of life and property still must continue doing their work, though these "excepted" employees do not receive pay, and other furloughed workers were forbidden from reporting for work. The rules OMB uses are based on the Antideficiency Act and subject to differing interpretations in different administrations.[77] As the 2018–2019 shutdown dragged on, the Trump administration ordered OMB to reinterpret its policies to allow workers to return to perform functions that were having a highly visible impact; for example, to process tax refunds, to clean up national parks, etc. None of the workers in the affected agencies received their pay during the shutdowns, though Congress appropriated their back pay after the shutdown. Government shutdowns disrupt the agencies that implement programs; they waste resources; and they have serious economic consequences. CBO estimated that the 2018–2019 partial shutdown delayed $18 billion in federal spending and cost the economy about $11 billion.[78]

In addition to shutdowns, threats to not increase the debt limit further increase budgetary uncertainty. The statutory limit on the national debt was created in 1917 in reaction to the need to provide continuing funding for World War I. Before that, Congress had to pass separate authorizations when additional borrowing was needed, in order for the Treasury to borrow money. In contemporary times, however, the statutory debt limit has been used as a "fiscal suicide vest" in which the full faith and credit of the United States is put at risk for one party to extract concessions on fiscal policy. Treasury Secretary Jack Lew observed: "the debt limit has morphed into a weapon that irresponsible actors in Congress can wield against our economic well-being."[79]

From 2011 to 2019 the debt limit was approached several times. In these cases the Treasury Department shifted cash balances and took extraordinary measures (that is, shifting funds among accounts; for example, from Social Security and Medicare trust funds) to pay its ongoing expenses. In the final resolution of each of these disputes, Congress suspended the debt ceiling until a specific date, when a new round of negotiating over fiscal policy had to begin.[80]

Permanent legislation could provide for automatic increases in the debt ceiling, allowing the United States to pay the debt it has incurred. But some members of Congress have refused to pass such legislation to be able to hold the full faith and credit of the United States hostage to get their way on policy issues. Automatic CRs would deprive some members of a powerful tool to get their way. The problem, of course, is that in such hostage showdowns, the hostages (that is, U.S. citizens, the full faith and credit of the U.S. government, and the economy) suffer.

The Rise of Mandatory Spending

Funds that are provided through the appropriations process are considered discretionary, or "controllable," and must be passed annually. Mandatory, or "uncontrollables," spending is authorized by substantive committees and is not subject to the regular appropriations process. To reduce mandatory spending, which comprises most of federal spending, Congress must pass new legislation that changes the level of benefits and/or the number of beneficiaries in entitlement programs (or increases offsetting collections netted against that spending).[81]

The largest entitlement programs are Social Security (about 24 percent of federal spending) and Medicare/Medicaid (about 27 percent of federal spending); their costs are increasing rapidly due to an aging population.[82] Other mandatory spending includes government retirement programs, unemployment insurance, and the Supplemental Nutrition Assistance Program (SNAP, formerly food stamps). These types of uncontrollable, mandatory spending amounted to 63 percent of total outlays in fiscal year 2017. In addition, interest on the national debt, which amounted to about 7 percent of annual spending in 2017, must be paid, leaving discretionary spending at 30 percent of outlays. In 2018, CBO projected that by 2028 mandatory spending would be 64 percent of outlays with net interest of 13 percent, leaving discretionary spending at 23 percent (table 2-6).[83]

Although defense spending is technically discretionary, spending has been increasing steadily and is unlikely to be cut; in 2019, it was more than $700 billion and amounted to more than half of all discretionary spending. The total of mandatory spending, interest on the national debt, and defense spending amounted to about 85 percent of the federal budget. Without cuts to the defense budget, by 2028 nondefense discretionary spending (that is, most of what the federal government does) will shrink even further from its 2018 level of 15 percent of outlays.

Consequently, cuts in nondefense discretionary spending would not put much of a dent in the deficit or debt. This leaves appropriations committees fighting more and more over less and less. Insofar as future budget battles are concerned with the overall health of the economy and the ratio of debt-to-GDP, they will have to be focused on uncontrollable spending and revenues. This leaves OMB's greatest influence relevant to a smaller portion of total federal spending. OMB career staff have considerable expertise in the financing of entitlement programs, and if Congress decides to enact changes to achieve cost savings, OMB will play a major role. But Congress has not often been willing to address such change in recent years. Congress and presidents have squandered opportunities to deal with the broader trends of fiscal policy, making the inevitable reckoning with budgetary and economic reality more traumatic.

TABLE 2-6. **Uncontrollables Increasingly Dominate the Budget**

Category	% Annual Outlays in 2017	% Annual Projected Outlays in 2028
Mandatory spending	63	64
Interest on the debt	7	13
Total uncontrollables	70	77

Source: Congressional Research Service, "The Federal Budget: Overview and Issues for FY 2019 and Beyond" (May 21, 2018), p. 7 (author name redacted).

CONCLUSION

After the creation of the executive budget in 1921, the Bureau of the Budget served as the primary tool for presidential control of the federal budget and, as such, the overall contours of the executive branch. In its first half-century, presidents used BOB to control discretionary spending through bottom-up budgeting, but also to respond to changing national priorities, such as the Great Depression, World War II, and Great Society programs.

During its second half-century, the Office of Management and Budget adapted to accommodate presidential concerns about budget deficits. In doing so, its approach shifted from a bottom-up focus on programs and agencies to the top-down imperative to reduce deficits. Although OMB maintained its expertise in and control over agency budgets, its leadership shifted the primary focus from controlling spending by programs and agencies to shepherding the president's budget through Congress. Discretionary (controllable) spending was overwhelmed by the demands of mandatory spending programs (uncontrollables). The leadership of OMB became more political (with more than fifty political appointees in 2018), and directors worked closely with White House staff to implement the president's political and policy priorities.

In the twenty-first century, deficits increased; as the gross national debt exceeded $22 trillion, and as the net debt approached 80 percent of GDP, OMB could not assert control. The staff of OMB shared the concern of many informed observers, including CBO, CRS, and GAO, that current fiscal trends were not sustainable. Less than 30 percent of annual outlays were subject to annual appropriations, and half of those funds went to the defense budget. Thus, career OMB expertise in agency oversight and control, while important for executive branch effectiveness and efficiency, could not impose rational budget decisions on a polarized Congress and presidency. As former OMB professional Kathleen Peroff observed, "the concern of presidents and Congress about deficits has diminished. OMB has often lost in the White House debate over the importance of fiscal constraint versus the inexorable political dynamics of the welfare/warfare state."[84]

The COVID-19 pandemic that was declared in March 2020 severely affected the economic outlook of the United States and the rest of the world. Within ten weeks more than 36 million workers in the United States filed for unemployment compensation, about 15 percent of the total workforce. Subsequently, the unemployment rate increased to the highest rate since the Great Depression, when unemployment was about 25 percent. Decreasing revenue from tax payments, in addition to automatic payments from safety net programs and the $2.2 trillion Coronavirus Aid, Relief, and Economic Security (CARES) Act, ensured that deficits for fiscal years 2021 and 2022, which were already projected to be more than $1 trillion (4.5 percent of GDP), would be much higher. These deficits would increase the national debt to 100 percent of GDP by 2021. The stimulus spending and decreased revenue would drive the deficit higher than the previous post–World War II record deficit of 9.8 percent of GDP in fiscal year 2009. It is also possible that deficits would approach those during World War II, when they ranged from 21 percent to 29.6 percent of GDP from 1943 to 1945.[85]

At the end of the budget bureau's first century, the United States was on an unsustainable fiscal path. OMB projected years of deficits of $1 trillion, and because of the recession caused by the COVID-19 pandemic, the debt to GDP ratio would hit 100 percent in 2021. Without significant changes, the trust fund for Medicare would be depleted and revenues would cover only 91 percent of spending by 2026. Ten years after that, Social Security disability and old age insurance would face the same fate.[86]

Politicians and experts have considered a range of reforms of the budgetary process, hoping to address the fiscal crisis. But as former CBO director Rudy Penner observed, "the process is not the problem; the problem is the problem." Both political parties must compromise, because only painful political decisions that reduce spending and increase taxes can begin to reduce deficits and address the national debt.

Notes

The author would like to thank the following friends and colleagues for their advice and assistance in writing this paper: scholars of the federal budget process Meena Bose, Jim Carter, Matt Dickenson, Phil Joyce, David Lewis, Siona Listokin, Roy Meyers, Iwan Morgan, Elouise Pasachoff, Irene Rubin, Andy Rudalevige, and Joe White; OMB career professionals Barry Clendenin, Martha Coven, Phil Dame, Bernie Martin, Kathy Peroff, Steve Redburn, and Jeffrey Weinberg.

    1. For details, see James P. Pfiffner, *The President, the Budget, and Congress: Impoundment and the 1974 Budget Act* (Boulder, CO: Westview Press, 1979), pp. 9–20.

    2. For a detailed analysis of the development of the 1921 Budget and Accounting Act, see John Dearborn, "The 'Proper Organs' for Presidential Repre-

sentation: A Fresh Look at the Budget and Accounting Act of 1921," *Journal of Policy History* 31, no. 1 (2019), pp. 1–41.

3. Budget and Accounting Act of 1921, Section 207, quoted in Fritz Morstein Marx, "The Bureau of the Budget: Its Evolution and Present Role," Part I, *American Political Science Review* 39, no. 4 (1945), p. 668. In an address to budget representatives in departments and agencies, President Harding emphasized Dawes' authority: "He is going to have all the authority of this government back of him. There will be many heart burnings." Charles W. Dawes, *The First Year of the Budget of the United States* (NY: Harper and Brothers, 1923), p. 20.

4. Dawes, *The First Year of the Budget of the United States*, p. 178. Dawes went on, "Again I say, we have nothing to do with policy. Much as we love the President, if Congress in its omnipotence over appropriations and in accordance with its authority over policy, passed a law that garbage should be put on the White House steps, it would be our regrettable duty, as a bureau, in an impartial, nonpolitical and nonpartisan way to advise the Executive and Congress as to how the largest amount of garbage could be spread in the most expeditious and economical manner."

5. Larry Berman, *The Office of Management and Budget and the Presidency, 1921–1979* (Princeton University Press, 1979), pp. 7–8.

6. Philip R. Dame and Bernard H. Martin, *The Evolution of OMB* (Middletown, DE: Create Space Publishing, 2009), p. 93.

7. See Allen Schick, "The Budget Bureau That Was: Thoughts on the Rise, Decline, and Future of a Presidential Agency," *Law and Contemporary Problems* 35, no. 3 (1970), p. 522.

8. Berman, *OMB and the Presidency*, p. 9.

9. Richard E. Neustadt, "Presidency and Legislation: The Growth of Central Clearance," *American Political Science Review* 48, no. 3 (1954), p. 644. For an incisive analysis of contemporary legislative clearance and the enrolled bill process, see Jeffrey Weinberg, "The View from the Oval Office: Understanding the Legislative Presidency," *Journal of Legislative Studies* 24, no. 4 (2018), pp. 1–15.

10. For an analysis of BOB's role in administrative management, see James P. Pfiffner, "OMB: Professionalism, Politicization, and the Presidency," in *Executive Leadership in Anglo-American Systems*, edited by Colin Campbell and Margaret Wysomirski, pp. 195–218. On this era, see also Matthew Dickinson and Andrew Rudalevige, "Presidents, Responsiveness, and Competence: Revisiting the 'Golden Age' at the Bureau of the Budget," *Political Science Quarterly* 119, no. 4 (2004–2005).

11. Pfiffner, "OMB: Professionalism, Politicization, and the Presidency," pp. 201–05.

12. Dame and Martin, *The Evolution of OMB*, p. 93.

13. Ibid.

14. See Matthew Dickinson and Andrew Rudalevige, "Presidents, Responsiveness, and Competence: Revisiting the 'Golden Age' at the Bureau of the Budget," *Political Science Quarterly* 119, no. 4 (2004–2005), p. 653.

15. Dickinson and Rudalevige, "Presidents, Responsiveness, and Competence," p. 648.

16. Statement by Elmer Staats, who chaired the panel meeting of the Presidency Project of the National Academy of Public Administration (May 17, 1988). The author was present.

17. Congressional Budget Office, "The Budget and Economic Outlook: 2018–2028 (April 2018), table 1.3.

18. Aaron Wildavsky, *The New Politics of the Budgetary Process* (NY: Little Brown, 1988), pp. 166–68.

19. Richard Fenno, *The Power of the Purse* (Boston: Little Brown, 1966), pp. 100–02.

20. Schick, "The Budget Bureau That Was," p. 533.

21. The 80 percent comes from *The Office of Management and Budget: An Insider's Guide*, edited by Steve Redburn and Paul Posner (Washington: White House Transition Project, 2016), p. 12. The 20 percent comes from OMB: Congressional Budget Submission, FY 2020, p. OMB-8, EOP-9.

22. Reorganization Plan No. 2, 1970. Title 5, Chapter 9, U.S. Code, Appendix, p. 200 (italics in the original).

23. See Dame and Martin, *The Evolution of OMB*, p. 30.

24. James P. Pfiffner, *The President, the Budget, and Congress: Impoundment and the 1974 Budget Act* (Boulder, CO: Westview Press, 1979), pp. 9–20.

25. Quoted in Louis Fisher, *Presidential Spending Power* (Princeton University Press, 1975), p. 52.

26. Berman, *OMB and the Presidency*, pp. 117–25.

27. The author observed executive branch panic in reaction to Stockman's hit list from the office of the director of the Office of Personnel Management in 1980.

28. For a detailed analysis of Reagan's first year budget, see James P. Pfiffner, "The Reagan Budget Juggernaut: The Fiscal 1982 Budget Campaign," in *The President and Economic Policy*, edited by James P. Pfiffner (Philadelphia: ISHI Publications, 1986).

29. Stockman, *The Triumph of Politics* (New York: Harper & Row, 1986), p. 109.

30. Reagan's tax cut was known as the Economic Recovery Tax Act of 1981. For an excellent and thorough analysis of the specific budget and economic data of the Reagan presidency, see Iwan Morgan, *The Age of Deficits: Presidents and Unbalanced Budgets from Jimmy Carter to George W. Bush* (University Press of Kansas, 2009), pp. 76–121.

31. Stockman, *The Triumph of Politics*, p. 268.

32. Ibid., p. 133.

33. Morgan, *Age of Deficits*, p. 119. The tax increase was known as the Tax Equity and Deficit Control Act of 1982.

34. Congressional Budget Office, "The Budget and Economic Outlook: 2018–2028 (April 2018), table E-1, p. 144.

35. Morgan, *Age of Deficits*, p. 56.

36. Interview with Barry Anderson by Steve Redburn of the George Mason University Center on the Public Service, October 16, 2015, www.youtube.com/watch?v=COMVBSWPvqw.

37. Stockman, *The Triumph of Politics*, p. 159.

38. See Irene Rubin, *Balancing the Federal Budget* (New York: Chatham House, 2003), pp. 37–45.

39. Joe White, "The President's Budget vs. Congressional Budgeting," in *Rivals for Power: Presidential-Congressional Relations*, edited by James A. Thurber (NY: Roman and Littlefield, 2013), pp. 185, 189.

40. Morgan, *The Age of Deficits*, pp. 137–49.

41. For details, see James P. Pfiffner, "President Clinton, Newt Gingrich, and the 104th Congress," in *On Parties: Essays Honoring Austin Ranney*, edited by Nelson W. Polsby and Raymond E. Wolfinger (Berkeley, CA: Institute of Governmental Studies Press, 2000). pp. 135–68.

42. For a detailed analysis of the battles between President Clinton and the 104th Congress, see James P. Pfiffner, "President Clinton, Newt Gingrich, and the 104th Congress," pp. 135–68.

43. Irene Rubin, "The Great Unraveling: Federal Budgeting, 1998–2006," *Public Administration Review* (July/August 2007), pp. 608–23. See, also, Irene Rubin, "Budgeting during the Bush Administration," *Public Budgeting and Finance* (2009).

44. "O'Neill says Cheney told him, 'Deficits don't matter,'" *Chicago Tribune,* January 12, 2004.

45. See the testimony and answers to questions by Martha Coven, Committee on the Budget, House of Representatives, 115th Congress, 2nd Session, Legislative History of the Joint Select Committee on Budget and Appropriations Process Reform, December 19, 2018, pp. 88–90.

46. Email to the author from Barry Clendenin, former OMB deputy associate director for the Health Division from 1994 to 2008. See, also, Joe White, "The President's Budget vs. Congressional Budgeting," in *Rivals for Power,* p. 242.

47. Congressional Budget Office, *The Budget and Economic Outlook: 2018–2028* (April 2018), table 1.3.

48. Ibid., Appendix E-1, p. 145.

49. For a detailed analysis, see Roy T. Meyers, "The Implosion of the Federal Budget Process: Triggers, Commissions, Cliffs, Sequesters, Debt Ceilings, and Shutdown," *Public Budgeting and Finance* (2014).

50. Congressional Budget Office, "The Budget and Economic Outlook 2019–2029" (March 2019), p. 105. See also Alicia Parlapiano, "How Congress Has Worked to Avoid the 'Sequester' Spending Caps," *New York Times,* October 29, 2015.

51. Congressional Budget Office, "Finding for Overseas Contingency Operations and Its Impact on Defense Spending (October 2018) ("At a Glance" box, no page number).

52. U.S. Government Accountability Office, Letter to Senators John McCain and Mac Thornberry, January 10, 2018, updated by Seamus P. Daniels, "Bad Idea: Moving OCO Back into the Base Budget (While Negotiating a Budget Deal)," CSIS, November 2918, pp. 1–6.

53. Aaron Blake, "Trump Won't Even Try to Balance the Budget Anymore," *Washington Post,* February 12, 2018.

54. William G. Gale and others, "Effects of the Tax Cuts and Jobs Act: A Preliminary Analysis," Brookings (June 13, 2018).

55. Michael Rainey and Yuval Rosenberg, "Trump Says National Debt Is Not His Problem," *Fiscal Times,* December 5, 2018.

56. Jared Bernstein, "Mick Mulvaney Says 'Nobody Cares' about Deficits," *Washington Post,* February 6, 2019.

57. Colby Itkowitz and David A. Fahrenthold, "Trump Privately Told Donors New Details about Soleimani Airstrike at Mar-a-Lago Fundraiser, *Washington Post,* January 18, 2020.

58. Congressional Budget Office, "The Budget and Economic Outlook: 2019–2029" (January 2019), p. 1; Congressional Budget Office, "The 2019 Long-Term Budget Outlook" (June 2019), p. 2.

59. Congressional Research Service, "The Federal Budget: Overview and Issues for FY 2019 and Beyond," (May 21, 2018), p. 7 (author name redacted), pp. 20–22.

60. Ibid.

61. For an insightful and thorough analysis of OMB's budgetary influence

on departments and agencies, see Eloise Pasachoff, "The President's Budget as a Source of Agency Policy Control," *Yale Law Journal* (2016), pp. 2182–290.

62. Shelley Lynne Tomkin, *Inside OMB: Politics and Process in the President's Budget Office* (NY: M. E. Sharp, 1998), p. 115.

63. The 686 number comes from Dame and Martin, *The Evolution of OMB*, p. 93. The 480 and 450 numbers come from OMB: Congressional Budget Submission, FY 2020, p. OMB-8.

64. U.S. House of Representatives, Committee on Oversight and Government Reform, 114th Congress, 2nd Session, *Policy and Supporting Positions* (Plum Book), (December 1, 2016), pp. 5–7.

65. See Martha Coven, "OMB's Role within the White House," Paper Presented at the Conference, Serving President and Presidency: The Role of the Office of Management and Budget in Presidential Policy Making, Hofstra University, April 11–12, 2019. Clinton appointed Leon Panetta; Bush 43 appointed Josh Bolten; Obama appointed Jack Lew; and Trump appointed Mick Mulvaney (acting).

66. *The Office of Management and Budget: An Insider's Guide*, edited by Steve Redburn and Paul Posner (Washington: White House Transition Project, 2016), p. 10. OMB-wide support offices had 174. The rest of agency personnel worked in statutory offices of Office of Information and Regulatory Affairs (OIRA, 1980); Office of Federal Financial Management (OFFM, 1990); Office of Federal Procurement Policy (OFPP, 1974); Office of E-Government & Information Technology; and Intellectual Property Enforcement Coordinator (2002).

67. Email to the author from Barry Clendenin, former OMB deputy associate director for the Health Division from 1994 to 2008.

68. Bill Heniff Jr., "Congressional Budget Resolutions: Historical Information," Congressional Research Service (November 16, 2015).

69. Molly E. Reynolds and Peter Hanson, "There Might Not be a Government Shutdown this Year. This Is Big News," *Washington Post*, Monkey Cage, September 19, 2018.

70. This analysis is based on Peter Hanson, "Restoring Regular Order in Congressional Appropriations" (Washington: Brookings Economic Studies, November 2015).

71. James Saturno and Jessica Tollestruup, "Omnibus Appropriations Acts: Overview of Recent Practices," Congressional Research Service (January 14, 2016).

72. Molly Reynolds, "There Might Not be a Government Shutdown this Year" (Washington: Brookings, September 19, 2018).

73. All data from James V. Saturno and Jessica Tollestrup, "Continuing Resolutions: Overview of Components and Recent Practices," Congressional Research Service (January 14, 2016).

74. Chris Cillizza, "2,322 Reasons to Hate Congress (Washington: CNN Politics, March 22, 2018).

75. On the costs of continuing resolutions and shutdowns, see the compelling analysis by Phillip Joyce in "The Costs of Budget Uncertainty: Analyzing the Impact of Late Appropriations" (Washington: IBM Center for the Business of Government, 2012), p. 9.

76. Well into the 2018–2019 shutdown, OMB Director and Acting White House Chief of Staff Mick Mulvaney said, "I found out for the first time last night that the person who technically shuts the government down is me, which is kind of cool." Veronica Stracqualursi, CNN, "White House Budget Director: 'Kind of Cool' to be in Charge of Government Shutdown," January 21, 2018.

77. For an analysis of OMB's role in the shutdown process, see chapter 4 in this volume.

78. Congressional Budget Office, "The Effects of the Partial Shutdown Ending in January 2019," January 2019; Niall McCarthy, "The Government Shutdown Cost the U.S. Economy $11 Billion," *Forbes*, January 30, 2019.

79. James Carter and Robert Bixby, "The Debt Limit is the Nation's Appendix—Get Rid of It," *The Hill* (October 12, 2017).

80. Congressional Research Service, "The Debt Limit Since 2011" (December 20, 2018).

81. Email from Stevens Redburn, who was a career professional in OMB until he retired in 2006.

82. "Present Trends and the Evolution of Mandatory Spending," Congressional Research Service (January 31, 2017), name of author redacted.

83. Congressional Research Service, "The Federal Budget: Overview and Issues for FY 2019 and Beyond" (May 21, 2018), p. 7 (author name redacted).

84. Email to the author. Kathleen Peroff, winner of four presidential rank awards, was deputy associate director of the National Security Division of OMB from 2000 to 2013.

85. OMB, Historical Tables, "Table 1.2: Summary of Receipts, Outlays, and Surpluses or Deficits as Percentages of GDP, 1930–2025," www.whitehouse.gov/omb/historical-tables/.

86. Government Accountability Office, "The Nation's Fiscal Health" (June 2018), GAO-18-299SP.

THREE

The Office of Management and Budget and the Congressional Budget Process

The View from Capitol Hill

MOLLY E. REYNOLDS

The foundation of the relationship between Congress and the president's budget office—known first as the Bureau of the Budget—was laid in the agency's originating statute, the Budget and Accounting Act of 1921. In addition to charging the bureau with assisting the president in the preparation of the budget proposal he would submit to Congress, it was to "at the request of any committee of either House of Congress having jurisdiction over revenue or appropriations, furnish the committee such aid and information as it may request."[1] Since then, interactions between the agency, known since 1970 as the Office of Management and Budget (OMB), and Congress have evolved. The emergence of the modern congressional budget process in 1974—and the degree to which that development represented an assertion by Congress of itself as an equal participant in the development and execution of the federal budget—fundamentally reshaped this relationship; as one historian of the office described it, "the growing emergence of the Congress as more of a co-equal partner . . . forced to look to OMB to increasingly track and communicate with congressional staff... such involvement had been minimal in the Bureau of the Budget before 1970."[2]

This chapter examines four specific ways in which Congress and OMB interact in the contemporary budget process; this is not an exhaustive list, but it is an illustrative one. First, I examine the role of what OMB produces in the form of the president's annual budget request in the broader congressional budget process of which it is the first stage. Second, I discuss how OMB has been involved—especially since the mid-1980s—at the other end of Congress's work on the budget, as the enforcer of certain fiscal limitations Congress has attempted to impose on itself. Third, I describe when and how Congress periodically attempts to oversee and influence the operations of OMB, just as it does with other components of the executive branch. Finally, I explore one of the key sources of conflict between Congress and OMB in recent decades: debates over OMB's role as a provider of budgetary information. Each section will address how the partisan politics of the contemporary American political system have shaped the institutional relationship between Congress and OMB as a component of the executive branch.

OMB AS AGENDA SETTER: THE PRESIDENT'S BUDGET

The president's budget, scheduled to be submitted in February of each calendar year, is perhaps OMB's most consistent, highest profile interaction with Congress. Indeed, scholars have argued that preparing the request is OMB's "first and most fundamental function"[3] and that the document is singularly identified with the president.[4] Given that evidence from recent years suggests a proposal closely connected to the president is more likely to polarize members of Congress merely because of its association with the president, the request is especially susceptible to partisan forces in the contemporary Congress.[5]

The preparation and transmission of the president's budget has the potential to serve a number of agenda-setting functions. Within the executive branch, the process is a key mechanism by which agencies and the White House negotiate and establish presidential spending and policy priorities; OMB has several tools available to influence agency policymaking through the preparation of the budget submission.[6] (At the same time, evidence suggests that, more broadly, presidential policies on which agencies have had more input are more successful in Congress and undergo less revision by the legislative branch.[7]) It is important to note that preparing the document extends beyond setting budgetary levels and also formalizes what agencies and the White House plan to emphasize in terms of agency management, initiatives that often involve substantive policy choices.[8] Once completed, it represents an important statement for Congress of the administration's priorities that cuts across various policy areas and agencies.

The conventional wisdom among many in Washington, however, is that the document plays little role in shaping the ultimate outcome of the congressional budget process. Media coverage of the proposal's release often contains language like "dead on arrival,"[9] says the proposal "isn't really a budget,"[10] and notes that the president's request is "going nowhere."[11] Scholars have shared this assessment, attributing the increasingly contentious relationship between Congress and the president in episodes of divided government as responsible for the dynamic.[12]

This notion that the president's budget matters little when it is released to Congress is not an especially recent development. One scholarly treatment pronounced the president's budget "which once had served as [a] definitive foundation . . . for congressional decision making . . . [as] frequently considered moribund on arrival to Capitol Hill."[13] A second academic analysis characterized the fiscal year 1984 proposal as "*another* dead budget" (emphasis added).[14] Legislators began using this framing as early as the 1980s. In 1986, for example, some legislators referred to President Ronald Reagan's budget as a nonstarter, especially if the president attempted to use it to lobby for spending cuts that Congress had previously rejected.[15]

Political scientists have taken up this question of whether the president's budget does, in fact, affect the ultimate outcomes of the appropriations process, exploring the degree to which the president does or does not "win" in spending negotiations with Congress. Some evidence suggests that, generally, the president's influence over the process is likely asymmetric, with the president more likely to get Congress to accede to his request when he prefers less spending than the legislative branch than when he requests more.[16] Other research that attempts to isolate the difference between external factors that might affect the president's budget request from his own policy priorities counters this claim, however. In arguing that between the early 1960s and the late 2000s, the president's personal preferences mattered more than external conditions, George

Krause and Ian Cook (2015) find no evidence of asymmetric effects; the president's partisan areas of focus are, they argue, "highly influential in shaping budgetary outcomes, irrespective of whether Congress seeks to limit such executive influence by limiting spending."[17]

In addition, to the extent a relationship does exist between presidential requests and congressional outcomes, it is not necessarily constant across policy areas. Work by Brandice Canes-Wrone, William Howell, and David Lewis (2008) finds that, between 1969 and 2000, enacted appropriations tended to better reflect the president's budget request for spending on foreign policy than on domestic.[18] This pattern appears to be driven by the fact that Congress is especially likely, relative to domestic policy, to go along with the president's requests for military spending (the Department of Defense and the nuclear weapons component of the Department of Energy); no similar trend is present for appropriations for the State Department and related agencies relative to domestic spending.[19] At the same time, other work indicates that while voting in the House and Senate tends to support the president on foreign policy to a greater degree than on domestic policy, the extent to which it does so on appropriations is smaller than on other foreign affairs issues.[20]

There is also some evidence that, historically, Congress used legislative tools available to it strategically to ensure that the final level of spending reflects its preferences. Work on the period between the late 1950s and the mid-1980s, for example, suggests that Congress would deliberately underfund accounts of importance to the president during the regular appropriations process, choosing instead to invest in areas of value to Congress and assuming that the president would submit a subsequent supplemental appropriations request to ensure his priorities were funded.[21]

The ability of the president's budget to shape the appropriations process depends, in part, on the actual information contained in the document; research also suggests that has changed over time in a way that has made it harder for Congress to use the information OMB is giving it. As one veteran of the congressional appropriations process told political scientist Joseph White during an interview about the development of spending legislation during the President George W. Bush administration, OMB had stopped supplying the kind of analysis that would provide "a sense of how our agencies are doing."[22] Similarly, a former OMB staffer who had since moved on to the Government Accountability

Office described the George W. Bush administration's approach to the congressional budget justifications as "blatant disregard for an extremely important document."[23]

One of the reasons the detailed information in congressional budget justifications is crucial is because of the role it plays in another component of the budget request's role as an agenda setter on Capitol Hill: hearings. The president's budget request provides important fodder for congressional hearings, which serve not only as a way for committees to review the administration's future plans but also its existing operations. In addition, even when the content of these hearings veers away from simply discussing the budget request, they still serve as a way to compel leaders of executive branch agencies to appear before congressional committees and discuss the conditions at their agencies more generally.

Using data from the Policy Agendas Project's Congressional Hearings data set, figure 3-1 displays the estimated share of hearings in each chamber that deal with the administration's budget request between the 94th Congress (1975–1976) and the 113th Congress (2013–2014).[24] Each hearing in the overall data set is coded by the policy area it addresses; relevant hearings, then, were identified using a combination of the category that includes the administration's annual budget request and a series of key words to capture hearings held by committees of jurisdiction on the proposal.

Data for the House is displayed in black, while data for the Senate is depicted in gray. For the House, the share has varied over time, ranging from a low of roughly 4.5 percent in the 94th Congress—the first one conducted under the contemporary congressional budget process—to roughly 11 percent. Two congresses saw that level of focus on the president's budget proposal in the House: the 98th Congress (1983–1984) and the 108th Congress (2003–2004). There is not, however, a consistent time trend in the amount of attention House committees appear to have paid to the annual budget request from the executive branch.

In the Senate, meanwhile, the levels are lower at the start of the time series, with the three congresses with least attention occurring in the first years after the advent of the current budget process, between 1975 and 1980. Since then, however, the share of the Senate's hearing attention devoted to the president's budget proposal has generally increased, with the two highest levels coming in the two most recent congresses measured here, the 112th Congress (2011–2012) and the 113th Congress

FIGURE 3-1. **Percentage Share of Congressional Hearings Dealing with President's Budget Proposal, 1975–2014**

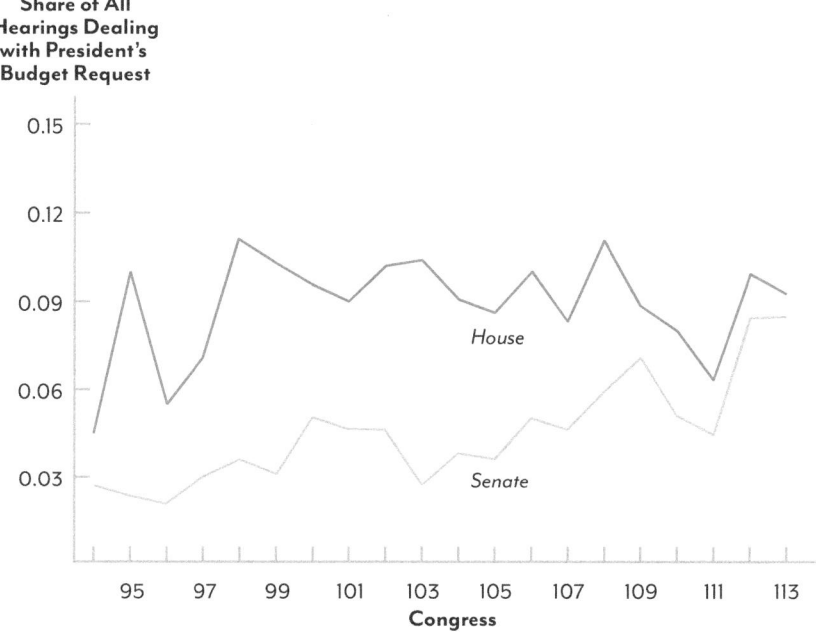

Information on hearings derived from Hearings, the Policy Agendas Project at the University of Texas at Austin, 2019, www.comparativeagendas.net. Hearings were considered to deal with the president's budget request if their titles contained the following terms: "budget proposal," "budget request," "budget justification," "FY + budget," "administration + budget," "president + budget," "FY + request," "administration + request," and "president + request." Hearings within the policy area that include the president's budget request were also included if their titles contained the following words: "administration proposal," "president + proposal," and "budget for." A hearing that satisfied one of the other conditions but had a title that included "authorization" or "concurrent resolution" was excluded.

(2013–2014). This trend is particularly notable since the total number of hearings held in the Senate as measured using the Policy Agendas Project data has not seen a similar trend; indeed, the same three early congresses displayed here as having low levels of attention to the president's proposal (94th, 95th, and 96th) had three of the four highest overall levels of activity. Even if the request does not dictate policy outcomes, it still appears to play a role in structuring the congressional agenda as measured through hearings.

If one function of the president's budget in the contemporary period is to serve as an articulation of the president's policy priorities, it is also worth considering whether media coverage of the document has changed. The degree to which the document can set a broader agenda beyond Capitol Hill depends on how much notice it receives, as "attention is one of the most powerful resources in the political system."[25] One way to measure the amount of interest devoted to the president's budget is to examine media coverage of it, captured in figure 3-2 by examining the *New York Times* coverage of the document. Traditionally, the *Times* runs an article summarizing the major highlights of the budget and the politics surrounding it the day after it is released. Figure 3-2 displays the length of these articles between fiscal years 1982 and 2019; darker bars indicate pieces that appeared on the front page of the newspaper, while lighter bars correspond to those that did not.

In figure 3-2, there is no clear linear over-time trend; there were years in the 1980s when the budget request received relatively short treatment and more recent years in which the length of the article was close to the average for the full time series (1,447 words). There is some indication, however, that fiscal year 2009—the last year of the George W. Bush administration—represents something of a turning point in media attention to the budget request, at least as measured in this way. On one hand, it might be expected that the final year of a two-term presidency—as fiscal year 2009 was—would see a shorter article, as attention is less focused on the outgoing president. Indeed, of the other two similarly situated requests prior to fiscal year 2009, Reagan's fiscal year 1989 proposal also received a relatively short treatment, at 1,206 words. The other analogous year—fiscal year 2001—was longer than average, however, at 1,547 words. It is important to note that fiscal year 2009 was also the first time in which the summary article was not on the front page, appearing instead on A20. The other three instances in which the treatment was relegated beyond the front page (fiscal years 2011, 2013, and 2017) also occurred since fiscal year 2009. In addition, the post-fiscal year 2009 articles have typically been shorter than those published for fiscal year 2008 or earlier; the more recent articles average approximately 1,301 words, while earlier treatments average roughly 1,506 words.[26] These data are consistent with other, interview-based evidence that highlights the degree to which administration officials had largely disappeared from the traditional Sunday talk show circuit in conjunction with the release of the budget request by the end of the George W. Bush administration.[27] As a result, while the president's budget request still plays an important agenda-setting role on Capitol Hill, a natural conclu-

FIGURE 3-2. **Number of Words in *New York Times* Summary Stories on President's Budget, 1982–2019**

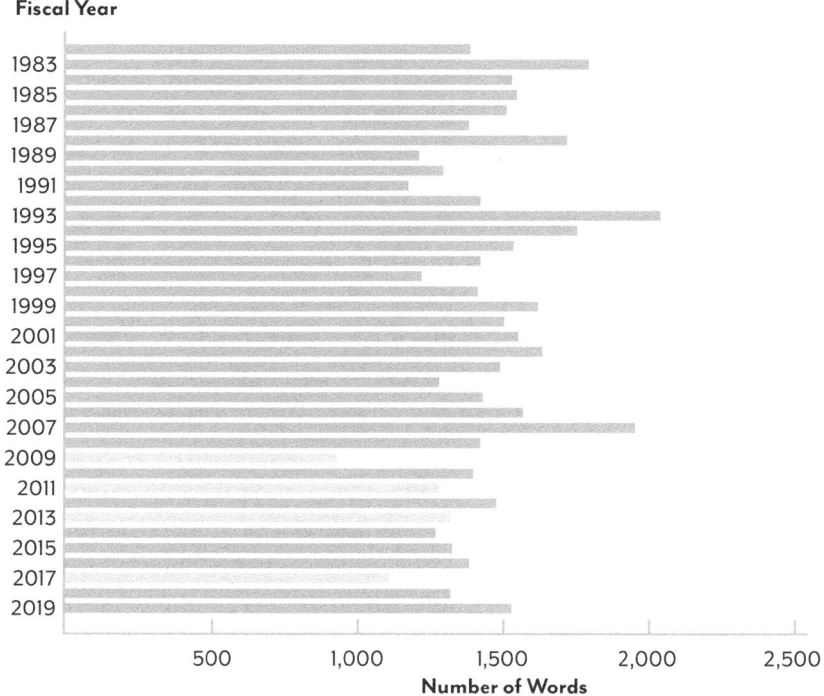

Data for article length provided by Nexis Uni. For years 1996 to 2006, articles were identified using New York Times Front Page, the Policy Agendas Project at the University of Texas at Austin, 2019, www.comparativeagendas.net. For articles prior to 1996 and after 2006, I identified the date of the release of the budget and then examined the front page stories for the following day. Budget release dates for fiscal years 1982–2014 taken from Michelle D. Christensen, "The President's Budget: Overview of Structure and Timing of Submission to Congress," Congressional Research Service 25 (July 2013). Budget release dates for 2015 to the present were taken from the Government Printing Office. In three cases (1982, 1994, and 1995), the front page story preceded the official release of the budget.

sion is that it has received lower levels of media attention in recent years.

While the president's budget proposal continues to be important in agenda setting, its reception is by no means immune from partisan politics. In 2016, for example, when President Obama released his final budget request, congressional Republicans—who controlled both chambers—elected not to schedule hearings with OMB Director Shaun Donovan to discuss it; this was the first time since the passage of the Congressional Budget and Impoundment Control Act of 1974 (CBA) that the House and Senate Budget Committees had declined to hold such hearings.[28] In addition, during the Obama administration, congressional Republicans also frequently used available legislative tactics to force Democrats to vote on measures identical to the president's proposal, largely to force vulnerable Democrats to go on record on an issue closely identified with the president.[29]

OMB AS THE ENFORCER OF CONGRESSIONAL CHOICES

Since the mid-1980s, OMB has played a second important role in the contemporary congressional budget process: that of enforcer of fiscal decisions—often unpleasant ones—made by Congress. This role dates to 1985 and the passage of the Balanced Budget and Deficit Reduction Act of 1985, more commonly known as Gramm-Rudman-Hollings (GRH).[30] After winning reelection in 1984, President Reagan proposed a budget for fiscal year 1986 with large defense spending increases and significant domestic spending cuts, but the proposal was generally seen as a nonstarter in Congress. Both parties in Congress were generally interested in reducing the deficit; however, they disagreed on how to do it.

Senate Republicans believed entitlement cuts were necessary, and proposed a budget resolution with limited cost-of-living adjustments (COLA) for beneficiaries. House Democrats, meanwhile, sought deficit reduction through defense cuts. The ultimate compromise, adopted just before the start of the August recess, pleased neither party but set the stage for a new round of negotiations, led by Senators Fritz Hollings (D-S.C.), Warren Rudman (R-N.H.), and Phil Gramm (R-Tex.). Gramm had been advocating for a sequestration approach to address the deficit—under which mandatory across-the-board cuts would be used to address the problem—since 1981, when he was in the House (and a Democrat). Hollings, meanwhile, had favored a budget "freeze" as an approach to reducing the deficit. The trio's basic approach was as follows: Congress would set five years of deficit targets up front and if, in subsequent years, Congress failed to abide by those limits with its fiscal decisions, sequestration would be implemented. The goal, proponents argued, was not that the mandatory reductions would necessarily be realized but that the *threat* of their implementation would be sufficient to alter congressional behavior.

The Republican-controlled Senate adopted an initial version of GRH in October, and after negotiations with the House, in which Democrats had a majority, the final legislation was signed into law in December. The mechanics of sequestration, as ultimately adopted, involved the Congressional Budget Office (CBO) and OMB issuing a joint report each August that would estimate the deficit for the next fiscal year, relying on a set of assumptions laid out in the statute. The final determination of the deficit would then be made by the comptroller general; if the president certified that a deficit exceeding the allowable level specified in the law existed for the next fiscal year, he would issue an initial sequestration order by September 1. Congress would then have a month to try to address the "excess deficit," but if it failed to do so, the president would issue the final sequestration order by October 15.

Much of the political conflict during the development of GRH had been over what, if any, programs would be exempt from the across-the-board cuts, but the biggest initial obstacle to the law's implementation was a constitutional one, involving the mechanism through which sequestration was triggered. Congress had recognized that if it were responsible for executing the sequestration process, it would likely be tempted to undo it when actually faced with the prospect of implementing across-the-board cuts. At the same time, legislators were apprehensive about delegating the authority to the executive branch; Congress was "flatly unwilling to leave control of this powerful machinery exclusively in the hands of the president or his OMB."[31] The alternative on which congressional negotiators settled, then, was to delegate the responsibility to the head of the General Accounting Office, the comptroller general. Immediately after GRH was signed into law, however, Representative Mike Synar (D-Okla.) filed a lawsuit alleging the law was unconstitutional because, while the comptroller general is appointed by the president, he or she can be removed from office by Congress. By vesting the comptroller general with the responsibility for triggering the sequester, Synar argued, Congress was delegating to itself the power to execute a law.[32] The Supreme Court agreed in 1986, holding that "the structure of the constitution does not permit Congress to execute the laws; it follows that Congress cannot grant to an officer under its control what it does not possess."[33]

This decision established an important precedent for efforts by Congress to tie its own hands in fiscal decisionmaking: that OMB—a creature of the executive branch—would be central to implementing those choices. Indeed, Congress took this approach the following year, when it adopted the Balanced Budget and Emergency Deficit Control Reaffirmation Act of 1987 (GRH II), which delegated to OMB the responsibility for both "reporting deficits that exceeded the targets and for determining the actual cuts"[34] in accordance with a revised formula. Three years later, after GRH II had failed to meaningfully address the deficit (largely because of its reliance on *estimated* deficits, which could be gamed by using "systematically optimistic forecasts"[35]), Congress and the president enacted the Budget Enforcement Act (BEA) of 1990. Rather than establishing deficit targets that would be enforced via sequestration, the BEA implemented spending caps on discretionary programs and pay-as-you-go (PAYGO) procedures designed to limit tax cuts and increases in mandatory spending.

Both involved implementation actions by OMB. In the case of the discretionary caps, the law established separate limits for defense, international, and domestic spending for three years, to be followed by a single, overall cap for two more years. If Congress breached these limits, "a sequester would be issued at the end of the session, although a sequester order could also be made within a session if supplemental appropriations increased spending above the current spending cap during the current year."[36] Estimates of potential sequestration were to be completed by CBO and OMB periodically throughout the year under a set timetable, but ultimate compliance by Congress with the caps was to be determined by OMB, with CBO's estimates serving as merely consultative.[37] OMB was implicated in enforcing compliance with PAYGO requirements; the deficit effects of any new mandatory spending or revenue provisions enacted by Congress would be entered on a PAYGO "scorecard" by OMB. If, at the end of a given session, the scorecard indicated a net increase in the deficit, across-the-board cuts to mandatory programs would be implemented by OMB (with some programs exempt from cuts, as under GRH). Congress extended this approach to fiscal hand-tying twice, with OMB continuing this enforcement responsibility until 2002, when the 1997 law extending the BEA expired.[38]

In 2010, Congress re-enlisted OMB as enforcer of its attempt at spending restraint when it enacted the Statutory Pay-As-You-Go Act of 2010, which takes the same general approach as the BEA to mandatory spending and revenue.[39] Under the Statutory PAYGO Act, OMB maintains two scorecards (one covering five years and the other ten) recording the effects of any changes to revenue and mandatory spending provisions. While OMB maintains these tabulations, it has less influence over the measurement of budgetary effects for PAYGO purposes under the 2010 law than it did under the BEA. As long as Congress follows a set of procedures set forth in the Statutory PAYGO Act—in which CBO generates a PAYGO estimate—Congress's assessment is the one entered on the scorecard. If Congress fails to follow these procedures, then OMB determines the budgetary consequences of the legislation at hand. At the end of a congressional session, if OMB certifies that either of the scorecards reflects a positive balance, the president proceeds to issue a sequestration order mandating across-the-board cuts in a set of direct spending programs (with many programs exempt from the sequester.)[40]

Congress re-enlisted OMB as the enforcer of discretionary spending caps in 2011 with the passage of the Budget Control Act (BCA). Under the BCA, if appropriations legislation is enacted that exceeds specified, separate limits on defense and nondefense spending, OMB is responsible for issuing a sequestration order within fifteen calendar days after the end of the congressional session. (Sequestration can also be triggered during the second or third quarter of a given fiscal year if appropriations bills are enacted that breach the caps.) In addition, OMB was implicated in two other elements of the BCA. The original legislation provided for a congressional Joint Select Committee on Deficit Reduction charged with developing recommendations that would reduce the deficit by $1.2 trillion over ten years. When that panel failed to achieve that goal, the BCA required reductions in the underlying spending limits; the size of those reductions is calculated by OMB. OMB is also responsible for determining sequestration levels for a set of non-exempt mandatory spending programs in which the BCA also imposed cuts.[41]

As the case of the BCA demonstrates, the implication of OMB as Congress's enforcer is not necessarily limited to the agency's mechanical involvement in estimating and imposing sequestration; that process can be subject to additional political conflict between Congress and OMB as an arm of the executive branch. In August 2012, for example, Congress passed, and President Obama signed, the Sequestration Transparency Act, which required OMB to report on how each "program, project, and activity" (PPA) would be affected by the pending sequester.[42] Though the bill ultimately passed by unanimous consent in the Senate and with a large bipartisan majority in the House, all of its sponsors in both chambers were Republicans, who generally emphasized President Obama's role in causing the across-the-board cuts when discussing the bill. One of the measure's lead sponsors in the House, Representative Jeb Hensarling (R-Tex.), argued that the "American people deserve to know how their commander-in-chief intends to implement half a trillion dollars in cuts to our national security" and that "sunlight [would be] provided by this new law."[43] When OMB released a report the following month, however, it did not contain information on the projected cuts at the PPA level; according to the report, the law's "reporting deadline of just 30 days, the large number of PPAs across all agencies and budget accounts, and inconsistencies in the way PPAs are defined"[44] made short-term compliance impossible.

Congress's efforts to use OMB's involvement in the process to try to shift blame to the president for the cuts that were to come did not end with the Sequestration Transparency Act, however; rather, they continued into early 2013. Some members questioned publicly whether agencies could choose which programs to target;[45] in one House hearing about Medicare anti-fraud efforts, Representative Bill Cassidy (R-La.) argued that, if the Center for Medicare and Medicaid Services let cuts to the Health Care Fraud and Abuse Program go into effect ahead of other initiatives, "it calls into question the wisdom of your management."[46] Congressional Republicans went as far as to draft a plan that would have, according to Senator Pat Toomey (R-Pa.), "give[n] the president and agency heads the discretion to proceed with cuts in a better way."[47] Doing so, however, would have likely increased the degree to which the White House was seen as responsible for the cuts—or at least made it easier for congressional Republicans to levy such charges.[48] The proposal ultimately failed in the Senate, 38 to 62, but it serves as an important example of how the required design of a particular spending constraint to include executive branch implementation affects the politics between Congress and OMB.[49]

Just because Congress has enlisted OMB to enforce certain budgetary limits does not mean, of course, that Congress cannot undo the underlying decision to tie its own hands. In 2002, for example, Congress passed, and President George W. Bush signed, legislation that would set the balance on the PAYGO scorecard to zero for fiscal years 2003 through 2006—effectively terminating the procedures.[50] The discretionary spending caps imposed as part of the 2011 BCA, meanwhile, have been delayed once and relaxed four times by statutes passed by Congress.[51] While Congress may find ways to escape the restraints, OMB's implication in their enforcement—required by the Supreme Court's *Bowsher v. Synar* decision—has been an important component of the relationship between OMB and Congress in the post-GRH era.

CONTROLLING OMB

Congress's efforts to control OMB's budgetary work through the Sequestration Transparency Act of 2012 are far from the only attempt in recent decades by the former to dictate the latter's behavior. The idea that OMB was an actor that Congress could control—or at the very least, affect the operations of—dates to at least the 1960s. While some of these efforts have involved the management rather than the budgetary functions of the agency, it is worth reviewing them briefly here for context. In 1965, for example, the Bailey Task Force on Intergovernmental Program Coordination proposed reinstating a set of Bureau of the Budget (BOB) field offices that had been eliminated during the Eisenhower administration. Congress, however, refused to provide the necessary appropriations to implement this recommendation, concerned about increasing the agency's power. Roughly a decade later, Congress also took several steps—including passing the CBA, which will be discussed at length in the next section—to increase its influence over OMB's operations. One involved the creation of a new Office of Federal Procurement Policy within OMB, to be led by a Senate-confirmable—and thus theoretically more accountable—director; this change was motivated by the desire among some legislators for OMB to engage in more centralized review of procurement policy. A second reform required Senate confirmation of both the OMB director and the agency's deputy directors in order to enhance Congress's ability to oversee their behavior.[52]

Notably, Congress has not always been successful in its efforts to shape the agency's organizational choices. When BOB was reorganized into OMB in the early 1970s, for example, Congress sought to influence the process but was largely unsuccessful. Because President Nixon was seeking to implement the reorganization using a statute that provided for congressional review of the plan, legislators were able to weigh in explicitly on the president's design choices. Among Congress's concerns were the transfer of responsibilities from within the BOB to the president himself, which, members argued, would be more difficult to oversee. Along similar lines, some legislators also argued that the selection process for the executive director of the newly-created Domestic Council violated a requirement of the underlying reorganization statute that any new position created by a reorganization plan must be Senate-confirmable or part of the competitive civil service. After vigorous lobbying from the White House, however, the House of Representatives failed to disapprove the plan, allowing it to go into effect.[53]

Importantly, decisions by Congress that have imposed additional workload on OMB in non-budgetary areas have consequences on the agency's ability to do its fiscal work. As seen in figure 3-3, the number of full-time equivalent staff at the agency has generally—though not exclusively—fallen since the early 1980s. The number of political appointees at OMB, meanwhile, fell slightly between the mid-1980s and mid-1990s but generally has increased since then, as demonstrated in figure 3-4. While an increasing number of political appointees does not necessarily mean the agency has become more politicized—though scholarly evidence suggests it has—the fact that the two staff trends have generally proceeded in opposite directions has likely had consequences for how the organization handles its workflow.[54]

As these staff levels have generally declined, the remaining staff have been responsible for more tasks. While some of these, like the Program Assessment Rating Tool (PART) under President George W. Bush, were imposed by the president himself, others were the result of choices made

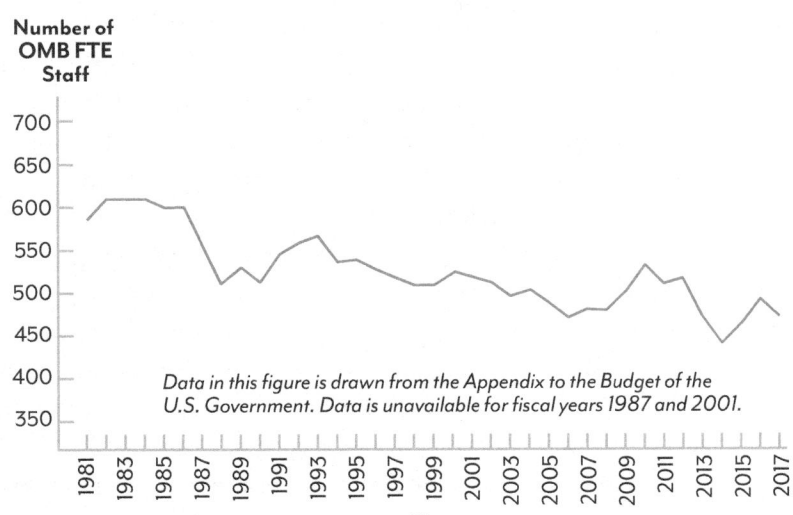

FIGURE 3-3. OMB Full-Time Equivalent Staff, 1981–2017

Data in this figure is drawn from the Appendix to the Budget of the U.S. Government. Data is unavailable for fiscal years 1987 and 2001.

FIGURE 3-4. Political Appointees at OMB, 1984–2016

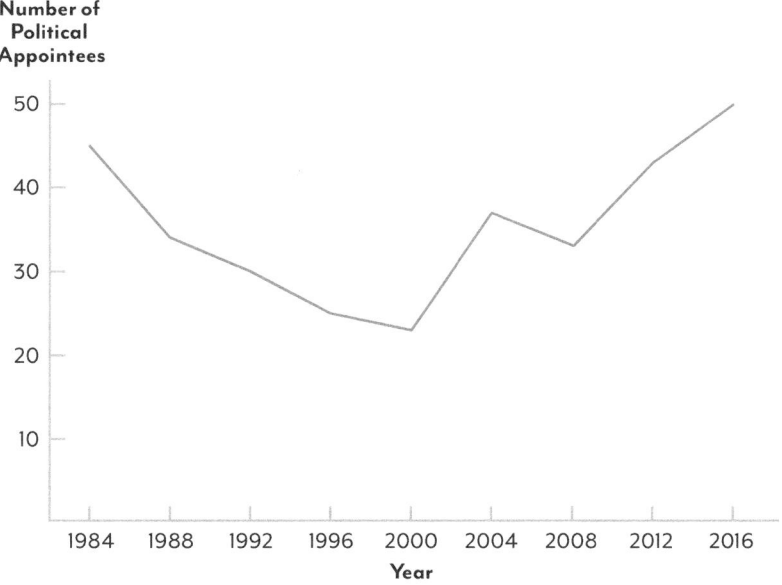

Note: Political appointees are defined as Presidential Appointments with Senate confirmation (PAS), non-career Senior Executive Service (SES), and Schedule C appointees; see David E. Lewis, The Politics of Presidential Appointments: Political Control and Bureaucratic Performance (Princeton University Press, 2008). Data is from "Policy and Supporting Positions: United States Government"—colloquially known as the Plum Book—published alternately by the Senate Committee on Homeland Security and Governmental Affairs and House Committee on Government Reform every four years.

by Congress, like the Government Performance and Results Act of 1993 (GPRA). As part of that legislation, Congress required OMB to oversee the preparation by agencies of annual performance plans and to review those strategies once they were submitted to OMB. The OMB director was given responsibility for approving them, and the agency would then draft a government-wide performance plan based on the agency submissions.[55] In addition, appropriations legislation passed by Congress can also impose reporting requirements on the agency, increasing its workload, and place restrictions on its conduct via appropriations riders.[56] As a result, one OMB employee described the situation as one where "you've got fewer people and you're engaged in doing more things," while another argued that "a substantial amount of examiners' time . . . is consumed with responding to requirements that are either mandated or legislated on the institution."[57] Even decisions made by Congress that involve the agency's non-budgetary responsibilities, then, have shaped its capacity to carry out its fiscal policy-related responsibilities—which, in turn, can affect OMB's relationship with Capitol Hill on those issues.

Indeed, Congress has used tools at its disposal to express this frustration. As previously discussed, legislators have argued that the quality of information provided to them by OMB has declined—which has sometimes led them to take action. In 2004, for example, the report accompanying the appropriations bill for the Department of Transportation and Treasury and independent agencies—which, at the time, funded OMB—contained language explicitly criticizing the agency's provision of budgetary information. "Many of the detailed tables providing breakdowns of requested funds by activity or by office have been discontinued," the report argued. "In place of critical budget-justifying material, the Committee is provided with reams of narrative text expounding on the performance goals and achievements of the various agencies."[58] In connection with this criticism, the bill cut OMB's funding by almost 12 percent. Such a change is especially notable given that Republicans enjoyed control of both Congress and the White House; congressional Republicans were so frustrated with a president of their own party that they were willing to endorse retaliatory budget cuts.[59]

OMB AND THE POLITICS OF BUDGETARY INFORMATION

When Congress fundamentally reshaped the budget process by passing the CBA in 1974, it also profoundly altered its relationship with OMB, especially in regard to the agency's influence as a source of information for Congress. The legislation was, more generally, part of a broader conflict between Congress and the executive branch over the latter's power. As Alice Rivlin, the founding director of the Congressional Budget Office described it, the CBA:

> had to do with the conflict between President Nixon, who was a Republican, and a Democratic Congress. It was very much like some recent controversies. Nixon wanted more for defense and less for domestic programs. And he was quite defiant of Congress about it. He did something which Congress was very upset by, namely, he did not spend some of the domestic appropriations that had already been appropriated by Congress and signed by him, and he just said I'm not

spending that. And that galvanized the Congress. They had the power of the purse and they realized that they didn't have a good way of organizing their own budget decisions.[60]

To address this problem, Congress created a new congressional budget process. It would start with the release of the president's budget proposal in February, to be followed by adoption by both the House and Senate of a concurrent resolution on the budget. This measure, which would not need to be signed by the president, would set out levels of revenue and spending in broad categories. The original act provided for two budget resolutions, a preliminary one early in the year and a final one just before the start of the new fiscal year. (Congress last considered two budget resolutions for fiscal year 1982 and eliminated the requirement for a second in 1985.) New budget committees in both chambers, created by the act, would be responsible for drafting the budget resolutions. The CBA also provided for the expedited budget reconciliation process, though it was not used for the purpose with which it is now associated—that is, passing filibuster-proof legislation that favors the majority party—until the early 1980s.[61]

Of particular importance for Congress's relationship with OMB was the law's creation of the CBO to provide the legislative branch with an in-house source of budgetary and fiscal analysis. The specific notion that Congress needed its own informational capacity as part of the budget process had been raised two years earlier as part of a report from the Joint Study Committee on Budget Control (JSC), comprised of thirty-two members of Congress and charged with making recommendations about "the procedures which should be adopted by the Congress for the purpose of improving congressional control of budgetary outlay and receipt totals."[62] When the JSC issued its interim report in 1973, it included an analysis from the Congressional Research Service in which budget expert Allen Schick made the case that Congress "lack[ed] sufficient information, and time" to make a unified set of decisions about the budget and that Congress's reliance on OMB for information put the legislative branch at a specific institutional disadvantage.[63]

The expansion of congressional budget expertise recommended by the Joint Study Committee was relatively circumscribed. A new, professional, nonpartisan staff was to support the new budget committees and the new budget process by generating estimates of the budgetary baseline and of the cost of new legislation; it was not seen as an "independent source of analysis."[64] By the time the CBA was finalized, however, the provisions setting up the office were broader; rather than staffing the budget committees only, an agency would serve the entire Congress, though with preference given to supporting the "money" committees (Budget, Appropriations, House Ways and Means, and Senate Finance). The authorizing law also left open the possibility that the CBO would potentially provide other types of information "necessary or appropriate . . . for the performance of their duties and functions"[65] to Congress. As the agency organized in its early years, Rivlin repeatedly argued for this broader notion of the CBO's role, even as the House and Senate Budget Committees interpreted the agency's mission more narrowly. This vision included a defense of the agency's production of self-initiated reports rather than focusing only on requests that came from congressional committees. This choice meant the CBO would be better equipped to stand as an informational counterweight to OMB. (By the late 1970s, however, the agency figured out that having at least nominal requestors of its products would generate more institutional buy-in.) Rivlin was also careful to ensure that the agency established a reputation for being nonpartisan, including making clear that the CBO's reports would not contain policy recommendations.[66]

In the four-plus decades since the CBO's creation, the agency has consistently provided a check on the executive branch's influence through its role as a provider of information to Congress. As one longtime participant in the budget process described it, "before CBO was created, OMB was the only game in town. It had developed a certain amount of credibility, but it was largely understood that OMB necessarily worked for the president."[67] The existence of two major players in the informational space often means competing scores of various proposals.[68] The differences in these estimates result from a range of factors, including different assumptions about the future state of the economy and program participation and different timelines over which consequences are estimated.[69] While both institutions and their staffs have an incentive to be seen as credible, "neither can avoid some entanglement in the politics of budgeting."[70]

This conflict between OMB and the CBO has sometimes been significant enough to, in the words of budget expert Allen Schick, "explode into the open."[71] During the deliberation over President Reagan's proposals for spending and tax cuts early in his first term, for example, the CBO produced analyses that challenged an exceptionally favorable set of assumptions—often referred to as "rosy scenarios"—made in OMB projections. Indeed, in retrospect, some observers have argued that CBO could have been more forceful than it was in countering the accuracy of OMB's analysis.[72]

The Clinton administration saw another round of these "forecasting wars"[73] between OMB and the CBO.[74] In 1993, President Clinton had made a notable move, announcing he would use the CBO's estimates of his deficit reduction plan rather than OMB's. In doing so, his goal was to reduce the potential for debates over his proposal's costs. By the time Republicans assumed control of both the House and Senate for the first time in forty years after the 1994 elections, however, the Clinton administration had returned to relying on its own information produced by OMB for budget proposals. As both congressional Republicans and the president advanced balanced budget plans in 1995 and early 1996, this conflict over whether the CBO's or OMB's estimates would be the basis for judgment played a major role in the overall legislative fight, including that year's discretionary appropriations process.

When President Clinton and congressional Republicans agreed to reopen the government after a short shutdown in November, the measure included language directing the president and Congress to enact balanced budget legislation and stipulating that the "agreement shall be estimated by the Congressional Budget Office . . . following a thorough consultation and review with the Office of Management and Budget and other government and private experts."[75] The White House and Congress disagreed on the meaning of that language, however. Just before the short-term spending bill that had been enacted in November expired in December, congressional negotiators walked away from the negotiating table because President Clinton "refused to meet the Republicans' one precondition—that the President submit a plan that could be shown on paper to lead to a balanced budget within seven years using the calculations of the Congressional Budget Office."[76] (The entire episode was eventually resolved in January 1996 when President Clinton presented a balanced budget plan that had been "certified" by CBO, though Congress did not take subsequent action on it.)

Some scholars have argued that this Clinton-era conflict between CBO and OMB information functioned as a cover for intractable partisan and ideological disagreement over the underlying policy.[77] Indeed, rising partisan conflict has also shaped the relationship between the CBO and OMB in other ways. One involves the CBO's own internal capacity and standing. Just as OMB's ability to fulfill congressionally mandated responsibilities has been affected by its own staff levels, CBO's internal capacity also waxed and waned over time—often as the result of changing political dynamics. As seen in figure 3-5, CBO staff levels have remained somewhat more consistent over time than OMB's. Total employment at the CBO was higher in fiscal year 2016 than in fiscal year 1980, but is below both a 1980s high-water mark and a more recent maximum level of 250 in fiscal year 2010.

When staff levels have increased in response to changing political conditions, though, they have not necessarily been maintained. In 2008, when Congress was beginning the development of what would eventually become the Affordable Care Act (ACA), the CBO "became concerned that it did not have sufficient resources to analyze policy changes regarding health care delivery and financing that were emerging as a critical issue in the Congress."[78] Congress approved an increase in the CBO's authorized staff levels of approximately twenty positions, but following overall cuts in discretionary spending beginning in 2011, CBO staff levels fell.[79] The CBO remains highly influential in the congressional budget process—including as an institutional counterweight to the executive branch—but its ability to do so depends on maintaining sufficient capacity of its own.

In the current hyper-partisan environment, where frequent changes in party control of Congress and a tendency toward gridlock make legislating difficult, the incentives for parties to take advantage of narrow windows for policymaking success have increased. The height of these stakes mean that conflicts about budgetary information sometimes spill beyond just disputes between OMB and the CBO; it also means the CBO has been the target of attacks on its credibility and usefulness from within its own branch of government. Take, for example, the 2017 legislative fight over repealing and replacing the ACA in 2017. The debate certainly had the potential for conflict between the CBO and OMB. Early in the year, as the House prepared to consider its version of the legislation, congressional Republicans continued their repeated attacks on the CBO's ACA-related work; as Representative Dave Brat (R-Va.) put it, "CBO has scored everything wrong forever so they're a minor concern."[80] Republican legislators indicated that OMB was expected to release its own

FIGURE 3-5. CBO Staff, 1980–2016

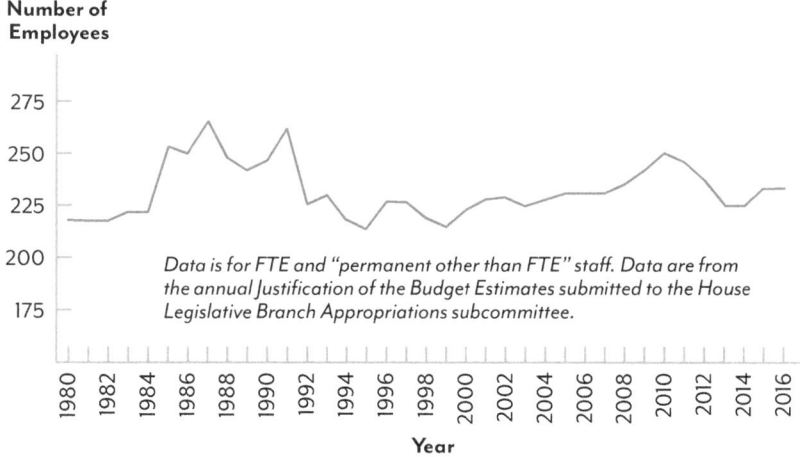

Data is for FTE and "permanent other than FTE" staff. Data are from the annual Justification of the Budget Estimates submitted to the House Legislative Branch Appropriations subcommittee.

estimates of the plan,[81] but subsequent press reports indicated that an OMB analysis of the repeal legislation "show[ed] even steeper coverage losses than the projections by CBO."[82]

As the Senate prepared to consider the repeal legislation later in the year, however, the chief informational conflict was not between the CBO and OMB; it involved discussions around whether to circumvent CBO entirely in favor of a non-congressional source as the provider of a budgetary estimate of a proposal offered by Senator Ted Cruz (R-Tex.). Cruz's plan would have allowed for the sale of insurance coverage that did not comply with many of the ACA's provisions aimed at protecting consumers under certain conditions.[83] The CBO indicated that the complexity of the proposal meant it would need at least a month to produce an estimate of its effects.[84] Wanting to move more quickly than that would allow, Republicans reportedly considered using an alternative score, and produced a contractor for the Department of Health and Human Services to measure its budgetary consequences for enforcement purposes.[85] The use of agency-prepared analyses as part of legislative debates was by no means novel, but the prospect of using a non-CBO source for budget enforcement purposes was abnormal. Ultimately, they elected not to do so, but the episode illustrates an important way in which contemporary budgetary information conflicts do not only involve OMB and the CBO.

POLITICS AND PARTISANSHIP IN OMB'S SECOND CENTURY

As OMB moves into its second century, these partisan dynamics that have shaped the various interactions between the agency and Congress are unlikely to abate absent broader change in the American political system. Partisan conflict has contributed to Congress's struggles with completing its budget and appropriations work on time in recent years, and it has frequently foregone adopting the annual budget resolution altogether.[86] Instead, the post-2011 BCA era has seen, effectively, a series of two-year budget agreements that set topline figures in the context of relaxing the law's discretionary spending caps. The president's identity as the central actor in American politics shapes a wide range of what might otherwise be expected to be unrelated political activity, including gubernatorial and even state legislative elections.[87] Given the much closer identification of OMB and the president's budget with the chief executive, the agency and its work are likely to continue to be targets of partisan conflict with Congress, especially in the periods of divided government that have become more common in recent decades.

Exactly how these dynamics play out will depend in part on what budgetary course Congress chooses to chart for itself in the coming years. The discretionary spending caps enacted as part of the BCA, for example, expire at the end of fiscal year 2021—and with them, the role of OMB in enforcing sequestration in the event the discretionary limits are exceeded. The BCA was the product of particular political circumstances—a Democratic president willing to negotiate with a Republican Speaker of the House over entitlement cuts on the brink of a default on the federal debt—that seem unlikely to repeat themselves in 2021. But whatever congressional budgeting regime does follow the BCA may have consequences for the first branch's relationship with OMB.

While known events, like the expiration of the BCA's discretionary spending caps, are likely to interact with partisan forces to shape the relationship between Congress and OMB in the decades to come, so, too, are newly arising episodes that current observers might not expect. Take, for example, the role OMB has played in the events related to President Donald Trump's impeachment. Among the actions enumerated in the articles of impeachment adopted by the House of Representatives was the president's attempt to condition "the release of $391 million of United

States taxpayer funds that Congress had appropriated on a bipartisan basis for the purpose of providing vital military and security assistance to Ukraine."[88] In addition, the list of means through which President Trump was alleged to have abused the power of his office included directing OMB to withhold documents and instructing two OMB officials—Acting Director Russell Vought and Associate Director of National Security Programs Michael Duffey—not to comply with congressional subpoenas. A subsequent decision issued by the Government Accountability Office just before the start of the impeachment trial found that OMB had acted in violation of the Impoundment Control Act of 1974 in withholding funds from Ukraine; the reservation of the assistance, GAO concluded, had been done by OMB for policy, not programmatic, reasons.[89]

Reactions to the GAO report illustrate well the degree to which assessments of OMB and its role have become heavily influenced by partisanship. Even senators with particular institutional interests in ensuring congressional spending decisions are effectuated assessed the situation through a partisan lens. Senator Richard Shelby (R-Ala.), chair of the Senate Appropriations Committee, for example, called the fact that the report was released just before the start of the Senate's impeachment trial "suspicious"[90] and said, "I don't think [GAO] should be deciding who broke the law."[91] As Congress and OMB move into the agency's second century, then, we should only expect the partisanship that has come to shape their interactions to increase.

Notes

1. Public Law 67-13 §212.
2. Shelley Lynne Tomkin, *Inside OMB: Politics and Process in the President's Budget Office* (Armonk, NY: M. E. Sharpe, 1998), p. 8.
3. Tomkin, 1998, p. 3.
4. Louis Fisher, "Federal Budget Doldrums: The Vacuum in Presidential Leadership," *Public Administration Review* 50, no. 6 (November/December 1990), pp. 693–700.
5. Frances Lee, *Beyond Ideology: Politics, Principles, and Partisanship in the U.S. Senate* (University of Chicago Press, 2009).
6. Eloise Pasachoff, "The President's Budget as a Source of Agency Policy Control," *Yale Law Journal* 125, no. 8 (June 2016), pp. 2182–2290.
7. Jose D. Villalobos, "Agency Input as a Policy-Making Tool: Analyzing the Influence of Agency Input on Presidential Policy Success in Congress," *Administration and Society* 45, no. 7 (September 2013), pp. 837–74.
8. Pasachoff, 2016; Andrew Rudalevige, *The New Imperial Presidency: Renewing Presidential Power After Watergate* (University of Michigan Press, 2005).

9. Jordain Carney, "McCain: Trump's Budget 'Dead on Arrival,'" *The Hill* 23 (May 2017); David Jackson, "Obama Budget Likely 'Dead on Arrival,'" *USA Today,* February 1, 2015.

10. S. V. Date, "Why Federal Budgets Aren't What You Think They Are," *NPR,* March 17, 2015.

11. Russell Berman, "All the Trump Budget Cuts Congress Will Ignore," *The Atlantic,* February 12, 2018.

12. Paul L. Posner, "Budget Process Reform: Waiting for Godot," *Public Administration Review* 69, no. 2 (March/April 2009), pp. 233–44.

13. Tomkin, 1998, p. 95.

14. Joseph White and Aaron Wildavsky, *The Deficit in the Public Interest: The Search for Responsible Budget in the 1980s* (University of California Press, 1989), p. 360.

15. Karen Tumulty and Paul Houston, "Reagan to Ask Budget Cuts Rejected by Congress in '85," *Los Angeles Times,* January 22, 1986.

16. Sarah E. Anderson and Jonathan Woon, "Delaying the Buck: Timing and Strategic Advantages in Executive-Legislative Bargaining over Appropriations," *Congress & the Presidency* 41, no. 1 (February 2014), pp. 25–48; D. Roderick Kiewiet and Mathew D. McCubbins, "Presidential Influence on Congressional Appropriations Decisions," *American Journal of Political Science* 32, no. 3 (August 1988), pp. 713–36.

17. George A. Krause and Ian P. Cook, "Partisan Presidential Influence over U.S. Federal Budgetary Outcomes: Evidence from a Stochastic Decomposition of Executive Budget Proposals," *Political Science Research and Methods* 3, no. 2 (May 2015), pp. 243–64, p. 262.

18. Brandice Canes-Wrone, William G. Howell, and David E. Lewis, "Toward a Broader Understanding of Presidential Power: A Reevaluation of the Two Presidencies Thesis," *Journal of Politics* 70, no. 1 (January 2008), pp. 1–16.

19. Helen V. Milner and Dustin Tingley, *Sailing the Water's Edge: The Domestic Politics of American Foreign Policy* (Princeton University Press, 2015).

20. Eric Paul Svensen, "Structure-Induced Deference or Equal and Coordinate Actor: Congressional Influence on American Foreign Policy," *American Politics Research* 47, no. 1 (January 2019), pp. 88–118.

21. Christopher Wlezien, "The President, Congress, and Appropriations, 1951–1985," *American Politics Quarterly* 24 (January 1996), pp. 43–67.

22. Joseph White, "Presidents, Congress, and Budget Decisions," in *Rivals for Power: Presidential-Congressional Relations,* 5th edition, edited by James A. Thurber (Lanham, MD: Rowman and Littlefield, 2013), pp. 179–200; p. 190.

23. Scott Lilly and Eleanor Hill, "Broken Budgeting: A View of Federal Budget Making from the Trenches," *Center for American Progress,* August 2012, https://cdn.americanprogress.org/wp-content/uploads/issues/2012/08/pdf/broken_budgeting.pdf, p. 27.

24. I use the share of all hearings to control for overall changes in the size of Congress's hearing workload over time.

25. Amber E. Boydstun, *Making the News: Politics, the Media, & Agenda Setting* (University of Chicago Press, 2013), p. 9.

26. A difference of means test on these averages yields a p-value of p = 0.01.

27. Joseph White, "The President's Budget vs. Congressional Budgeting," in *Rivals for Power: Presidential-Congressional Relations,* 4th edition, edited by James A. Thurber (Lanham, MD: Rowman and Littlefield, 2009), pp. 229–49.

28. Jackie Calmes, "Congressional Republicans Balk at Obama's Budget, Sight Unseen," *New York Times,* February 8, 2016.

29. See, for example, Hannah Hess, "Senate Ditches Obama Budget: Plan Earns Only 1 'Yes'," *Roll Call,* March 24, 2015; Erik Wasson and Daniel Strauss, "Senate Rejects Obama Budget in 99-0 Vote," *The Hill,* May 16, 2012.

30. This discussion of the development and adoption of GRH in this and the following paragraph is drawn from Lance T. LeLoup, *Parties, Rules, and the Evolution of Congressional Budgeting* (Ohio State University Press, 2005), chapter 4 and White and Wildavsky, 1989, chapter 19.

31. John B. Gilmour, *Reconcilable Differences: Congress, the Budget Process, and the Deficit* (University of California Press, 1990), p. 209.

32. Ibid.

33. *Bowsher v. Synar* 478 U.S. 714 (1986).

34. LeLoup, *Parties, Rules, and the Evolution of Congressional Budgeting,* p. 105.

35. Statement of Philip G. Joyce before the Committee on the Budget, U.S. House of Representatives, 28 July 2015.

36. Megan Suzanne Lynch, "Statutory Budget Controls in Effect Between 1985 and 2002," Congressional Research Service, July 1, 2011, p. 9.

37. LeLoup, *Parties, Rules, and the Evolution of Congressional Budgeting.*

38. Lynch, "Statutory Budget Controls in Effect Between 1985 and 2002."

39. Separately, the Senate has PAYGO rules that are enforced on a bill-by-bill basis for certain legislation; see Bill Heniff Jr., "Budget Enforcement Procedures: The Senate Pay-As-You-Go (PAYGO) Rule," *Congressional Research Service,* January 9, 2018. The House had a similar rule between 2007 and 2011 and reinstated it as part of the rules package for the 116th Congress in January 2019.

40. Robert Keith, "The Statutory Pay-As-You-Go Act of 2010: Summary and Legislative History," Congressional Research Service, April 2, 2010.

41. Grant A. Driessen and Megan S. Lynch, "The Budget Control Act: Frequently Asked Questions," Congressional Research Service, February 23, 2018.

42. Roy T. Meyers, "The Implosion of the Federal Budget Process: Triggers, Commissions, Cliffs, Sequesters, Debt Ceilings, and Shutdown," *Public Budgeting & Finance* 34, no. 4 (Winter 2014), pp. 1–23.

43. Jennifer Epstein, "Obama Signs Sequestration Transparency Act," *Politico,* August 7, 2012.

44. "OMB Report Pursuant to the Sequestration Transparency Act of 2012 (P.L. 112-155)," September 2012, p. 9.

45. Meyers, "The Implosion of the Federal Budget Process."

46. Emily Ethridge, "Sequester Bites into Medicare Abuse Savings," *CQ Weekly,* March 18, 2013, p. 495.

47. Alexander Bolton, "Rival Sequester Bills Teed Up in the Senate," *The Hill,* February 26, 2013.

48. Jonathan Weisman and Michael D. Shear, "G.O.P. Plan to Give Obama Discretion on Cuts," *New York Times,* February 25, 2013.

49. Vote #26, 113th Congress, 1st session.

50. Keith, "The Statutory Pay-As-You-Go Act of 2010."

51. Driessen and Lynch, *The Budget Control Act: Frequently Asked Questions*; Emily Cochrane, Alan Rappeport, and Jim Tankersley, "Federal Budget Would Raise Spending by $320 Billion," *New York Times,* July 23, 2019, p. A1.

52. Tomkin, 1998.

53. Louis Fisher, *Presidential Spending Power* (Princeton University Press, 1975).

54. For discussions of the increasing politicization of OMB, see Matthew J. Dickinson, "The Executive Office of the President: The Paradox of Politi-

cization," in *The Executive Branch*, edited by Joel D. Aberbach and Mark A. Peterson (Oxford University Press, 2005), pp. 135–73; Judith E. Michaels, *The President's Call: Executive Leadership from FDR to George Bush* (University of Pittsburgh Press, 1997); James P. Pfiffner, "OMB: Professionalization, Politicization, and the Presidency," in *Executive Leadership in Anglo American Systems*, edited by Colin Campbell and Margaret Jane Wyszomirski (University of Pittsburgh Press, 1991).

55. Bill Heniff, Jr., "The Role of the Office of Management and Budget in Budget Development," Congressional Research Service, August 28, 2003.

56. Curtis W. Copeland, "Congressional Influence on Rulemaking and Regulation Through Appropriations Restrictions," Congressional Research Service, August 5, 2008.

57. Both quotes from OMB staffers are from White, 2009, p. 242.

58. This report is discussed by Lilly and Hill, 2012, pp. 20–21. For the original text, see House Report 108-671, "H.R. 5025: Department of Transportation and Treasury Appropriations Bill, 2005," Committee on Appropriations, U.S. House of Representatives, 108th Congress, 2nd session, September 8, 2004.

59. Lilly and Hill, 2012.

60. Interview with Alice Rivlin, *Brookings Cafeteria Podcast*, March 8, 2019, www.brookings.edu/wp-content/uploads/2019/03/20190308-Alice-Rivlin-Transcript.pdf.

61. Molly E. Reynolds, *Exceptions to the Rule: The Politics of Filibuster Limitations in the U.S. Senate* (Washington, D.C: Brookings Institution Press, 2017).

62. Public Law 92-599, § 301(b)(1).

63. Allen Schick, "Analysis of Proposals to Improve Congressional Control of Spending," *Congressional Research Service*, in Joint Study Committee on Budget Control, "Improving Congressional Control Over the Budget: Interim Report," Committee on Governmental Affairs, U.S. Senate, 93rd Congress, 1st session; quoted in Nooree Lee, "Congressional Budget and Impoundment Control Act of 1974, Reconsidered," *Harvard Law School Federal Budget Policy Seminar*, Working Paper 34, April 2008, p. 15.

64. Philip G. Joyce, *The Congressional Budget Office: Honest Numbers, Power, and Policymaking* (Georgetown University Press, 2011), p. 17

65. Public Law 93-344, § 202(e)(2), quoted in Joyce, 2011, p. 19.

66. Joyce, 2011.

67. Interview with Susan Irving, U.S. Government Accountability Office, quoted in Joyce, 2011, p. 210.

68. For proposals affecting the tax code, the Joint Committee on Taxation represents a third informational player.

69. Cheryl D. Block, "Pathologies at the Intersection of the Budget and Tax Legislative Process," *Boston College Law Review* 43, no. 4 (2002), pp. 863–964; Christopher J. Puckett, "Is the Experiment Over? The OMB's Decision to Change the Game Through a Shortening of the Forecast," *Georgetown Journal on Poverty Law and Policy* 11, no. 1 (Winter 2004), pp. 169–90; Allen Schick, *The Federal Budget: Politics, Policy, Process* (Washington, D.C.: Brookings Institution Press, 2000).

70. Schick, 2000, p. 55.

71. Ibid., p. 54.

72. For a discussion of these events, see Joyce, 2011, pp. 56–58.

73. Tomkin, 1998, p. 270.

74. For a discussion of these events, see Tomkin, 1998, chapter 10 and Joyce, 2011, chapter 3.

75. Public Law 104-56, § 203(b).

76. David E. Rosenbaum, "With No Budget, Clinton and Republicans Pass the Blame," *New York Times*, December 17, 1995.

77. Tomkin, 1998.

78. "Legislative Branch Appropriations for 2011: Part 1: Justification of the Budget Estimates," Subcommittee on the Legislative Branch, Committee on Appropriations, United States House of Representatives, 2010, p. 329. See also Paul Starr, *Remedy and Reaction: The Peculiar American Struggle Over American Health Care Reform* (Yale University Press, 2011).

79. "CBO's Appropriation Request for Fiscal Year 2017," Subcommittee on the Legislative Branch, Committee on Appropriations, United States House of Representatives, March 22, 2016.

80. Jennifer Haberkorn, "GOP Slams Budget Scorekeeper as Repeal Bill Moves Forward," *Politico*, March 7, 2017.

81. Haberkorn, 2017.

82. Paul Demko, "White House Analysis of Obamacare Repeal Sees Even Deeper Insurance Losses than CBO," *Politico*, March 13, 2017.

83. Sarah Kliff, "The Trump Administration Produced This Misleading Report to Sell Its Heath Care Bill," *Vox*, July 20, 2017.

84. Matt Fuller, "The Senate Health Care Bill Is Still Not Dead," *HuffPost*, July 17, 2017.

85. Anna Maria Barry-Jester, "The Republicans Have Three Health Care Bills and No Clear Path Forward," *FiveThirtyEight*, July 20, 2017; Haley Byrd, "Senate Republicans Are Considering Alternative Scoring for Cruz Amendment Instead of Waiting for CBO," *Independent Journal Review*, July 13, 2017.

86. Bill Heniff Jr., "Congressional Budget Resolutions: Historical Information," Congressional Research Service, November 16, 2015; James V. Saturno and Jessica Tollestrup, "Continuing Resolutions: Overview of Components and Recent Practices," *Congressional Research Service*, January 14, 2016; Congressional Research Service, "Appropriations Status Table," August 2019, https://crsreports.congress.gov/AppropriationsStatusTable.

87. Daniel Hopkins, *The Increasingly United States: How and Why Political Behavior Nationalized* (University of Chicago Press, 2018); Steven Rogers, "National Forces in State Legislative Elections," *Annals of the American Academy of Political and Social Science* 667, no. 1 (2016), pp. 207–25.

88. H. Res. 755, 116th Congress, 1st session.

89. U.S. Government Accountability Office, "Decision: Matter of: Office of Management and Budget—Withholding of Ukraine Security Assistance," January 16, 2020, www.gao.gov/assets/710/703909.pdf.

90. Emily Cochrane, Eric Lipton, and Chris Cameron, "G.A.O. Report Says Trump Administration Broke Law in Withholding Ukraine Aid," *New York Times,* January 16, 2020.

91. Andrew Desiderio, Kyle Cheney, and Caitlin Emma, "White House Violated the Law by Freezing Ukraine Aid, GAO Says," *Politico*, January 16, 2020.

FOUR

The President's Budget Powers in the Trump Era

ELOISE PASACHOFF

Presidents are often portrayed as bit players in the budget process. Congress has the constitutional power of the purse, it is said, so presidents are relegated to two basic jobs when it comes to the budget: proposing budgets that then tend to be pronounced dead on arrival in Congress, and occasionally threatening to veto appropriations legislation over a major policy disagreement. On this logic, the Office of Management and Budget (OMB) sounds like an office for bean-counting technocrats, but not much more.[1]

This view is incorrect. The Trump administration's actions are revealing a little understood fact about the budget process: Through the work of OMB, the budget process provides many tools for presidents to control the executive branch and to effectuate their goals.

The goal of this chapter is to disaggregate the tools of the executive budget power in distinct legal frameworks and to illustrate the ways in which the Trump administration is making use of each one. While every president uses these tools, and, indeed, their proper use is a critical part of the administrative state's operation, the story told in the first part of this chapter is not a run-of-the-mill one. More than simply using generally available budget tools, political officials in this administration are pushing some of them to their statutory limits and beyond, while suggesting off the record that these actions are "part of a broader effort to defend the president's authority to spend money at any time and in any manner that he determines appropriate."[2]

The administration has not articulated a fleshed-out constitutional argument for unbounded executive authority over the budget, but it may be heading in that direction. Such an argument would be dangerous, subverting democracy, accountability, and our system of checks and balances.[3] It would also be wrong.[4] As it is, some of the administration's statutory arguments and application of those arguments to the facts at hand seem questionable at best.

But while many have suggested that courts can and should police the boundaries of the executive budget power, experience and logic point in the other direction. The second part of the chapter takes up this issue. After identifying the limits of judicial oversight, this part identifies potential legislative responses to the assertion of broad executive budget authority, seeking ways to curb presidential overreach while still leaving room for the executive budget discretion a functioning government requires. The chapter takes a long view in this regard. Political alignments change, turning the politically implausible into the institutionally obvious.

THE TRUMP ADMINISTRATION'S USE OF PRESIDENTIAL BUDGET LEVERS

The 1921 Budget and Accounting Act created OMB's predecessor, the Bureau of the Budget, and set forth the basic contours of the presidential budgeting regime to rationalize what had previously been a disjointed process driven by individual agencies.[5] The 1974 Congressional Budget Act provides the currently operative version of the process.[6] Under this act, the president must present to Congress by the first Monday in February a proposal for the national budget for the next fiscal year, which starts on October first.[7] In anticipation of this deadline, agencies spend the spring and summer preparing budget proposals to submit to OMB, which then spends the fall considering and revising them. This is the budget preparation process. After the congressional appropriations process works its course, agencies must implement whatever appropriations deal has been reached. OMB oversees this process, too: the process of budget execution. OMB also administers management initiatives throughout the executive branch, including through the President's Management Agenda.

As the largest component of the Executive Office of the President (EOP), in recent years between 435 and 465 employees, OMB is unusual in the EOP because the vast majority of its employees are civil servants, with only a thin layer of political officials on top.[8] The high caliber and professionalism of this office is important, for OMB's work in putting together the president's budget, overseeing the execution of appropriations, and implementing management initiatives plays a valuable role in coordinating the work of the executive branch, at its best making it more efficient and more effective. At its best, this work also locates accountability for government operations in the White House, as budget preparation, budget execution, and the management agenda provide OMB, and the White House more generally, with a variety of tools for centralized control of decisionmaking, in a "buck stops here" manner. But these same tools of control can also lead to executive aggrandizement, obfuscation, and partisan politicization in a way that is harmful to the national interest.

This part of the chapter shows how the Trump administration is capaciously, and controversially, using these tools. When it comes to budget preparation and management initiatives, it is largely just the policies the administration is pursuing that are controversial, not the use of the tools themselves. When it comes to budget execution, however, the administration has been not only pushing controversial policies but also engaging in controversial uses of these tools, straining their statutory basis and using them to the president's own personal political advantage.

Budget Preparation

When President Trump has sent his budget proposal to Congress, a common refrain has been that it is "dead on arrival."[9] After Congress and the president have finally reached a budget deal lacking features the president had requested, it is said that the latter has been "rebuked."[10] But this view is too simplistic. The budget preparation process includes a variety of ways to control agency priorities—indeed, this was part of Congress's goal in creating the centralized presidential budgeting process in the first place—and the president's focus helps set the agenda for congressional action. This is as true in the Trump administration as it is in any other.

OMB's directives are generally issued through OMB Circular A-11, The Preparation, Submission, and Execution of the Budget, and memoranda from the OMB director. The Trump administration's revisions to the former include, for example, deletion of references to agency climate change plans that are no longer required.[11] As examples of the latter, consider President Trump's first OMB director Mick Mulvaney's instructions to agencies seeking research and development funds, directing them to focus on such familiar presidential priorities as "American Military Superiority" and "American Manufacturing."[12]

To maximize the chances that OMB will approve an agency's budget requests, agencies give their component parts budget instructions that reflect the administration's policy agenda. For example, in 2017, the Department of Health and Human Services (HHS) instructed its offices to avoid the words "vulnerable, diversity, [and] entitlement" in their budget requests.[13] When employees at the Centers for Disease Control and Prevention asked whether they could use the words "transgender," "fetus," "evidence-based," and "science-based" in their budget proposals, HHS officials suggested it might be wise to avoid those words to obtain budget approval in this administration.[14]

To be sure, not all instructions will result in the requested policy effects, either because agencies convince OMB and the president not to follow through on a certain demand, or because Congress ultimately rejects the budget proposal. The fact that initial instructions do not always become final policy does not diminish the power of the instructions to begin with. The need to get OMB's approval for congressional budget justifications works to secure overall policy conformity; if agencies do not comply with OMB budget instructions, OMB may simply provide the answers it requested in the first place.[15] Agencies may spend so much time working toward an ultimately fruitless presidential goal that they sideline other aspects of their mission.[16] OMB's approval authority is strengthened by its rules on the confidentiality of internal budget deliberations, which restrict agencies from talking to Congress and the public about different budget priorities they may have.[17] This is not to say this requirement is never breached but, rather, that it is a powerful baseline tool of control.[18]

More generally, a president's budget proposal sets the terms of the debate. President Trump's focus on building a wall at the Mexican border has elevated it to a major issue Congress must attend to. His persistence in demanding the creation of a Space Force led to the funding of the first new military branch in over seventy years.[19] His embrace of deficit spending (over the contrary views of his OMB directors) has become the mainstream Republican position, leaving the Tea Party days behind.[20] The budget preparation process has, thus, played an important role in elevating President Trump's policy vision.

Budget Execution

Budget execution is not simply ministerial. There is room in budget execution to make discretionary decisions of substance. This section focuses on four tools of control in budget execution on which the Trump administration has been relying: apportioning appropriated funds; proposing rescissions and deferrals of funds, and avoiding doing so; transferring and reprogramming funds; and managing the government shutdown.[21]

Apportioning Appropriated Funds   One of the central tools of budget execution is apportionment, the authority to specify by time period and by project how agencies may spend their appropriations. The governing law for apportionments is the Antideficiency Act, which provides that the president "shall apportion in writing" appropriations before agencies have access to any funds.[22] OMB has long been delegated this task, which is typically conducted by a senior civil servant.[23] The purpose of apportionment is effective funds management. For annual appropriations, OMB is tasked with apportioning spending to prevent running out of funds, while for indefinite appropriations (such as for certain public health emergency and disaster relief programs), OMB's job is to apportion them "to achieve the most effective and economical use."[24] To further these goals, the OMB official making the apportionment has the authority to specify by time period or by project in whatever combination "the official considers appropriate."[25]

Apportionment is a powerful tool of control over agencies because of the regularity with which OMB must review apportionments—at least four times each year—and because OMB may use its discretion to specify how the agency must spend its appropriation in more detail than Congress did.[26] Moreover, OMB's apportionments have the force of law under the Antideficiency Act, which spells out administrative or even criminal consequences for government employees who violate the act.[27]

At the same time, this control is not unfettered. Apportionment may not be used to withhold sums from programs the administration does not like. The Antideficiency Act specifies narrow grounds on which an apportionment may reserve funds, and all reserves must be reported to Congress.[28] Nor does the Antideficiency Act treat the power to apportion as an independent source of executive policy development. In fact, Congress narrowed the apportionment power in the wake of President Nixon's efforts to do just this.[29] Moreover, Congress has tasked the Government Accountability Office (GAO) with issuing decisions on the propriety of certain executive branch actions under appropriations law in light of the Antideficiency Act and other statutes.[30]

While OMB exercises its apportionment authority all the time, and most uses reflect unremarkable authority over agencies to ensure efficient funds management, the Trump administration is developing a broad view of the apportionment power as a tool of presidential control. For example, one of the administration's early arguments for opposing the Consumer Financial Protection Bureau's (CFPB) status as an independent agency is that the CFPB ought to be "subject to OMB apportionment" to "facilitate additional oversight by the President."[31] Separately, the administration floated the idea of using its apportionment authority to support its efforts (as discussed further later) to reorganize the executive branch without going through Congress, although it did not, in the end, rely on apportionment in this way.[32]

The most significant and controversial effort to use apportionment to further the administration's goals occurred in July and August 2019, when OMB placed holds on Department of State, United States Agency for International Development (USAID), and Department of Defense foreign aid funding, including to Ukraine, with no immediately discernable funds management reasons, and in a way that ultimately jeopardized the agencies' ability to spend at least some of the money before it was to have expired at the end of the fiscal year on September 30. In each instance, a political appointee took over the apportionment decisions from the career official who would normally have signed the apportionments.[33] For fifteen separate accounts, the appointee issued a reapportionment totaling somewhere between $2 and $4 billion, instructing the agencies to freeze spending on those programs until three days after the agencies provided OMB with an accounting of all unobligated funds.[34] Reports emerged that this reapportionment targeted foreign aid programs the administration did not like while protecting programs favored by administration insiders.[35] Separately, the same appointee reapportioned all the available amounts appropriated for the Ukraine Security Assistance Initiative.[36] While OMB eventually offered as justification for the reapportionment the need to go through an interagency process before releasing the funds in light of endemic corruption in Ukraine, a CIA whistleblower detailed concerns that the president had himself demanded the funds be withheld until the Ukrainian president agreed to investigate President Trump's Democratic political rival Joe Biden.[37]

This whistleblower complaint became the basis for impeachment hearings during the fall of 2019, culminating in a House vote in December 2019, almost entirely along party lines, to impeach the president for abuse of power in soliciting foreign interference in the United States presidential election to benefit his reelection and conditioning American aid on that support.[38] In February 2020, the Senate voted to acquit the president, almost entirely along party lines as well.[39] But while the parties ultimately divided on the relevance of the president's actions to impeachment, there was immediate bipartisan congressional opposition to the reapportionments that withheld this foreign aid, and all of the temporarily withheld funding was ultimately released.[40]

Releasing the funding did not ease concerns about the legality of the apportionments at issue; as one observer noted, it appeared the administration "created an irregular budgetary process to match its irregular foreign policy process with respect to Ukraine."[41] It later emerged that career officials inside OMB and the affected agencies had strenuously raised legal objections.[42] Two OMB staff members, including a lawyer, appear even to have resigned over concerns that the use of apportionment authority in the Ukraine situation was illegal.[43]

In December 2019, days before the House impeachment vote, OMB General Counsel Mark Paoletta issued a letter responding to a request from the GAO general counsel Thomas Armstrong to offer an opinion about the legality of the Ukraine apportionments. While the Paoletta letter did not fulsomely make the constitutional case for the president's ability to override statutory limits on presidential spending, the Paoletta letter nonetheless placed the president's statutory apportionment authority in the broad context of his constitutional duty to "take Care that the Laws be faithfully executed."[44] Calling "pausing before spending a necessary part of program execution" so that OMB can confirm and approve agencies' plans, the letter seemed to contemplate a broad use of apportionment authority for policy reasons, ignoring Congress's Nixon-era rejection of this rationale.⁴⁵ The letter also asserted that the apportionment action was appropriate in light of the need "to ensure that funds were not obligated prematurely in a manner that could conflict with the President's foreign policy," again gesturing toward the president's constitutional role as commander-in-chief.⁴⁶

GAO rejected this view in a January 2020 decision concluding that OMB's Ukraine apportionments were illegal. "Faithful execution of the law does not permit the President to substitute his own policy priorities for those that Congress has enacted into law," the decision held, citing *Clinton v. City of New York*, the Supreme Court's 1998 decision that struck down the Line Item Veto Act on the ground that nothing in the Constitution allows the president to unilaterally amend a statute.⁴⁷ GAO raised the constitutional stakes further, noting that OMB and the State Department had failed to provide sufficient information to allow GAO to assess the legality of a subset of the Ukraine apportionments that ran through the State Department rather than the Department of Defense, and stating, "We consider a reluctance to provide a fulsome response to have constitutional significance" in light of GAO's own role in "ensuring respect for and allegiance to Congress' constitutional power of the purse."⁴⁸ The president's legal brief in the Senate impeachment trial did not address these appropriations law issues.⁴⁹

A conflict is thus brewing between OMB and GAO about the scope of presidential budget powers under the Constitution and relevant statutes, not only on apportionment but far more broadly. Indeed, Paoletta has recently reiterated in another context the executive branch's view that none of GAO's legal opinions on appropriations law are binding on the executive branch, as GAO is a legislative agency.⁵⁰

Rescinding, Deferring, and Impounding Funds   There is a second statute in addition to the Antideficiency Act that limits apportionment and presidential spending power more generally: the Impoundment Control Act. Congress passed this act in 1974 as part of an overhaul of the federal budget process in response to the Nixon administration's widescale refusal to spend appropriated funds.⁵¹ To limit "policy impoundments"—presidential attempts to withhold funds based on a policy disagreement with Congress—the Impoundment Control Act contains only two mechanisms for a president to withhold funds or delay spending: rescission and deferral.⁵² Under rescission, the president proposes to cancel certain spending, for reasons that may include policy disagreements.⁵³ But the president cannot do so unilaterally; he must transmit a "special message" prepared by OMB to Congress, and if Congress does not pass a rescission bill within forty-five days, the administration must make the funds available as Congress had previously specified.⁵⁴ Under deferral, the administration proposes to delay spending specific sums of money; here, however, the proposed reasons may not include policy disagreements.⁵⁵ The president must again transmit a special message prepared by OMB explaining the reasons for the proposed deferral.⁵⁶ Congress then has the opportunity to consider an "impoundment resolution" through streamlined procedures under which it "expresses its disapproval" but does not stop the delay, and the delay may last no longer than the current fiscal year.⁵⁷

The Trump administration is both reinvigorating and engaging in expansive interpretation of presidential authority under this act.

As to reinvigorating, the Trump administration attempted to use the rescission procedure for the first time since the Clinton administration.⁵⁸ In May 2018, shortly after signing an omnibus appropriations bill in March to which the president objected as including too much domestic spending, he submitted a special message to Congress proposing rescission of $15.4 billion from thirty-eight separate, largely domestic, programs, slightly revised a month later.⁵⁹ When Congress narrowly rejected the proposal, however, the administration followed the procedures required by the Impoundment Control Act and released the funds for obligation.⁶⁰

As to expansive interpretation, the administration is pursuing two different lines of reasoning. One argument involves interpreting rescission implicitly to permit unilateral cancellation if Congress does not have enough time to act on a rescission proposal before the end of the fiscal year. In both summer 2018 and summer 2019, the administration took steps to effectuate such a result, both times targeting foreign aid accounts (including the accounts in State and USAID whose apportionment a political appointee had taken over in 2019).⁶¹ In both years, bipartisan congressional opposition led the administration to drop the effort.⁶² But it did not drop the legal interpretation of its authority to run out the clock on rescission. To the contrary, when GAO issued a legal opinion concluding that the Impoundment Control Act did not allow presidents to withhold funds through their date of expiration and thereby cancel funds without congressional approval, OMB disagreed.⁶³ Instead, OMB offered a reading of the act that took silence as a grant of presidential authority.⁶⁴

A second expansive argument offered by the administration reads deferral to exclude the non-statutory category of "programmatic delay." On this reading, as explained in the Paoletta letter on the administration's withholding of funds to Ukraine, while the executive branch may not engage in "policy deferrals" to avoid implementing a law with which it disagrees, it may engage in temporary programmatic delays "to determine the best policy for the efficient and effective use of funds *consistent with* the intent of the statute."⁶⁵ Noting that GAO has itself recognized this category as being distinct from deferral, the Paoletta letter nonetheless distanced itself from GAO's view that the agency's intent in delaying spending is relevant to the question of legality, implying that where the executive branch says its delay is programmatic rather than a policy deferral, that ends the matter.⁶⁶

This reading contributed to the growing dismay of civil servants in OMB and elsewhere that the administration's hold on Ukraine funds without notifying Congress through a special message with a valid justification violated the deferral provisions of the Impoundment Control Act.⁶⁷ GAO's January 2020 decision agreed with the civil servants' view, holding that the Ukraine apportionments constituted an unlawful deferral. GAO also rejected OMB's definition of programmatic delays. As a matter of law, GAO explained that such delays are permissible only "because of factors external to the program," and where the agency is otherwise "taking necessary steps to implement" it. Such delays are not permissible where the executive branch delays spending "to ensure compliance with presidential policy prerogatives."⁶⁸ As applied to the facts of the Ukraine apportionments, GAO concluded there was no programmatic delay because it was OMB's own direction, not any external factor, that caused the delay, and because the program's execution was already underway when OMB decided to halt it.⁶⁹

The administration's actions and its interpretation of its authority under the Impoundment Control Act indicate another inflection point toward an even broader assertion of presidential spending powers, and another conflict with GAO over the proper scope of such powers.

Transferring and Reprogramming Funds If the Impoundment Control Act represents congressional limits on the executive's ability to withhold money, the appropriations concepts of "transfer and reprogramming" represent congressional authority for the executive to change the terms on which appropriations are made.[70] The idea behind this authority is that Congress cannot always specify with enough knowledge of future events exactly how funds should be spent, and so the executive branch needs some ability to modify spending as circumstances change.[71] Exercising this authority always reflects centralized executive branch control, in that OMB oversees agency efforts to transfer and reprogram funds.[72] But the Trump administration is taking a particularly broad view of this presidential authority in size, in scope, and in rejecting traditional congressional oversight in this arena.

Both transfer and reprogramming involve changing the funding allocations set forth in a given appropriations law, but the two terms have different definitions and legal frameworks. A transfer moves funds between different appropriations, and an agency may transfer funds only with specific statutory authority.[73] In contrast, a reprogramming changes the allocation of funds within a single appropriation, and an agency is generally free to reprogram funds as long as it does so consistent with the relevant appropriations act's restrictions.[74] Common, uncontroversial restrictions include how much an agency may move, permissible purposes for which funds may be moved, and a timeframe for moving funds or for using moved funds.[75] Also common, but more controversial, are requirements and practices around committee notice and approval. Some committees expect advance notification when transfers or reprogramming above a certain amount are planned, while others expect that no transfers or reprogramming will take place without advance approval, sometimes not only by the appropriations committees but by the authorizing committees as well.[76]

President Trump is not the first president to reject congressional claims that committee approval can be legally required before funds may be transferred or reprogrammed.[77] As President Obama and others asserted before him, the idea that a single congressional committee can veto an executive action violates the modern understanding of the separation of powers.[78] In the 1983 decision *INS v. Chadha*, the Supreme Court held that a law permitting one House of Congress to invalidate an executive action violates the Constitution's framework for legislation, which requires the agreement of both Houses of Congress ("bicameralism") and subsequent presidential action ("presentment").[79] After *Chadha*, as the

GAO explains, "statutory committee approval or veto provisions are no longer permissible. However, an agency may continue to observe committee approval procedures as part of its informal arrangements."[80]

Appropriations act statements that an agency must receive committee approval before transferring or reprogramming funds thus serve as a political limit rather than a legal one. These statements are part of an ongoing relationship between agencies and their congressional appropriators and authorizers, in which it is understood that transferring or reprogramming funds against the committee's wishes may have negative consequences in the next year's appropriation or in other aspects of the administration's relationship with Congress. Although the Trump administration has not (yet) made an across-the-board decision to fully ignore committee expectations of obtaining approval, it seems increasingly willing to accept the risk of those consequences. At the same time, Congress seems increasingly unwilling to impose them.

The Trump administration used transfers and reprogramming to support its policy goals well before its large-scale reliance on that strategy to begin construction on a border wall in 2019. For example, in the summer of 2018, the Trump administration used these tools to support its immigration policies, shifting hundreds of millions of dollars from other Homeland Security programs to Immigrations and Customs Enforcement (ICE),[81] and from other HHS programs to its Unaccompanied Alien Children program.[82] The administration also used these tools that summer to accomplish foreign aid priorities, moving hundreds of millions of dollars away from the West Bank and Gaza[83] and away from civilian support in Syria.[84] Although Democrats in Congress decried these actions, Congress did not take action to stop them.

The largest assertion of presidential authority in transfer and reprogramming, however, has unfolded under the administration's efforts to build the border wall. In December 2018, President Trump refused to sign a budget that did not include $5 billion he had requested for wall funding, beginning a shutdown that lasted for thirty-five days, the longest in the nation's history.[85] When he and congressional Democrats finally agreed on a budget, it included only $1.375 billion for the construction of limited fencing at the border.[86] Yet on the same day he signed the budget in February 2019, he announced he would obtain the rest of the funds he wanted for the wall, and more, through executive action.[87] He identified three additional sources of funds. He would tap over

$600 million from the Treasury Forfeiture Fund, whose statutory authorization includes the ability to transfer funds "in connection with the law enforcement activities of any Federal agency or of a Department of the Treasury law enforcement organization."[88] He would transfer up to $2.5 billion in Department of Defense funds under a statutory provision providing "support for counterdrug activities and activities to counter transnational organized crime," including via "Construction of roads and fences and installation of lighting to block drug smuggling corridors across international boundaries of the United States."[89] Finally, he would reprogram $3.6 billion from Department of Defense military construction projects by using the National Emergencies Act to declare an emergency at the southern border.[90]

These actions provoked immediate opposition, but none was successful in stopping the administration's use of these funds. The Democratic-led House Appropriations Committee denied the reprogramming plans, to no avail.[91] In a rare bipartisan formal rejection, both the House and Senate voted to overturn the president's emergency declaration, but the president vetoed the resolution in the first veto of his administration, and there were not enough votes to override.[92] A contentious supplemental appropriations battle over additional funds for humanitarian needs at the border during the summer of 2019 did not address the reprogramming.[93] And although fiscal year 2020 began with two continuing resolutions rather than an actual budget, the appropriations law that President Trump finally signed in December 2019 contained no repercussions for his actions to build the wall; it provided the same amount of funding for limited fencing and did not include any additional restrictions on his ability to transfer or reprogram funds for the wall.[94] The administration almost immediately announced new plans to shift an additional $7.2 billion in the Pentagon's 2020 budget toward building the wall.[95]

Nor were any of the numerous legal challenges to the president's authority successful in stopping the wall's construction throughout the course of 2019. Despite some isolated injunctions over the course of the year, none was kept in place by an appeals court, and several lawsuits foundered on "standing" grounds—that is, plaintiffs had difficulty establishing a legally cognizable injury that would be redressable by a favorable decision.[96] Moreover, on the merits, in a rare instance of GAO's approval of OMB's assertions of presidential budget authority, GAO issued a decision in September 2019 concluding that the administration's wall-directed transfer of funds for counterdrug activities was permissible.[97]

The challenges to the president's transfer and reprogramming authority did not stop the administration from using those tools more broadly to support its policy goals in areas beyond the wall. As 2019 unfolded, for example, the State Department announced plans to redirect foreign assistance away from the Latin American countries the president blamed for the flow of migrants, while the Department of Homeland Security announced its intention to shift money away from its other work into ICE.[98]

The Trump administration has thus used transfer and reprogramming to support its policy goals even where Congress seems to have taken steps to stop it, through persistence that seems to have resulted in Congress's eventual tacit approval of the status quo, and in a manner that courts have been unable to control.

Managing the Government Shutdown It may seem counterintuitive to identify a government shutdown as a site of presidential control over agencies, as there may seem to be little left to control if the government is shut down. In actuality, however, because of OMB's role in managing a shutdown, shutdowns provide an opportunity for presidential control.[99] The Trump administration's assertion of presidential budget power through a shutdown is notable in three ways: because it presided over the longest shutdown in history and then maneuvered its way to victory on the issue over which it had shut down the government even though the shutdown ended without Congress providing that money; through expansive interpretations of both the law governing shutdowns and the applicable facts; and through escalating responses to GAO's determination that its actions during the shutdown violated the Antideficiency Act. Given the attention in the previous section to the administration's border wall maneuvers, this section focuses on the second two issues.

The legal authorities governing a shutdown are both constitutional and statutory. When Congress and the president are unable to reach agreement on a budget deal, as has been increasingly frequent, the end result is a gap in funding, which, if it lasts long enough, results in a government shutdown.[100] This is because the government cannot operate without appropriations. As the Constitution states, "No Money shall be drawn from the Treasury, but in consequence of Appropriations made by Law."[101] The Antideficiency Act effectuates the Appropriations Clause by forbidding government officials from making commitments to pay without appropriations.[102] It also provides important exceptions to this restriction. While in general a government "officer or employee . . . may not" commit the government "for the payment of money before an appropriation is made," such an action is possible where "authorized by law."[103] In addition, the act provides an "except[ion] for emergencies involving the safety of human life or the protection of property."[104] In news accounts, this second exception is often described as whether an employee is "essential" and can therefore be called to work without pay during a shutdown, but the formal legal term is whether the employee is "excepted" on one of these grounds.[105]

Defining which activities are "authorized by law" and which employees and activities are "excepted" is an important means of executive branch control during shutdowns. Typically, the job of making these determinations falls to OMB. While there is discretion embedded in the determination of who goes to work to do what tasks during a shutdown, the discretion is bounded both by longstanding interpretations from the Office of Legal Counsel (OLC) and the text of the Antideficiency Act itself. OLC has identified several categories of activities as "authorized by law," including not only those that are expressly authorized but also those that are "authorized by necessary implication."[106] As for the emergency exception, the Antideficiency Act further clarifies that "the term 'emergencies involving the safety of human life or the protection of property' does not include ongoing, regular functions of government the suspension of which would not imminently threaten the safety of human life or the protection of property."[107]

Different administrations have made different decisions about what to keep running during shutdowns. Some differences are due to the extent, timing, and length of the shutdown. For example, the circumstances of the complete two-day shutdown of the government over a weekend in January 2018 were quite different from the thirty-five-day shutdown the following year, when some agencies had been funded in a previous appropriations law.[108] Other differences are influenced by political considerations, as every administration is involved in a negotiation with Congress over the terms of the budget deal prompting the shutdown in the first place, while also trying to win public support. Contrast, for example, President Trump's acting OMB director's description of the administration's goal during the 2018–2019 shutdown ("to make this shutdown as painless as possible, consistent with the law") with President Clinton's OMB director's reflections about the administration's goal during the 1995 shutdown ("We were trying to emphasize the pain so it would be over").[109] Decisions about what to shut down that are sensitive to the political environment while still within the bounds of the law are to be expected.

At the same time, budget insiders across party lines questioned whether the Trump administration's decisions in the 2018–2019 shutdown crossed the line from politically aware but permissible to politically driven and illegal. As the Associated Press summarized, "if you're a sportsman looking to hunt game, a gas company planning to drill offshore or a taxpayer awaiting your refund, you're in luck: This shutdown won't affect your plans."[110] One former Clinton OMB official suggested that the Trump administration's "focus on services that reach rural voters, influential industries, and voters' pocketbooks is intended to protect Republicans from blowback" about the shutdown.[111] A former Republican budget committee aide had a similar interpretation: The Trump administration's strategy for what to keep running during the shutdown "does not sound legal, and it is so transparent what they're doing. . . . It's pretty obvious the entire agenda is political."[112] This inference was strengthened by the president's tweets emphasizing his belief that most of the furloughed government workers were Democrats and therefore in need of no sympathy.[113]

The Antideficiency Act serves as something of a deterrent against the executive branch making patently illegal decisions during a shutdown. In addition to the potential for individual liability already mentioned, the act requires agency heads to "report immediately" any violation of the act to the president and to Congress with an explanation of "all relevant facts and a statement of actions taken."[114] But if the agency heads and the president are the ones pushing the boundaries of the Antideficiency Act, such requirements are not likely to be effective. Reports to Congress will have an effect only if Congress is willing to rebuke the president at the time of the report. And it appears that no one has ever actually been criminally charged under the act.[115]

The limits of relying on the Antideficiency Act as a backstop to assertions of presidential authority during a shutdown became apparent in a series of conflicts between OMB and GAO throughout the last half of

2019. As GAO began to investigate the legality of the administration's shutdown decisions in response to requests from congressional Democrats, OMB revised the reporting obligations under the Antideficiency Act that it had previously required of agencies. For decades, OMB had required agencies to report to the president and Congress any such violations of that act that the GAO had identified, along with the agencies' views, regardless of whether the agencies agreed with the GAO's determinations.[116] In June 2019, however, OMB changed the instruction. Now, agencies no longer needed to report any GAO determination unless, "in consultation with OMB," the agencies agree with the GAO.[117] Agencies need not articulate any response at all if they (or, it appears, OMB) disagree.

This new rule became immediately relevant as GAO issued a series of decisions over the course of fall 2019, finding numerous Antideficiency Act violations during the shutdown, including Interior's decision to keep the national parks open, Treasury's decision to process tax refunds, and even OMB's own decision to continue reviewing certain regulations.[118] GAO directed the agencies not only to report the violations but also to update their accounting and explain how they will avoid such violations going forward, further noting that GAO would treat future similar violations as "knowing and willful" and thus subject to the Antideficiency Act's provisions for fines and imprisonment.[119] GAO followed these decisions with a memorandum directly to all agency general counsels objecting to OMB's new interpretation of their Antideficiency Act reporting obligations and emphasizing that GAO would notify Congress of any agency's failure to report a violation found by GAO.[120]

It was in this context that OMB's general counsel Paoletta issued what he termed a "reminder" to agency general counsels that GAO's legal opinions are not binding on them.[121] Citing OLC precedent, Paoletta defended OMB's revisions to Antideficiency Act reporting requirements as "better reflect[ing] the separation of powers," and in compliance with the plain text of the law.[122] Agencies *can* respond to Congress, but there is no need for them to affirmatively comment on GAO's determinations if they (or, again, it appears, OMB) disagree.

The Trump administration has thus indicated a broad interpretation of the law governing shutdowns to accommodate its political interests and to favor executive authority, including the role of OMB, in determining whether Antideficiency Act violations exist. The conflict over shutdown management and the Antideficiency Act reflects continued tension between OMB and GAO over the scope of the executive budget power.

The President's Management Agenda

The renaming of the Bureau of the Budget as OMB under President Nixon underscored the importance of the office's work on supervising the executive functions of the administrative state—the "M" for "Management." Congress has recognized the value of OMB's focus on management by continually delegating responsibility for new management programs to that office.[123] At the same time, the President's Management Agenda (PMA) can provide an opportunity for an administration to accomplish substantive goals through the budget process without going through Congress. This is because the budget process incorporates OMB's management work; many management initiatives reflect substantive policy goals; and these initiatives provide another lever for centralized control over agency action.[124] (As President Nixon's political advisers explained privately in justifying OMB's new name, the "M" was to stand for "management in the get-the-Secretary-to-do-what-the-President-needs-and-wants-him-to-do-whether-he-likes-it-or-not sense."[125])

For an illustration of the Trump administration's assertion of policy control through its management agenda, consider its proposals for government reorganization. While the administration has not succeeded in all of its reorganization goals, it has nonetheless accomplished some reorganizations with policy implications by avoiding, and in some cases ignoring, Congress.

Two months after taking office, President Trump issued an executive order calling for a "Comprehensive Plan for Reorganizing the Executive Branch."[126] Shortly thereafter, OMB director Mulvaney followed up with an implementing memorandum that called for agencies to participate in the development of reorganization plans through the budget process, and required agencies to undertake a series of actions, including meeting with OMB officials to obtain approval of their plans.[127] After a long, behind-closed-doors process, the administration announced thirty-two major reorganization proposals in the summer of 2018.[128] Among the most controversial were merging the Departments of Education and Labor, moving the food stamp program out of the Department of Agriculture and into a newly renamed "welfare" agency with other human service programs in HHS, privatizing the postal service, and dismantling the Office of Personnel Management (OPM), moving its policy shop on federal employees into the EOP.[129]

Some of the reorganization proposals sounded familiar to nonpartisan "good government groups" who work on public administration, and, indeed, OMB explained that many came from GAO proposals, either directly or modified.[130] But others sounded policy-driven in various ways, including the proposal to merge the welfare programs, which was based on a Heritage Foundation proposal and raised the potential of ultimately cutting or eliminating the programs once merged, and the proposal to bring federal employee policy into the White House, which struck some observers as part of a broader presidential plan to politicize civil service hiring.[131] For some, even the proposals that sounded more technocratic than others, like civil service reform, were troublesome because of the president's self-promotion as "dismantler-in-chief" out to "drain the swamp."[132]

Proposed legislation in the fall of 2018 to authorize the White House to move forward with presenting the reorganization plans to Congress did not get very far.[133] In contrast, Congress acted in a series of appropriations laws to place limits on executive branch reorganization.[134] But these limits were placed on individual agencies or individual programs rather than the executive branch as a whole.[135] The limits were not all bans; some of them, echoing reprogramming language, simply said that the relevant congressional committee must be notified, or must give approval, for any agency move to take action on a particular reorganization proposal.[136] Some limits were general enough that not everyone agreed about what restrictions they actually placed.[137]

The White House continued to push forward on reorganization in a number of ways in 2018 and 2019 in spite of these restrictions. OMB asserted that many of the reorganization proposals could be entirely accomplished administratively, without any new authority from Congress.[138] An independent assessment by the Congressional Research Service suggested that this was partially true.[139] As to the appropriations restrictions, when a 2019 inspector general report concluded that a planned agency move violated a 2018 appropriations act requirement to receive congressional committee approval before spending any money on agency relocation, the administration disagreed, citing *Chadha* for the proposition that requiring committee approval is unconstitutional, and announced its intention to continue with its plans.[140]

While the administration eventually dropped its effort to move part of OPM into the White House as a result of bipartisan resistance, after almost two years of taking increasingly controversial steps to do so, other efforts to reorganize were more successful.[141] The Federal Labor Relations Authority closed two of its seven regional offices.[142] The Education Department consolidated several offices and elevated the Office of Nonpublic Education, which promotes private school options, to report directly to the secretary.[143] The Environmental Protection Agency (EPA) revealed plans to consolidate various science offices.[144] The Citizenship and Immigration Services explained that it planned to close all of its overseas offices.[145] The Interior Department announced a plan to relocate the headquarters of the Bureau of Land Management from D.C. to west of the Rockies.[146] The Department of Agriculture began to move the Economic Research Service and National Institute of Food and Agriculture out of D.C. to Kansas City.[147]

It is not difficult to see how these reorganization proposals embed substantive policy choices on every issue represented by the agencies in question, topics on which the president has staked out public and controversial positions. The elements of these proposals also suggest another lever of control over policy through management choices: changing the composition of the workforce through attrition by making it unpleasant for employees who disagree with the choices to stay. This interpretation gained traction when Mulvaney, by this point the acting White House chief of staff, highlighted as a positive example of "draining the swamp" the decision to quit made by more than half the workforce in the Department of Agriculture offices slated to move.[148] Some observers suggested further that particular agency efforts to reorganize were designed to retaliate against units that had conducted research with findings that ran counter to the administration's policies by pushing the offending civil servants out.[149]

LAW, POLITICS, AND ACCOUNTABILITY

As the flurry of lawsuits filed after the president's emergency declaration indicates, some have expressed optimism in the ability of the courts to constrain executive overreach on budget issues. As time goes on, however, it should be clear that such optimism is misplaced. Given the unceasing nature of the executive budget process and the slow pace of litigation, there is no way for courts reliably to police executive budget decisions. Many actions, especially in the reprogramming and transfer space, are committed to executive discretion, with no justiciable issue at all. The more courts get involved in what are essentially political disputes, the more the public loses faith in the impartiality of courts, a true crisis for a country committed to the rule of law. And, of course, those seeking to enlist the courts to police the bounds of the budgeting power may well be disappointed as a practical matter. The concerns about standing mentioned earlier are only one reason courts are not a fruitful source of control in this arena. Even should a decision get to the merits, the Supreme Court may end up blessing expanded presidential action, as it did in *Trump v. Hawaii*, the case upholding the president's travel ban, or weakening the tools for congressional oversight, as it did in *Chadha*.[150]

Instead, the only realistic source of regular control over the presidential budget process rests with political actors in Congress, as bolstered by the public and other civic institutions.[151] To be sure, in the highly polarized post-impeachment era, with President Trump in office and the Senate in Republican control, it may be difficult to envision effective congressional resistance to expanded executive budget power. The stark divide between congressional Republicans and Democrats throughout the impeachment proceedings is one indicator of these difficulties. Congress's failure to respond to the president's 2019 wall reprogramming in the 2020 budget is another.

But the story told in this chapter actually indicates a number of instances in which there was bipartisan congressional agreement to reject expanded executive action and where, as a result, the administration complied. Consider the bipartisan pushback on the administration's apportionment foreign aid holds, which resulted in the release of the funds; the bipartisan rejection of the administration's efforts to run out the fiscal year clock and avoid the requirements of the Impoundment Control Act, which resulted in the administration's decision not to pursue that path; and the bipartisan rejection of the administration's efforts to move OPM into the White House, which resulted in the administration's dropping that effort. Even in these polarized times, Congress has acted to limit executive budget authority. Over time, as political alignments change, more opportunities to do so seem likely.

There are many ways in which Congress could usefully act to cabin executive overreach in budget execution. Several amendments to the Antideficiency Act would be helpful. To limit efforts to use apportionment to support presidential policymaking or partisan gain, Congress should clarify that the apportionment authority is not a general delegation of authority but is only for the purposes of efficient funds management. To ensure that apportionments are kept within these bounds, Congress should further require that signed apportionments ought to be disclosed as a matter of course on OMB's website; they are final decisional documents with the force of law, and it is difficult to justify their current nondisclosed status in a rule of law regime. To cabin shutdown management choices, Congress should require that agencies report not only actual Antideficiency Act violations but also external allegations or decisions on violations, along with a written response.

Several amendments to the Impoundment Control Act would also be valuable. To avoid unilateral administrative cancellation of funds, Congress should clarify that the act does not permit rescission proposals that would allow funds to expire at the end of the fiscal year if Congress does not act in time. To cabin administrative efforts to avoid the act by labeling any apportionment hold a programmatic delay, Congress ought to develop a clear definition of that term that distinguishes it from a deferral. To bolster civil servants' motivation and ability to refuse to violate the act at the behest of a political official, Congress should import into the act the potential administrative and criminal penalties currently reserved for the Antideficiency Act.

As to reprogramming and transfer authority, the underlying rationale for those concepts—the need for executive flexibility as circumstances change—remains valid, so Congress should not attempt any generalized overhaul. In light of the administration's rejection of notice and approval requests, however, Congress ought to impose more specific limitations in appropriations laws. It also ought to require regular and public disclosure of all administration reprogramming and transfer actions; as with apportionments, these final decisional documents ought not be subject to occasional, piecemeal, targeted releases.

Finally, Congress ought to strengthen its capacity to analyze budget matters by expanding its staff with such expertise. Just as the 1974 overhaul to the federal budget process created the Congressional Budget Office and the House and Senate Budget Committees to develop the ability to push back at the Nixon administration's assertion of presidential budgeting power, so another expansion is in order.[152] GAO's decisions on appropriations law are instructive but not self-executing, and Congress itself has a further role to play. While congressional staff members will never be as numerous as the staff in OMB and agency budget offices, the extent of the current imbalance makes it difficult to review and respond to administrative budgeting actions in a timely fashion.[153] Such an expansion would be especially important if the president articulates the broad constitutional view of executive budget authority toward which he has been gesturing and if the Supreme Court ends up blessing it. The president can only take actions that politics will bear, and congressional analysis of disclosed information will help determine those limits.

CONCLUSION

None of these reforms would undercut OMB's valuable role. Instead, they would protect OMB's ability to conduct what is valuable about its work in support of the presidency and the nation by limiting the potential for executive aggrandizement and partisan hackery. Historically, when presidents have used OMB in such a dangerous manner, Congress has responded by cabining such misuse and restoring the balance of powers.[154] This time should be no different.

Notes

I received helpful comments during presentations at Hofstra, UC-Hastings, the American Bar Association annual administrative law conference, the American Political Science Association annual conference, and the Association of American Law Schools annual conference; from current and former OMB and congressional appropriations staff members; and from Matthew Lawrence and David Vladeck. Thanks also to Matthew Angelo, Brooke Schwartz, and Sara Divett for research assistance.

1. I set forth this standard view along with the framework for some of the views expressed in this chapter in Eloise Pasachoff, "The President's Budget as a Source of Agency Policy Control," *Yale Law Journal* (2016).
2. Emily Cochrane and Annie Karni, "Administration Threatened Veto over Ukraine Aid in Spending Package," *New York Times*, December 20, 2019.
3. Peter Shane, *Madison's Nightmare* (University of Chicago Press, 2009).
4. Zachary S. Price, "Funding Restrictions and Separation of Powers," *Vanderbilt Law Review* 71 (March 2017), pp. 357–464.
5. Public Law No. 67-13, 42 Stat. 20 (1921).
6. Public Law No. 93-344, tit. I–IX, codified at 31 U.S.C. § 1101 et seq.
7. 31 U.S.C. § 1102.
8. Administrative Conference of the United States, Sourcebook of United States Executive Agencies, 2nd edition (2018), pp. 20–24; Pasachoff, "The President's Budget," p. 2195.
9. Susan Ferrechio, "Trump's Budget Dead on Arrival in the House, Says Democratic Appropriator," *Washington Examiner*, March 11, 2019; Gabrielle

Levy, "Lindsey Graham: Trump Budget 'Dead on Arrival' in Congress," *U.S. News & World Report*, February 28, 2017.

10. Julie Hirschfeld Davis, "Spending Plan Passed by Congress is a Rebuke to Trump. Here's Why," *New York Times* March 22, 2018; Charles S. Clark, "The 19 Agencies Trump Tried to Kill Aren't Going Away," *Government Executive*, March 22, 2018.

11. Compare Circular A-11, at § 31, p. 6 (2016) with Circular A-11 (2018).

12. M-17-30, FY 2019 Administration Research and Development Budget Priorities, August 17, 2002, p. 2; M-18-22, FY 2020 Administration Research and Development Budget Priorities, July 31, 2018, p. 3.

13. Elizabeth Cohen, "The Truth about Those 7 Words 'Banned' at the CDC," *CNN.com*, January 31, 2018.

14. Ibid.

15. Pasachoff, "The President's Budget," pp. 2213–23.

16. Lisa Rein and Josh Dawsey, "After Bipartisan Pushback, Trump Ditches Effort to Kill Major Federal Agency," *Washington Post*, December 11, 2019.

17. Pasachoff, "The President's Budget," pp. 2224–27.

18. Valerie Strauss, "Education Department Threatens to Suspend Employee Who Provided *The Post* with Budget Data," *Washington Post*, September 11, 2019.

19. Robert Burns, "Space Force Will Start Small but Let Trump Declare a Big Win," *AP News*, December 21, 2019.

20. Robert Costa, " 'It's Depressing, Isn't It?': With Little Protest, GOP Succumbs to Trump on Spending," *Washington Post*, December 19, 2019; Joseph Zeballos-Roig, "The New Federal Budget Shows How Republicans Went From Being Thrifters to Big Spenders on Deficits in the Trump Era," *Business Insider*, August 3, 2019.

21. There are initial signs that the administration will begin to rely on another tool, Administrative PAYGO, to cut spending connected to regulations. Executive Order on Increasing Government Accountability for Administrative Actions by Reinvigorating Administrative PAYGO, October 10, 2019; M-20-06, Revoking OMB Memorandum M-05-13 and Providing Other Information on Administrative PAYGO Implementation Guidance, December 16, 2019. Language in these documents seems to suggest the administration may use this mechanism to impound funds in a way that may violate the Impoundment Control Act, discussed later in this chapter. This is an area to watch in 2020.

22. 31 U.S.C. § 1513(b).

23. OMB Circular A-11 § 120.1; Pasachoff, "The President's Budget," pp. 2199–201.

24. 31 U.S.C. § 1512(a).

25. 31 U.S.C. § 1512(b)(2).

26. 31 U.S.C. § 1512(d); Allen Schick, *The Federal Budget: Politics, Policy, Process*, 3rd edition (Brookings: 2007), p. 277.

27. 31 U.S.C. §§ 1349, 1350.

28. 31 U.S.C. § 1512(c).

29. GAO, *Principles of Federal Appropriations Law*, Volume II, 3rd edition (2006), pp. 6-122–6-125.

30. 31 U.S.C. §§ 712, 3526, 3529; GAO, *Principles of Federal Appropriations Law*, 4th edition (2016), pp. 1-12–1-17.

31. U.S. Department of the Treasury, *A Financial System that Creates Economic Opportunities*, June 2017, p. 89.

32. Nicole Ogrysko, "2020 Budget Sheds Little Light on Details behind the Proposed OPM Reorganization," *Federal News Network*, March 19, 2019.

33. Andrew Duehren and Gordon Lubold, "White House Shifted Authority Over Ukraine Aid Amidst Legal Concerns," *Wall Street Journal*, October 10, 2019.

34. Edward Wong, "U.S. Orders Freeze of Foreign Aid, Bypassing Congress," *New York Times*, August 7, 2019.

35. John Hudson, "U.S. Officials Shield Ivanka Trump's and Mike Pence's Projects in Review of Foreign Aid," *Washington Post*, August 14, 2019.

36. Eric Lipton, Maggie Haberman, and Mark Mazzetti, "Behind the Ukraine Aid Freeze: 84 Days of Conflict and Confusion," *New York Times*, December 29, 2019.

37. Ibid.

38. Art. I, H. Res. 755 (116th Cong. December 15, 2019); House Roll Call Votes 695, 696, December 18, 2019.

39. Senate Roll Call Votes 33, 34, February 5, 2020.

40. Lipton and others, "Behind the Ukraine Aid Freeze"; Caitlin Emma, "Trump's Budget Office Ends Foreign Aid Pause," *Politico*, August 9, 2019; Catie Edmondson and Edward Wong, "White House Lifts Mysterious Hold on Military Aid to Lebanon," *New York Times*, December 2, 2019.

41. Sam Berger, "Trump's Hold on Ukrainian Military Aid was Illegal," *Just Security*, November 26, 2019.

42. Kate Brannen, "Exclusive: Unredacted Ukraine Documents Reveal Extent of Pentagon's Legal Concerns," *Just Security*, January 2, 2020.

43. Michael D. Shear and Nicholas Fandos, "White House Budget Official Said 2 Aides Resigned Amid Ukraine Aid Freeze," *New York Times*, November 26, 2019.

44. Letter from Mark Paoletta, General Counsel, OMB, to Tom Armstrong, General Counsel, GAO, December 11, 2019, p. 3; Lipton and others, "Behind the Ukraine Aid Freeze."

45. Letter from Mark Paoletta, General Counsel, OMB, to Tom Armstrong, General Counsel, GAO, p. 5.

46. Ibid., p. 9.

47. GAO, B-331564, *Office of Management and Budget—Withholding of Ukraine Security Assistance*, January 16, 2020, pp. 1, 5.

48. Ibid., p. 9.

49. Trial Memorandum of President Donald J. Trump, In Proceedings Before the United States Senate, January 20, 2020.

50. Mark Paoletta, Memorandum for Agency General Counsels, Reminder Regarding Non-Binding Nature of GAO Opinions, November 11, 2019.

51. Pub. L. No. 93-344, tit. X, codified at 2 U.S.C. § 681 et seq.

52. Louis Fisher, *Presidential Spending Power* (Princeton, 1975), pp. 175–201.

53. 2 U.S.C. § 683(a).

54. 2 U.S.C. §§ 682(3), 683(b).

55. 2 U.S.C. § 684(b).

56. 2 U.S.C. § 684(a).

57. 2 U.S.C. §§ 682(4), 688.

58. GAO, B-330019, *Rescission Statistics*, September 18, 2018, Enclosure 2, pp. 1–2.

59. Charles S. Clark, "Trump Readies a Vaguely Nixon-Like Package of Spending Clawbacks," *Government Executive*, April 23, 2018; Letter from Donald J. Trump to the Congress of the United States, May 8, 2018; Letter from Donald J. Trump to the Congress of the United States, June 5, 2018.

60. Eric Katz, "House Passes Bill to Rescind $15 Billion from Federal Agencies," *Government Executive*, June 7, 2018; Eric Katz, "Senate Rejects Bill to Rescind $15 Billion from Federal Agencies," *Government Executive*, June 20, 2018; U.S. Government Accountability Office, Letter from Thomas H. Armstrong, General Counsel, to the Hon. Michael R. Pence and the Hon. Paul Ryan, B-330045.3, July 3, 2018.

61. "U.S. Senators Pledge to Fight Trump Push to Cut Aid Funding," *Reuters*, August 16, 2018; Sarah Ferris, "GOP Senators Balk at White House Foreign Aid Cutbacks Tactic," *Politico*, August 21, 2018; Edward Wong, "U.S. Orders Freeze of Foreign Aid, Bypassing Congress," *New York Times*, August 7, 2019; Hudson, "U.S. Officials Shield."

62. Ferris, "GOP Senators"; Carol Morello and Erica Werner, "Administration Decides Not to Roll Back Foreign Aid Funds," *Washington Post*, August 28, 2018; John Bresnahan and others, "Trump Kills Plan to Cut Billions in Foreign Aid," *Politico*, August 22, 2019.

63. GAO, B-330330, *Impoundment Control Act*, p. 1-2.

64. Ibid., p. 8.

65. Paoletta Letter to GAO, p. 7 (emphasis in original).

66. Ibid., p. 7 n. 18.

67. Lipton and others, "Behind the Ukraine Aid Freeze"; Brannen, "Unredacted Ukraine Documents."

68. GAO, B-331564, p. 7.

69. Ibid.

70. Schick, *The Federal Budget*, pp. 281–84.

71. Fisher, *Presidential Spending Power*, pp. 261–62.

72. Ibid., pp. 12–13; Pasachoff, "The President's Budget," p. 2231.

73. 31 U.S.C. § 1532; GAO, *Principles of Federal Appropriations Law*, p. 2-38.

74. *Lincoln v. Vigil*, 508 U.S. 182, 192 (1993); GAO, *Principles of Federal Appropriations Law*, p. 2-44.

75. Congressional Research Service, *Transfer and Reprogramming*, pp. 9–11.

76. Schick, *The Federal Budget*, pp. 282–83; 31 U.S.C. § 1534.

77. Administration of Donald J. Trump, Statement on Signing the Consolidated Appropriations Act, 2017, May 5, 2017, 2017 U.S.C.C.A.N. S22, 2017 WL 8116422, P.L. 115-31, at S24.

78. Note, "Omnibus Appropriations Act, 2009—President Obama Issues First Constitutional Signing Statement, Declares Appropriations Bill Provisions Unenforceable," *Harvard Law Review* (2010), pp. 1053–54; Irene Rubin, "Budgeting During the Bush Administration," *Public Budgeting and Finance* (Fall 2009), p. 9.

79. 462 U.S. 919, 944–51 (1983).

80. GAO, *Principles of Federal Appropriations Law*, p. 2-46.

81. Isaac Stanley Becker, "Trump Administration Diverted Nearly $10 Million from FEMA to ICE Detention Program, According to DHS Document," *Washington Post*, September 12, 2018; Department of Homeland Security, FY 2018 Transfer and Reprogramming Notifications, pp. 29–30.

82. Letter from Secretary of Health and Human Services Alex M. Azar II to the Honorable Patty Murray, Ranking Member, Subcommittee on Labor, Health, and Human Services, Education and Related Agencies, Committee on Appropriations, September 5, 2018; Tal Kopan, "Trump Admin Moves $260M from Cancer Research, HIV/AIDS and Other Programs to Cover Custody of Immigrant Children Costs," CNN.com, September 20, 2018.

83. Matthew Lee, "U.S. Cuts Aid to Palestinians by More than $200 Million," *AP*, August 24, 2018.

84. Krishnadev Calamur, "The U.S. Will Spend Billions in Syria—Just Not on Rebuilding It," *The Atlantic*, August 20, 2018.

85. Andrew Restuccia and others, "Longest Shutdown in History Ends as Trump Relents on Wall," *Politico*, January 25, 2019.

86. Public Law No. 116-6, 2019 Appropriations Act, February 15, 2019, §230(a)(1).

87. President Donald J. Trump's Border Security Victory, White House, February 15, 2019.

88. 31 U.S.C. § 9705(g)(4)(B).

89. 10 U.S.C. § 284(b)(7).

90. Proclamation 9844 of February 15, 2019, Declaring a National Emergency Concerning the Southern Border of the United States, 84 Fed. Reg. 4949 (invoking 10 U.S.C. § 2808); 10 U.S.C. § 2808 (providing authority to engage in "military construction projects" once a national emergency has been declared).

91. Letter from Peter J. Visclosky, Chairman, Defense Subcommittee, House Appropriations Committee, to David L. Norquist, Under Secretary of Defense, Controller, March 27, 2019.

92. Michael Tacket, "Trump Issues First Veto after Congress Rejects Border Emergency," *New York Times*, March 15, 2019; Erica Werner, "House Fails to Override Trump Veto on Southern Border Emergency," *Washington Post*, March 26, 2019.

93. Emily Cochrane, "The House and Senate Have Separate Plans for Border Aid. Here's What's Different," *New York Times*, June 24, 2019; Julie Hirschfeld Davis and Emily Cochrane, "House Passes Senate Border Bill in Striking Defeat for Pelosi," *New York Times*, June 26, 2019.

94. Public Law No. 116-93, 2020 Appropriations Act, December 20, 2019, §§ 209(a), 8005.

95. Nick Miroff, "Trump Planning to Divert Additional $7.2 Billion in Pentagon Funds for Border Wall," *Washington Post*, January 13, 2020.

96. *Trump v. Sierra Club*, 140 S. Ct. 1 (2019); *El Paso v. Trump*, No. 19-51144 (5th Cir. January 9, 2020); *U.S. House of Representatives v. Mnuchin*, 379 F. Supp. 3d 8 (D.D.C. 2019).

97. GAO, B-330862, *Department of Defense—Availability of Appropriations for Border Fence Construction*, September 5, 2019.

98. Teresa Walsh, "Following Review, US 'Will Not Provide New Funds' to Central America," *Devex*, June 18, 2019; Felicia Sonmez and Maria Sacchetti, "Trump Administration Will Divert Disaster Relief Funds to U.S.-Mexico Border Enforcement, Prompting Outcry from Democrats," *Washington Post*, August 27, 2019.

99. Pasachoff, "The President's Budget," pp. 2232–35.

100. Congressional Research Service, *Federal Funding Gaps: A Brief Overview*, March 26, 2018, pp. 1–2.

101. U.S. Const. Art. I, cl. 7.

102. 31 U.S.C. §§ 1341, 1342, 1349–51, 1511–19.

103. 31 U.S.C. § 1341(a).

104. 31 U.S.C. § 1342.

105. Congressional Research Service, *Shutdown of the Federal Government: Causes, Processes, and Effects*, December 10, 2018, p. 10.

106. Ibid., p. 6.

107. 31 U.S.C. § 1342.

108. Congressional Research Service, *Shutdown of the Federal Government*, Summary; Congressional Research Service, *Past Government Shutdowns: Key Resources*, February 7, 2019, Summary.
109. Juliet Linderman, "Selective Shutdown? Trump Tries to Blunt Impact, Takes Heat," *AP*, January 13, 2019.
110. Linderman, "Selective Shutdown?"
111. Ibid.
112. Charles S. Clark, "OMB's Shutdown Improvising Draws Fire from Budget and Legal Experts," *Government Executive*, January 15, 2019.
113. Tom Shoop, "Trump: Most Furloughed Employees Are Democrats," *Government Executive*, December 28, 2019; Tal Axelrod, "Trump: 'I Don't Care' that Most Federal Employees Working Without Pay 'are Democrats,'" *The Hill*, January 5, 2019; Joe Davidson, "Unpaid Federal Employees Recalled So that They Can Pay Federal Contractors," *Washington Post*, January 25, 2019.
114. 31 U.S.C. § 1351.
115. GAO, *Principles of Federal Appropriations Law*, p. 6-144.
116. GAO, B-331295, *Agency Reporting of GAO Determinations of Antideficiency Act Violations*, September 23, 2019.
117. OMB Circular A-11, § 145.8, June 28, 2019.
118. GAO, B-330776, *Department of the Interior—Activities at National Parks during the Fiscal Year 2019 Lapse in Appropriations*, September 5, 2019; GAO, B-331093, *U.S. Department of the Treasury—Tax Return Activities during the Fiscal Year 2019 Lapse in Appropriations*, October 22, 2019; GAO, B-331132, *Office of Management and Budget—Regulatory Review Activities during the Fiscal Year 2019 Lapse in Appropriations*, December 19, 2019.
119. Eric Katz, "Trump Officials Threatened with Fines, Jail Time over Illegal Spending During Shutdown," *Government Executive*, September 6, 2019.
120. GAO, B-331295, *Agency Reporting of GAO Determinations*.
121. Paoletta, *Reminder*.
122. Ibid.
123. Pasachoff, "The President's Budget," pp. 2237–38.
124. Ibid., pp. 2238–43; Eric Katz, "White House to Meet with Agencies to Ensure Enactment of Trump's Agenda," *Government Executive*, April 25, 2018.
125. Pasachoff, "The President's Budget," p. 2239.
126. Executive Order 13781, Comprehensive Plan for Reorganizing the Executive Branch, March 13, 2017.
127. M-17-22, Comprehensive Plan for Reforming the Federal Government and Reducing the Federal Civilian Workforce, April 12, 2017; M-17-28, Fiscal Year (FY) 2019 Budget Guidance, July 7, 2017.
128. Eric Katz, "Trump's Reorganization of Feds: Relocations and Reskilling, But Not Job Cuts," *Government Executive*, June 21, 2018; Eric Katz, "White House Produces No Evidence It Considered Public Input on Reorganizing Government," *Government Executive*, May 2, 2018.
129. Eric Katz and Erich Wagner, "Proposed OPM Reorganization Draws Widespread Criticism," *Government Executive*, June 22, 2018; Donald F. Kettl, "Reorganizing Welfare Programs Is a Very Big Deal," *Government Executive*, June 6, 2018; Danielle Douglas-Gabriel, "Merging the Labor and Education Departments Won't Accomplish Much, Say Experts," *Washington Post*, June 21, 2018; Eric Katz, "Groups Launch Six-Figure National Ad Campaign to Oppose Postal Privatization," *Government Executive*, March 11, 2019.
130. Charles S. Clark, "After a Slow Start, Trump's Civil Service Reformers Connect with Experts," *Government Executive*, September 24, 2018.

131. Charles S. Clark, "White House Proposes a Massive Reorganization of Federal Agencies," *Government Executive*, June 21, 2018; Helena Bottemiller Evich and Andrew Restuccia, "Trump Seeks to Reorganize the Federal Government," *Politico*, June 6, 2018.

132. Paul C. Light, "It's Dismantlers v. Rebuilders on the Government Reform Front," *Government Executive*, August 27, 2018; Katz and Wagner, "Proposed OPM Reorganization."

133. Reforming Government Act of 2018, H.R. 6787 (introduced September 12, 2018), S.3137 (reported out of committee November 26, 2018).

134. Eric Katz, "Omnibus Puts Kibosh on White House Efforts to Unilaterally Reorganize Agencies, Shed Workers," *Government Executive*, March 22, 2018; Eric Katz, "Congress Begins Formally Blocking Trump's Government Reorganization Plan," *Government Executive*, September 12, 2018.

135. Katz, "Congress Begins Formally Blocking."

136. Ibid.; "Congress Weighing Restrictions on Agency Reorganizations," *FEDweek*, June 5, 2018.

137. Eric Katz, "Bipartisan Senate Group Demands Trump Team 'Immediately Cease' Shrinking of Federal Labor Relations Authority," *Government Executive*, May 1, 2018.

138. Eric Katz, "Tempers Flare as White House Defends Reorg Proposal against Accusations of Stonewalling," *Government Executive*, July 18, 2018.

139. Eric Katz, "These Are the 15 Trump Reorganization Proposals Agencies Can Advance Without Congress," *Government Executive*, October 16, 2018.

140. USDA Office of Inspector General, *USDA's Proposal to Reorganize and Relocate the Economic Research Service and National Institute of Food and Agriculture*, August 2019, pp. 6–10.

141. Rein and Dawsey, "After Bipartisan Pushback"; Nicole Ogrysko, "Trump Administration Takes Another Baby Step to Advance OPM-GSA Merger," *Federal News Network*, July 30, 2019; Eric Yoder and Lisa Rein, "Trump Abruptly Replaces Federal Personnel Director after Just 7 Months," *Washington Post*, October 5, 2018; Eric Katz, "Behind the Trump Administration's 'Brutal' Decision to Remove Its Federal Personnel Chief," *Government Executive*, October 9, 2018; Eric Katz, "OPM Begins Planning Its Reorganization Despite Pushback From Lawmakers," *Government Executive*, July 23, 2018.

142. Nicole Ogrysko, "Rent Costs, Caseloads Prompt FLRA to Close Second Regional Office," *Federal News Network*, November 2, 2018; Katz, "Bipartisan Senate Group Demands."

143. Maria Biery, "Betsy DeVos Poised to Reorganize, Consolidate the Education Department," *Washington Examiner*, October 31, 2018.

144. Josh Siegel, "EPA Announces Major Reorganization Plan for Science Research Office," *Washington Examiner*, March 7, 2019.

145. Yeganeh Torbati and Mica Rosenberg, "U.S. Immigration Agency to Close Its Overseas Offices," *Reuters*, March 12, 2019.

146. Juliet Eilperin and Lisa Rein, "Interior to Move Most of Bureau of Land Management's D.C. Staff Out West as Part of Larger Reorganization Push," *Washington Post*, July 15, 2019; John Sadler, "Environmentalists Express Worry over BLM Reorganization; Bureau Downplays Concerns," *Las Vegas Sun*, August 14, 2019.

147. Ben Guarino, "USDA Research Agencies Will Move to Kansas City Despite Oppositions," *Washington Post*, June 13, 2019; Erich Wagner, "Lawmaker on USDA Office Relocations: 'This Fight is Not Over'," *Government Executive*, August 7, 2019.

148. Ben Guarino, "USDA Science Agencies' Relocation May Have Violated Law, Inspector General Report Says," *Washington Post*, August 6, 2019.

149. Maya Earls, "Whistle-Blower Complaint Highlights CDC Turmoil on Climate," *Scientific American*, August 14, 2019; Sam Fossum, "USDA Moving Ahead with Reorganization Plan Opponents Argue Would 'Eviscerate' Research Units," *CNN.com*, May 31, 2019.

150. *Trump v. Hawaii*, 138 S. Ct. 2392 (2017).

151. Josh Chafetz, *Congress's Constitution: Legislative Authority and the Separation of Powers* (Yale University Press, 2017); Mariano-Florentino Cuéllar, "From Doctrine to Safeguards in American Constitutional Democracy," *UCLA Law Review* 65 (2018), pp. 1398–1428.

152. Chafetz, *Congress's Constitution*, pp. 63–64.

153. Official Congressional Directory, 115th Congress (2017), pp. 349–51; Pasachoff, "The President's Budget," p. 2195.

154. Pasachoff, "The President's Budget," pp. 2286–86.

PART II

CENTRAL CLEARANCE

FIVE

OMB's Role Inside the White House

MARTHA B. COVEN

I served for the first three years of the Obama administration as a special assistant to the president at the Domestic Policy Council and for the next three as an associate director at the Office of Management and Budget (OMB). It took two minutes to move to my new office—a quick trip down a flight of stairs and around a corner. That's how embedded this tiny but mighty federal agency is in the larger operation called the Executive Office of the President. Or as it is less formally known, the White House.

OMB has been in the thick of White House decisionmaking for decades. In 1990, *Washington Post* writer Marjorie Williams described OMB as "the central nervous system of domestic policy" under the leadership of legendary Reagan-era director David Stockman and George H. W. Bush-era director Richard Darman.[1] Each of the last four presidents has asked an OMB director to serve as White House chief of staff, and four of their OMB directors have also served as cabinet secretaries.[2]

This chapter explores that central nervous system, seeking to answer two related questions: What role does OMB play inside the White House, and how do White House staff perceive OMB? It then illustrates the relationship between OMB and the rest of the White House with two brief

101

case studies: preparing the president's State of the Union address and responding to a major crisis like a natural disaster.

The observations in this chapter are drawn from domestic policymaking experiences in the Obama administration, with some references to prior administrations.[3] However, they appear to remain largely true in the Trump administration, judging from the limited public and private reflections available to me from individuals serving in that administration.

WHAT ROLE DOES OMB PLAY INSIDE THE WHITE HOUSE?

OMB may be small by federal agency standards, but it is a big part of the Executive Office of the President (EOP). The EOP was created in 1939 by President Franklin Roosevelt, when he transferred the Bureau of the Budget (as OMB was then called) from the Treasury Department to his office.[4] The EOP has grown since that time and now includes more than a dozen offices, but OMB is the single largest component.

In 2019, OMB employed one in four EOP staff, with an estimated 480 full-time equivalent positions.[5] Other large EOP components include the 450 people formally classified as employees of "the White House," as well as the Office of Administration (which provides support services) and the Office of the U.S. Trade Representative, each of which employs about 250 people.

The National Security Council (NSC) appears large, but only because many agency personnel are detailed or assigned to work there temporarily.[6] In 2019, the NSC and the companion Homeland Security Council directly employed just fifty-eight people, while the total NSC professional staff is capped by law at 200.[7] NSC staff is now shrinking; in October 2019, President Trump's national security advisor announced plans to reduce the number of people serving in policy roles at the NSC from 174 to under 120.[8]

The vast majority of OMB staff are based in the New Executive Office Building (NEOB, or "the Red Building," in OMB parlance), located half a block from the Eisenhower Executive Office Building (EEOB, or "the Gray Building") where most White House staff work. OMB staff have badges permitting them to enter the secure perimeter bounded by Pennsylvania Avenue that includes not only the EEOB but also the White House building itself. Like other EOP staff, OMB employees are among the privileged few who can give West Wing tours to their friends and family. From most outward appearances, they seem like other White House staff.

Yet they are different. While most White House staff are politically appointed, approximately 90 percent of OMB staff are civil servants, also known as career staff, whose jobs continue even after a president leaves office.[9] This is also true of the people employed by the Office of Administration and other operational units within the White House, but unlike those other units, OMB gets deeply involved in developing and carrying out the president's policy agenda. It does so in three central ways: by helping to operationalize the agenda, by connecting White House staff with agency experts, and by spotting issues as they arise across the executive branch.

Helping to Operationalize the President's Agenda

Even before a new president is elected, OMB career staff are already preparing to turn campaign promises into implementable government policies. In a practice dating back at least to the Eisenhower administration, OMB staff are permitted during a presidential election year to spend time studying the proposals put forward on the campaign trail by the full array of candidates, regardless of party, even when an incumbent president is running for reelection.[10] The idea is that as soon as a president is elected, the transition team will be scrambling to figure out how to put an agenda together, and OMB can get ahead of that process by cataloging the proposals, filling in programmatic details often missing from big-picture campaign ideas, identifying the agency best positioned to implement each proposal, and determining whether funding is already available or needs to be requested from Congress in the president's first budget.

OMB continues to play this role of operationalizing the president's agenda throughout an administration. OMB is well-positioned to do this, because it has more than 200 program experts (on the "B" side), as well as experts in management issues like procurement and IT (on the "M" side), lawyers (in the general counsel's office), and regulatory experts (in the Office of Information and Regulatory Affairs) who can be mobilized to figure out how to solve a particular problem. OMB also has institutional memory, because it employs so many career staff, and can draw on experiences from prior administrations. It does so carefully, without violating confidences. There is even a separate network drive on the OMB computer system for historical files that political appointees cannot access.

It is, therefore, not surprising that the Trump plan to declare a national emergency at the Southwest border in 2019 came out of OMB as a potential solution to the president's problem that Congress was not providing the funding he desired for a border wall. The *Washington Post* reported that Acting White House Chief of Staff Mick Mulvaney "initially formulated the idea in his role as director of the Office of Management and Budget and presented the president with a lengthy memo describing how it would work."[11]

Why doesn't all the work of operationalizing the president's agenda happen in the policy councils, in coordination with executive branch agencies? The EOP houses several of these policy offices, which are led and staffed by political appointees with substantial subject matter expertise. Among them are the Domestic Policy Council, the National Economic Council, and the National Security Council, as well as a handful of other offices. The policy councils do take the lead on major initiatives, in coordination with other senior White House staff. For example, President Obama's plan to solve the problem of childhood obesity within a generation—which was the policy complement to the First Lady's "Let's Move!" initiative—was developed by an interagency task force chaired by the head of the Domestic Policy Council.[12]

But the policy councils pick and choose what to focus on. This is, in part, because their small staff size limits their capacity; there were only a couple dozen people on the Domestic Policy Council staff during my time there. It is also because they don't have statutory responsibilities to carry out—their agenda is entirely self-created. If the policy councils want to get involved in the weedy aspects of governing, they can. If they prefer to spend their time on more communications-driven activities, they can do that, too. They know they can rely on OMB and the agencies to get the rest of the work done.

Other parts of the White House play an even more limited role in policy implementation. Outside of the policy councils and the White House counsel's office, most White House staff focus on stakeholder engagement, congressional relations, communications, or event-planning, and are less experienced in the technical aspects of governing. OMB provides the operational expertise and fills in the gaps to keep the president's agenda moving along.

Connecting White House Staff with Agency Experts

OMB staff frequently play the role of connecting their White House colleagues with experts in executive branch agencies. This is particularly needed in the beginning of an administration, when the agencies have few political appointees in place. Of the roughly 1,200 positions requiring Senate confirmation, just over 200 nominees had been confirmed six months into the George W. Bush and Obama administrations, and only fifty at the same point in the Trump administration.[13] OMB's career staff, meanwhile, are constantly interacting with their counterparts across the executive branch on budget, regulatory, and management matters. They often identify the relevant agency experts to pull in to advise or assist White House staff.

Identifying Issues as They Arise across the Executive Branch

OMB functions as the "eyes on the enterprise" for the White House across the vast executive branch. At any point in time, there is an extraordinary volume of activity happening in this multi-trillion-dollar operation. Although agencies often chafe at OMB's outsized role in overseeing the executive branch, it is the formal OMB review and clearance process for regulations, testimony, and legislation—as well as the informal, ongoing dialogue between OMB and the agencies about budgets and other matters—that ensures the president's agenda is consistently carried out throughout government.

On the B side of OMB, program examiners, each of whom is tasked with monitoring a specific set of federal programs, projects, and activities, are often the first in the EOP to become aware of a new policy question or controversial implementation issue arising within an agency. Program examiners report such developments to their direct manager (a branch chief, who in turn reports to a deputy associate director, or DAD), who decides whether to inform their political appointee (the program associate director, or PAD), through an email, phone call, or impromptu meeting.

Depending on the nature of the issue, the PAD may call it to the attention of the policy councils or other White House staff, so they can weigh in on how to proceed. If the issue seems particularly sensitive or likely to attract media attention, the PAD may choose to brief the OMB director or deputy director, who will either provide on-the-spot guidance or raise the issue with other senior White House staff.

A similar sequence unfolds in other parts of OMB, with career staff flagging critical developments for political appointees (often referred to as policy officials), who decide what further communications are necessary inside the White House. In theory, the White House Office of Cabinet Affairs could play this role of gathering information from agencies and determining what needs to be shared with others. In practice, it has a small staff who generally focus on the highest-profile issues at cabinet-level agencies. Here, too, OMB fills in gaps in the White House staffing structure.

HOW DO WHITE HOUSE STAFF PERCEIVE OMB?

The relationship between OMB and the rest of the White House evolves over the course of a presidency. It begins with some caution on the part of White House staff, but over time they come to appreciate the expertise OMB can provide, and rely on OMB staff in many internal deliberative processes. By the end of a president's first term, more often than not, the staffs are working closely together.

White House staff regard OMB career staff with some caution, especially at the beginning of a new administration. When you work in politics, you pick a team and stick with it. So it can be difficult for White House staff, who often come from having worked on a campaign or on Capitol Hill, to trust a group of people whose loyalties shift with each election. This is particularly the case when the previous president is from a different political party than the incoming president. But it can happen even when there is no change in party control of the White House. Very likely, the incoming president had to distinguish him or herself on the campaign trail from the outgoing president, whether in style or substance or both, and that can lead to tensions between their staffs even if they are from the same political party.[14]

White House staff soon learn to look to OMB career staff for assistance, however. This is partly borne of necessity. As noted, it can take time for executive branch agencies and even the White House itself to staff up at the beginning of an administration. OMB's career staff are on the job on day one, and likely have already been engaging with the president's transition team. OMB's political appointees are typically in place on day one as well, or soon thereafter. Few OMB political appointments require Senate confirmation (and on the B side, where most staff work, only the director and deputy director are Senate-confirmed), and getting OMB leadership in place early is a priority given the agency's broad mission and responsibilities.[15] These responsibilities include helping the president fulfill the requirement in the Congressional Budget Act to deliver a budget request on or before the first Monday in February, though this date often slips.[16] So even in the first few weeks after a new president is inaugurated, OMB and White House staff are starting to get to know one another and work together, which helps to build trust.

There are rare exceptions. While most OMB career staff are consummate professionals and give their best advice regardless of whether they agree with the policy agenda being pursued, a handful will do what they can to steer the agenda in a conservative or progressive direction, or use their position to slow-walk a presidential initiative instead of facilitating its implementation. But if the organization is well managed, these individuals do not end up wielding much influence. Moreover, career staff who feel they cannot in good faith support the president's agenda usually choose to leave, though OMB generally does not experience substantial turnover after a change in party control of the White House. Even after the dramatic shift from President Obama to President Trump, OMB staff remained fairly stable.

Some White House staff underestimate OMB staff, and assume they are "just" focused on money. As Paul O'Neill, a former deputy OMB director who went on to be President George W. Bush's Treasury secretary, once noted, "If you are responsible for advising the President about numbers, you are—de facto—in the stream of every policy decision made by the federal government."[17] Not everyone realizes this. As a result, White House staff may get far into a policy development process before they figure out that OMB has a role.

Some White House staff perceive OMB staff narrowly, as accountants rather than policy experts, and assume the only lens they bring to a discussion is a green eyeshade. This is not a fair description of most OMB staff, though there are some budget examiners who mainly oversee salaries and expense accounts and pay little attention to an agency's broader policy agenda. Similarly, while many Office of Information and Regulatory Affairs (OIRA) career staff are skilled at shaping policy compromises, some limit their scope to process-related matters.

OMB staff also place themselves in the background in White House meetings in a way that can end up downplaying their role. EEOB meeting rooms are set up with one large conference table surrounded by chairs and a second ring of chairs behind them. OMB career staff nearly always select those back-benching "staff chairs." While they do so out of respect for the chain of command, it disconnects them from the discussion, particularly if they don't speak during the meeting. This adds to the misleading impression that their role in a policy process is limited and perhaps merely dollar-driven.

The "No-MB" reputation is at times deserved. OMB is usually respected but not exactly beloved by executive branch agencies. Often, OMB has to tell an agency it cannot do something it wants to do, like make a specific budget request of Congress or put a particular provision in a final regulation. The "No-MB" moniker didn't come out of nowhere.

This perception of OMB can also exist inside the White House. White House staff tend to think in terms of big ideas and public-facing messages, while OMB staff are trained to think through all the operational details of a program or policy. As a result, OMB often ends up explaining why an action White House staff want to take is not feasible. Similarly, OMB's edits on documents that circulate internally for review are among the most pointed.

OMB often says no for good reasons—when the law simply doesn't permit an action to be taken, for example, or a proposed policy shift is being announced before it has been vetted and agreed to through the OMB-led interagency clearance process. In those cases, the PAD or another OMB policy official may have to play the heavy, pushing back on White House colleagues who want to ignore the substantive or procedural objections. But there are times when OMB career staff reflexively say no rather than creatively deploying their problem-solving skills to find a way to get to yes.

As time goes on, White House staff often—but not always—engage OMB career staff in policy development processes. OMB's political appointees are almost always at the table in White House policy processes. Indeed, OMB political appointees are virtually indistinguishable from other White House staff. During the Obama administration, the OMB director attended the daily early morning meeting of the most senior White House staff. PADs and other senior political appointees at OMB have security badges that permit them to move freely around the West Wing and they have dining privileges at the Navy Mess, a restaurant in the West Wing open only to senior staff.

There is a good reason for this. OMB's political appointees cannot do their jobs well if they are not strongly connected to the rest of the White House, since every day they are making judgment calls and decisions on behalf of the president and applying a political filter to determine what developments in the agencies need to be called to the attention of White House colleagues. At least one person has even served simultaneously as both OMB staff and White House staff. In the final year of the Clinton administration, OMB's Education, Income Maintenance, and Labor PAD also served as deputy director of the White House Domestic Policy Council.[18]

OMB's political appointees have broad, cross-cutting portfolios that give them a role in a wide range of policy domains. The director and deputy director oversee all federal agencies and, therefore, have a hand in nearly every domestic or foreign policy matter. PADs each oversee approximately one-fifth of federal spending. The OIRA administrator reviews all regulatory actions determined to be "significant," as well as a variety of other matters.

Whether OMB career staff have a seat at the policy development table in the White House, however, is left to the discretion of OMB's political appointees, though some administrations have had a de facto policy of routing all communication with OMB through appointees. Career staff who bring technical expertise, historical context, or agency relationships are more likely to be invited to join policy discussions. This happens more and more as an administration goes on and people get to know one another.

Sometimes, policy councils even start to treat OMB career staff as their own, which can be useful to both sides, though it can also result in too much work being piled on OMB staff on top of their ordinary responsibilities. It makes sense for OMB program examiners to help work through the mechanics of how an initiative or program would be implemented, but branch chiefs may see it as crossing a workload line if their staff are asked to draft White House factsheets or reports. And while OMB staff are known for putting in long hours in crunch times, they may resist requests from White House staff that require after-hours work on short notice, unless it is truly necessary to carry out the president's agenda.

In some circumstances, OMB political appointees will choose not to bring their career staff into a policy conversation. This is particularly likely when a discussion is politically sensitive and White House colleagues may feel uncomfortable having OMB career staff in the room. Nor would career staff necessarily want to be there. This could happen, for example, if there was expected to be discussion of how various policy options would affect public perceptions of the president or the president's standing with interest groups. In these situations, OMB political appointees might be prepped in advance by or report back to their career staff. But it is not unusual for career staff to be left in the dark entirely, unaware that a policy discussion is even happening or what was decided, often to their frustration.

Most White House staff come to value OMB staff; by the end of a president's first term, the two teams generally work seamlessly together. The relationships between White House staff and OMB staff deepen over time, and trust builds with each successful interaction and partnership. If an administration lasts into a second term, OMB career staff also increasingly play the role of serving as that president's institutional memory. This is particularly true of DADs and branch chiefs, who typically stay in their jobs longer than White House staff or OMB program examiners.[19] Looking around the room at a goodbye party for a White House policy staffer, one finds several OMB faces. The White House and OMB staffs, by the end of an administration, almost become a single team.

TWO CASE STUDIES

The case studies that follow illustrate the role OMB plays inside the White House in two different kinds of situations. The first is the political, public act of delivering the annual State of the Union address. The second is the apolitical task of mobilizing the government to respond to a crisis such as a natural disaster. In both cases, OMB plays a role inside the White House that is not well known outside of the executive branch.

Preparing the President's State of the Union Address

The President's State of the Union address is typically the biggest speech of the year, so one would expect the policy, political, and communications experts in the White House to take the lead in developing it, in consultation with the president. The process is indeed driven by the policy councils, the president's speechwriters, and other senior advisers.

But OMB also plays a role in the policy dimensions of the State of the Union. Political appointees, such as the director, deputy director, and PADs, are most likely to be involved, but occasionally career staff are pulled in, too, given their expertise. The words of the speech itself are tightly held throughout the drafting process, and OMB career staff are not given the opportunity to review or comment on the text—nor are many political appointees, for that matter. But the policy content bears OMB's imprint.

Why is OMB at the table for discussions of the policy deliverables in the State of the Union address? In part, it is because policy proposals almost always have budgetary effects. OMB is needed to make sure there are resources available or requested to support a proposal the president is announcing, to make it credible.

The calendar, however, is the main reason OMB is involved in the State of the Union process. Though the Constitution does not specify a date for the State of the Union, and only requires "Information of the State of the Union" to be given to Congress "from time to time," by long tradition, the president delivers the State of the Union as an address to a joint session of Congress in January or February.[20] Meanwhile, the Congressional Budget Act requires the president's budget to be submitted on or before the first Monday in February.[21]

On paper, this suggests that the State of the Union would be developed in parallel with the president's budget request for the next fiscal year. In practice, the budget development process begins much earlier—as early as the spring of the previous year at the agency level. OMB has made nearly all decisions about the policy direction and major initiatives in the budget by late November or December, when the State of the Union process begins. This makes sense, because preparing a detailed $4 trillion budget is a far more complex task than writing a speech. Even in years when the budget release is delayed—for example, because the previous year's appropriations process has run particularly late—OMB usually has wrapped up most of its work by the end of December.

This gives OMB a jump on the State of the Union process. OMB can even end up driving the discussion around a major initiative being considered for the address, since it has to have been baked into the budget or else the president won't appear to have been serious about it when the budget is released. Initiatives presented in the budget are developed in consultation with the policy councils and with direction from the president, of course. But they are usually developed through the OMB-led budget process, not in the subsequent White House-led process of crafting a State of the Union address. Indeed, the address often previews proposals presented in more detail in the budget submitted to Congress shortly thereafter.[22]

Admittedly, some White Houses have felt freer than others to promote funding requests not actually built into the president's budget. For example, the OMB-prepared budget for fiscal year 2019 requested $1.6 billion for the Southwest border, and even though no budget amendment was submitted, President Trump began advocating for more than $5 billion in a high-stakes maneuver that led to the longest government shutdown in history.[23] But the expectation that the budget and presidential statements will be consistent with one another has generally held.

Crisis Response in the White House

When a crisis like a natural disaster happens, the White House's focus appropriately turns to overseeing the federal government's response. The Federal Emergency Management Agency is in charge of immediate on-the-ground measures, and can tap resources in the short term from the Disaster Relief Fund, but a more comprehensive effort is often needed to address large-scale disasters.

OMB's relationships with agency personnel, understanding of the flow of funds, and programmatic expertise all position it well to engage quickly and gather information in a crisis situation. One of the tools OMB can use is to issue a "data call" (called a Budget Data Request, or BDR) across the executive branch to collect information about how a crisis like a natural disaster is affecting federal operations, grants, and contracts.

As one example of an impact that might not be identified quickly without a comprehensive inquiry across the executive branch, 2012's

Hurricane Sandy damaged several Head Start centers supported by grants from the U.S. Department of Health and Human Services. Disaster response isn't generally thought of as a concern for Head Start, but OMB helped surface this issue, among many others. The seventy-seven-page supplemental budget request submitted by OMB to Congress six weeks after Sandy struck included a $100 million request to serve displaced Head Start children and to repair and rebuild centers affected by the storm.[24]

The White House, with its limited staff and uneven expertise, would have difficulty collecting and assessing information from across the government in an efficient and timely manner. The partnership with OMB on tasks like this in a crisis ensures that the job gets done, while permitting White House staff to focus on the political and communications aspects of the response.

CONCLUSION

Nestled within the EOP, OMB plays a critical role in advancing the president's policy agenda. OMB staff—the largest component within the EOP—help operationalize the agenda, connect White House staff with agency experts, and spot issues as they arise across the executive branch.

The relationship between the politically-appointed White House staff and the civil servants at OMB can be awkward, particularly at the start of an administration. OMB's role in policy development and implementation is also sometimes overlooked by White House staff who misperceive OMB staff as bean counters. And OMB's cautionary tendencies can frustrate White House staff at times. But over time, White House staff learn to trust and rely on OMB, and often engage career staff directly in policy development.

As a result, OMB has a hand in nearly every policy-related process in a White House, from influencing the proposals put forward in the president's State of the Union address to managing the response to a crisis like a natural disaster.

Notes

1. Marjorie Williams, "The Long and the Short of Richard G. Darman," *Washington Post*, July 29, 1990, p. SM10. Reprinted as Marjorie Williams, "The Pragmatist (Richard Darman)," in *The Woman at the National Zoo: Writings on Politics, Family, and Fate* (New York: PublicAffairs, 2005), pp. 30–54.

2. In the Clinton administration, Leon Panetta served as OMB director from 1993 to 1994 and as chief of staff from 1994 to 1997; in the George W. Bush administration, Josh Bolten served as OMB director from 2003 to 2006 and as chief of staff from 2006 to 2009; in the Obama administration, Jack Lew served as OMB director from 2010 to 2012 (after having served as OMB director in the Clinton administration from 1998 to 2001) and as chief of staff from 2012 to 2013; and in the Trump administration, Mick Mulvaney served as OMB director starting in 2017 and as acting chief of staff starting in 2019. Clinton-era OMB director Leon Panetta later served as Secretary of Defense under President Obama; two Obama-era OMB directors went on to head cabinet departments (Sylvia Burwell, who went to the Department of Health and Human Services, and Jack Lew, who later headed the Department of the Treasury); and one Obama-era OMB director had previously served as a cabinet secretary (Shaun Donovan, at the Department of Housing and Urban Development).

3. For a discussion of how OMB staff interact with others in the EOP on national security matters, see Gordon Adams, Rodney Bent, and Kathleen Peroff, "The Office of Management and Budget: The President's Policy Tool," in *The National Security Enterprise: Navigating the Labyrinth*, 2nd edition, edited by Roger Z. George and Harvey Rishikof (Georgetown University Press, 2017), pp. 57–78.

4. See Franklin D. Roosevelt, Message to Congress on the Reorganization Act, April 25, 1939, www.presidency.ucsb.edu/documents/message-congress-the-reorganization-act, and Executive Order 8248, September 8, 1939.

5. See Executive Office of the President, "Fiscal Year 2020 Congressional Budget Submission," www.whitehouse.gov/wp-content/uploads/2019/03/EOP_FY20_Congressional_Budget_Submission.pdf, p. EOP-9.

6. See Adams, Bent, and Peroff, "The Office of Management and Budget: The President's Policy Tool," p. 73 ("Most NSC staff are nonpermanent representatives from DOD, State, Homeland Security, and the IC").

7. See 50 U.S.C. 3021(e)(3).

8. See Robert C. O'Brien, "Here's How I Will Streamline Trump's National Security Council," *Washington Post*, October 16, 2019, www.washingtonpost.com/opinions/robert-c-obrien-heres-how-i-will-streamline-trumps-national-security-council/2019/10/16/2b306360-f028-11e9-89eb-ec56cd414732_story.html.

9. See U.S. Senate Committee on Homeland Security and Governmental Affairs, "United States Government Policy and Supporting Positions" (Washington: U.S. Government Publishing Office, 2016), commonly referred to as the Plum Book, pp. 5–7 (listing fifty-two politically appointed positions at OMB).

10. See Bradley H. Patterson, *To Serve the President: Continuity and Innovation in the White House Staff* (Brookings Institution Press, 2008), p. 99 (describing a practice in the then Bureau of the Budget during the 1960 presidential campaign of compiling two catalogues, a "Jacklopedia" and a "Dicklopedia," summarizing the campaign promises of candidates John F. Kennedy and Richard M. Nixon, respectively).

11. Matt Zapotosky and Josh Dawsey, "How President Trump Came to Declare a National Emergency to Fund His Border Wall," *Washington Post*, February 15, 2019, www.washingtonpost.com/world/national-security/how-president-trump-came-to-declare-a-national-emergency-to-fund-his-border-wall/2019/02/15/3e9f4348-3152-11e9-8ad3-9a5b113ecd3c_story.html.

12. See The White House, "Presidential Memorandum—Establishing a Task Force on Childhood Obesity," February 9, 2010, https://obamawhitehouse

.archives.gov/the-press-office/presidential-memorandum-establishing-a-task-force-childhood-obesity.

13. See Jan Diehm and others, "Tracking Trump's Nominations," CNN Politics, December 31, 2017, www.cnn.com/interactive/2017/politics/trump-nominations. This includes an interactive graphic showing the total nominations and confirmations at each point in the first two years of the Bush, Obama, and Trump administrations.

14. See, for example, John F. Harris, "Clinton and Gore Clashed over Blame for Election," *Washington Post*, February 7, 2001.

15. In total, seven OMB political appointees must be confirmed by the Senate: the director; deputy director; deputy director for management; intellectual property enforcement coordinator; administrator, Office of Information and Regulatory Affairs; controller, Office of Federal Fiscal Management; and administrator, Office of Federal Procurement Policy. See Senate Committee on Homeland Security and Governmental Affairs, "United States Government Policy and Supporting Positions," pp. 5–6.

16. See 2 U.S.C. 631.

17. See Shelley Lynne Tomkin, *Inside OMB: Politics and Process in the President's Budget Office* (New York: Routledge, 1998), p. 4 (quoting a speech given by O'Neill to OMB staff in 1988).

18. See Biography of Barbara Chow, www.csg.org/2012NationalConference/EducationLegislativeBriefing.aspx (noting that "From 1997 to 2001, Barbara worked in the Office of Management and Budget, where she was the program associate director for education, income maintenance, and labor. Starting in 2000, she kept the OMB position and added the position of deputy director of the White House Domestic Policy Council.").

19. See Eloise Pasachoff, "The President's Budget as a Source of Agency Policy Control," *Yale Law Journal* (June 2016), n. 326.

20. Article II, Section 3 of the U.S. Constitution. For the actual dates of the in-person delivery of State of the Union addresses dating back to George Washington, see Office of the Historian, U.S. House of Representatives, "List of In-Person Annual Message and State of the Union Addresses," https://history.house.gov/Institution/SOTU/List/ (showing that the last president to deliver the address in a month other than January or February was Calvin Coolidge, in 1923).

21. See 2 U.S.C. 631.

22. See, for example, "Remarks by the President in State of the Union Address: January 20, 2015," https://obamawhitehouse.archives.gov/the-press-office/2015/01/20/remarks-president-state-union-address-January-20-2015 ("My plan will make quality childcare more available and more affordable for every middle-class and low-income family with young children in America—by creating more slots and a new tax cut of up to $3,000 per child, per year"), which previewed the FY 2016 budget proposals delivered to Congress two weeks later, on February 2, 2015. See "Fiscal Year 2016 Budget of the U.S. Government," www.govinfo.gov/content/pkg/BUDGET-2016-BUD/pdf/BUDGET-2016-BUD.pdf, pp. 34, 53 (summarizing the child care spending and tax proposals).

23. For the original budget request, see "An American Budget: Fiscal Year 2019," www.whitehouse.gov/wp-content/uploads/2018/02/budget-fy2019.pdf, p. 16. While no budget amendment was submitted, the acting OMB director eventually sent a letter to Congress on January 6, 2019, three months after FY 2019 had already begun, describing the $5.7 billion figure. See Letter to Senate Appropriations Committee Chairman Richard Shelby from acting OMB direc-

tor Russell T. Vought, January 6, 2019, www.whitehouse.gov/wp-content/uploads/2019/01/Final-Shelby-1-6-19.pdf. For a description of the shutdown, see, for example, Kristina Peterson, Michael C. Bender, and Rebecca Balhaus, "Shutdown Breaks Record for Longest in Modern History," *Wall Street Journal*, January 13, 2019, www.wsj.com/articles/trump-plays-down-emergency-option-to-get-wall-funding-11547238564.

24. See Letter to House Speaker John Boehner and Senate Majority Leader Harry Reid from OMB Deputy Director for Management Jeffrey Zients (then performing the functions of the OMB director), December 7, 2012, https://obamawhitehouse.archives.gov/sites/default/files/supplemental__december_7_2012_hurricane_sandy_funding_needs.pdf.pdf, p. 16.

SIX

Projects Worth the Price

OMB and the Central Clearance of Legislation and Executive Orders

ANDREW RUDALEVIGE

In 1935, Labor Secretary Frances Perkins had a question for President Franklin Delano Roosevelt. "Why should one refer to the Bureau of the Budget a question of policy?" she wondered. "It seems a peculiar thing to do.... You say the Director of the Budget passes upon the question as to whether the project is worth the price?"

Roosevelt quickly demurred. Non-budgetary items would be passed on to his Cabinet-level National Emergency Council, he said: "[If] it is a fiscal matter involving the expenditure of money, one way or the other, it clears through the Director of the Budget.... He gives me factual information about finances, that is all."[1]

Yet the administrative and budgetary landscape had been dramatically changed by the Depression and New Deal; as the Brownlow Committee would soon conclude, "the president needs help."[2] Roosevelt craved information and coordination, the ability to unite the executive branch behind his priorities and preferences, a government-wide view, and the ability to coordinate a wide-flung bureaucracy. In 1946, as Budget director Harold Smith summed up: "To help [the president] work out the program of the Government . . . it would be absolutely necessary to have a separate staff operating in a detached, objective atmosphere to supply him with information and to check all information that came in . . ." Where Cabinet officers were concerned, "neither their judgments nor their facts can be altogether trusted—not because they are in any way dishonest men, but because their facts and their judgments are colored by personal ambitions and their operating experience in only a segment of the government. [The president] must be so well-equipped that [he] can direct the heads of departments and say, 'here's what I want done and here's what I do not want done.' "[3]

This need translated into a number of distinct services—but most of them wound up in a newly fortified Bureau of the Budget (BOB), which moved from the Treasury department to become the bulwark of a new Executive Office of the President in 1939.[4] It would provide enhanced analysis of budgetary and fiscal matters, organizational and managerial concerns, and the substance of policies and programs. Tying all this together was a new mechanism of "central clearance"—of legislation, enrolled bills, departmental testimony, and executive orders—that could impose a chokepoint on transactions between the White House, the executive branch, and Congress. It would provide information about what the departments were up to as well as a substantive sense of the worth of those endeavors. In short: it would determine whether the "project was worth the price."

This chapter examines the history and practice of central clearance as implemented for legislation and executive orders. (Proposed regulations would be added to the roster later, a development discussed elsewhere in this volume.) It traces the rise of a presidential legislative program, and the need for coordination that engendered, before turning to the practice of clearance in the formulation of executive orders. These histories draw heavily on archival documents as well as on research by and interviews with participants in the process.

The chapter concludes with an assessment of the state and utility of central clearance generally as a tool of present-day presidential management. "Over the years, the basic purpose of the central legislative clearance requirement has remained the same," as an internal Office of Management and Budget (OMB) manual put it in 1993, namely "to ensure that Presidential policies are reflected correctly on legislative matters before the Congress."⁵ Or, as longtime OMB legislative attorney Jeffrey Weinberg noted in a recent article, "The process has been used, basically unchanged, by all modern presidents, because it is such an effective tool."⁶

MANAGING A PRESIDENT'S PROGRAM

As William McKinley prepared to take office near the end of the nineteenth century, a contemporary scholar acidly observed that "the President has . . . so slight a share in initiating the legislative policy. His message to Congress is really an address to the country and has no direct influence upon Congress."⁷ Yet fifty years later, by the time of the Truman administration, direct presidential involvement in the legislative process had become a given. In the wake of Franklin Roosevelt's tidal wave of New Deal bills, the president was dubbed "legislator-in-chief" and the legislative branch suddenly deemed a very junior partner in the initiation of legislation. Congress might or might not be inclined to dispose, but the president was certainly expected to propose. As Truman's election loomed, such proposals became presidential strategy; as White House counsel Charles Murphy noted, in 1948, the White House "wanted to have a special message ready to go to Congress every Monday morning."⁸

This is the genesis of the president's program as we know it today, a package of recommendations comprehensive in subject matter, specific in prescription, and bounded in scope. As Richard Neustadt puts it, the program serves as "a comprehensive and coordinated inventory of the nation's current legislative needs, reflecting the President's own judgments, choices, and priorities in every major area of Federal action."⁹ Sporadic recommendations became a systematic agenda, and both Congress and the executive agencies adapted to the new institution. When, in 1953, the new Eisenhower administration was slow in producing its program, a House committee chair took offense: "Don't expect us to start from scratch on what you people want. That's not the way we do things here—*you* draft the bills and *we* work them over."¹⁰ Likewise, in 1965, Senate majority leader Mike Mansfield wrote to President Lyndon Johnson pleading for him to "prevail upon the Departments to get the relevant draft legislation to the Senate as soon as possible." After all, "time is now being lost, when Committees could be working on significant parts of your program." By the late 1970s, presidential aides were almost fatalistic about these demands. "Since we must propose legislation which will be the embodiment of our governmental programs," one staffer wrote, "we cannot avoid sending up draft legislation."[11]

In short, what Stephen Wayne would later dub "the legislative presidency" had arrived, and was here to stay.[12] But this demanded a capacity for centralized policy formulation and evaluation. That, in turn, was provided by the legislative clearance functions centered in the BOB.

Institutional Innovations

The Budget Bureau had been created by the Budget and Accounting Act of 1921 and placed in the Treasury, though reporting directly to the president, who was in turn charged by the act with the annual presentation of a consolidated executive budget. At the time, departments and agencies sent their funding requests directly to Congress, giving little scope for centralized management or, for that matter, a coherent sense of how each program fit into national needs and priorities. Creating the BOB was a nod toward the best principles of contemporary public administration, which (with no little wishful thinking) viewed the president as a true chief executive in the sense that phrase applied in the private sector. As a 1921 business journal put it, the president must "successfully administer the biggest business in the world despite the interferences of Congress." Yet "by the standards of business he cannot successfully do any such thing. . . . A dozen big business men combined into one could not do it—because he hasn't the instruments with which to work."[13]

The first director of BOB, Charles Dawes, saw an opportunity for what he called "the reorganization of the routine business of government through the use by the president of the Budget Bureau as an agency of executive pressure, and the creation . . . of coordinating machinery."[14] In December 1921, a BOB circular (already #49 in a series) told executive branch agencies that any proposal, "the effect of which would be to create a charge upon the public Treasury. . . . should be first submitted" to BOB, which would determine whether it was "in accord with the financial program of the President."[15] (Worried about departmental evasion of the new act, congressional leaders did not object to this extra-statutory power play.) Under the Republican administrations of the 1920s, the process was used mainly to keep down expenditures. But it took on broader meaning with the flurry of policy proposals that marked the start of the New Deal.[16]

The range of policies subject to BOB review began to expand as well.

In late 1935, President Franklin Roosevelt directed that the bureau should receive copies of all executive-proposed legislation, prompting some pushback—including the colloquy between Roosevelt and Secretary Perkins quoted earlier.[17] But when the Cabinet-level National Emergency Council was phased out in 1937, BOB took over not only its records but its coordinating functions.[18] Indeed, it created a Division of Coordination in 1938. Such a development was consonant with Dawes's focus on the Bureau's use as "an agency of executive pressure" and the importance of administrative "machinery"—a word Roosevelt himself had used as early as 1919 when, as assistant secretary of the Navy, he had testified to Congress about strengthening presidents' ability to direct the actions of the wider executive branch.[19]

The scope of BOB's duties would greatly expand thereafter, especially with its shift from the Treasury Department into the new Executive Office of the President (EOP) and the appointment of Harold D. Smith as budget director, both in 1939. Executive Order 8248 confirmed that the BOB's job as part of the EOP included "assist[ing] the President by clearing and coordinating departmental advice on proposed legislation and by making recommendations as to Presidential action on legislative enactments, in accordance with past practice" (as well as the "consideration and clearance and, where necessary, in the preparation of proposed Executive orders and proclamations," as discussed later.)[20]

Smith, a professional public administrator and aggressive advocate of executive-centered leadership in government, created a Legislative Reference Division (LRD) to replace the Division of Coordination. "Reference" sounded less threatening to legislators, Smith thought, but the idea was for the new LRD to be more powerful, not less.[21] In 1939, it processed departmental comments on some 2,400 pending bills (up from 300 in 1935), and on over 400 drafts of proposed legislation (up from 170). As Smith reminded Roosevelt several years later, "recognition of the necessity for coordination was the basic reason for transferring" BOB into the EOP, enhancing presidential leverage "in all fields of governmental activities."[22]

By 1945, the process of central clearance required that Legislative Reference review ("clear") all administration-proposed legislation to determine its relationship to the president's agenda. It designated whether the proposed law was "in accord" with, "consistent with" (or "not consistent with"), or "not in accord" with the president's own priorities. A fourth category registered "no objection to" the proposal from the president's perspective. Departmental testimony on any legislation pending before Congress also required clearance, as well as enrolled bills (that is, those approved by Congress and awaiting presidential action). As discussed later in more detail, key to the process was the LRD's efforts to seek out all agencies across the executive branch that might have an interest in the legislation at hand, both to inform them and to solicit their comments. But at this stage, departments were not yet sold. As Smith told President Truman, as late as 1946, "clearances—if at all—were more by accident than by design." The exception was in the area of enrolled bills awaiting presidential signature or veto. Gathering comment on these provided the Bureau with a wealth of information across different policy areas as well as forging new departmental contacts.[23]

As noted, after World War II, the Bureau modified and expanded the clearance process to identify, develop, and promote a priority set of presidential legislation: in short, to manage a presidential program. Note that BOB was not the only institutional actor competing for this role.[24] Reprising Perkins's critique, trusted Truman aide John Steelman, then director of the EOP's Office of War Mobilization and Reconversion (OWMR), said, "I simply do not see why *policy* is any business of the *Budget* Bureau."[25] But when, in December 1945, Truman asked Steelman "to coordinate the whole administration program on legislation," the assignment was fumbled. As public administration scholar Luther Gulick observed, the OWMR was fine at resolving interagency conflict but not at developing a systematic positive program.[26] So when the 1946 Employment Act required the president to present an agenda for governmental action across the economy—harmonized with the State of the Union and Budget messages, BOB director Jim Webb lobbied the president to let his staff do the job. Both the lobbying and the coordination proved successful.

After the 1946 elections, Webb named career civil servant Roger Jones to head Legislative Reference. As Jones recalled in an oral history, given the new congressional majority, "quite naturally he looked for someone who was known to be a Republican. Through sheer accident, I was known to be a Republican. . . . This was the start of what . . . became a rather substantially institutional type of channel."[27] Since no White House legislative affairs staff yet existed (that began under Eisenhower), Jones and others in LRD expanded the division's ability to conduct legislative monitoring, track program items' status, learn of forthcoming congressional plans, and even mobilize what one staffer called "spot salvage operations" on troubled legislative proposals.[28] "We established for the first time a formal office for legislative analysis," Jones recalled, as LRD sought to extend its role in evaluating agency proposals for the White House.[29] This, Neustadt (then at LRD) argued, was "the only way to do a good job on this thing and keep our own hand in properly."[30] It was even suggested that BOB work to place candidates in congressional committee staff positions to give it better legislative connections, though "the initiative will have to, at least, have the appearance of coming from Congress."[31] More generally, as Assistant Director Elmer Staats wrote, BOB needed to give the president advice not only on the issues themselves (after they were "thoroughly canvassed") but on the "scope and relative emphasis in the messages on program, timing of introduction, relative administration priority, form of and responsibility for Congressional presentation, and possible upward or downward effects on budget allowances." This meant that even then Budget staffers—remember that only a handful at this stage were political appointees and none were Senate-confirmed—had to be sensitive to Truman's political interests as they identified items as part of the president's legislative program, compiled the proposals made by each department, and made substantive and strategic assessments of each.[32]

All of this culminated in BOB efforts during the 1948 campaign discussed earlier; as the campaign progressed, LRD produced a checklist of items to be considered by the (mostly White House) drafters of 1949 messages even before the agency programs arrived. Budget Circular A-19 was released on October 25, 1948, detailing the requirements for coordination and clearance procedures.[33] Then, in 1949, departments and agencies were asked for both a preliminary legislative program (along with their budget estimates) and a "final" program in conjunction with the president's annual messages. With this, a call for legislative proposals for the president's program became an annual ritual.[34]

Thus, a decade after the Coordination Division came into being, coordination—that is, legislative clearance—was finally routine, institutionalized in departmental and presidential expectations. This can be seen partly in the exceptions that proved the rule, or at least the energy expended in enforcing it. "It should be called to your attention," Roger Jones informed BOB director Percival Brundage in 1958, "that the

Bureau of the Budget did not participate in any way in the development of the President's message on extension of the Reciprocal Trade Act, or in the coordination and clearance of the bill that was sent to the Congress by the Secretary of Commerce . . . Such handling is clearly contrary to the President's instructions."[35] In a 1959 self-study, BOB concluded that "of the major Bureau functions, legislative coordination is second only to budget review in terms of demands upon division staff time." No wonder. The same study reported that, in 1958, the LRD had to clear 385 draft bills, more than 3,000 agency reports on legislation, and nearly a thousand congressional requests for information on bill status—as well as more than 1,100 enrolled bills en route to the president's signature or veto.[36]

Legislative Clearance Today

OMB Circular A-19 is still in effect, most recently revised in 1979, and continues to detail clearance procedures for pending, proposed, and enrolled substantive legislation. Agencies are bound by the substance approved by the process, which can put them in hot water with interested congressional committees.[37]

Longtime OMB civil servant Bernard Martin, who headed LRD for a time, wrote in 2008 that "the process is essentially the same for each type of proposal":

> LRD sends the document for comment to other agencies and to offices in OMB and the EOP that have a substantive interest in the document. It circulates the comments received to all relevant parties, identifies issues, and seeks to resolve them . . . frequently under short deadlines. Finally, LRD assures that disputes are resolved either by negotiation among the various parties, or by decisions from politically appointed policy officials.[38]

As the OMB's 1993 manual on clearance notes, the issues raised by the process "can be policy, program, management and organization, technical, financial, legal, or constitutional in nature."[39] This requires significant horizontal integration across OMB's different program divisions, drawing on divergent expertise. The LRD uses those divisions, the Resource Management Offices (RMOs), quite extensively. The RMOs' work undergirds the basic substantive decisions. "No LRD analyst could keep up with the multitude of issues" raised within the universe of administration legislation," Martin notes.[40] But while that does imply a sorting and rerouting function, that does not make LRD staff the "OMB equivalent of postal clerks."[41] Most are former budget examiners themselves and have a broad institutional vantage on past legislative proposals and agency perspectives.

Indeed, the process also assists the agencies.[42] That is important and sometimes overlooked, but it is one reason central clearance was able to gain traction and (mostly) cooperation across the executive branch. Agencies receive the chance to give input and OMB has the opportunity to reconcile divergent views in a sort of peer review. But it is also an early warning system. As the examples given in the next section (on executive order clearance) make clear, this informational service helps agencies find out what their colleagues are up to—and to protect themselves against any self-aggrandizement those colleagues might attempt. This, in turn, helps OMB protect the president.

Despite this continuity, some things have, indeed, shifted over time. One important change is that far fewer legislative drafts are produced by the executive branch overall these days—and beginning with George W. Bush, administrations transmitted far fewer draft bills as specific manifestations of their legislative programs. As Jeffrey Weinberg notes, in 2001 George W. Bush did not send Congress a full draft of his No Child Left Behind education reform but, instead, a "blueprint," nor did Barack Obama do so for the legislation that became the Affordable Care Act. Donald Trump's version of the 2017 Tax Cuts and Jobs Act was, similarly, a one-page outline of his goals for the legislation. This practice gives Congress more autonomy—and presidents some political flexibility, especially when the House and Senate may have very different ideas of what a good bill might look like.[43] In Obama's case, the fate of the 1,400-page health care proposal sent to Congress by Bill Clinton also played a cautionary role—the devils of the legislative process were, indeed, summoned by the details.

This shift—arguably a diminution in the LRD's role and a loss in agenda-setting power for the presidency overall—led to another; in about 2012, the long series of periodic reports that the division had compiled to keep tabs on the progress presidential program items were making in Congress came to an end, at least temporarily. This document, titled "Status of Administration Legislative Proposals," had served as a valuable catalog of the White House view of what constituted its program in a given session. Current LRD director Matt Vaeth notes that though the division continued to compile the underlying data, the shift made the system "very different from what we'd done for years and years and years."[44]

Even as the drafting function has ebbed, the tracking side of the process has become more extensive. As noted, BOB had stepped into the role of legislative liaison back in the 1940s and 1950s, before a bespoke White House staff specialized in that function. The periodic reports on the status of administration legislation kept broad tabs on the progress of the president's program as it moved through Congress. But OMB was not necessarily present in the rooms where that happened; as former staffer Bruce Johnson notes, LRD and budget analysts "often learned the outcome of subcommittee deliberations from agency officials."[45]

Under OMB director David Stockman (in that position from 1981 to 1985), agency staffers began to return to following the labyrinthine legislative process in real time. In the summer of 1982, Stockman formed bill-tracking teams that attended the subcommittee and committee markups of appropriations bills. The bill trackers "ferret[ed] out information on how the committees arrived at their estimates, and prepar[ed] their own estimates on projected costs of each proposal."[46] This allowed for "Stockman . . . to be more forceful and direct in conveying the Administration's views at all stages," as Bernard Martin puts it—for communication from OMB to the committee (though formal "views letters" are more rare these days), and to House and Senate leadership.[47] As the Reagan administration progressed, "demand from the OMB Director for more sophisticated bill statements grew" at every stage of the appropriations process, and the range of alerts to troublesome bills expanded. As Stockman reacted to those alerts, a new formal means of communication resulted: what became known as Statements of Administration Policy (SAPs).[48] In 1985, Stockman extended SAPs to nonappropriations bills.

An SAP may be issued just before House or Senate floor consideration of a bill, whether part of the president's legislative program or not.[49] It can be used to request specific changes to the legislation, as well as to convey veto threats at various levels of severity. Samuel Kernell and his coauthors identify eight different levels of endorsement for or opposition to a bill, ranging from "the administration strongly supports" to "no objection" to "senior advisors will recommend" a veto to a flat "the president will veto."[50]

As with other cleared items, SAPs reflect comments from across the executive branch and ensure an unambiguous transmission of presidential preferences to members of Congress. OMB's standardization of language for SAPs (and for that matter items cleared in other ways) helps ensure a clear signal is given. This is important given the "noise" often involved in such negotiation, as Charles Cameron's work on "veto bargaining" stresses. Indeed, recent White House–legislative engagement has sometimes foundered on Trump administration staffers' inability to speak definitively on behalf of the president.[51]

At the conclusion of the legislative process comes one more round of review, this time for the bills that have passed Congress. As those head to the president's desk, LRD elicits recommendations as to whether a bill should be signed into law or vetoed (as well as for draft texts of potential signing statements and veto messages). An OMB analyst—normally, whoever has helped track the bill through the legislative process—is responsible for surveying the relevant departments (and other parts of OMB), compiling their input, and drafting the "enrolled bill memo." As part of this, the Justice Department is always asked to weigh in as to the constitutionality of the bill's provisions.

The subsequent memo to the president from the OMB director lists the recommendations of the departments surveyed—after OMB's own recommendation—and then summarizes their substantive comments. It also provides a description of the major provisions of the pending bill. As a result, it is allowed to go past the informal two-page limit traditionally imposed on decision memos headed to the Oval Office.[52] While framed as a decision memo, by the time it reaches the president, the key choice—sign or veto—has already been made. The enrolled bill memo process is thus one that helps decide an outcome and then memorializes and formalizes its rationale, rather than one that tees it up *de novo*.

EXECUTIVE ORDERS

Executive orders (EOs) are not mentioned in the Constitution but have been used since the Washington administration as an implication of "the executive power" vested in the presidency by Article II. As Kenneth Mayer argues, they "have played a critical role in the development and exercise of presidential power."[53] They are aimed within (and binding on) the executive departments and agencies, thus relating directly to presidential control of the bureaucracy. As a widely-cited 1957 congressional study puts it:

> Executive orders and proclamations are directives or actions by the President. When they are founded on the authority of the President derived from the Constitution or statute, they may have the force and effect of law.... In the narrower sense executive orders and proclamations are written documents denominated as such.... Executive orders are generally directed to, and govern actions by, Government officials and agencies. They usually affect private individuals only indirectly.[54]

Of course, even an indirect impact can be important. When changing how stringently cost-benefit analysis is applied to regulatory review, or when requiring that government contractors and subcontractors provide a minimum wage to their employees or enforce anti-discrimination standards, for instance, EOs can certainly influence the private sector economy. The scale of that influence varies with the scope of the federal government. It is perhaps not surprising, then, that recent studies have found an upswing in the number of "significant" EOs issued by presidents over time. Federal contracts alone contribute some $500 billion to the economy annually.[55] Further, as legislative achievement became harder, administrative unilateralism became more politically and substantively attractive.

Given the importance of executive orders, then, presidents needed to manage their formulation and issuance. As noted, FDR's EO 8248 specified the BOB's role in that function, too. But that codified already-existing practice. In August 1933, Roosevelt had issued EO 6247, requiring that "the draft of an Executive order or proclamation shall first be submitted to the Director of the Bureau of the Budget," and if approved at BOB, to the Attorney General. The latter was given the job of analyzing the order "for form and legality," a task normally delegated to Justice's Office of Legal Counsel. From Justice, the order went on to State, to check on formatting and style, before the president finally received an official copy to sign.[56] Three years later, State's role was superseded as the newly-created *Federal Register* became the official publisher of most executive orders.

In February 1936, FDR issued an EO formalizing that change and making two other key amendments as well. EO 7298 required proposed

EOs to cite the statutory or constitutional authority justifying their issuance. And it strengthened the veto points at Budget and Justice: "If [the proposed order] is disapproved by the Director of the Bureau of the Budget or the Attorney General," Roosevelt directed, "it shall not thereafter be presented to the President unless it is accompanied by the statement of the reasons for such disapproval."[57]

That is the basic process in place today, updated by several additional executive orders. The most crucial is John F. Kennedy's EO 11030, "Preparation, Presentation, Filing and Publication of Executive Orders and Proclamations," issued in 1962. This order is the governing authority now cited for the clearance process. By contrast, other changes to central clearance have been largely cosmetic. In 1987, Ronald Reagan finally removed the term "Bureau of the Budget" from operative executive orders, replacing it with "Office of Management and Budget" a mere seventeen years after the agency changed its name. It was not until 2006 that George W. Bush removed the requirement that items be "typewritten," and allowed them to be submitted on standard legal-size paper. The only shifts in the formulation procedure were in 1978, when OMB was authorized to send commemorative proclamations (honoring "National Safe Boating Week" and the like) directly to the president without requiring the Attorney General's approval, and in 2014, when preparation of the highly technical trade proclamations issued under the 1974 Trade Act was vested in the United States Trade Representative rather than OMB.[58]

EO 11030 was issued because EOs frequently come from departments—they almost never spring complete from the pen of the president, despite the way we often think of "unilateralism."[59] And BOB, as it told the White House in 1962, frequently did not have "from the agencies adequate information in support of the proposed order. . . . Such information has frequently been meager and has necessitated requests for additional material."[60] Thus, to Roosevelt's "machinery," Kennedy added the requirement that those seeking issuance of an order include documentation "explaining the nature, purpose, background, and effect of the proposed Executive order or proclamation and its relationship, if any, to pertinent laws and other Executive orders or proclamations." BOB general counsel Arthur Focke stressed to Kennedy aide Ted Sorensen the need for an orderly process that would allow all aspects of an issue to be considered before an order was "presented to the President. In most cases," Focke went on, "a proposed order . . . handled under this procedure can be issued more expeditiously, and with greater protection to the President, than one which is presented and processed outside the normal channels."[61]

In early 1969, likewise, Focke was at pains to explain to the incoming Nixon administration the value of clearing orders through BOB rather than issuing them directly from the White House. The clearance process, he told new chief of staff H. R. Haldeman, would warn the president of budgetary, management, and organization implications raised by a draft order, and provide "the best judgment of the Administration as a whole." It would also avoid "the confusion and embarrassment" that could result from endorsing a request without wider coordination and consultation. Chief of Staff Haldeman, always nervous that the bureaucracy would try to put one over on the Nixon insiders, tersely noted in reply that "the procedure outlined by Mr. Focke . . . should become standard procedure immediately."[62]

What is that procedure in practice? It is similar to legislative clearance, though normally conducted by the OMB general counsel's office instead of by LRD. As a 2001 template used by the George W. Bush administration lays out, it normally follows several basic steps, which can be tracked by the documents that are supposed to be included in the OMB's file on a given proposed order. Those include the:

1. White House Office or Executive Agency Request for Executive Order

2. Memorandum Requesting White House and Agency Comments on the Proposed Executive Order

3. White House and Agency Comments on the Proposed Executive Order

4. OMB Executive Order Package Containing: Abstract of OMB officials approving the order, Memorandum from OMB Director to the President describing the order and requesting signature of the order, Letter from OMB General Counsel to Attorney General requesting review and approval of the proposed Executive Order, and a copy of the order

5. Department of Justice (OLC) Form and Legality Documents for the Order[63]

The various stages of this sequence are worth briefly discussing. When a proposed EO is received, the general counsel's office will often ask personnel in OMB's Resource Management Offices for their feedback. Those staffers may already have caught wind of the order from ongoing work with "their" agencies. In some cases, the originator will have worked with OMB and/or one of the White House-centered policy councils in advance of providing the draft. Often, or even usually, then, what OMB formally receives is not the very first draft of the order.

Even so, some proposals wind up rejected out-of-hand. Late in the Carter administration, a White House aide sent OMB a "draft EO that Stu would like to have signed as soon as possible," name-dropping top domestic policy adviser Stuart Eizenstat. An OMB counsel recorded subsequent phone calls with passive-aggressive pleasure: "Told him this doesn't look, smell, or read like an Executive order. . . . [He] said he would talk to 'Stu' and call back." When he did, he "says 'Stu' still wants an Executive order. I told him to dream up something to put in it and contact me next week."[64] The first question, in short, is whether a proposal should *be* an executive order.

The second question deals with drafting. The general counsel's office formulates some orders and seeks to edit others. One common effort is to rein in departmental efforts at self-promotion. In 1963, for example, a BOB attorney observed that "the occupancy of a proper foreign policy role by the Department of State should not be dependent upon constant reiteration of statements of that role."[65] Another common edit attempts to cut down on florid preamble language more suitable to a press release. For instance, the submitted draft of the 2001 EO creating an Office of Faith-Based and Community Initiatives started: "Government can rally a military, but it cannot put hope in our hearts or a sense of purpose in our lives . . . The indispensable and transforming work of faith-based and other charitable service groups must be front and center." The issued order was more circumspect: "Faith-based and other community organizations are indispensable in meeting the needs of poor Americans . . ."[66] Of course, as the eight first-person pages prefacing July 2019's EO 13880 on the federal census suggest, presidents who want self-promotion will get it; OMB has to pick its battles on style as well as substance.

In general, OMB has an eye out for the ramifications of an order on presidential power, following from its focus on "greater protection to the president" already noted. Consider, for instance, a Kennedy administration draft EO to create a Water Resources Council. The BOB weighed in, noting:

> As a matter of policy, we believe it is preferable for such interagency coordinating bodies to be created by Executive Order rather than by statute. . . . [The] legislative route has no advantage over an Executive Order, but it has the major disadvantage of tying the President's hands with respect to establishing the most appropriate method for coordinating executive agencies and revising the method as need arises without resort to Congress.[67]

As with legislative clearance, OMB requests input on the draft order from any executive agencies (including multiple separate offices within the EOP) with a potential interest in its issuance. Even White House-driven orders are subject to this process. The time allowed for comment varies a fair bit, depending on the importance of the order, whether it is being issued because of an external event or deadline, and departmental or White House pressure. That last can be gamed; as one BOB lawyer put it, the "pressing of the [department] for rapid action should be preceded by knowledge as to actual urgency."[68] Such deadlines can be imposed by political needs, too—frequently by the presidential scheduling office, when White House aides decide the president's announcement of a new EO will give heft to an impending event. In such cases, the clearance process speeds up dramatically, to OMB's dismay. As one recent general counsel noted, "You say, 'seriously? Can't you just pretend you're signing something?'"[69]

Comments returned by the agencies are tabulated and assessed, recording everything from fierce opposition to solid support to a sort of baffled apathy. Sometimes agencies will stress they have no *formal* objection while making clear their true feelings in other ways. For one 2002 order proposed by the Advisory Council on Historic Preservation (linked to the Interior Department), seeking to "promote the preservation and effective use of the many historic properties held by Federal agencies," the Commerce Department requested a meeting. OMB's handwritten notes record the result: "our econ[omic] development people say this isn't needed," Commerce said, careful to note this was an "unofficial" view. As the OMB notetaker put it, Commerce wanted to know how the political winds were blowing. "Is there some W[hite] H[ouse] interest[?] They will go if *White House* staff wants it. But if it's staff at [the Advisory] Council then we are much less concerned."[70]

Agency comments can lead to rapid internal sign-off of the EO; to more edits; or to a request that the originator defend the extant draft against criticism, perhaps with a revised draft sent out once more for repeated review. A good deal of negotiation occurs as comments come in. OMB has generally centered on gaining consensus—on ensuring the wider executive branch agrees, to the extent possible, on the text of an order moving forward. That can spur a long process of sequential appeasement. Acting BOB director Percival Brundage put it nicely in a letter to agencies in 1954. In the preparation of a contemporary EO, he said, "the comments of the various affected agencies with respect to earlier drafts of these documents have been taken into consideration and have been accommodated as far as appears to be practicable, bearing in mind particularly the sum total of agency views and the sometimes opposed views of agencies upon the same point."[71]

Consider Bill Clinton's issuance of EO 13045 on children's health on April 21, 1997, requiring agencies to "make it a high priority to identify and assess" environmental risks to children and to "ensure" those risks were addressed by "its policies, programs, activities, and standards"—by adding this requirement as a hook to the regulatory review function conducted by OMB's Office of Information and Regulatory Affairs.[72] The EO began life in an August 1996 memo from the Environmental Protection Agency (EPA), which sent a draft order to OMB in January 1997. During the clearance process, some seventeen executive agencies and EOP staff offices became involved as EPA lobbied to "generat[e] support within the White House" for its text. Agencies uniformly claimed to support the idea of protecting children from environmental hazards, of course, but raised many objections to the mechanisms for doing so in the draft order. Among other things, they argued that the EO put a "kick-me sign" on their own backs—how, for instance, the Department of Health and Human Services asked, was the department supposed to say why tobacco remained a legal product? Banning it would clearly be better for children's health.

A series of negotiations ensued over four months of meetings; "we have made significant drafting changes to accommodate concerns," Domestic Policy Council (DPC) staffers reported. Those concerns came from within the EOP as well as the wider bureaucracy; indeed, a DPC memo to White House chief of staff Erskine Bowles that same month noted that the DPC, the National Economic Council (NEC), the Council of Environmental Quality (CEQ), and the Office of Science and Technology Policy (OSTP) were all involved. It was not until late March that staff could note: "I think we have resolved all the kids e.o. issues *among WH offices*."[73] And then, "serious last-minute objections" from the agencies remained. Notes by DPC from an April 1 meeting note EPA's objections to Treasury "nervousness" and to others' continued queries: "we've redone [the order] to address concerns. Weakened already."

The next step is for an order to gain approval as to "form and legality" from the Justice Department. As noted, this task is normally delegated to the OLC, which prepares a memorandum certifying the order. This can consist of one substantive sentence ("The proposed Executive order is acceptable as to form and legality") or, in the case of Ronald Reagan's famous 1981 EO formalizing regulatory review in OMB, eighteen single-spaced pages.[74]

"Form" simply means the EO adheres to stylistic norms and standards and that it makes correct reference to the statutes or constitutional authorities relied upon in the order.[75] As William Rehnquist, then the head of the OLC, put it in a 1971 memo to White House Counsel John Dean, "We will review orders and proclamations with avoidance of unnecessary legal gobbledygook in mind." He noted the "legal requirements respecting the style of executive orders" but assured Dean that "ponderous language" was not actually required.[76]

Questions of "legality" are far less standardized. Technically, as Acting Attorney General Sally Yates put it in 2017, "OLC's review is limited to the narrow question of whether, in OLC's view, a proposed Executive Order is lawful on its face and properly drafted. . . . it does not address whether any policy choice embodied in an Executive Order is wise or just."[77] Still, as Clinton administration OLC attorney Beth Nolan notes, almost all orders, other than those that are "kind of copying another executive order," have "some legal issue that goes beyond the form part." These issues may arise far earlier than their allotted slot in the sequence would imply. According to Charles Cooper, who headed OLC in Reagan's second term, "typically executive orders don't make it even to the drafting stage unless legal issues have been identified and pretty well-thought through."[78]

Finally, with agency feedback and OLC sign-off in hand, OMB writes a customized version of an enrolled bill memo to the president providing its formal approval of the order. This begins by "forwarding for your consideration a proposed executive order that was prepared by"—filling in the relevant organizational author—and summarizing the order's text and background. It also provides the views of "affected agencies and staff." That may be a long list of executive departments, agencies, and White House offices. For one relatively trivial 2003 order, for example, the list usefully highlights the somewhat paranoiac nature of the clearance process—it includes forty-two staff units, nineteen of them within the EOP, ranging from the Department of State to the White House Office of Administration, all of whom "do not object."[79] At times, departments do object, though, in which case OMB may justify why those issues were not dispositive; in some cases, OMB also provides a blow-by-blow history of the order in the background information section. Even the director's endorsement can be fervent or lukewarm. As far back as 1944, for instance, Harold Smith complained to FDR that time pressures had curtailed analysis: "Under the existing circumstances I think the draft is reasonably satisfactory. Under other circumstances the concept . . . might have been more fully developed and the delineation of its functions more fully matured before the issuance of the Order."[80]

Since under EO 11030 an order that does not receive OMB approval is not supposed to make its way to the president, at this stage the formal recommendation is almost always favorable.[81] Even so, the president doesn't always choose to issue the proposed order, or requests changes. In the children's health order noted earlier, for instance, on his note approving the order President Clinton requested still more changes aimed at addressing agencies' remaining objections—"might want to ease burden a bit," he scrawled. One more revision thus ensued before the order was issued.

CONCLUSIONS: CENTRAL CLEARANCE AND BUREAUCRATIC MANAGEMENT

The idea of central clearance remains, well, central to the function of OMB—as a manager of, and protector of, presidential preferences. As OMB director Richard Darman briefed his incoming successor Leon Panetta in late 1992 on clearance in the legislative arena, it provides a process that

> permits the coordinated development, review, and approval of legislative proposals needed to carry out the President's legislative program;

provides a mechanism for reviewing agency legislative proposals which the president may wish to include in his legislative program; helps the agencies develop draft bills that are consistent with and that carry out the president's policy objectives; identifies for Congress those bills that are part of the President's program and the relationship of other bills to that program; assures that Congress receives coordinated and informative agency views on legislation which it has under consideration; assures that bills and position statements submitted to Congress by one agency properly take into account the interests and concerns of all affected agencies; [and] provides a means whereby divergent agency views can be reconciled.[82]

There are certainly cases where central clearance is (as a BOB staffer put it in 1957) "a rather pro forma ratification of action already announced," or where it is rushed to meet a real or artificial deadline for PR or other purposes.[83] There are others where it is evaded entirely, by negligence or by craft. A former OMB branch chief told his boss, Deputy Associate Director Barry Clendenin, that into the early 1990s "several Administrations didn't want to deal with the executive order process, which had become so ritualized and process-oriented, that it was 'easiest' to just issue a memorandum, which didn't go through [OMB assistant general counsel] Mac Reed's processes . . ."[84] Clendenin himself recalls reviewing multiple drafts of EOs; when it came to the final draft, Reed "would personally walk around for sign-off on a cover sheet. For the memoranda, it was more of a pickup game."[85] (OMB higher-ups took notice, perhaps. By the time of the Clinton administration, most presidential memoranda had been folded into the formal clearance process.)

Or canny agency heads may simply take their case directly to the president. In 2001, Vice President Dick Cheney famously obtained President Bush's signature on a four-page directive concerning enemy combatants "with emphatic instructions to bypass staff review." Secretary of State Colin Powell, one of those bypassed, found out about the order from CNN. "What the hell just happened?" he barked.[86] Back in 1962, Secretary of Defense Robert McNamara did much the same thing. The entirety of the BOB file for EO 11058, which modified eligibility for the armed services' Ready Reserve, consists of a single index card, which notes that the order was not cleared by the Bureau—or anyone else. The card's text reads rather plaintively:

The Secretary of Defense brought the order to the White House on October 23rd and took it back to the Pentagon with him after obtaining the President's signature. Someone in his office then transmitted it to the Federal Register the next morning, when we became aware of its existence for the first time. A request has been made of the Defense Department for any file or papers that may have accompanied it but as yet none have been received. This [card] constitutes the file so far.[87]

Central clearance is designed to avoid just that outcome. It aims to shield the president from being tempted or pressured into the "oh, by the way" decision made on the fly in informal bilateral encounters with administration officials—something that Cheney in other circumstances warned strongly against.[88] As Neustadt describes it, it "sought to protect both President from agencies and agencies from one another."[89] The latter is because agencies also benefit from getting advance information about their peers' activities and plans. And we might include Congress here, too, as a beneficiary: "Although Congress periodically questions OMB's central clearance role," OMB staff noted in the 1980s, "its continued endurance and success may be attributed to the fact that it meets Congress's needs as much as the President's or the agencies'" by ensuring legislators get coordinated agency views across different legislative vehicles.[90]

Does all this risk the "neutral competence" for which OMB is revered? After all, central clearance does lead to decisions with clear political implications, and since the 1970s, at least, political appointees—notably the program associate directors layered above the substantive program divisions—have played a larger role in decisionmaking. As Martin notes, "all recent administrations, regardless of party, have clearly decided that positions on legislation pending before Congress are the exclusive province of political appointees."[91] Yet in contemporary cases, it is the absence of clearance that has proved most problematic—see, for instance, the Trump "travel ban" issued in early 2017, about which Senator Lindsey Graham (R-SC) reportedly told the president that "some third grader wrote it on the back of an envelope," and which proved to be substantively unworkable. (It was the third iteration of the "ban" that, after much bureaucratic intervention, was upheld by the Supreme Court in 2018.)[92]

In any case, the process represents both policy and politics, and always has—because that is what the president needs. More than seventy years ago, a member of Congress told BOB director Fred Lawton,

"You are the President's man. We cannot consider your judgment wholly objective. It is a reflection of presidential policy. . . . We get a little suspicious because you do represent the President."[93] That is exactly the job of central clearance.

Notes

1. Quoted in *New Deal Mosaic: Roosevelt Confers with his National Emergency Council, 1933–1936*, edited by Lester G. Seligman and Elmer E. Cornwell Jr. (University of Oregon Books, 1965), pp. 492–93.

2. See Matthew J. Dickinson, *Bitter Harvest* (Cambridge University Press, 1997), p. 86 and chapter 3 generally.

3. Meeting of February 8, 1946, Franklin D. Roosevelt Library, Harold Smith Papers, *Conferences with President Truman (1946)*.

4. Dickinson, *Bitter Harvest*, chapter 3.

5. Legislative Reference Division, Office of Management and Budget, *Legislative Clearance* (January 1993).

6. Jeffrey A. Weinberg, "The View from the Oval Office: Understanding the Legislative Presidency," *Journal of Legislative Studies* 24 (2018), p. 400.

7. Mary Parker Follett, *The Speaker of the House of Representatives* (New York: Longmans, Green, 1896), p. 325. For overarching accounts of presidential involvement in the legislative process, see Wilfred E. Binkley, *President and Congress*, 3rd revised edition (New York: Vintage, 1962); James L. Sundquist, *The Decline and Resurgence of Congress* (Washington, D.C.: Brookings Institution, 1981), chapter 6. This section is largely drawn from Richard E. Neustadt, "Presidency and Legislation: Planning the President's Program," *American Political Science Review* 49 (December 1955), pp. 980–1021, especially pp. 996–1013, and Andrew Rudalevige, *Managing the President's Program: Presidential Leadership and Legislative Policy Formulation* (Princeton University Press, 2002), chapter 3.

8. Quoted in Francis H. Heller, editor, *The Truman White House: The Administration of the Presidency, 1945–1953* (Regents Press of Kansas, 1980), p. 90. See also Neustadt, "Presidency and Legislation," pp. 999–1000.

9. Neustadt, "Presidency and Legislation: Planning the President's Program," p. 980.

10. Ibid., p. 1015.

11. Mansfield, quoted in Rudalevige, *Managing*, p. 41; Al Stern to Stu Eizenstat, "96th Congress," Memo of November 27, 1978, Jimmy Carter Library, White House Central Files: Subject Files, Box LE-2, *11/1/78-12/31/78*. The context is "the beating we took in the 95th Congress."

12. Stephen J. Wayne, *The Legislative Presidency* (New York: Harper and Row, 1978).

13. Quoted in Matthew J. Dickinson and Andrew Rudalevige, "'Worked Out in Fractions': Neutral Competence, FDR, and the Bureau of the Budget," *Congress and the Presidency* 34 (Spring 2007), p. 3. For a broader discussion of the history leading to the Budget and Accounting Act, see Peri Arnold, *Making the Managerial Presidency: Comprehensive Reorganization Planning, 1905–1996*, 2nd revised edition (University Press of Kansas, 1998); Larry Berman, *The Office of Management and Budget and the Presidency* (Princeton University Press, 1979), chapter 1.

14. Charles A. Dawes, *The First Year of the Budget of the United States* (New York: Harper & Brothers, 1923), p. ix.

15. Richard E. Neustadt, "Presidency and Legislation: The Growth of Central Clearance," *American Political Science Review* 48 (September 1954), pp. 644–46. Budget Circular 49, December 19, 1921. Related materials can be found in the National Archives (College Park, Maryland) [hereafter NARA], Record Group [RG] 51, Entry A1-27, General Records (Additional Series), 1921–40: Records regarding the Clearance of Legislation and Executive Orders, 1929–39 (Series 21.6e), Box 1, *Procedures for Handling Clearance of Proposed and Pending Legislation and Executive Orders*.

16. Neustadt, "Presidency and Legislation: Growth of Central Clearance," p. 648. He notes that FDR's first budget director, Lewis Douglas, was not fully versed in the "old orders," which went unenforced in 1933, but that Roosevelt himself revived the issue in 1934.

17. Budget Circular 336 (December 21, 1935). Again, note that FDR had already directed in 1934 that the BOB receive copies of all fiscally-related legislative proposals.

18. See EO 7709-A (September 16, 1937).

19. Dickinson and Rudalevige, "'Worked Out in Fractions,'" pp. 8–9.

20. EO 8248 (September 8, 1939), www.archives.gov/federal-register/codification/executive-order/08248.html.

21. For more detail on this evolution, see Andrew Rudalevige, "Inventing the Institutional Presidency: Entrepreneurship and the Rise of the Bureau of the Budget, 1939–1949," in *Formative Acts: American Politics in the Making*, edited by Stephen Skowronek and Matthew Glassman (University of Pennsylvania Press, 2007). Note that over time LRD has also been called the Office of Legislative Reference (OLR), so I will generally refer to "Legislative Reference" below.

22. Harold Smith to the President, "Section 4 of August 28 Draft of Executive Order," Memo of September 1, 1942, NARA, RG 51, Entry 24-A, Division of Legislative Reference: History of Executive Orders, 1939–1946 (Series 39.1a), Box 14 [EO 9250].

23. On clearance statistics and the process in general, see Neustadt, "Presidency and Legislation: Growth of Central Clearance," pp. 641–71; Harold Smith, notes of February 8, 1946, Harry S. Truman Library (HSTL), Smith papers, *Conferences with President Truman*; Don K. Price, "Staffing the Presidency," *American Political Science Review* 40 (December 1946), pp. 1160–61.

24. See Rudalevige, "Inventing the Institutional Presidency," pp. 327–36.

25. Quoted in Neustadt, "Presidency and Legislation: Growth of Central Clearance," p. 658.

26. Herman Somers, *Presidential Agency: OWMR* (Harvard University Press, 1950), p. 75; Luther Gulick, "War Organization of the Federal Government," *American Political Science Review* 38 (December 1944), p. 1174.

27. Roger W. Jones, Oral History Interview, August 14, 1969, Harry S. Truman Library, p. 6.

28. See Rudalevige, "Inventing," quoting Richard Neustadt to Roger Jones, "Weekly Reports on Anticipated Congressional Schedules," Memo of May 15, 1950, NARA, RG 51, Series 39.39, Box 4, Legislative Program—82nd Congress, 1st session.

29. Jones, Oral History, p. 14.

30. MacPhail and Neustadt to Jones, "Bureau Procedure For Utilizing

Agency Legislative Programs Submitted Under Sec. 86," Memo of September 6, 1949, NARA, RG 51, Series 39.39, Box 4, Legislative Program—81st Congress, 2nd session.

31. See Rudalevige, "Inventing," quoting Staats to Director, "Some Immediate Issues in Relation to the President's Legislative Program for the Forthcoming Session," Memo of November 12, 1948, HSTL, Neustadt Papers, Box 10, Addendum: Budget Policy and Legislative Program, 1948–1949.

32. Staats to Stauffacher, Martin, and J. W. Jones, "Review of Legislative Proposals prior to Convening of 81st Congress," Memo of December 6, 1948, HSTL, Neustadt papers, Addendum: Budget Policy and Legislative Program, 1948–49; Dickinson and Rudalevige, "Golden Age," pp. 641–42; Neustadt, "Presidency and Legislation: Planning the President's Program," pp. 1003–07.

33. Neustadt, "Presidency and Legislation: Growth of Central Clearance," p. 642 n4. This codified earlier directives such as those already discussed. Note that the process for enrolled bills was in Circular A-9. The two circulars were merged in 1960 into a revised Circular A-19.

34. Frank Pace Jr. to Heads of Executive Departments and Establishments, "The Preliminary Legislative Program Requested in the 1951 Call for Estimates," Bureau of the Budget Bulletin 50-5, August 31, 1949. See Rudalevige, *Managing*, p. 46; Neustadt, "Presidency and Legislation: Planning the President's Program," p. 1008.

35. Jones to Director, Untitled Memo, February 7, 1958, NARA, RG 51, Legislative Reference Division Subject Files, 1939–70 (series 39.39), Box 5, Legislative Program 85th [Congress]. See, too, the extended battle between BOB and the Department of Agriculture recounted in Rudalevige, *Managing*, pp. 55–56.

36. *Staff Study Group Report to the Director: A Self-Study of the Bureau of the Budget*, May 1, 1959, and attached material, NARA, Records Relating to the Administrative Management of the Bureau of the Budget, 1952–60, Series 52.2; Entry 9-C, Box 6 [B1-13/2]. See especially pp. 31 and 37A.

37. A-19 does not apply to independent regulatory agencies, nor budget and appropriations testimony, which is governed by circular A-11 and managed by staff in the OMB's substantive budget divisions. Further, the Pentagon's annual responses to congressional inquiries about Defense items not funded in the president's budget are not cleared by OMB at all.

38. Bernard Martin, "The Legislative Clearance Process," Standing Panel on Executive Organization and Management, National Academy of Public Administration, August 2008, 5.

39. OMB, "Legislative Clearance," p. 5.

40. Martin, personal communication with author, August 27, 2019. Thanks to Mr. Martin for his hugely useful feedback on this chapter.

41. Ibid.

42. OMB, "Legislative Clearance," pp. 2, 4.

43. Weinberg, "View from the Oval Office," p. 397; Steven Brill, *America's Bitter Pill* (New York: Random House, 2015), p. 90.

44. Samuel Kernell, Roger Larocca, Huchen Liu, and Andrew Rudalevige, "New Data for Investigating the President's Legislative Program: OMB Logs and SAPs," *Presidential Studies Quarterly* 49 (June 2019), p. 338, and see p. 338n14.4

45. Bruce Johnson, "Analyst to Negotiator: OMB's New Role," *Journal of Policy Analysis and Management* 3 (1984), p. 502.

46. Shelley Lynne Tomkin, *Inside OMB: Politics and Policy in the President's Budget Agency* (Armonk, NY: M. E. Sharpe, 1998), p. 156.

47. Martin, "Legislative Clearance," p. 7. Weinberg writes that "Since the Obama Administration, views letters have not been regularly transmitted." See "View from the Oval Office," p. 403.

48. Meghan Stuessy, *Statements of Administration Policy*, CRS Report R44539 (Congressional Research Service, 2016). See also Weinberg, "View from the Oval Office," 404-05; OMB, "Legislative Clearance," p. 8, noting that the Budget Review and Concepts staff was responsible for SAPs on appropriations bills and for "scoring" a bill's cost.

49. The OMB manual noted that "particular attention is focused on Administration-sponsored legislation and on bills that deviate substantially from Administration policy." See "Legislative Clearance," p. 7.

50. Kernell and others, "New Data," p. 8.

51. Charles Cameron, *Veto Bargaining* (Cambridge University Press, 2000). On Trump, see, for example, Amber Phillips, "Five Tough Lessons Congress Learned in the Year of Trump," *Washington Post*, December 27, 2017; Jonathan Swan, "Trump Dressed Down Mulvaney in Front of Congressional Leaders," Axios.com, January 13, 2019, www.axios.com/donald-trump-mick-mulvaney-government-shutdown-meeting-7d84ea72-5aaf-45e0-a707-5f955836070e.html.

52. Weinberg, "View from the Oval Office," pp. 407, 411 n25. Weinberg notes that this rule was relaxed during the Obama administration.

53. Kenneth Mayer, *With the Stroke of a Pen: Executive Orders and Presidential Power* (Princeton University Press, 2001), p. 31.

54. House Committee on Government Operations, 85th Cong., 1st Sess., Executive Orders and Proclamations: A Study of a Use of Presidential Powers, December 1957.

55. For studies of significant orders over time, see Mayer, *Stroke of a Pen*; William Howell, *Power without Persuasion* (Princeton University Press, 2003). For contracting data, see Daniel Gitterman, *Calling the Shots: The President, Executive Orders, and Public Policy* (Washington, D.C.: Brookings Institution, 2017), p. 10.

56. Herbert Hoover had sought to standardize EOs' format and, since so many were lost or uncollated over the years, mandated that copies of all orders be sent to the State Department. See EO 5220 (November 8, 1929).

57. EO 7298 (February 18, 1936).

58. EO 12608 (September 9,1987); EO 13403 (May 12, 2006); EO 12080 (September 18, 1978); EO 13683 (December 11, 2014). For the sake of completeness, reference should be made also to EO 10006 (October 9, 1948) and EO 11354 (May 23, 1967), which made minor technical changes regarding spelling, printing, and formatting to the Roosevelt and Kennedy orders, respectively.

59. See Andrew Rudalevige, "Executive Branch Management and Presidential Unilateralism: Centralization and the Formulation of Executive Orders," *Congress and the Presidency* 42 (Winter 2015), pp. 342–65; more broadly, see Rudalevige, *By Executive Order* (Princeton University Press, forthcoming), from which much of this section is drawn.

60. Arthur Focke to Director, "Proposed Executive Order," Memo of February 4, 1962, and Arthur Focke to Ted Sorensen, Memo of April 19, 1962, NARA, RG 51, Executive Orders and Proclamations, 1961–1965 (Series 61.4), Box 4, Preparation, Presentation, Filing and Publication of Executive Orders and Proclamations—E5-3/62.1 (E18-4/60.1).

61. Focke to Sorensen, April 19, 1962.

62. Focke, "Pending Executive Orders," Memo of January 17, 1969 and H.

R. Haldeman to Ken Cole, no title, Memo January 27, 1969, both in Richard Nixon Library, WHCF, Box 7, EX FE6: Executive Orders.

63. "Executive Order Process—Documents," no date [January 2001], Washington National Records Center (Suitland, Maryland) [hereafter WNRC], accession #51-06-0013, OMB: OGC: Ex. Orders/Proc. 2001-2004, MR 2001: Faith-Based Initiatives.

64. William Nichols, memoranda for the record, December 9 and 12, 1980, NARA, RG 51, Executive Order Files FY81, Entry UD-WW 63, Box 3, Small Business Conference Commission.

65. F. E. Levi, "Foreign Policy Role of the Secretary of States," Notes of January 9, 1963, NARA, RG 51, Series 61.4, Box 12, *EO 11077/R6-5.65.2*.

66. John Bridgeland to Mitch Daniels, "Office of Faith-Based Executive Orders," memo of January 26, 2001, and attached material, WNRC, 51-06-0013, OMB: OGC: Ex. Orders/Proc. 2001-2004, EO 13199. One former OMB staffer noted of the original: "there was a lot of eye-rolling at the time." (Personal communication with author.)

67. Schwartz and Seidman to Elmer Staats, "Proposed Executive Order Creating a Water Resources Council," Memo of May 3, 1962, and attached material, NARA, RG 51, Series 61.4, Box 18, Creating a Water Resources Council—EO Proposed—P4-6/62.1.

68. Fred Levi, handwritten note of November 2, 1959, NARA, RG 51, Series 53.2E, Box 17, EO 10893.

69. Interview with former OMB general counsel, September 23, 2016.

70. The OMB general counsel's office said "there *is* senior WH staff interest." After some significant revision, EO 13287 was issued in March 2003. See John L. Nau III to Mitch Daniels, Letter of May 9, 2002, and additional notes and documents in WNRC, 51-06-0013, OMB: OGC: Ex. Orders/Proc. 2001-2004 Box 4 [EO 13287—Preserving America's Heritage]. Emphasis in original.

71. Percival Brundage to nine agency heads, letter of August 25, 1954, NARA, RG 51, Executive Orders and Proclamations, 1953–1961 (Series 53.2E), Box 25, EO 10560.

72. This case is drawn from Andrew Rudalevige, "Executive Orders and Presidential Unilateralism," *Presidential Studies Quarterly* 42 (March 2012), pp. 138–60. See the cites therein; the documents used are from Elena Kagan's Domestic Policy Council and Counsel files, available online at the William J. Clinton Presidential Library. For more on OIRA and regulatory review, see chapter 6 in this volume.

73. Emphasis added. Even at this point, the CEA and the NEC were at best unenthusiastic.

74. Larry Simms (Assistant Attorney General, OLC) to David Stockman, "Proposed Executive Order on Federal Regulation," Memo of February 12, 1981, NARA, RG 51, Records of the Office of the General Counsel—Executive Order Files FY81, Box 1, EO 12291.

75. Tobias T. Gibson, "The Office of Legal Counsel and the Presidency: The Legal Strategy of Executive Orders," Ph.D. dissertation (Washington University, St Louis, MO, May 2006), p. 62.

76. William Rehnquist to John Dean III, "Wording of Executive Orders," Memo of February 16, 1971, GFL, Office of the Counsel to the President: Kenneth A. Lazarus Files, Box 2, FE 6—Executive Orders (1).

77. Sally Yates, Letter of January 30, 2017, reprinted in Jonathan Adler, "Acting Attorney General Orders Justice Department Attorneys Not to Defend Immigration Executive Order," Volokh Conspiracy blog, *Washington Post*, January

30, 2017, www.washingtonpost.com/news/volokh-conspiracy/wp/2017/01/30/acting-attorney-general-orders-justice-department-attorneys-not-to-defend-immigration-executive-order/.

78. Interviews of Beth Nolan and Charles Cooper by Gibson, quoted in "Office of Legal Counsel and the Presidency," pp. 63–64.

79. Mitch Daniels to the President, "Proposed Executive Order Entitled 'Amendment to Executive Order 10448, Establishing the National Defense Service Medal,'" Memo of March 25, 2003, WNRC, OMB: OGC: Ex. Orders/Proc. 2001-2004, #51-06-0013, Box 4, EO 13293.

80. Smith to President, "Reemployment and Retraining of Veterans and War Workers," Memo of February 24, 1944, NARA, RG 51, Series 39.1a, Box 17, EO 9427.

81. This is not universally the case, though; in 1975, for instance, President Ford was sent competing drafts of an EO expanding predator control on federal lands and asked to choose between them.

82. Richard Darman, "General Outline: OMB Roles and Responsibilities," transition briefing book provided by Richard Darman to Leon Panetta, December 16, 1992, Leon Panetta Institute Archives, OMB Files, Box 28, File 10.

83. Titus to Ellington, Handwritten note of December 17, 1957, NARA, RG 51, Executive Orders and Proclamations, 1953–1961 (Series 53.2E), Box 22, EO 10747.

84. Personal communication from Barry Clendenin, December 17, 2014, passing along an excerpted email from "a branch chief who worked for me." For far earlier examples of evasion, see Neustadt, "Presidency and Legislation: Growth of Central Clearance," pp. 651–52.

85. Ibid.

86. Barton Gellman and Jo Becker, "A Different Understanding with the President," *Washington Post*, June 24, 2007, p. A1.

87. Memorandum for the file of October 27, 1962, JFKL, Box 599, ND 4-1 Manpower.

88. Quoted in Terry Sullivan, editor, *The Nerve Center: Lessons in Governing from the White House Chiefs of Staff* (Texas A&M Press, 2004), p. 104.

89. Neustadt, "Presidency and Legislation: Growth of Central Clearance," p. 650.

90. "OMB's Legal Authority to Review Transcripts of Agency Testimony," NARA, RG 51, OMB General Counsel Subject Files (Entry UD-UP 65), Box 4 [Weinstein Files: OMB Authority to Review Transcripts and Legislation].

91. Martin, "Legislative Clearance," p. 9. But he argues strongly that OMB remains an analytic arbiter rather than a partisan tool, "unable to find a single instance in which any evidence . . . was produced to sustain the often-heard charge that OMB career staff are now routinely engaged in preparing politically-slanted analysis of budget, management, or legislative issues. . . . Though the visibility of OMB's engagement in the political process may have increased, nothing substantive has changed about the institution's involvement." See pp. 8–9.

92. Quoted in Bob Woodward, *Fear* (New York: Simon & Schuster, 2018), p. 100. See, too, the extensive discussion of the EO's formulation in Julie H. Davis and Michael Shear, *Border Wars* (New York: Simon & Schuster, 2019); *Trump v. Hawaii*, 585 U.S. ___ (2018).

93. Staff Meeting Minutes of September 29, 1948, HSTL, Lawton papers, BOB—Staff Meetings.

SEVEN

Learning from Failure

A "Failure CV" for the Office of Information and Regulatory Affairs

RACHEL AUGUSTINE POTTER

Writing in the *Harvard Law Review* in 2012, law professor Cass Sunstein sought to educate readers about how the Office of Information and Regulatory Affairs (OIRA), a small office within the White House Office of Management and Budget responsible for centralized review of agency regulations, actually functions in practice.[1] His fundamental concern was that "the role of OIRA and the nature of the OIRA process [remains] poorly understood."[2] Sunstein was well-suited for the task, having just come off a three-year stint serving as the OIRA administrator, the office's politically appointed head.

Sunstein had a point. OIRA rarely makes above-the-fold news, or any news for that matter. OIRA staffers carefully avoid the spotlight. On the occasions when the office does capture the attention of journalists, however, hyperbole and misinformation rule the day. The office has been described as "obscure, but powerful,"[3] "one of the most powerful bureaucracies inside the Beltway,"[4] "a black box inside a black hole,"[5] the "cockpit of the regulatory state,"[6] and the "killing ground for agency regulations."[7] Shapiro notes that OIRA's shadowy image is further perpetuated by media references to the office's leader, the OIRA administrator, as the president's "regulatory czar."[8] These journalistic accounts feed into the misperception that OIRA's power is absolute and unchallengeable. Academic work tends to cement this view rather than correct it. For example, law professor Lisa Heinzerling, who served as a political appointee in the Environmental Protection Agency during the Obama years, recalls "[OIRA] was calling the shots. [It] decided what to review, offered line-by-line edits of regulatory proposals, convened meetings with outside parties, mediated disputes among the agencies, decided whether an agency's benefit-cost analysis was up to snuff, and more."[9] This narrative is further entrenched by academic studies where scholars model OIRA's power to audit draft regulations,[10] alter them,[11] and veto them[12] as near absolute.

Like all stylized narratives, this characterization of OIRA is, of course, false. However, it is perhaps so false as to be misleading rather than clarifying. In a separation of powers system, the power of all political institutions is circumscribed, and OIRA is no different.[13]

Since its creation, OIRA's path has been marked by both successes and failures. This chapter chronicles the office's institutional highs and lows. OIRA's successes are highly visible and relatively well known to observers, thus documenting them is, in some sense, par for the course. Its failures, however, are harder to observe and less widely known. Failing to document them, however, contributes to the false sense of the institution's super-capabilities.

A recent trend in academia is for highly successful scholars with remarkable professional accomplishments listed on their curriculum vitae (CV) to publish a second CV, a "failure CV," that records their failures, including rejected applications, work that was never published, etc. The purpose of a failure CV is to "balance the record and provide some perspective,"[14] by showing that even the most successful scholars routinely encounter failure and must overcome adversity. Failure CVs recalibrate for outside observers what "success" really looks like from the inside.

The aim here is similar; not to recast OIRA as either a failed or failing institution—it clearly is not—but, instead, to evaluate the extent to which OIRA's power has grown over time and, where possible, to identify places where the office could or should have succeeded but did not. Observing and documenting failures remedies the selection bias that emerges from focusing exclusively on success. In bringing to light areas in which OIRA has either struggled or failed entirely, this essay uncovers the commonalities that unite these incidents and elucidates patterns among them. The aim, therefore, is a practical one. The lessons of failure can guide OIRA's leaders and policy practitioners in steering the institution toward future successes. This correction can also help media and academic observers better understand the place of OIRA in the separation of powers system.

This more accurate perspective on success and failure reveals that OIRA has at times studiously avoided giving agencies detailed guidance on how to manage important aspects of the regulatory process. This laxity arises from a desire by OIRA leaders and its rank-and-file to maintain maximum institutional flexibility and autonomy, but it comes at the cost that agencies can fill in the gray areas with less than desirable (in an analytical or normative sense) policy. This reveals lessons for future administrations that hope to further enhance OIRA's successes.

A BRIEF HISTORY OF OIRA

OIRA emerged on the scene in 1980 when Congress passed the Paperwork Reduction Act,[15] which created the office for the purpose of reviewing agency information collections. Seizing the opportunity, President Reagan shortly thereafter, in 1981, issued an executive order giving OIRA the power to review drafts of agency proposed and final rules.[16] The stated goal of Executive Order (EO) 12291 was "to reduce the burdens of existing and future regulations, increase agency accountability for regulatory actions, [and] provide for presidential oversight of the regulatory process."[17] For major rules, those the order defined according to their economic impact, agencies were required to prepare a Regulatory Impact Analysis (RIA), which included an evaluation of the draft rule's potential costs and benefits, and submit it to OIRA for review.[18]

After some fits and starts (discussed in the next section outlining the office's successes), OIRA got up and running and, throughout the Reagan and George H. W. Bush administrations, it reviewed all draft regulations issued by executive branch agencies. Shortly after taking office in 1993, President Bill Clinton revoked Reagan's order and issued a new order revising the scope of OIRA's purview. EO 12866 kept the basic framework for regulatory review intact but refocused OIRA's work so that, instead of reviewing all agency draft rules, the office would review only those deemed "significant," a determination that OIRA (not the agency) was to make.[19] It also increased the amount of time allotted for OIRA review and extended the RIA requirement to cover all significant rules reviewed by OIRA, not just those with a sizable economic impact.

Since 1993, the basic setup established by EO 12866 has stabilized, albeit with some notable tweaks. Each successive president has issued executive orders to refine the process (and in some cases undo the reforms of other presidents). For instance, President George W. Bush issued an order that extended OIRA's review to include subregulatory guidance documents, an action that added to the office's already substantial workload. That order, however, was subsequently revoked by President Obama.[20] In 2017, President Trump issued an order, EO 13771,[21] that required agencies to remove two existing regulations for each new one generated, a requirement that OIRA was charged with implementing. While this did not change the scope of OIRA's review, it instituted another additional workload.

OIRA is typically overseen by one Senate-confirmed presidential appointee, the OIRA administrator, and employs roughly forty-five "desk officers," who are career staff analysts with advanced degrees in policy analysis, economics, and scientifically relevant fields (for example, epidemiology). In 2018, the most recent year for which data are available, the office reviewed ninety-one draft "economically significant" rules (that is, those with an annual economic impact of $100 million or more) and another 269 "significant" draft rules (that is, those that raised "novel legal or policy issues" or met one of the other significance criteria laid out in EO 12866) from twenty-six agencies,[22] in addition to performing a number of government-wide oversight responsibilities relating to paperwork, information technology, and statistical reporting. Stepping back, one must conclude that, since its founding, OIRA has flourished; among the cognoscenti, it is perceived as having tremendous influence in the regulatory process. This does not mean, however, that it has achieved favorable outcomes at every turn. Instead, the tale has been one of both success and failure.

EVALUATING SUCCESS AND FAILURE

The idea of a failure CV originated with Melanie Stefan, a neurobiologist. Writing in the journal *Nature*, she argued that, "As scientists, we construct a narrative of success that renders our setbacks invisible both to ourselves and to others. Often, other scientists' careers seem to be a constant, streamlined series of triumphs."[23] She argued that scholars should keep a running tally of their professional failures and, if their position afforded them the opportunity, make it public. Doing so would allow others to see that success was often a function of not just talent but also effort. Her argument sparked a conversation within the academy, and others quickly followed suit, posting their "failure CVs" online alongside their traditional CVs.

Looking at OIRA, its successes are also highly visible—they are what gave rise to the descriptions of the office's supposedly incontestable power that introduced this chapter, and they have become ingrained in the historical narrative of what the office is and what it does. However, like Stefan found in academia, its failures are harder to observe, either because they were not very public to begin with—unsurprising given the technocratic nature of regulatory matters and the office's penchant for operating under the radar—or they have been obscured by the passage of time. Regardless, this lowered visibility helps foster the illusion that the office is somehow infallible or omnipotent.

To remedy this, I construct OIRA's failure CV. "Failure" in this context means one of two things: either OIRA tried to expand its power in some way and that attempt failed or was not sustained over a longer period or, alternatively, OIRA missed a major opportunity to grow and meaningfully expand its power.[24] Most of the failures discussed herein fall within the latter category, but both types of failure run counter to the prevailing narrative about OIRA.

Of course, an organization's failures only make sense in the context of its successes, since the one is inevitably measured in relation to the other. Therefore, the next section briefly highlights OIRA's successes. By success, I mean that OIRA launched an initiative that made the office more powerful by tangibly expanding the scope of its review power or enhancing its reputation in some way.

Underlying this evaluation of OIRA's success and failures is an implicit assumption that, as an organization, OIRA is able to influence its own trajectory. This assumption builds on work from both political science and the field of organization studies showing that bureaucrats themselves are often pivotal actors in charting their organization's course.[25] Theories of "bureaucratic autonomy" do not imply that external influences do not matter. For instance, in OIRA's case, the OMB director, the president, Congress, the courts, and some powerful interest groups certainly have influenced the organization's path. Instead, the concept of bureaucratic autonomy suggests that an organization that is more autonomous can overcome the constraints imposed by these external factors and prevail in establishing its own reputation and power sources. For OIRA, this means that it should not *a priori* be viewed as a pawn that is manipulated by and set to carry out the instructions of, say, the current OMB director or the current administration. This may be an accurate characterization of the organization if it is not able to exercise bureaucratic autonomy. However, if the organization is viewed as more autonomous, an ambitious and strategic OIRA administrator or set of career OIRA staffers may be able to shape the office, its reputation, and, ultimately, the policies it pursues.

ACCOUNTING FOR OIRA'S SUCCESSES

When and where has OIRA been successful? There are many achievements that could be highlighted; for instance, OIRA has implemented the Paperwork Reduction Act for almost four decades. By nearly all accounts, this has been a successful undertaking; agencies comply with OIRA's oversight, and despite the massive amount of information managed under this law, there are very few violations of the law reported each year.[26] Instead, this chapter focuses on three of OIRA's higher profile accomplishments: the retention and expansion of regulatory review functions, the institution of core principles of regulatory review, and the balancing of transparency with the need to accomplish policy goals.

OIRA's foremost success lies in its very survival. OIRA is nothing if not controversial, and by many accounts it is a marvel the office has endured for nearly forty years. Writing in 1982, the chairmen of five House committees with jurisdiction over regulatory agencies opined: "Unless it is checked, the program embodied in [Reagan's] Executive Order 12291 will fundamentally damage the administrative process by which our laws are implemented, the legislative system by which our laws are enacted and monitored, and the separation of powers upon which our system of government rests."²⁷

While OIRA's history is often recounted in matter-of-fact terms, as if its current status was a matter of certain destiny, there has been a near-constant struggle for OIRA's survival between those who have wanted to enhance the scope of the office and those who have wanted to eviscerate it. As the quote from House overseers illustrates, this struggle was particularly acute at the outset.

At many points in its history, it was not at all clear that OIRA would persist into the next administration, or even the next year.²⁸ The fault lines were not necessarily partisan, either; while initially it seemed that Republicans supported OIRA and Democrats opposed it (since its first decade was under the auspices of Republican administrations), Democrats became more supportive and Republicans less so when President Clinton assumed office in 1993.

Despite this opposition, OIRA endured and even grew in its power. For instance, early on, many assumed that OIRA would be eliminated as soon as Clinton took office. Instead of doing away with OIRA, however, Clinton issued EO 12866, which consolidated and enhanced OIRA's powers. Each subsequent president has continued to reaffirm OIRA's place in the regulatory process, and its power—and its reputation—has grown in kind.

Political scientist Terry Moe argues that presidential reliance on institutions like OIRA is part of a broader trend wherein presidents centralize power into the Executive Office of the President to more closely oversee the bureaucracy.²⁹ While OIRA certainly fits this pattern, it is also true that any president could have scrapped OIRA and replaced it with another institution more to their liking. Instead, each has left OIRA largely unchanged and even worked to empower it. These actions are a testament to the demonstrated value of centralized review in OIRA, as well as to the office's reputation for professionalism and competency.

OIRA's second chief success has been its ability to dictate and sustain the central principles of regulatory review. There are two core tenets of regulatory review in the United States, both of which were instituted at OIRA's founding and have become more firmly entrenched over time. The first is the idea that regulations should be created only when there is a demonstrated need for them (that is, the burden is on the agency to demonstrate why a particular regulatory action is warranted). The second is that, at least for the most important regulations, their effects should be evaluated in terms of their costs and benefits.

It is entirely possible that OIRA by itself could have survived and these principles could have fallen by the wayside or been superseded by other approaches. That is, while these principles are considered doctrine today, it was not at all clear in the early years that they would be durable or thrive. The introduction of benefit-cost analysis as a mandatory and systematic component of regulatory review was particularly controversial. As one *New York Times* article explained: "The intensity of opposition to the use of cost-benefit analysis in the regulatory process ranges from those who oppose any application on the ground that, once adopted, it would reduce all decisions to simple-minded weighing of dollars, to those who think it is a useful tool for administrators but worry about its rigid application."[30]

Given these doubts, it was uncertain that benefit-cost analysis would be faithfully taken up by the agencies and therefore endure. Public criticism of the methodology presented opportunities for agencies to avoid implementing benefit-cost analysis, which they had reason to avoid due to resource constraints and an aversion to additional measures of political control.

Despite these challenges, today these two principles remain central to OIRA's work. In a recent public speech, former OIRA administrator Neomi Rao reiterated the first principle, remarking that "we're not in the business of just regulating for the sake of it."[31] Her remarks also reaffirmed the centrality of benefit-cost analysis, a point frequently reiterated by OIRA's top brass.[32] Again, the fact that these principles have endured is evidence of OIRA succeeding in an area where success was by no means foreordained.

A third institutional success is how OIRA has managed transparency around its review process and engagement with the public. Throughout its history, OIRA has regularly been criticized as "too secretive and subject to influence by private interests."[33] It might have been tempting for OIRA officials to ignore or disregard pointed critiques like this. Yet, doing so ran the risk of inviting more criticism, and potentially even exacerbating the aforementioned threat to the office's existence. Instead, OIRA has consistently responded by increasing the transparency of its review process, but in very limited and strategic ways.

Information about draft regulations and information collections that are currently under review is posted online at www.reginfo.gov. Additionally, meetings that OIRA holds with private stakeholders about regulations that are under review (called "12866 meetings" after the same-numbered EO) are also posted on this web platform, along with any documents presented by the stakeholders during the meeting. Notably, while this approach offers a window into OIRA's operations, there are many more things OIRA could do to provide transparency, but which it does not. For instance, OIRA could post versions of draft rules before and after its review, which would give outsiders a fuller sense of what changed during the course of review. Technically, both versions of these documents are considered part of the public domain[34] and can be viewed in person at OIRA's docket library in Washington, D.C.; however, OIRA chooses to limit their visibility. Similarly, many have noted that 12866 meetings tend to be the province of well-heeled groups.[35] OIRA could potentially remedy this by prominently posting its policy regarding the meetings (that is, that they are available to all stakeholders) and also explaining the process for requesting a meeting. This information is provided on a government website,[36] but it is buried deep within a "Frequently Asked Questions" page and not prominent by any means.

These transparency decisions are not accidental; OIRA's moves have been carefully calibrated. After all, if OIRA were to make all or even most aspects of its review process transparent, it would be limited in what it could accomplish for two reasons. First, much of what OIRA does is political; offering too much transparency might stymie the office's ability to accomplish political goals, as disaffected parties could certainly find grievance with the particulars of how individual rulemaking cases were handled. Such grievances might even become part of future litigation against agency rules, thus working against OIRA's intent to make lasting regulatory policy. Second, as discussed later, the size of OIRA's staff has been relatively fixed, and managing transparency on a wide scale would inevitably involve trade-offs in terms of staff time and resources. Put differently, policies aimed at increasing transparency also have workload implications. Seen in this light, OIRA's strategy for managing transparency has been highly successful. The office has been able to balance the need to conduct some of its business behind closed doors with the need to placate those who allege that the office was too opaque (particularly in its early years).

These three aspects of OIRA—survival, principle entrenchment, and transparency—are key pillars of the office's success. Of course, the three successes highlighted here are not OIRA's only successes. For instance, one could readily point to the office's management of its paperwork reduction and statistical review responsibilities, both of which have been executed rather seamlessly over the years.[37] However, they are highly visible and have been critical to building institutional resilience.

OIRA'S FAILURE CV

Despite these notable successes, OIRA has not always prevailed at attempts to expand its jurisdiction, nor has it always wielded its power in the most effective manner. In several cases, OIRA did not take advantage of opportunities that had the potential to alter the institution's course in a positive direction. Following is an outline of four major failures, including the failure to routinize RIAs, the failure to systematically oversee guidance documents, the failure to standardize regulatory lookbacks, and the failure to build staff capacity. Each runs counter to the predominant narrative of OIRA as a highly successful institution, and together they form a more nuanced (and, arguably, more accurate) view of OIRA.

To be clear, these failures do not constitute the entirety of OIRA's failure CV. The extended failure CV would undoubtedly point out that two features designed to augment OIRA's power have fizzled out of existence. The return letter, a way OIRA could publicly shame agencies who submitted unpalatable rules for review, and the prompt letter, a way OIRA could publicly direct which issues agencies worked on, were to revolutionize OIRA's review when they debuted early in the George W. Bush administration. That dream has surely died now, as the last return letter was issued in 2011 and the last prompt letter was issued in 2006. Nevertheless, the failures focused on here are representative of the range and depth of OIRA's institutional shortcomings.

OIRA'S FAILURE TO ROUTINIZE RIA

While the conceptualization of benefit-cost analysis as a staple of regulatory review undoubtedly accrues to OIRA's success column, the particulars of how benefit-cost analysis has been implemented on the ground leave much to be desired. Thus, the implementation of benefit-cost analysis accrues to OIRA's failure column, because there are many things

OIRA could have done to standardize, and thus further entrench, the practice of benefit-cost analysis that it did not do. In practice, benefit-cost analysis is unevenly applied across agencies. This unevenness has led many observers to speculate that agencies manipulate benefit-cost analysis to favor their preferred policy alternatives.[38] Given its central location and oversight role, OIRA is well positioned and has the authority and expertise to promote and enforce a more standardized benefit-cost analysis process. In spite of this imperative, there are many things the office could (and arguably should) have done to routinize the practice of benefit-cost analysis that, instead, languished.

A recent study evaluating the quality of RIAs conducted by the Department of Education concludes that the "practice falls short of methodological standards in a number of ways. Cost estimates appear to be underestimated and lack transparency with respect to method and assumptions. Benefit estimates are very infrequent and analyses often lack sensitivity testing, proportionality, and a reasonable counterfactual."[39] This finding comports with those of numerous other studies that find that, except in the case of high-profile rulemakings, agencies fail to conduct RIAs in the first place or produce low quality analyses when they do.[40] This unevenness in implementation contributes to the perception that, rather than using benefit-cost analyses as an analytical tool, agencies use them to justify decisions that have already been made.

An example illustrates an area where OIRA could have, but has not, improved the quality of RIAs or standardized the benefit-cost analysis process. At present, there is no government-wide standard for the value of a statistical life (VSL), the monetary value that agencies attach to an individual life (in a statistical sense) when calculating the monetized benefits associated with a regulatory intervention that will reduce health or environmental risks and thus save lives. The current practice, laid out in broad brushstrokes in a 2003 guidance document,[41] is for agencies to individually determine the appropriate VSL for their agency (or, in some circumstances, for the individual rule). This means that, as of 2017, three agencies—the Department of Health and Human Services (HHS), the Department of Transportation (DOT), and the Environmental Protection Agency (EPA)—have guidance documents, which they periodically update, setting out the methodology and literature underlying their particular VSL. Unsurprisingly, these agencies arrive at different figures: when adjusted to reflect real 2015 dollars, a life is worth $9.5 million at

HHS,[42] $9.6 million at the DOT,[43] and $8.7 million at the EPA.[44] While these figures are roughly comparable (in real 2015 dollars), that has not always been the case.

Having individual agencies set their own VSLs is inefficient, since every agency reinvents the wheel.[45] It is also not theoretically necessary, as a recent EPA report found that the academic literature did not make a strong case for adjusting the VSL for idiosyncratic (or agency-specific) factors.[46] The case against agency-specific VSLs is furthered by speculation that the value is sometimes gamed to advance political goals. For instance, under the George W. Bush administration, the EPA devalued the VSL—from $7.8 million to $6.9 million per life—adopting a lower rate than had been used by the agency during the Clinton administration.[47] Just a few years later, under the more pro-regulatory Obama administration, several agencies made a change in the opposite direction, increasing their VSLs; for example, in 2010 the Food and Drug Administration raised its VSL to $7.9 million, up $5 million from its 2008 level.[48] These changes to the VSL align with the regulatory agenda of the respective administrations; a lower VSL—as the EPA's under Bush—makes it harder to justify the costs of strong safety and health protections, whereas higher VSLs—like those adopted under Obama's tenure—effectively make these regulations easier to justify. These kinds of politically convenient changes to what should be objective and consistent values reduce public confidence in the RIA process. OIRA has done little to nothing to limit the practice.

The VSL is just one small but illustrative example of where RIAs fall short. For instance, observers have repeatedly noted that, although Circular A-4 requires agencies to consider a range of alternatives in the RIA (in addition to the alternative the agency is proposing), agencies often consider only one other alternative (for example, the status quo) or fail to consider any alternative at all. Writing in 2007, Robert Hahn and Patrick Dudley found that, among a sample of rules where RIAs were required, "the percentage of RIAs that considered at least one alternative standard or level decreased from 85 percent during the Reagan administration to 74 percent during the Clinton administration."[49, 50]

Why doesn't OIRA scrupulously monitor how agencies conduct benefit-cost analysis? Or require more standardization of the process? There are many ways OIRA could have accomplished this. For example, a standing group of experts from agencies, academia, and regulated industry could have been established to provide regular updates to OMB Circular A-4 and to evaluate and update a government-wide VSL. Additionally, OIRA staff could provide more enforcement for the quality of RIAs conducted, ensuring they always include (for example) at least one alternative other than the status quo and the agency proposal. Doing some combination of these things would likely have diminished the political maneuvering—or at least the perceptions of political maneuvering—associated with the analytical parts of rulemaking.

By not pushing agencies to do a better job with benefit-cost analysis, either through rigorous monitoring or greater process standardization, OIRA relinquished an opportunity to both increase its power and enhance public confidence in the rulemaking process.

OIRA'S FAILURE TO OVERSEE GUIDANCE DOCUMENTS

OIRA has also had a strained and often ill-defined relationship with agency guidance documents, and specifically its role in overseeing them. Guidance documents are nonbinding policies issued by agencies, offered either in lieu of regulations or to further explicate how particular statutes or regulations should be implemented. In many ways, they are the bane of regulatory overseers, since regulated parties often treat them as gospel even though they are not legally binding and, therefore, not subject to the same procedural rigor and disclosure requirements as regulations created through notice-and-comment. Because of this, they are often described as "regulatory dark matter," and a recent House report describes them as having a "ubiquitous and nebulous character."[51]

At present, there is little standardization to the process of creating new guidance documents. Some agencies, like the FDA, have established their own practices, and others voluntarily follow the "good guidance" practices outlined in a memorandum issued by the George W. Bush administration, but many agencies do not. There is also no official inventory of guidance documents.[52] Further, OIRA's role in overseeing guidance is murky. While OIRA has long maintained that it has authority to review guidance documents, there is ambiguity surrounding that interpretation. At various points, presidents have attempted to assert OIRA's authority over guidance documents. Nonetheless, OIRA's oversight role has been at best incoherent and at worst nonexistent.

In OIRA's early years under Presidents Reagan and H. W. Bush, capacity constraints (that is, OIRA's limited staff and the expectation that the office review all rules issued by covered agencies) prevented the office from reviewing guidance documents. As Paul Noe and John Graham explain,[53] in practice this meant that OIRA "rarely called in guidance documents for review and did not have an established practice for doing so." Little changed in terms of reviewing guidance with President Clinton's issuance of EO 12866, as Administrator Sally Katzen later recounted that OIRA never reviewed a guidance document during her tenure (from 1993 to 1998).[54] This practice continued into the early George W. Bush years.

In 2007, President George W. Bush issued an order (EO 13422) designed to enhance OIRA's purview over guidance documents. Specifically, the order defined the term "significant guidance document," required agencies to give OIRA advance notice of such documents, and gave OIRA the authority to formally review these types of guidance. The order was controversial; many considered expanding OIRA review powers to guidance to be an unabashed power grab, not to mention the aspects of the order that politicized other facets of the rulemaking process.[55] Shortly after the EO was released, OMB followed up with guidance on "good guidance" practices.[56]

Perhaps because of the controversies surrounding Bush's order—particularly those unrelated to guidance[57]—upon assuming office, President Obama rescinded Bush's order.[58] Shortly thereafter, the OMB director issued a memorandum indicating that revocation of the EO returned the status quo to its pre-2007 state, where "OIRA reviewed all significant proposed or final agency actions, including significant policy and guidance documents. Such agency actions and documents *remain subject to OIRA's review under Executive Order 12866*" (emphasis added). This was a confusing turn of events, because if OIRA had the authority to review guidance documents under EO 12866 then Bush's order was superfluous in the first place. Not to mention that Clinton-era Administrator Katzen claimed to never have reviewed a guidance document during her five-year tenure. Further confusing matters, a congressional investigation uncovered that implementation of guidance review during the Obama years was spotty; between 2008 and 2017, a time when all significant guidance documents should have been reviewed by OIRA, less than two-thirds of significant guidance documents were sent to the office for review.[59]

More recently, a flurry of developments has affected OIRA's oversight role in guidance creation. In the spring of 2019, OMB issued a memorandum "clarifying" that all guidance was to be reviewed by OIRA.[60] The memo tied OIRA's review authority to existing authorities the office had under the Congressional Review Act (CRA), not EO 12866 as prior administrations had claimed. This was, instead, a new interpretation of the CRA, a law that had been passed more than twenty years prior. Yet, despite the grandiose claims of the memo, details about how implementation would work under the new guidance regime were initially quite sparse. Then in the fall of 2019, President Trump signed two executive orders on guidance.[61] These orders require agencies to make a number of changes to their current guidance practices, including: stating explicitly that guidance is nonbinding, posting all guidance to a centralized, searchable web platform; establishing a process for the public to petition to repeal guidance; and increasing overall transparency regarding guidance document usage.

By increasing standardization of guidance production, the Trump administration's actions promise to address some of the low-hanging fruit with respect to guidance and OIRA's role in it. But much remains unanswered. Does EO 12866 cover guidance documents, or does only the CRA do so? Should agencies still follow the Bush-era memorandum regarding good guidance practices?[62] What are the consequences if agencies do not alert OIRA before issuing a new guidance document? The net result is that, at present, it is difficult to definitively state OIRA's official stance on guidance documents.

One can be forgiven for failing to comprehend all the twists and turns in OIRA's complicated guidance saga. The path has been anything but straightforward. What is clear is that the office has tried—and repeatedly failed—to develop a workable guidance oversight system. It is also clear that many of the issues surrounding guidance are deeply entrenched. It remains to be seen how the Trump administration's approach to guidance will be implemented. While the administration's actions clearly put OIRA into a more definitive oversight track, they come at a time when the administration is also asking OIRA to take on many other new responsibilities (for example, review of independent agency regulations, major deregulation-related tasks). Stepping back, it is too early to conclude whether these actions mark a clear inflection point in OIRA's relationship with guidance. Historically speaking, however, OIRA's approach to guidance has been ill-defined and unevenly implemented and, as such, it definitively accrues to the organization's failure column.

OIRA'S FAILURE TO STANDARDIZE REGULATORY LOOKBACKS

OIRA has also failed to establish a system for managing regulatory lookbacks. A regulatory lookback, sometimes referred to as a "retrospective review," is the idea that agencies should periodically scour their portions of the Code of Federal Regulations and eliminate outdated or ineffective regulations.

When President Trump assumed office in 2017, he made headlines by promising to eliminate "75% maybe more" of existing regulations to reduce the burden on regulated entities. While Trump is unique in the scale of his promised lookback, his desire to remove ineffective and outdated regulations from the books is not unique.[63] Every recent president, regardless of their political orientation, has attempted to do some version of this. As Cary Coglianese explains, "the second Bush White House issued three separate requests for nominations of existing rules to modify or rescind. President Barack Obama launched a government-wide regulatory 'lookback' initiative that gave priority to reviews that could generate 'significant quantifiable monetary savings or significant quantifiable reductions in paperwork burdens.'"[64] And President Trump's "1 in 2 out" order certainly is associated with retrospective review, since it requires agencies to eliminate existing regulations when creating new ones.

Despite these presidential initiatives, there is widespread agreement that retrospective regulatory review has been a failure.[65] One recent academic report noted, "that every administration feels compelled to call anew for retrospective review suggests that these repeated attempts at regulatory look-back have not been sufficient."[66] The complaints are numerous: that the general approach focuses on costs rather than benefits,[67] that the process is not transparent enough to the public,[68] that agencies lack sufficient data to do the job well,[69] or that the approach is necessarily ad hoc.[70]

Again, OIRA is uniquely positioned to improve the way agencies conduct retrospective reviews, but it has failed to establish a standardized way for agencies to evaluate what is on the books. Instead, each new administration has come up with a slightly different take on what these lookbacks should look like, who should do them, how they should do them, and how often. This is unquestionably an organizational failure, as a more standardized process would have provided agencies with certainty and afforded them the opportunity to plan accordingly. It would also make OIRA central in that process. OIRA's failure is not one of imagination, either, as observers have suggested numerous ways to improve lookbacks: requiring regulatory sunsets (which would force agencies to reevaluate regulations at predetermined intervals); requiring agencies to include data collection plans in their proposed rules so as to facilitate future evaluations of a rule's effectiveness; and convening government-wide panels that would offer agencies expertise in improving their existing regulatory framework and help them to develop a comprehensive plan.[71]

OIRA'S FAILURE TO BUILD STAFF CAPACITY

OIRA's staff is responsible for numerous tasks, including not only reviewing draft regulations from dozens of agencies but also reviewing information collections from these agencies under the Paperwork Reduction Act, managing privacy and statistical standards for the federal government, and coordinating sundry activities within the executive branch. Doing all these tasks requires skilled staff familiar with the policy and technical issues at play. Historically, most OIRA desk officers have held advanced degrees in their respective areas, be it economics, epidemiology, public policy, public health, or statistics.

Having enough staff in place is critical to OIRA performing its work effectively and efficiently. Prior work has shown that in periods where OIRA staff has been more limited, the time OIRA spends reviewing individual regulations increases.[72] Staff shortages are likely to impact other aspects of OIRA's work as well, such as the number of agency regulations OIRA is able to bring in for formal review and the quality of the reviews it does conduct.[73] Despite this centrality, OIRA's staff size has been relatively stagnant over the last several decades. In many regards, the other failures already noted may trace their origins to this underlying capacity deficit.

OIRA's staff levels peaked in its first decade. With ninety full-time equivalent (FTE) employees, OIRA had its largest staff in 1981. However, the imposition of EO 12866 in 1993 cut OIRA's workload by changing its review purview from all agency regulations to a subset of the most significant ones, and OIRA's staff numbers were reduced accordingly. Since 1994, OIRA's total FTEs—a figure that includes both desk officers and administrative staff—has hovered at around fifty, as shown in figure 7-1.

Meanwhile, as also illustrated in figure 7-1, the office's workload—in terms of total rules reviewed— also has remained somewhat constant during this period.

While OIRA's staff numbers have leveled off, regulatory agencies have experienced large increases in staff sizes.[74] Increases in regulatory agency staff are potentially indicative of many things (for example, increased inspections or industry oversight), but one possibility is that the sophistication of the rules produced by these agencies may have increased. This suggestion, supported by some observers,[75] would mean OIRA's primary task of regulatory review has become more difficult over time.

Additionally, concurrent with these trends within OIRA, the number of tasks delegated to the office has grown over time. For instance, during George W. Bush's administration OIRA took on new responsibilities related to improving the quality of data used in regulatory analyses. President Trump also required OIRA to monitor the implementation of his "1 in 2 out" order, again increasing the workload without corresponding staff increases. For some time during the Bush administration and under a recent change during the Trump administration, OIRA has been tasked

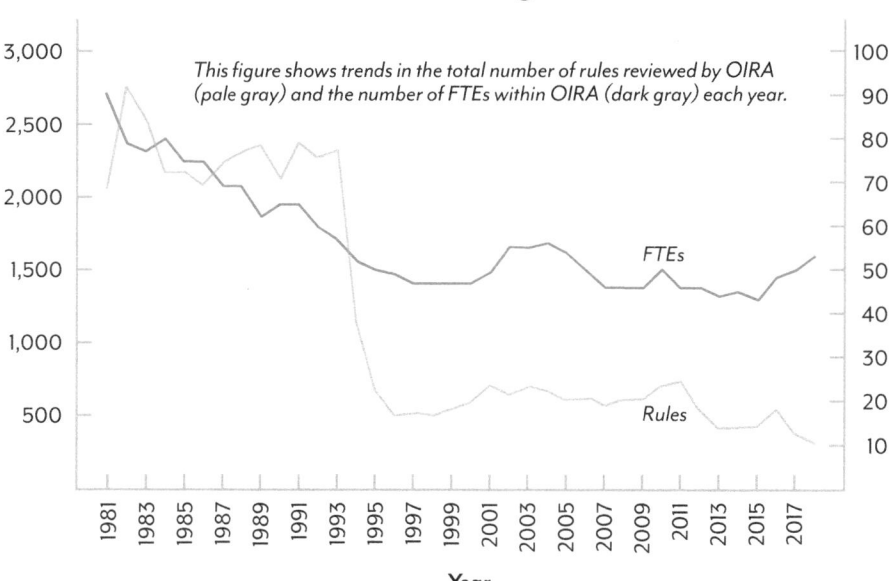

FIGURE 7-1. **OIRA's Staff Size Has Stagnated in Recent Years**

Source: Regulatory review counts are drawn from www.reginfo.gov. OIRA's FTE count is reported in OMB's annual congressional budget justifications.

with reviewing a considerable volume of agency guidance documents. The same Trump memo that gave OIRA authority to review guidance documents[76] also extended OIRA's purview to rules from independent agencies, a potentially large workload increase.

It is clear, then, that OIRA would be well served with a much larger staff, one at the level of its earliest staffing figures. Increased capacity would be transformative, giving the institution the bandwidth to take on many of the issues laid out in this chapter, including reviewing guidance documents and improving the implementation surrounding agency RIA practice.

Yet, while calls for increasing OIRA's staff size have been near constant throughout its history,[77] the actual numbers have not meaningfully budged.[78] Of course, increasing an agency's staff size is not entirely within its own purview, since monies for staff must come from congressional appropriations. However, that does not exonerate OIRA, and its leadership in particular, from the failure to add the needed FTEs. Scholars have long recognized that growing an agency in terms of both its budget and its staff is the hallmark of highly effective bureaucratic leaders.[79] Thus, while staff enhancement is not a unilateral action that OIRA leaders could have taken, it is something that should have been a priority for each administrator. Each should have made the case for a larger OIRA, publicly, privately, and repeatedly. While the historical record indicates that many OIRA administrators have, in fact, argued for more staff, none has expended the required capital to actually accomplish change. This is perhaps the organization's most fundamental failure.

As several chapters in this volume highlight, the failure to advocate for increased staff is an OMB-wide issue and is by no means limited to OIRA. This hesitation stems from deeply held beliefs; as one former OMB staffer noted, OMB directors have sought to be "purer than Caesar's wife" when it comes to asking Congress for more staff. The underlying concern is one of perception. OMB cannot ask other agencies to cut back while growing in its own right. While certainly a difficult needle to thread, the failure to make the political case for capabilities commensurate with the growth in responsibilities has not served OIRA's, OMB's, or the public's interest in the long term.

CONTRASTING SUCCESS AND FAILURE

Why did OIRA fail in these endeavors? More generally, what distinguishes OIRA's successes from its failures? Answering these questions is critical in putting OIRA's failure CV to work, using insight about failures in a constructive fashion to craft a more effective institution.

Looking across this accounting of OIRA's successful and unsuccessful initiatives, several patterns emerge. To begin, OIRA's successes—its survival, principled focus, and approach to transparency—are all things OIRA's leadership has tackled head-on and repeatedly reinforced. No one administration or administrator can reasonably claim these successes as their own but, rather, they are the amalgamation of a consistently-prioritized and shared vision about what OIRA is and how it should work. OIRA's failures also do not owe to one particularly ineffective administration or administrator; each of the failures—be it with RIAs, guidance, retrospective review, or staff shortages—has been a longstanding issue that multiple generations of leaders have either ignored or failed to effectively tackle. The lesson is one of the importance of organizational leadership and continuity of vision across leadership transitions.

Additionally, OIRA seems to have been successful when expectations regarding both agency and OIRA responsibilities are made clear. Consider, for example, that from the agency's perspective, it is clear what will transpire at a 12866 meeting (that is, it will be a "listening session" that will be disclosed on the Internet afterward). This stands in contrast to OIRA's policy and expectations regarding the level of analytical rigor required for any individual RIA, the expectations surrounding the creation and review of new guidance documents, or the expectations for retrospective review in any given year. In each of these cases, agencies cannot be reasonably sure of what to expect for any particular action, given the variation in experiences across individual actions and across different administrations.

OIRA's failure CV also highlights the institution's laxity in terms of formalizing many aspects of its rulemaking duties. Arguably, OIRA's work would be easier if agencies were given more instruction about what would be expected for, say, retrospective review every year for the next several years or if OIRA clarified exactly what a good RIA should include. Yet, OIRA seems reluctant to spell these things out, perhaps out of a concern such formalization would hinder its own discretion and flexibility.[80] This, however, is not cause enough to justify avoiding formalization altogether, as the benefits of doing so may be considerable in the long term even if it may reduce flexibility in individual instances. With more informed expectations, agencies may start doing a better job at preparing RIAs and guidance documents, planning for retrospective reviews, and the like.

How OIRA chooses to handle this formalization is important. These are highly technical matters and OIRA will need expertise as well as buy-in from the agencies. Here, the Obama administration's approach to developing a government-wide standard for the Social Cost of Carbon (SCC) provides an instructive example. In 2009, President Obama established an interagency working group to determine a government-wide value of the SCC. The working group was composed of six executive branch offices (including OIRA) and six regulatory agencies, and included experts who evaluated the science and came up with a single set of government-wide values of the cost per ton of carbon. The SCC values, which were to be used across all agency RIAs, were developed in 2009 and 2010 and updated by the working group in 2013 and 2015. This interagency working group format provides a model for not only developing a government-wide VSL but also for updating OMB Circular A-4 (governing RIA practices more generally), for handling guidance practices, and for developing a workable system for conducting regulatory lookbacks.

Of course, considering the SCC interagency working group raises an important consideration about durability. That group was convened by order of a memorandum issued by President Obama, and when President Trump took office, he disbanded the group and essentially gutted the role of the SCC in RIAs. Perhaps if Obama had used an EO, which carries greater weight, the group might have gotten better treatment from Trump, but it is unlikely. As this discussion of OIRA's history has underscored, EOs seem to be a favored vehicle for making changes to the regulatory review process. But presidents seem to have no compunction about undoing the orders of their predecessors, meaning these policy instruments may not be long-lasting. Therefore, to establish durability, OIRA should consider other avenues to take up these issues, such as leaning on legislative allies to create standing groups via statute.

Before concluding, a final note on prioritization is warranted. This section has focused entirely on failures that are rooted around specific issues (for example, guidance practices). The other failure discussed in depth is OIRA's lack of staff capacity; this should be considered OIRA's first order of business. Growing staff is a political problem and one that an ambitious OIRA administrator should take on before addressing the other failures discussed herein.

The notion of a failure CV suggests that every person—and institution—suffers setbacks. Starting a conversation about OIRA's institutional shortcomings is important because it reveals a more accurate picture of OIRA and identifies concrete ways the institution can improve. Without a doubt, OIRA is a powerful institution, but it nevertheless has problems, problems that are not easy to solve. However, the suggestions offered here are oriented toward moving OIRA to a more streamlined and effective regulatory review process, one that instills confidence among both agencies and the public.

Notes

I thank the Center for the Study of Democratic Politics at Princeton University for research support.

1. Cass R. Sunstein, "The Office of Information and Regulatory Affairs: Myths and Realities," *Harvard Law Review* 126 (2012), pp. 1838–79.
2. Ibid., p. 1839.
3. Dick Durbin, "Graham Flunks the Cost-Benefit Test," *Washington Post*, July 16, 2001, www.washingtonpost.com/archive/opinions/2001/07/16/graham-flunks-the-cost-benefit-test/4a4af210-df8b-4137-b9b3-03e8a82df9a1/?utm_term=.dfa1cb48142.
4. Leif Frederickson, "The Federal Agency that Few Americans Have Heard Of and Which We All Need to Know," *Washington Post*, September 28, 2017, www.washingtonpost.com/news/made-by-history/wp/2017/09/28/the-federal-agency-that-few-americans-have-heard-of-and-which-we-all-need-to-know/?utm_term=.b9307939cbcf.
5. Donald R. Arbuckle, "Obscure but Powerful: Who are Those Guys?" *Administrative Law Review* 63 (2011), pp. 131–34.
6. Sunstein, "The Office of Information and Regulatory Affairs."
7. Rena Steinzor, "Eye on OIRA: Regulation Goes Opaque," CPR Blog, Center for Progressive Reform, June 10, 2010, www.progressivereform.org/CPRBlog.cfm?idBlog=5C7955F2-A0D9-B017-5A5D963250256AAF.
8. Stuart Shapiro, "OIRA Inside and Out," *Administrative Law Review* 63 (2011), pp. 135–48; Stuart Shapiro and John F. Morrall III, "The Triumph of Regulatory Politics: Benefit-Cost Analysis and Political Salience," *Regulation & Governance* 6, no. 2 (2012), pp. 189–206.
9. Lisa Heinzerling, "Inside EPA: A Former Insider's Reflections on the Relationship between the Obama EPA and the Obama White House," *Pace Environmental Law Review* 31 (2014), pp. 314, 325–69.

10. Alex Acs and Charles M. Cameron, "Does White House Regulatory Review Produce a Chilling Effect and 'OIRA Avoidance' in the Agencies?" *Presidential Studies Quarterly* 43, no. 3 (2013), pp. 443–67.

11. Simon F. Haeder and Susan Webb Yackee, "Influence and the Administrative Process: Lobbying the US President's Office of Management and Budget," *American Political Science Review* 109, no. 3 (2015), pp. 507–22.

12. Rachel Augustine Potter, *Bending the Rules: Procedural Politicking in the Bureaucracy* (University of Chicago Press, 2019).

13. For example, Bolton and others discuss in detail how a limited capacity hinders OIRA's performance. Alexander Bolton, Rachel Augustine Potter, and Sharece Thrower, "Organizational Capacity, Regulatory Review, and the Limits of Political Control," *Journal of Law, Economics, and Organization* 32, no. 2 (2015), pp. 242–71.

14. Haushofer, as quoted in Scott Jaschik, "Sharing the Failures," *Inside Higher Ed* (May 2, 2016), www.insidehighered.com/news/2016/05/02/professors-failure-cv-prompts-discussion-what-constitutes-academic-success.

15. P.L. 96-511.

16. Before then, a series of less formalized and somewhat ad hoc organizations—from the Nixon administration's Quality of Life review program to the Carter administration's Regulatory Analysis Review Group—provided agencies with various levels of feedback on their rulemakings. For an account of these predecessor organizations, see Jim Tozzi, "OIRA's Formative Years: The Historical Record of Centralized Regulatory Review Preceding OIRA's Founding," *Administrative Law Review* 63 (2011), pp. 37–69.

17. Executive Order 12291 "Federal Regulation," February 17, 1981.

18. The order, however, did not require agencies to quantify all costs and benefits, an expectation that persists to this day.

19. Executive Order 12866 "Regulatory Planning and Review," October 4, 1993.

20. See Executive Order 13422 "Further Amendment to Executive Order 12866 on Regulatory Planning and Review," January 18, 2007; and Executive Order 13497 "Revocation of Certain Executive Orders Concerning Regulatory Planning and Review," January 30, 2009.

21. Executive Order 13771 "Reducing Regulation and Controlling Regulatory Costs," January 30, 2017.

22. Figures are from www.reginfo.gov.

23. Melanie Stefan, "A CV of Failures," *Nature*, November 17, 2010, www.nature.com/naturejobs/science/articles/10.1038/nj7322-467a.

24. Failure—or its converse, success—should not be defined merely in terms of size and power. Good policy outcomes, which in the case of OIRA means that regulations are improved as the result of its review, are an important marker of an organization's achievements. Policy outcomes are naturally more idiosyncratic and harder to systematically observe. Fortunately, for the purposes herein, OIRA's ability to effectuate good policy outcomes goes hand-in-hand with its size and power.

25. See, for example, Daniel P. Carpenter, *The Forging of Bureaucratic Autonomy: Reputations, Networks, and Policy Innovation in Executive Agencies, 1862–1928* (Princeton University Press, 2001); Morten Egeberg and Jarle Trondal, "Political Leadership and Bureaucratic Autonomy: Effects of Agencification," *Governance* 22, no. 4 (2009), pp. 673–88; John D. Huber and Charles R.

Shipan, *Deliberate Discretion?: The Institutional Foundations of Bureaucratic Autonomy* (Cambridge University Press, 2002).

26. For an accounting of the violations of this law, see the annual Information Collection Budget, which is published each year by OMB.

27. As quoted in David C. Vladeck, "Amending Executive Order 12866: Good Governance or Regulatory Usurpation?" Testimony before the House Committee on Science and Technology, February 13, 2007, https://scholarship.law.georgetown.edu/cgi/viewcontent.cgi?article=1075&context=cong.

28. See, for example, Philip Shabecoff, "Reagan Order on Cost-Benefit Analysis Stirs Economic and Political Debate," *New York Times*, November 7, 1981, www.nytimes.com/1981/11/07/us/reagan-order-on-cost-benefit-analysis-stirs-economic-and-political-debate.html.

29. Terry M. Moe, The Politicized Presidency, in *The New Direction in American Politics*, edited by John E. Chubb and Paul E. Peterson (Washington, D.C.: Brookings Institution Press, 1985), pp. 244–63.

30. Shabecoff, "Reagan Order on Cost-Benefit Analysis Stirs Economic and Political Debate."

31. Neomi Rao, "Assessing the Administrative State," Remarks at the American Enterprise Institute, June 19, 2018. Washington, D.C., www.youtube.com/watch?v=A6n9qEOByT4.

32. Ibid.; Neomi Rao, "What's Next for Trump's Regulatory Agenda? A Conversation with OIRA Administrator Neomi Rao," Brookings Institution, January 26, 2018. Transcript, www.brookings.edu/wp-content/uploads/2018/01/es_20180126_oira_transcript.pdf; Tozzi, "OIRA's Formative Years."

33. CRS, "Presidential Review of Agency Rulemaking," Congressional Review Service, April 5, 2005, Report #:RL32855, www.everycrsreport.com/files/20050405_RL32855_aea4443451f90263db284510507bc46d8f32eda7.pdf.

34. Indeed, some individual agencies post both versions on the web. See Haeder and Yackee, "Influence and the Administrative Process" for an analysis comparing document changes pre- and post-OIRA review.

35. Rena Steinzor, Michael Patoka, and James Goodwin, "Behind Closed Doors at the White House: How Politics Trumps Protection of Public Health, Worker Safety, and the Environment," Center for Progressive Reform, White Paper #1111, 2011, www.progressivereform.org/articles/OIRA_Meetings_1111.pdf.

36. See www.reginfo.gov/public/jsp/Utilities/faq.jsp/.

37. I do not spend more time outlining OIRA's numerous other successes as an institution since they have been so well documented elsewhere (Arbuckle, "Obscure but Powerful: Who are Those Guys?"; Shapiro, "OIRA Inside and Out"; Tozzi, "OIRA's Formative Years").

38. For example, Potter, *Bending the Rules*; Wendy E. Wagner, "The CAIR RIA: Advocacy Dressed Up as Policy Analysis," in *Reforming Regulatory Impact Analysis* (NY: Routledge: 2010), pp. 56–81.

39. Clive R. Belfield, A. Brooks Bowden, and Viviana Rodriguez, "Evaluating Regulatory Impact Assessments in Education Policy," *American Journal of Evaluation* (2018), pp. 1–19.

40. For example, Robert W. Hahn and Paul C. Tetlock, "Has Economic Analysis Improved Regulatory Decisions?" *Journal of Economic Perspectives* 22, no. 1 (2008), pp. 67–84; Shapiro and Morrall, "The Triumph of Regulatory Politics"; Stuart Shapiro and John F. Morrall III, "Does Haste Make Waste? How Long Does It Take to Do a Good Regulatory Impact Analysis?" *Administration & Society* 48, no. 3 (2016), pp. 367–89.

41. OMB, "Regulatory Analysis," September 17, 2003, Circular A-4, https://obamawhitehouse.archives.gov/omb/circulars_a004_a-4/.

42. HHS, "Guidelines for Regulatory Impact Analysis," Department of Health and Human Services document, 2016, https://aspe.hhs.gov/system/files/pdf/242926/HHS_RIAGuidance.pdf.

43. DOT, "Guidance on Treatment of the Economic Value of a Statistical Life (VSL) in U.S. Department of Transportation Analyses–2016 Adjustment," Department of Transportation memorandum, August 8, 2016, www.transportation.gov/sites/dot.gov/files/docs/2016 20Revised20Value 20of 20a 20Statistical%20Life 20Guidance.pdf.

44. EPA, "Mortality Risk Valuation," Environmental Protection Agency webpage, 2017, www.epa.gov/environmental-economics/mortality-risk-valuation.

45. This inefficiency is underscored by the fact that invoking VSLs is relatively rare; government-wide, only about a dozen rules per year involve VSL calculations; See Dave Merrill, "No One Values Your Life More than the Federal Government," Bloomberg News, October 19, 2017, www.bloomberg.com/graphics/2017-value-of-life/.

46. Merrill, "No One Values Your Life More than the Federal Government."

47. Associated Press, "Like the Dollar, Value of American Life has Dropped," *New York Times*, July 10, 2008, www.nytimes.com/2008/07/10/business/worldbusiness/10iht-10life.14401415.html?mcubz=1.

48. Binyamin Appelbaum, "As U.S. Agencies Put More Value on a Life, Businesses Fret," *New York Times*, February 16, 2011, www.nytimes.com/2011/02/17/business/economy/17regulation.html.

49. Robert W. Hahn and Patrick M. Dudley, "How Well Does the U.S. Government Do Benefit-Cost Analysis?" *Review of Environmental Economics and Policy* 1 (2007), pp. 192–211, 202.

50. See also Belfield, Bowden, and Rodriguez, "Evaluating Regulatory Impact Assessments in Education Policy."

51. "Shining Light on Regulatory Dark Matter," House Committee on Oversight and Government Reform, Majority Staff Report, March 2018, https://permanent.fdlp.gov/gpo110748/Guidance-Report-for-Issuance1.pdf.

52. Ibid.

53. Paul R. Noe and John D. Graham, "Due Process and Management for Guidance Documents: Good Governance Long Overdue," *Yale Journal on Regulation* 25, no. 1 (2008), pp. 103–12, 105.

54. Ibid.

55. The order also called for each agency to select a "regulatory policy officer" (RPO), who had to be a political appointee. The RPO would then be the point of contact for all the agency's important regulations. Many saw this as inviting even more politics into the rulemaking process.

56. Rob Portman, "Memorandum to Heads of Executive Departments and Agencies on Issuance of OMB's Final Bulletin for Agency Good Guidance Practices," Office of Management and Budget, January 17, 2007, www.whitehouse.gov/sites/default/files/omb/memoranda/fy2007/m07-07.pdf.

57. Robin Bravender, "Obama Tosses Bush Order, Eases OMB Grip on Rulemaking," *E&E News*, February 4, 2009, www.eenews.net/stories/73906.

58. Peter R. Orszag, "Memorandum to Heads and Acting Heads of Executive Departments and Agencies," Office of Management and Budget, March 4, 2009, https://tinyurl.com/thsenal; Heinzerling, "Inside EPA," pp. 314, 325–69.

59. Committee on Oversight and Government Reform, "Shining Light on Regulatory Dark Matter."

60. OMB, "Guidance on Compliance with the Congressional Review Act," April 11, 2019, Memo: M-19-14, www.whitehouse.gov/wp-content/uploads/2019/04/M-19-14.pdf.

61. See "Promoting the Rule of Law through Improved Agency Guidance Documents" (EO 13891; October 15, 2019, 84 FR 55235) and "Promoting the Rule of Law through Transparency and Fairness in Civil Administrative Enforcement and Adjudication" (EO 13892; October 15, 2019, 84 FR 55239).

62. According to the GAO, some agencies do seem to follow the guidance on good guidance practices. GAO found that among the four agencies studied, all identified standard practices to follow when developing guidance, but they addressed OMB's requirements on significant guidance to varying degrees. See GAO, "Federal Regulations: Opportunities to Improve the Effectiveness and Transparency of Regulatory and Guidance Practices," Government Accountability Office report, GAO-18-436T, 2015, www.gao.gov/assets/700/690650.pdf.

63. Trump also stands apart in his approach to deregulation; see Rachel Augustine Potter, Andrew Rudalevige, Sharece Thrower, and Adam L. Warber, "Continuity Trumps Change: The First Year of Trump's Administrative Presidency," *PS: Political Science and Politics* 52, no. 4 (2019), pp. 613–19.

64. Cary Coglianese, "It's Time to Think Strategically about Retrospective Benefit-Cost Analysis," *The Regulatory Review*, University of Pennsylvania, April 18, 2018, www.theregreview.org/2018/04/30/coglianese-think-strategically-retrospective-benefit-cost-analysis/.

65. Coglianese, "It's Time to Think Strategically"; Andrew M. Grossman, "An Administration Takes Sides," *Notice & Comment*, May 25, 2017, http://yalejreg.com/nc/an-administration-takes-sides-by-andrew-m-grossman/; Connor Raso, "Assessing Regulatory Retrospective Review under the Obama Administration," Center on Regulation and Markets, Brookings Institution, June 15, 2017, www.brookings.edu/research/assessing-regulatory-retrospective-review-under-the-obama-administration/.

66. Institute for Policy Integrity, "Strengthening Regulatory Review: Recommendations for the Trump Administration from Former OIRA Leaders," Report, New York University School of Law, 2016, www.thecre.com/oira/wp-content/uploads/2016/11/Report.pdf.

67. Coglianese, "It's Time to Think Strategically."

68. GAO, "Agencies Often Made Regulatory Changes, but Could Strengthen Linkages to Performance Goals," Government Accountability Office report, GAO-14-268, 2014, www.gao.gov/assets/670/662517.pdf.

69. Institute for Policy Integrity, "Strengthening Regulatory Review."

70. Grossman, "An Administration Takes Sides."

71. Arguably, the Trump administration has gone some way toward standardization on this last point with the creation of regulatory reform officer roles within agencies, but this approach is entirely focused on costs and it is not clear whether these roles will persist beyond the Trump administration.

72. Bolton, Potter, and Thrower, "Organizational Capacity, Regulatory Review, and the Limits of Political Control."

73. Shapiro and Morrall, "Does Haste Make Waste?

74. See Julie Balla, "Regulators' Budget: OIRA's Growth and the Future of Regulatory Reform," Report, Regulatory Studies Center at George Wash-

ington University, 2018, https://regulatorystudies.columbian.gwu.edu/regulators%E2%80%99-budget-oira%E2%80%99s-growth-and-future-regulatory-reform.

75. There is some sense among scholars that the level of rule sophistication has indeed increased over time. One key indicator is that the number of administrative requirements has grown; agencies must often evaluate the impact of a proposed rule on specific subpopulations, such as tribes, children, or small businesses. This is to say nothing of statute-specific procedural and analytical requirements imposed on individual agencies; see, for example, Jerry L. Mashaw, "Improving the Environment of Agency Rule-Making: An Essay on Management, Games, and Accountability," *Law and Contemporary Problems* 57 (1994), pp. 185–257; Thomas O. McGarity, "Some Thoughts on 'Deossifying' the Rule-Making Process," *Duke Law Journal* 41 (1992), pp. 1384–462; and Richard J. Pierce, "Seven Ways to Deossify Agency Rule-Making," *Administrative Law Review* 47 (1995), pp. 59–95. Additionally, regulatory impact analyses can involve highly technical analytical calculations; the sophistication level for these analyses has likely increased as the academic field of cost-benefit analysis has evolved over the years. Finally, while evaluating regulatory complexity is notoriously difficult, some studies have found increased complexity in areas where it is easier to directly measure, such as financial regulation; see James R. Barth and Stephen Matteo Miller, "On the Rising Complexity of Bank Regulatory Capital Requirements: From Global Guidelines to their United States (US) Implementation," *Journal of Risk and Financial Management* 11, no. 4 (2018), pp. 77.

76. OMB Memo M-19-14, 2019.

77. See Balla, "Regulators' Budget: OIRA's Growth and the Future of Regulatory Reform"; Institute for Policy Integrity, "Strengthening Regulatory Review"; Shapiro and Morrall, "Does Haste Make Waste?

78. There have been small staff increases at OIRA under the Trump administration, but they are not of the magnitude I suggest is necessary here. See Cheryl Bolen, "White House Regulatory Office Fully Staffed," *Bloomberg BNA*, September 15, 2017, www.bna.com/white-house-regulatory-n57982087934/; Rao, "Assessing the Administrative State."

79. For example, William Niskanen, *Bureaucracy and Representative Democracy* (NY: Aldine Press, 1971).

80. Indeed, this is consistent with my own experience serving as an OIRA desk officer from 2005 to 2007. Maximizing organizational flexibility so OIRA could treat individual cases on their own merits was considered sacrosanct by both leadership and by rank-and-file staff.

PART III

OMB—MANAGING THE BUREAUCRACY (AND ITSELF)

EIGHT

OMB in Its Management Role

Evidence from Surveys of Federal Executives

DAVID E. LEWIS
MARK D. RICHARDSON
ERIC ROSENTHAL

One of the defining features of the Trump presidency has been the chief executive's strained relationship with the departments and agencies of the government. The president has referred to the permanent government as part of the "swamp" and decried "deep state" resistance to his agenda.[1] He has publicly railed against government actors that have not carried out his orders and expressed frustration and surprise at instances where the agencies have pursued policies at variance with his own views.

President Trump is learning what other presidents before him understood: to be successful, presidents must effectively direct the activities of the executive branch and related agencies. The public holds presidents responsible for the actions of the departments and agencies of government even though presidents share authority with Congress and the courts. When a visible public problem emerges in national life, voters largely attribute to the president blame or credit.[2] This is particularly true when the problem exists in the bureaucracy. Presidents who want to fulfill their campaign promises should realize that civil servants are central to this effort. This is true whether the goals are those of President Trump, such as limiting new regulations or ramping up immigration enforcement, or those of President Obama, including efforts to expand health care access or combat climate change.

Presidents have adopted a number of strategies to secure control of the departments and agencies of government to define administration policy and ensure its effective implementation. The most prominent of these strategies are loosely defined as politicization and centralization.[3] Presidents use the careful selection and strategic placement of political appointees to help them direct the departments and agencies of government.[4] They also bring important decisions into the White House orbit.[5] The principal continuing staff agency at the center of presidents' efforts is the Office of Management and Budget (OMB). This modestly sized unit in the Executive Office of the President manages the formulation of the president's budget and provides oversight of agency spending post-appropriations. It reviews agency regulatory actions, provides guidance on procurement and grants, and to varying degrees drives presidential management initiatives across the government.

The OMB is central to the success of modern presidents, yet we have very little systematic understanding of how other agencies perceive OMB and respond to its leadership. This is important since the president's policy priorities are often implemented through circulars, memoranda, and management guidance issued by OMB and budgets superintended by OMB staff. Do agencies implement OMB memoranda with alacrity or delay? Are some agencies better able to circumvent OMB's oversight than others?

This chapter uses surveys of federal executives from 2007 and 2014 to answer these questions and to describe how federal executives inside and outside OMB perceive the degree of OMB influence over government policymaking. The data suggest that OMB's reach across the executive establishment is wide but its penetration varies. Among groups that compete for control of agency policy decisions, OMB trailed only political appointees in perceived influence over agency policy decisions. Survey respondents rate OMB as one of the top three most influential agencies in interagency processes, along with the National Security Council staff and the Office of the Secretary of Defense. Respondents that perceive OMB to be less influential tend to work in independent agencies, agencies whose policy views differ from the administration, and agencies with reputations for skilled workforces. The chapter concludes with the implications of these findings for the Trump administration's efforts to elevate OMB's management role.

PRESIDENTIAL MANAGEMENT AND OMB

One of the key features of the policy process in the United States is the central role of federal agencies. As the range and complexity of government work has grown, Congress has delegated increasing policymaking authority to government agencies so that the locus of policymaking activity has partly shifted away from Congress to executive agencies.[6]

The fundamental management challenge for any president is that the administrative state is enormous and complex. The federal government employs more than 2.7 million civilians (including the Postal Service) scattered throughout the United States and around the globe. Only 15 percent reside in the Washington, D.C., area. They work in distinct agencies performing remarkably different tasks, from protecting civil rights to landing planes to conducting scientific research. Each agency implements a variety of agency-specific and government-wide policies enacted by Congress. Some agencies perform well and others poorly; some are very responsive to presidential direction and others are less so.[7]

Presidents have sought to extend their influence over administrative agencies to ensure the activities of agencies are consistent with their views and that they are performing well.[8] They have increased the number and penetration of appointees and augmented and improved vetting processes in the White House.[9] They have also built capacity to review administrative policymaking centrally so that budgets, testimony, proposed regulations, and new executive orders are cleared prior to promotion.[10] Presidents have pursued reorganization plans and management agendas intended to rationalize administrative structure and management and to strengthen executive control.[11]

OMB has been central to virtually all the management efforts of modern presidents.[12] The success of OMB in implementing the president's agenda varies by agency.[13] OMB has a great deal of influence over some agencies, such as bureaus within the Departments of Commerce and Agriculture, and less influence over others, including the Office of the Comptroller of the Currency and the Federal Reserve. For example, some agencies are insulated from OMB control by virtue of their statutory structure as independent commissions.[14] These agencies are regularly omitted from centralized budgetary, testimony, and regulatory review. Other agencies compete with OMB for influence over policymaking and outcomes, and some are powerful enough to resist directions from OMB.[15] Indeed, in some cases, OMB is just one agency among many competing for power in interagency disagreements.[16] Even within the Executive Office of the President (EOP), agencies regularly disagree with OMB over the proper course of action and OMB is often overruled. Outside the EOP, large agencies like the Department of Defense can object to OMB decisions, and agencies often have powerful allies, including supporters in Congress and outside government. Such agencies also often have large staffs to conduct analyses that compete toe-to-toe with OMB staff.

WHY DO SOME AGENCIES RESIST OMB?

Beyond agency structures designed to limit political influence, scholars identify a number of reasons why some agencies are more or less likely to be influenced by OMB. One prominent source of variation among agencies is whether their policy views are similar or dissimilar to those of the presidential administration. Immigration policy is a good example. President Obama directed the Department of Homeland Security to create the Deferred Action for Childhood Arrivals (DACA) program partly in response to resistance from frontline workers to the president's immigration priorities.[17] The president and his Secretary of Homeland Security had a difficult time getting Immigration and Customs Enforcement (ICE) and Customs and Border Protection (CBP) to adopt their priorities in immigration enforcement, and the formalization of these priorities in DACA was the president's response. The unions for these agencies subsequently endorsed Donald Trump for president during the 2016 election, and after his election President Trump threatened to end DACA, publicly praised CBP and ICE workers, and worked to increase those agencies' budgets. These two presidents confronting ICE and CPB can expect different responsiveness to their policy priorities.

One of the defining features of modern civil service systems is the expectation of neutral competence among continuing professionals in government. Most career professionals aspire to serve any new administration faithfully. Yet, larger forces can give different agencies in government—like ICE or CBP—an ideological leaning. Congress assigns agencies tasks that have ideological content, such as cleaning the environment, providing national defense, or providing social services. Faithfully implementing these statutes produces ideological outcomes that are naturally political because elected officials still disagree about the wisdom of these laws. Agencies with ideological missions tend to attract and produce workers that support these missions.[18] So, while civil servants do their best to provide neutral competence, agency employees are naturally more enthusiastic about some policies than others, particularly if they involve the mission of those agencies.

More generally, agencies that share the president's views about policy—like ICE and CBP under the Trump administration—are likely to do what the president prefers with little oversight. Other agencies may hold policy views that differ significantly from the new administration and require attentive direction to ensure they faithfully implement the president's policies.

Beyond policy, some agencies are harder for a new administration to influence because of technical or esoteric skills and reputations for competence.[19] Agencies with highly skilled workforces that work in complex policy domains, such as the Centers for Disease Control or the Defense Advanced Research Projects Agency, are better able to connect proposed budgets and policies to potential outcomes than their often generalist overseers, and their informational advantage helps them in the budget and policymaking processes. Agencies with reputations for competence also invite political support from Congress and other stakeholders inside and outside the administration.[20] This provides agencies some additional influence in the competition for resources and influence since deciding against the agency may come with greater political costs. Agencies with skilled workforces may also invite less OMB scrutiny.

Other factors scholars deem important include an agency's constituency and its positional centrality within larger components of the government. With respect to the importance of an agency's constituency, scholars suggest that an agency that has a larger number of influential supporters (and a smaller number of influential enemies), such as the Department of Veterans Affairs or the Department of Agriculture, will tend to be powerful. Political scientist Matthew Holden states that the condition of power is "a favorable balance of constituencies."[21] Agencies that can escape harmful political attacks and enjoy the support of powerful constituencies interested in the agency's well-being have a better political position.[22] Any presidential efforts to direct an agency to take an action key stakeholders dislike will come with a cost, whether the vehicle of administration action is the White House, OMB, or agency appointees. According to this view, some agencies with powerful political support may be able to resist OMB more than other agencies if the White House determines their efforts through OMB are not worth the political cost.

One of the key factors in OMB's influence is not only their one-to-one relationship with an agency but also their unique role in the competition among agencies for resources and power. Competition among agencies for position, turf, and resources extends to all areas of government.[23] Law dictates that all agencies carry out mandates given by Congress and the president, but law does not provide agencies the power necessary to implement these mandates.[24] The success of an agency depends on its ability to control the definition of its tasks and secure the resources and support necessary to implement the agency's mission. A significant amount of government work involves more than one agency, whether the work is providing feedback on proposed legislation or policy initiatives, conducting joint rulemaking, or pursuing other interagency goals.[25]

OMB has an advantage in this larger competition among agencies because of its centrality and the key role it plays in providing resources and controlling agency planning and uncertainty. Within large organizations, the components that interact more with other parts of the organization (subunits that are pervasive) interact with other parts of an organization in ways that are essential for those parts to complete their tasks, and subunits that reduce uncertainty for other units will tend to be more powerful.[26] OMB fits this description because it has influence over other agencies' essential functions, namely budget formulation, rulemaking, and setting overall policy in spending, procurement, and management. It is pervasive in that it touches nearly every agency in the executive branch, and it has a big influence on the level of uncertainty in agencies' planning via its control of budgets and procurements.

In sum, the existing scholarship suggests that OMB should be perceived as influential with agencies whose views depart from those of the president and agencies whose workforces are less skilled and whose tasks are easier to oversee and understand. OMB should have a more difficult time influencing agencies with large supportive constituencies. In addition, OMB should be perceived as relatively influential among agencies in interagency processes.

HOW INFLUENTIAL IS OMB?

To evaluate OMB's position in the executive establishment, we rely on survey data from the two surveys on the future of government service.[27] These surveys were academic surveys conducted by university researchers with the help of university, not-for-profit, and government partners.

The 2014 survey was an online and paper survey of 14,698 appointed and career federal executives from across the executive establishment.[28] The survey targeted all components of the executive establishment that were headed by a Senate-confirmed appointee whose functions were not exclusively advisory.[29] The survey omits scholarship agencies, regional agencies, and nonprofits and cooperatives. Within agencies, researchers sent the survey to all political appointees,[30] all career members of the Senior Executive Service, U.S.-based members of the Senior Foreign Service, and other high-level executives who ran programs and agencies.[31] The survey included a number of questions about the backgrounds, experiences, and political views of federal executives, including questions about agency management and performance. The response rate was 24 percent (3,551 respondents). The 2007 survey targeted a similar population but with a smaller sample.[32] We primarily use data from the 2014 survey but reference the 2007 survey where questions are comparable.

Competing for Influence

A number of different actors compete to influence the policy decisions of government agencies, including OMB, but also agency political appointees, congressional committees, key interest groups, and others. We begin by comparing OMB's influence to these other actors. The survey asked respondents, "In general, how much influence do you think the following groups have over policy decisions in {your agency}? [A great deal, a good bit, some, little, none, Don't know]." The question then listed a number of actors, including:

- White House
- Office of Management and Budget
- political appointees
- senior civil servants

- congressional committees
- private sector or not-for-profit stakeholders (for example, regulated parties, advocacy groups)
- media
- Democrats in Congress
- Republicans in Congress
- contractors

The ordering of the groups was randomized, and the question was asked in grid format so that a comparison was implied.[33]

Figure 8-1 includes the average responses from *None* (0) to *A great deal* (4). Respondents reported that political appointees had the largest impact over policy decisions in their agencies. This is to be expected, since appointees fill the top executive positions and many statutes delegate policymaking authority to these positions or officials in statute. Respondents also reported that senior civil servants had a significant amount of influence over policymaking in their agencies. This confirms that career executives not only implement policy, they also make policy. They play a key role in decisions involving budgets, rulemaking, enforcement, the distribution of grants, and other issues. Interestingly, federal executives reported that OMB was the second most influential group when it came to policy decisions in government agencies, ahead of the White House and congressional committees. This confirms the important role OMB plays in presidential management of the executive branch.

More generally, federal executives report that the presidential administration, either through appointees, OMB, or the White House directly, had more influence on policymaking in their agency than Congress.[34] Among discrete groups in Congress, agencies reported that the committees had more influence than the parties, which is not surprising since agencies interact most directly with Congress via committees and their staffs. Federal executives reported that nongovernmental actors such as outside stakeholders, the media, and government contractors had less influence on agency decisions on average.[35]

These overall averages mask significant variation from agency to agency. Respondents in independent commissions notably provide different responses than their counterparts in executive agencies. They report

FIGURE 8-1. **How Influential Is OMB Relative to Other Political Actors?**

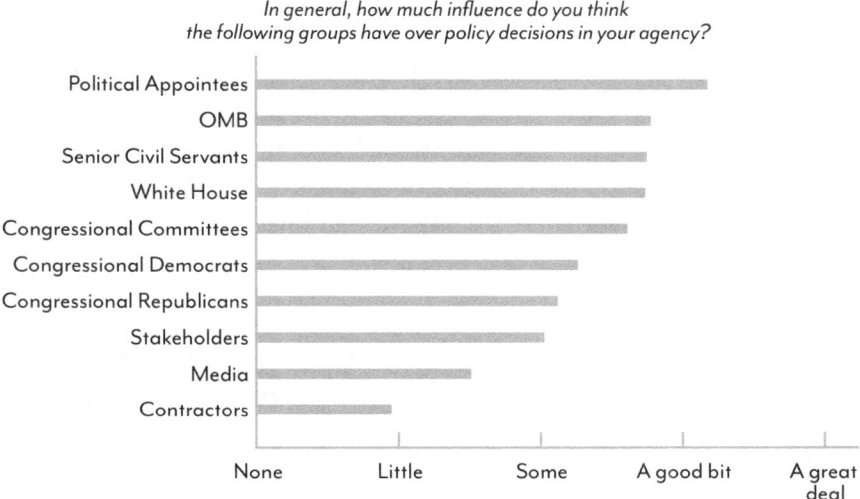

Source: Survey on the Future of Government Service (Center for the Study of Democratic Institutions, Vanderbilt University, 2014), www.vanderbilt.edu/csdi/research/sfgs.php.

less outside political influence in their decisions than executive agencies. They report less White House, OMB, and congressional influence over agency decisions than respondents in executive agencies.

Where independent commissions report outside influence, it is most likely to come from Congress. Respondents working in independent commissions report more congressional influence over agency decisions than either OMB or the White House. Members of Congress and their staffs may have more regular interaction with these agencies, and this is reflected in the relative influence of the branches. Previous congressional efforts to limit presidential influence over these agencies appear to have been successful. Interestingly, however, respondents in independent commissions report more appointee influence than their counterparts in executive agencies. This finding suggests that appointment politics may be a more significant battleground for control in the independent commissions than executive agencies.

Interagency Power and Influence

The choices agencies make are determined not just by directions from elected officials or feedback from clients or stakeholders. For government to function, agencies must participate in an increasing number of interagency processes. The data provide insight into how agencies—including OMB—fare in interagency disputes. Who wins or loses when agencies disagree with one another? The 2014 survey instrument provided respondents the following text and question:

> Government policy making often involves multiple agencies (e.g., commenting on proposed legislation, interagency task forces). When agencies participate in work that involves multiple agencies and diverse opinions, not all agencies operate on equal footing. Some have more influence than others.
>
> In your experience, how influential are the following agencies in interactions involving multiple agencies?

After the text and question, respondents were provided a list of five to eight agencies and a scale from 1 to 5. We populated each respondent's list of agencies based upon a combination of information provided by them and the agencies we chose. We asked respondents to identify the three agencies they work with the most. We included these agencies in their list, along with OMB and the Office of Personnel Management.[36] Online respondents were provided three additional agencies, other bureaus in their department (if they worked in a department) or independent agencies and executive departments, all chosen at random.[37] The low end of the scale (that is, 1) was labeled "Least influential" and the high end of the scale (that is, 5) was labeled "Most influential." Respondents could select values between 1 and 5 or "Don't know."

In figure 8-2, we include estimates of agency influence derived from aggregating all the ratings and adjusting for differences among raters.[38] The figure includes estimates of the influence of the fifteen most and fifteen least influential agencies sorted from highest to lowest (see online appendix for the full set of estimates).[39] The horizontal lines in the figure represent our uncertainty in the estimates of influence. Agencies with fewer ratings have more uncertainty as to their true influence.

Several aspects of the rank ordering of agencies by influence are worth mentioning. First, OMB is listed among the most influential agencies.

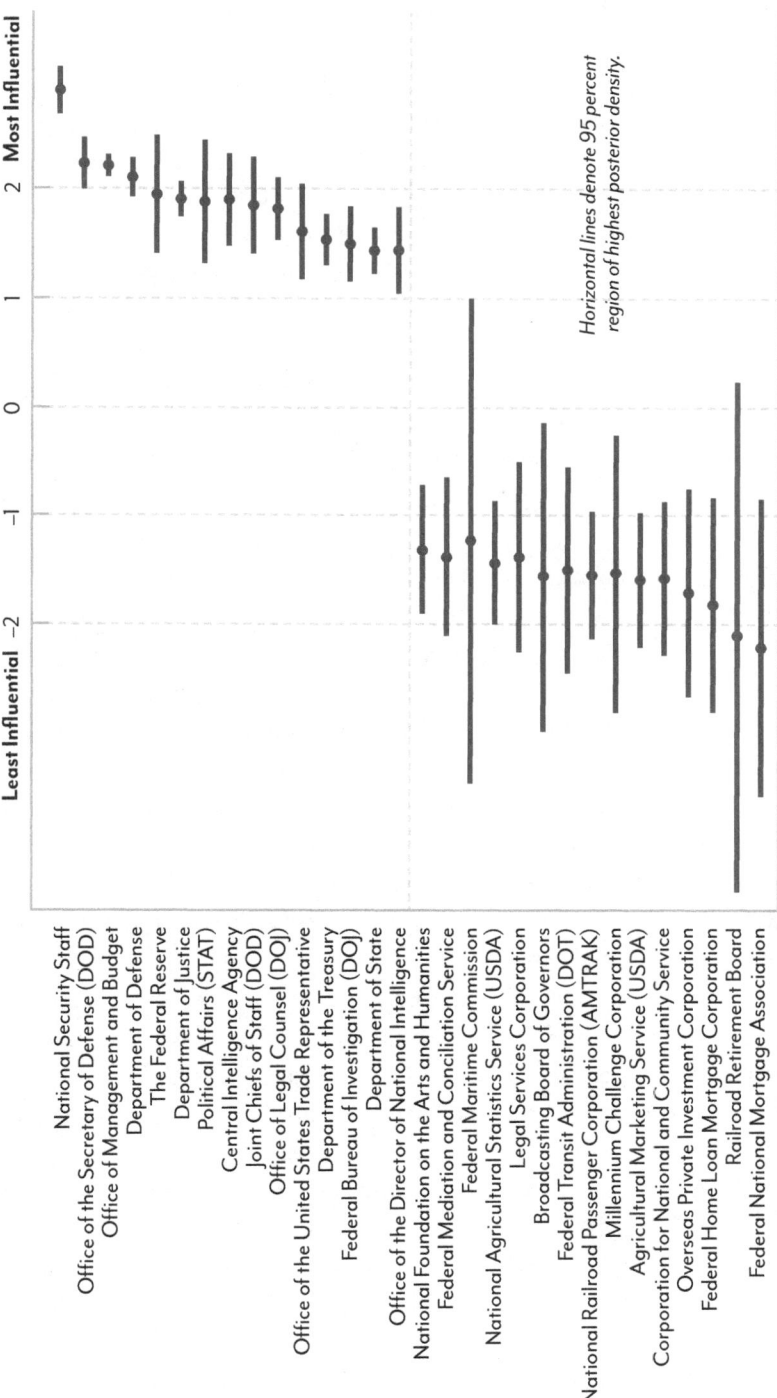

FIGURE 8-2. Fifteen Most and Fifteen Least Influential Agencies

Source: Survey on the Future of Government Service (2014).

OMB is rated the third most influential agency in government out of 165 agencies. Only the Office of the Secretary of Defense and the National Security Council staff are rated as more influential.

Second, among the most influential agencies are a number of agencies involved in foreign policy and national security, as well as the Federal Reserve and the Department of the Treasury. The presence of these agencies collectively may hint at one source of OMB esteem. One commonly identified cause of agency influence is an organization's expertise or skills.[40] The estimates for agencies involved in national security, intelligence, the macroeconomy, and law enforcement seem to confirm Francis Rourke's claim that organizations that have skills necessary for society's survival will be more influential.[41] In addition, national security and law enforcement agencies also have the ability to withhold information from other agencies, enhancing their power relative to other agencies. OMB's own technical skills and its key role in budget forecasting, preparation, and apportionment may provide it some additional influence.

Third, among the top ranked agencies are a few other smaller agencies, such as the Office of Legal Counsel (OLC). The OLC is the legal arbiter for the executive branch, rendering legal judgments in disputes among agencies. The OLC, like OMB, interacts with large numbers of other agencies, and their determinations influence the planning and resources of other agencies.[42] Another pervasive agency, the OPM, is also rated in the top twenty-five based on ratings by federal executives. The OPM makes decisions about allocations in the Senior Executive Service and makes determinations about appointment authority and pay for new positions across the executive.

Interestingly, no clientele agencies are among the most influential agencies. For example, the Agricultural Marketing Service is one of the least influential agencies, despite its mission to create domestic and international market opportunities for U.S. farmers. In addition, respondents rate some clientele agencies, such as those serving railroad retirees, Native Americans, and veterans, among the least influential (though not all in the bottom fifteen). Federal executives rate large service agencies, such as the U.S. Postal Service and the Social Security Administration, as lacking power. They are estimated to be in the bottom third of all agencies rated in influence. These estimates appear to contradict the authors who claim that agencies with strong constituencies will have greater influence. Perhaps the decline of strong and stable relationships between groups, agencies, and congressional committees (that is, iron triangles) and the growth of groups representing a diverse set of interests has reduced the influence of constituency dominated agencies.[43] One other possibility is that our respondents do not often come into conflict with these agencies and therefore rate them as slightly less influential simply for a lack of experience disagreeing with them in an interagency context.

Where Is OMB Influential?

Federal executives perceive OMB as quite important and powerful relative to other political actors and agencies. With this big picture in mind, we turn our attention to explaining variation: which agencies' executives report that OMB has a lot of influence and which executives report little OMB influence, and why? To explain variation, we look to the factors just suggested, including structural features that insulate agencies from administration control, agency policy views, and aspects of agency workforce skills.

In figure 8-3, we graph the average reported OMB influence by the degree of agency insulation from the president.[44] Specifically, we include continuous measures of the degree of agency insulation from politics based on the structural features of agencies on the x-axis and average agency reports of OMB influence on the y-axis. The figure includes two graphs based on two different types of insulation from political influence: the independence of decisionmakers (for example, fixed terms for appointees, party-balancing requirements) and the independence of agency policy decisions (for example, exemption from OMB budgetary review, independent funding, etc.).[45] These measures are a convenient way of disentangling more insulated agencies from less insulated, but we can also divide and compare agencies by whether they have specific structural features (see figure 8-3). Agencies higher in the figure report that OMB is very influential in policy decisions in their agencies. Agencies lower in the figure report that OMB is less influential. Agencies to the left in the graphs are designed to be more amenable to executive control, and those on the right are designed to be more insulated, either by rules related to who runs the agency or rules related to who gets to review agency policy decisions.

Among the agencies reporting the highest level of OMB influence in their agencies are the Employment and Training Administration (ETA), the Corporation for National and Community Service (CNCS), and

FIGURE 8-3. OMB Influence by Agency Structural Independence, 2014

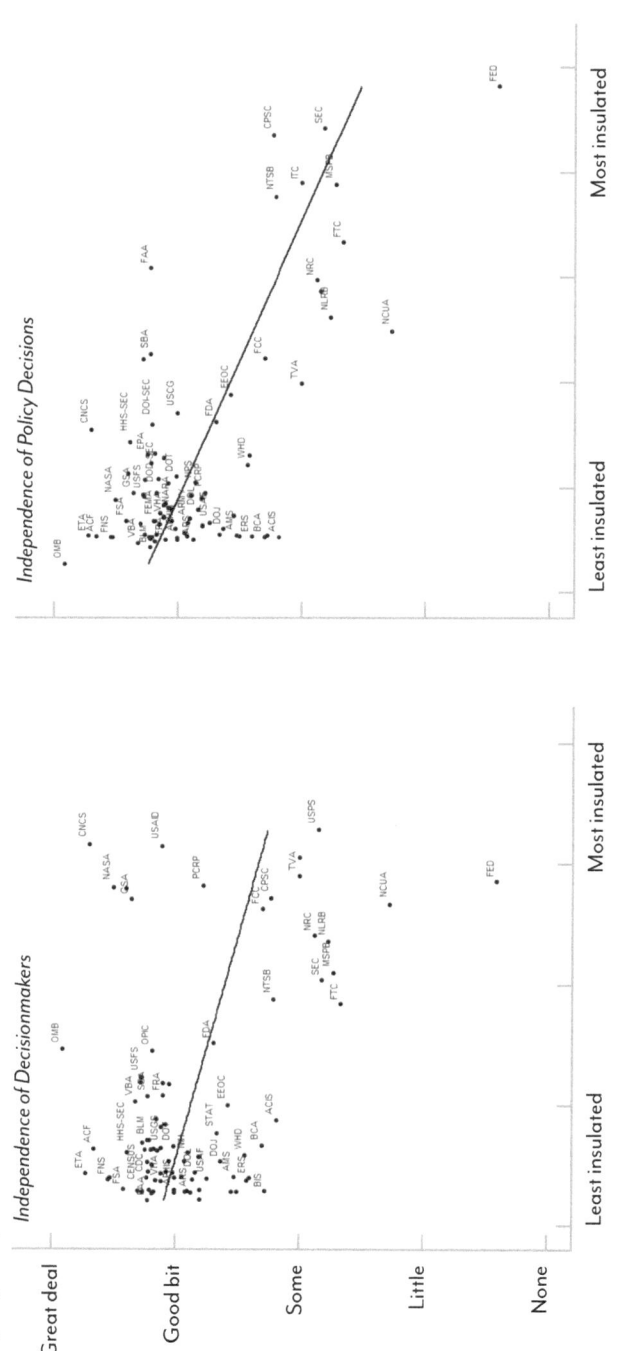

The figure includes agency average responses to the question "In general, how much influence do you think the following groups have over policy decisions in (your agency)? [A great deal, a good bit, some, little, none, don't know]" on the y-axis. It includes numerical estimates of two dimensions of agency insulation from Selin (2015) on the x-axis. Agencies listed include only those with at least ten respondents and thirty potential respondents. Some labels omitted in cases where labels overlap.

Source: *Survey on the Future of Government Service* (2014).

the Administration for Children and Families (ACF). All the executive departments report relatively high levels of OMB influence, with the Department of the Interior reporting the most and the Departments of Justice and Treasury the least. Not surprisingly, agencies that are not part of an executive department report the least OMB influence, including the Federal Reserve (FED), the Federal Trade Commission (FTC), and the National Credit Union Administration (NCUA). The downward sloping regression line suggests that respondents in more insulated agencies report less average OMB influence, as we would expect given design features intended to limit White House and OMB influence. The figures do exclude some very small independent agencies, and it is possible that these smaller and more vulnerable agencies are more responsive to OMB than larger independent agencies. If so, the actual lines in figure 8-3 would remain downward sloping but perhaps less steep.

Executives working in these agencies may perceive less OMB influence in independent commissions because the leadership in such agencies is less responsive due to features such as their commission structure, bipartisan composition, or statutory fixed terms. Alternatively, the lack of OMB leverage over agencies may be due to their exclusion from OMB budget and regulatory review. Agencies that depend on OMB a great deal for approval of budgets, regulations, or congressional testimony may need to defer to OMB more in interagency processes. In table 8-1 we dig deeper. The table includes respondent answers to questions about OMB influence broken down by some of the more prominent features of independent agencies.[46] Respondents in agencies with exemption from OMB review of budgets, regulations, and testimony report less OMB influence. Similarly, respondents in agencies with their own sources of funding outside the annual appropriations process and respondents in commissions with party balancing and "for cause" protections against removal report less OMB influence. The features leading respondents to report the least OMB influence include independent sources of funding and exemption from OIRA rulemaking review. Respondents working in agencies such as the U.S. Postal Service or the Tennessee Valley Authority, which have other sources of funds, or the independent regulatory commissions that do not require OMB approval of regulations are the least likely to report a good bit or great deal of OMB influence.

While structure explains some of the variation and does so in expected ways, it does not explain all of the variation. Presidents have

TABLE 8-1. How much influence do you think OMB has over policy decisions in your agency? (proportion selecting "A good bit" or "A great deal")

Insulating Mechanism	No	Yes
Exempt from OMB Budget Review	0.69	0.40
Exempt from OIRA Review of Rulemaking	0.71	0.24
Exempt from OMB Review of Testimony and Legislation	0.72	0.28
Independent Source of Funding	0.70	0.23
Explicit "For Cause" Protections	0.70	0.35
Party Balancing Requirements	0.71	0.36

worried that agencies with long histories and reputations for skill or competence can use this to their advantage, either by cultivating outside political support or by using their superior expertise to their advantage in discussions with OMB or the White House.[47] Figure 8-4 presents summary graphs of the extent of OMB influence in agency policy decisions by agency ideology, agency workforce partisanship, workforce skill, and the uniqueness of agency workforce skills. The measures of ideology and skill come from the survey and were estimated using the same method employed to generate numerical estimates of influence.[48] Specifically, the survey asked respondents:

> *Ideology:* Some agencies have policy views due to law, practice, culture, or tradition that can be characterized across Democratic and Republican administrations as liberal or conservative. This can be an important feature of the environment of public management in these agencies (which is why we ask about it). If you are willing, we would benefit from your assessment of the policy leanings of the following agencies to characterize this aspect of their management environment. As with other questions, you are free not to answer.
>
> In your opinion, do the policy views of the following agencies tend to slant liberal, slant conservative, or neither consistently in both Democratic and Republican administrations?
>
> *Skill:* In your view, how skilled are the workforces of the following agencies?

We then aggregated these ratings into numerical estimates of agency ideology and workforce skill. This figure also includes a graph of average respondent partisanship by agency (Democrat [0] to Republican [4]) and a graph that includes a measure of the uniqueness of agency workforce skills. Specifically, the survey asked respondents, "What percentage of the expertise that you have acquired in [your agency] can only be acquired by working in [your agency]?" The purpose of this question was to tap into the uniqueness of the skills of agency employees. Could the agency get the skills they needed on the open market for labor or could employees get these skills only by working in their agency? If a significant portion of an agency's expertise is specific to that agency and acquired by working there, other actors are less likely to have that expertise and are more likely to defer to the expertise of agency personnel.

The results are instructive. First, there appears to be little relationship between agency ideology or partisanship and reports of OMB influence. There is slight evidence that more conservative/Republican agencies (as perceived by federal executives in the survey) report a bit less OMB influence than liberal agencies, but the effect is small. There is more evidence that agencies with reputations for highly skilled workforces report less OMB influence over policy decisions. Agencies with a reputation for skill may both be harder for OMB to monitor and given more deference by OMB and elected officials. Finally, there is a clear relationship between the uniqueness of an agency's expertise and the reported influence of OMB. Respondents in agencies whose workforces are skilled and have expertise that is hard to acquire outside the agency are more likely to report less OMB influence.

The perspective of respondents is also influenced by their individual interactions with OMB. In figure 8-5, we include information on perceptions of OMB influence by the job of the executive. The black bar indicates the proportion of respondents working with budgets (top left), contracting (top right), grants (bottom left), and rulemaking (bottom right) in each response category. The gray bar includes the proportions for all respondents that do not work with these policymaking tools. The figure shows that federal executives involved in budgets, rulemaking, contracts, and grants all report more OMB influence than executives who are not—that is, the black bar is higher than the gray bar in response categories indicating "a good bit" or "great deal" of OMB influence over agency policy.[49] This could reflect the fact that executives who come in

FIGURE 8-4. OMB Influence by Agency Ideology, Partisanship, Workforce Skill, and Agency-Specific Skills, 2014

Influence of OMB Over
Agency Policy Decisions

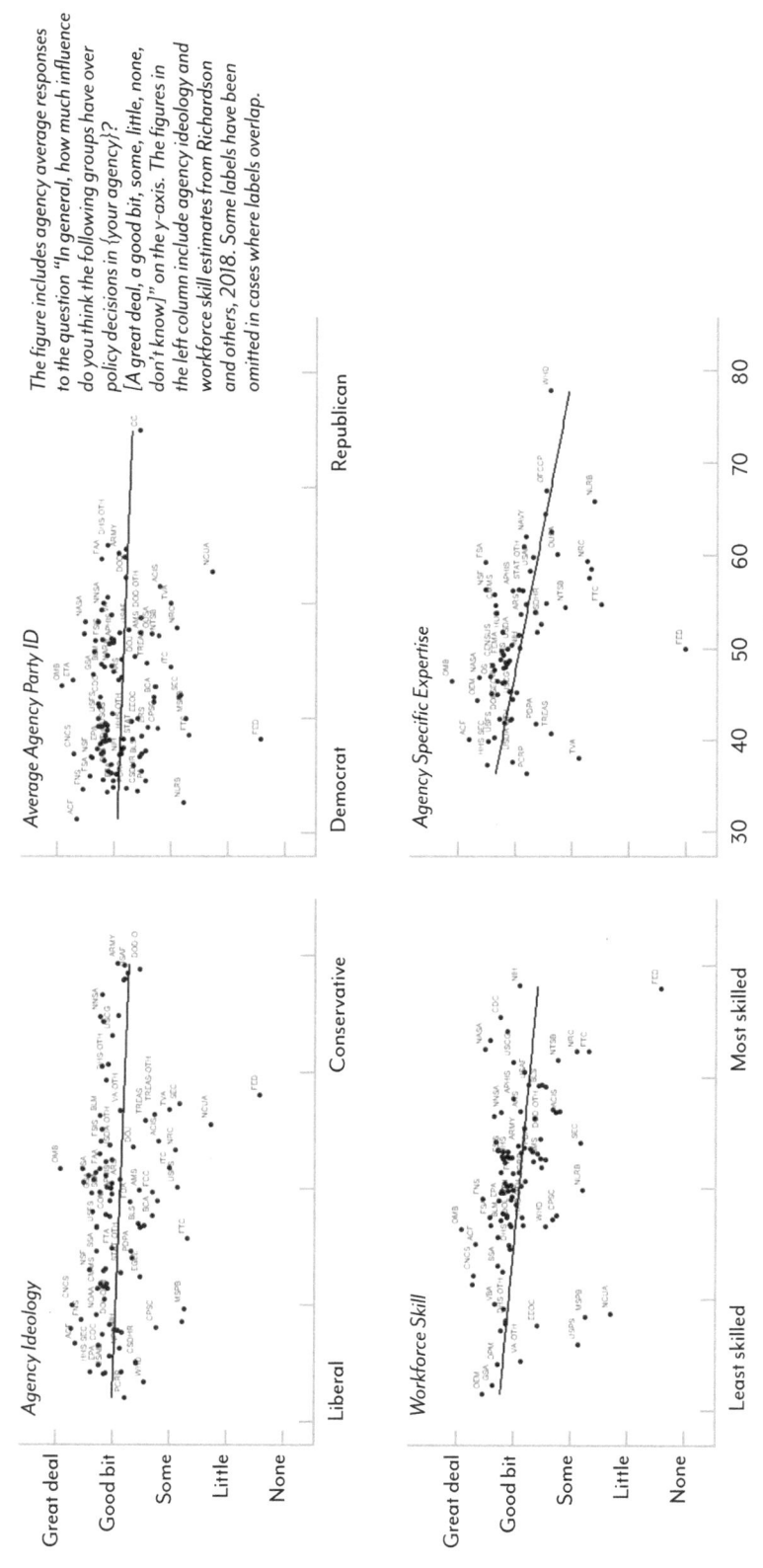

Source: *Survey on the Future of Government Service* (2014).

FIGURE 8-5. Perceptions of OMB Influence by Role of Executive, 2014

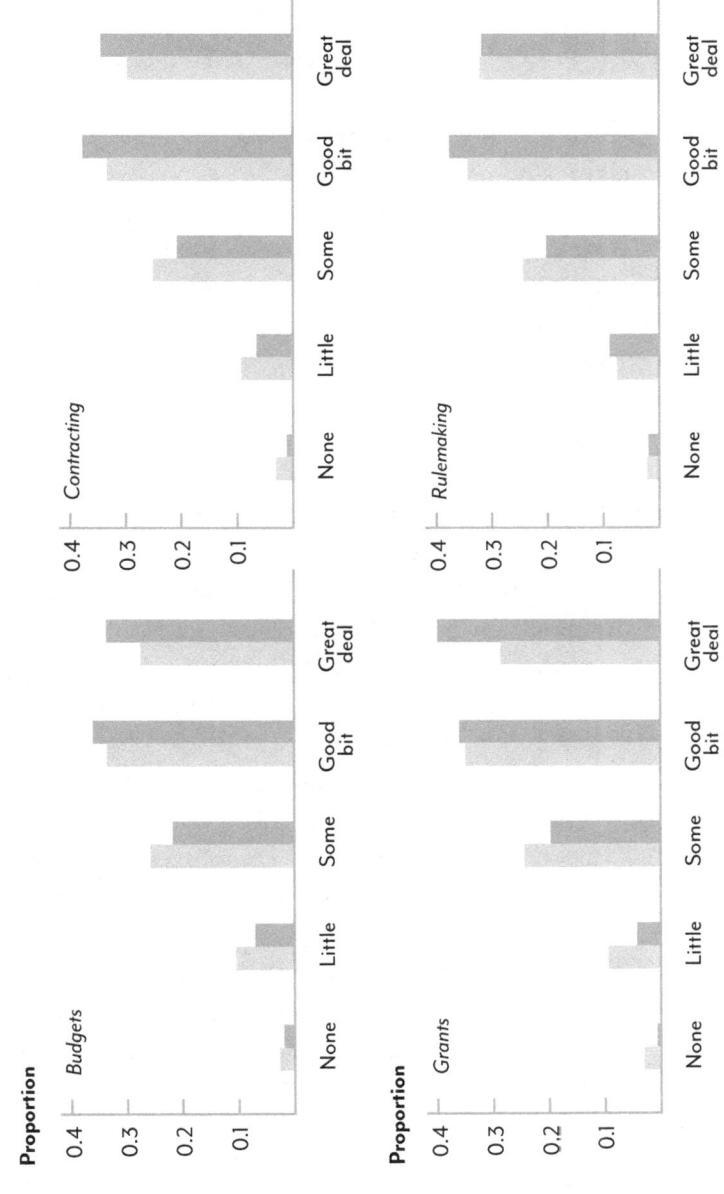

Source: *Survey on the Future of Government Service* (2014).

contact with OMB are more likely to understand how OMB is influential in their agency. Indeed, the respondents for whom OMB is pervasive are more likely to report a significant amount of OMB influence. This suggests that agencies whose day-to-day work does not involve rulemaking, procurement, or grants may perceive less OMB influence, both because employees deal with OMB less and because OMB has fewer levers of influence into agency decisions.

In total, there are a host of agency-specific and respondent-specific factors that explain why some federal executives perceive OMB as powerful and others do not. Of course, many of the agency-specific and individual factors correlate with one another (for example, agency size and agency ideology), and disentangling the unique effect of these factors requires a multivariate approach. In table 8-2, we regress responses to the question concerning OMB influence and the ratings of OMB influence on these factors and a number of controls. Specifically, we include the factors just mentioned[50] as well as controls for the size of the agency[51] and features of the respondents background, such as whether they are an appointee (0,1; 0.16), whether the respondent works in Washington, D.C. (0,1; 0.76), and the years the executive has worked for the federal government (Mean 23; SD 11.1).

A number of interesting results emerge. First, respondents working in conservative agencies and agencies with reputations for highly skilled workforces report less OMB influence over policy decisions in their agencies on average. A one-unit change in ideology or workforce skill is estimated to reduce the probability that a person reports that OMB has a "great deal" of influence from 33 percent to 30 percent. Not surprisingly, if a respondent works in an independent commission, the estimated probability they report a "great deal" of OMB influence is estimated to decrease from 33 percent to 5 percent. These agencies are more likely to have independent revenue streams and be able to bypass OMB budgetary and regulatory review. Respondents who work in agencies with large budgets and large staffs are estimated to report more OMB influence, on average, although only the size of the budget is estimated precisely in the following models.[52]

The coefficient estimates suggest that executives involved with budgets, contracts, and grants believe OMB to be more influential, although the estimates are not always estimated precisely enough to be distinguishable from zero with a high degree of confidence. Interestingly, those

TABLE 8-2. Regression Models of Respondent Perceptions of OMB Influence, 2014

Variable	OMB Influence, in Agency		OMB Influence, Interagency	
	B	SE	B	SE
Agency Characteristics				
Agency ideology (L-C; -2, 2)	−0.09	0.05*	−0.03	0.04
Agency skills (Least, Most; -2, 2)	−0.10	0.05*	−0.03	0.05
Independent regulatory commission (0,1)	−0.96	0.14**	−0.30	0.12**
Ln (2014 agency budget)	0.04	0.02*	−0.02	0.02
Ln (2014 employment)	0.02	0.03	0.01	0.02
Individual Characteristics				
Political appointee (0,1)	−0.03	0.14	−0.06	0.11
Salary (1–21, $10,000 increments)	−0.02	0.02	−0.03	0.02**
Party ID (D, R; 1, 5)	0.00	0.02	−0.05	0.02**
Washington, D.C. (0,1)	0.00	0.08	0.16	0.07**
Years of government experience	0.00	0.003	0.00	0.003
Job involves budget (0,1)	0.04	0.07	0.02	0.07
Job involves rulemaking (0,1)	−0.12	0.06*	−0.06	0.06
Job involves grants (0,1)	0.15	0.09	0.10	0.06*
Job involves contracts (0,1)	0.14	0.07**	0.10	0.07
Constant			4.88	0.36**
N	1,347		908	
X2, F (14 df)	188.30		4.12	

Note: **Significant at the 0.05; *significant at the 0.10 level in two-tailed tests. Robust standard errors clustered on bureau reported. Model 1 includes ordered probit estimates of responses to "In general, how much influence do you think the following groups [OMB] have over policy decisions in {your agency}? [A great deal, a good bit, some, little, none, don't know]." Cut point estimates from Model 1 omitted. Model 2 includes OLS estimates of ratings of OMB influence "In your experience, how influential are the following agencies in interactions involving multiple agencies?" [1 = Least influential; 5 = Most influential].

respondents whose jobs involve developing notices of proposed rulemaking, summarizing related comments, or writing final rules report less OMB influence than other executives without these responsibilities. It is possible that those executives involved in the details of rulemaking possess policy expertise that makes OMB staff more deferential.

With regard to perceptions of OMB interagency influence, respondents who work in independent commissions are also less likely to believe OMB is very influential in interagency processes. Conservative respondents and respondents with higher salaries (that is, higher in the hierarchy) rate OMB as less influential, while those working in Washington, D.C., rate OMB as more influential. It is possible that conservative executives higher in the hierarchy may be better able to see ways President Obama's OMB (survey fielded in 2014 during the Obama administration) did not get its way in interagency fights. Those executives outside Washington, D.C., may also not be able to perceive the ways OMB influences interagency processes, particularly those centered in Washington.

Changes in OMB Influence between 2007 and 2014

Of course, factors specific to the Obama administration rather than features of the agency or respondent may be the cause of perceptions in 2014. Fortunately, the 2007 survey asked the same question about OMB influence, allowing us to compare perceptions in 2007 with those in 2014 for a subset of agencies. These perceptions look relatively stable over time. Figure 8-6 includes agency average responses to the question "How much influence do you think OMB has over policy decisions in your agency?" in 2007 (x-axis) and 2014 (y-axis). If there was no change in the perceptions of OMB influence, all the agencies would line up along the 45-degree line in the figure. The figure illustrates some of the familiar patterns with the independent commissions reporting less OMB influence. Interestingly, there are a number of agencies that report significantly more influence in 2007 than 2014, including the United States Agency for International Development (USAID) and the Food and Drug Administration (FDA). The Bush administration paid significant attention to foreign aid, food safety, and drug approvals and this may help explain higher levels of OMB influence. In 2014, the OPM, the Army, and the National Science Foundation reported an uptick in OMB influence. The Office of Personnel Management (OPM) was the subject of substantial negative media attention due to retirement backlogs and a major breach of personnel information. The Army was at the center of President Obama's surge strategy in Afghanistan. These factors may have contributed to increased attention to these agencies during the Obama administration.

The higher values of some relatively conservative agencies in 2014 (for example, Army) and some relatively liberal agencies in 2007 (for example, USAID, the Department of Labor (DOL), the Environmental Protection Agency (EPA)) raise the natural question whether OMB directed more attention to agencies in these administrations based on their political leanings. In figure 8-7, we graph the difference in the average reported OMB influence over agency policy decisions (2014 versus 2007) by agency ideology, from liberal to conservative. Positive values represent an increase in reported OMB influence in 2014, and negative values indicate less OMB influence. We fit a locally weighted regression line to the data to help divine patterns. The results reveal that, comparing 2007 to 2014, OMB influence went down slightly overall. OMB influence appeared to decrease more for liberal agencies on average. It went up slightly for conservative agencies, although we cannot distinguish the estimated increase from no change at all. This evidence is suggestive that during the Obama administration OMB may have taken a different approach than the Bush administration, as least as it relates to specific liberal and conservative agencies. While the Obama administration had more influence over conservative agencies than the Bush administration, conservative agencies still reported marginally less influence by the Obama OMB than more liberal agencies. Other factors influence the change in OMB influence, including scandal and presidential priority, but agency policy leanings may play a role as well.

Summary

Overall, the data reveal that federal executives believe OMB is quite influential, both in their own agencies and in interagency processes. Among groups that compete for control of the executive branch, OMB trailed only political appointees in terms of actors that are influential in agency decisions. OMB is also one of the top three most influential agencies in processes involving multiple agencies. The agencies that perceive OMB to be less influential tend to be independent agencies, insulated

FIGURE 8-6. Respondent Perceptions of OMB Influence, 2007 and 2014

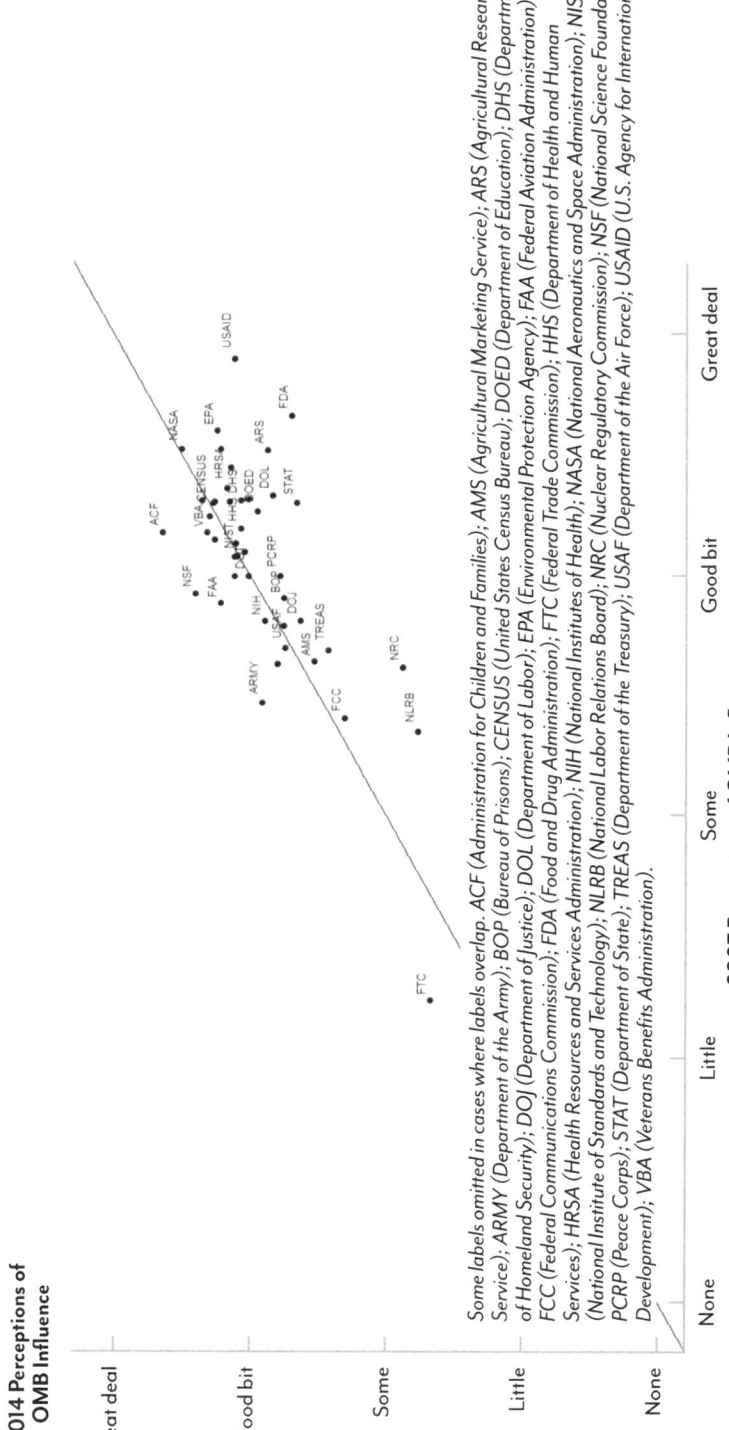

Source: Survey on the Future of Government Service (2007, 2014).

FIGURE 8.7. Change in Perceptions of OMB Influence by Agency Ideology, 2007 and 2014

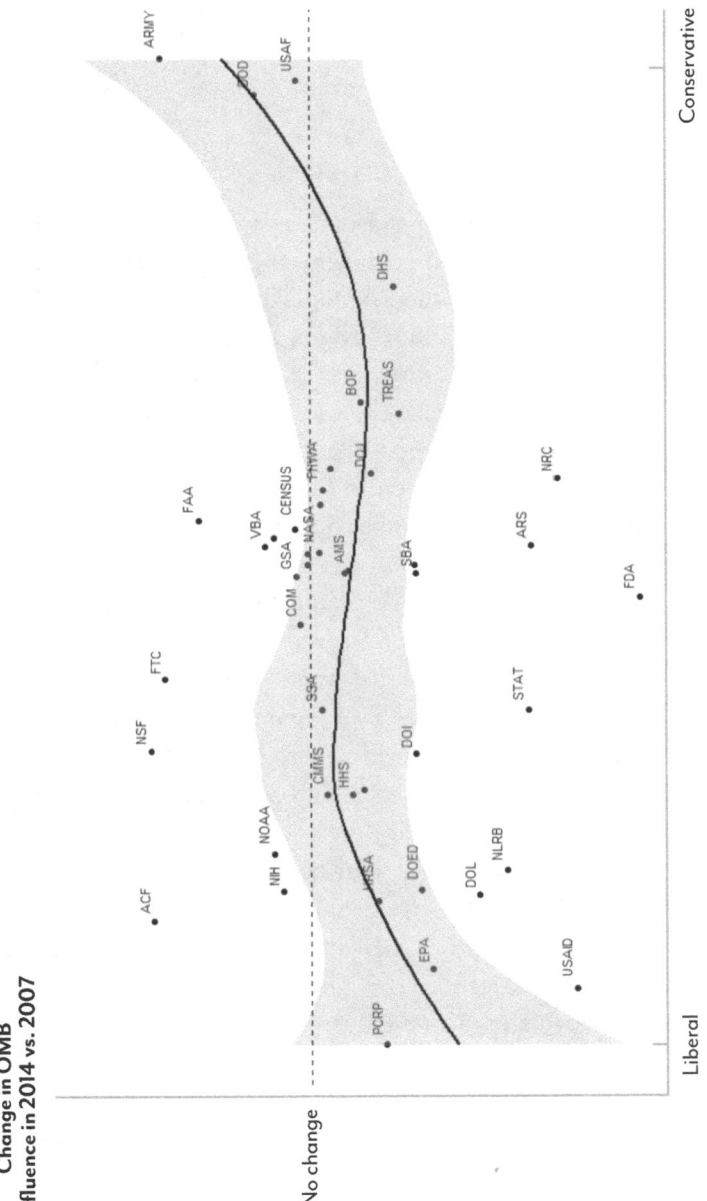

Source: Survey on the Future of Government Service (2014).

from OMB influence by design. Agencies with reputations for skilled workforces report modestly less OMB influence, as do agencies with policy views that differ from the presidential administration. Federal executives report broad OMB influence, but influence that goes deeper in some agencies than in others.

CONCLUSION

Like presidents before him, President Trump's OMB has been at the center of his policymaking and management goals. OMB has crafted the president's budget proposals, superintended his efforts to limit the promulgation of new regulations, and rolled out the administration's management agenda. OMB has also directed the president's efforts to cut the federal workforce and reorganize the executive branch.

Despite the importance of the agency to the president, it is not clear how responsive agencies have been to OMB's leadership, from adhering to OMB's role vetting agency budget documents prior to rollout to embracing the president's management agenda.[53] Some responses to OMB's actions are likely influenced by the leadership choices of the administration itself.[54] Others, however, are driven by longer-term forces that existed prior to the Trump administration. Some agencies provide less access to OMB by design. Others have reputations for skill or expertise.

An effective OMB is an important part of any president's efforts to direct the activities of the departments and agencies of government. Presidents would be well advised to take great care to select qualified appointees to run OMB and be attentive to its health and effectiveness. Notable in this administration is the president's decision to "double hat" two of his key appointees. Two of OMB's top appointees have taken other important management jobs in the administration while remaining in their jobs in OMB (that is, White House chief of staff and director of the OPM). This is a credit to them both but also a worrisome sign regarding the president's own understanding of OMB's historic role.

There are limits to what even an effective OMB can do by design. The data reveal some interesting patterns that suggest presidents should choose different strategies of control for different agencies. For example, presidents should attempt to influence independent, highly skilled, and more ideological agencies with carefully selected appointees to head those agencies rather than relying on centralized control. Indeed, the most influential actors in independent agencies were the appointees. It is, thus, surprising that President Trump has been slow to name appointees to a number of vacant positions in independent agencies.

It is also interesting that OMB is perceived as more influential than the OPM given longstanding tension between these two agencies regarding management. President Trump's fiscal year 2020 budget includes a proposal to split up the OPM, moving parts to the General Services Administration. This would further place OMB at the center of presidential management of the executive. One factor influencing this proposal is the OPM's relatively low esteem in government. The OPM is one of the lowest rated agencies in perceptions of workforce skill (that is, in the bottom ten) among all agencies. Federal executives report the OPM to be influential but also low-skilled. If the current trend toward increased OMB responsibility continues, this raises the stakes for understanding where OMB can be influential and where it is limited.

Notes

Paper prepared for presentation at the Hofstra University, Peter S. Kalikow Center Symposium on Prioritizing Presidential Policies: How Does the Office of Management and Budget Influence Executive Policy Making?, Hofstra University, April 11–12, 2019. We are grateful to the federal employees who shared their experiences and views via the survey. We thank Ed Freeland and Naila Rahman at the Princeton Survey Research Center for advice and survey support and the Center for the Study of Democratic Institutions at Vanderbilt University for financial support. We thank Meena Bose, Larry Matlack, Kathleen Peroff, and James Pfiffner for helpful feedback. The errors that remain are our own.

1. See Julian E. Barnes, Adam Goldman, and Charlie Savage, "Blaming the Deep State: Officials Accused of Wrongdoing Adopt Trump's Response," *New York Times*, December 18, 2018, nytimes.com/2018/12/18/us/politics/deep-state-trump-classified-information.html; Evan Osnos, "Trump vs. the 'Deep State': How the Administration's Loyalists are Quietly Reshaping American Governance," *New Yorker*, May 21, 2018, newyorker.com/magazine/2018/05/21/trump-vs-the-deep-state.

2. See, generally, Richard E. Neustadt, *Presidential Power: The Politics of Leadership* (New York: John Wiley & Sons, 1960).

3. For the classic treatment, see Terry M. Moe, "The Politicized Presidency," in *The New Direction in American Politics*, edited by J. E. Chubb and P. E. Peterson (Washington, D.C.: Brookings, 1985).

4. For a full description, see James P. Pfiffner, *The Strategic Presidency: Hitting the Ground Running*, 2nd revised edition (University Press of Kansas,

1996) and Thomas J. Weko, *The Politicizing Presidency: The White House Personnel Office* (University Press of Kansas, 1995).

5. The most detailed treatment of the centralization decision is Andrew Rudalevige, *Managing the President's Program: Centralization and Legislative Policy Formulation, 1949–1996* (Princeton University Press, 2002). See, also, William F. West, "The Institutionalization of Regulatory Review: Organizational Stability and Responsive Competence at OIRA," *Presidential Studies Quarterly* 35 (2005), pp. 76–93.

6. For classic treatments, see Theodore J. Lowi, *The End of Liberalism: The Second Republic of the United States* (New York: W. W. Norton, 1979); David Epstein and Sharyn O'Halloran, *Delegating Powers* (Cambridge University Press, 1999); and John D. Huber and Charles R. Shipan, *Deliberate Discretion?* (Cambridge University Press, 2002).

7. For evidence regarding different levels of responsiveness among civil servants and agencies, see, generally, Rosemary O'Leary, *The Ethics of Dissent: Managing Guerilla Government* (Washington, D.C.: CQ Press, 2005); Mark D. Richardson, Joshua D. Clinton, and David E. Lewis, "Elite Perceptions of Agency Ideology and Workforce Skill," *Journal of Politics* 80 (2018), pp. 303–08; and James Q. Wilson, *Bureaucracy* (New York: Basic Books, 1989).

8. For the classic works on this subject, see Richard Nathan, *The Plot that Failed: Nixon and The Administrative Presidency* (New York: John Wiley & Sons, Inc., 1975) and Richard W. Waterman, *Presidential Influence and the Administrative State* (University of Tennessee Press, 1989).

9. For details of changes in the number of appointees, see David E. Lewis, *The Politics of Presidential Appointments: Political Control and Bureaucratic Performance* (Princeton University Press, 2008). For a description of the changes in the White House personnel operation, see Carolyn R. Thompson and Roger G. Brown, "The Transfer of Political Functions from the National Party Committees to the White House: From Eisenhower to Nixon," *Southeastern Political Review* 25 (1997), pp. 27–47 and Weko, *The Politicizing Presidency*.

10. See, for example, Alex Acs and Charles Cameron, "Does White House Regulatory Review Produce a Chilling Effect on 'OIRA Avoidance' in the Agencies?" *Presidential Studies Quarterly* 43 (2013), pp. 443–67; Andrew C. Rudalevige, "Executive Branch Management and Presidential Unilateralism: Centralization and the Formulation of Executive Orders," *Congress and the Presidency* 42 (Winter, 2015), pp. 342–65; and Alan E. Wiseman, "Delegation and Positive-Sum Bureaucracies," *Journal of Politics* 71 (2009), pp. 998–1014.

11. For a detailed account of presidential reorganization, see Peri E. Arnold, *Making the Managerial Presidency: Comprehensive Reorganization Planning, 1905–1996*, 2nd revised edition (University Press of Kansas, 1998).

12. Some excellent histories of OMB include Larry Berman, *The Office of Management and Budget and the Presidency, 1921–1979* (Princeton University Press, 1979); John A. Dearborn, "The 'Proper Organs' for Presidential Representation: A Fresh Look at the Budget and Accounting Act of 1921," *Journal of Policy History* 31 (2019), pp. 1–41; and Shelley Lynne Tomkin, *Inside OMB: Politics and Process in the President's Budget Office* (New York: M. E. Sharpe, 1998). For a description of OMB in its current role in regulatory review, see Rachel Augustine Potter, *Bending the Rules: Procedural Politicking in the Bureaucracy* (University of Chicago Press, 2019); and Wiseman, "Delegation and Positive-Sum Bureaucracies."

13. An early accounting of differential levels of OMB influence is James W.

Davis and Randall B. Ripley, "The Bureau of the Budget and Executive Branch Agencies: Notes on Their Interaction," *Journal of Politics* 29 (1967), pp. 749–69.

14. For background on the history and structure of independent agencies, see Marshall J. Breger and Gary J. Edles, *Independent Agencies in the United States* (Oxford University Press, 2015) and Jennifer L. Selin, "What Makes an Agency Independent?" *American Journal of Political Science* 59 (2015), pp. 971–87.

15. Davis and Ripley, "The Bureau of the Budget and Executive Branch Agencies"; Norton E. Long, "Power and Administration," *Public Administration Review* 9 (1949), pp. 257–64; and Francis E. Rourke, "Variations in Agency Power," in *Bureaucratic Power in National Politics*, edited by Francis E. Rourke (Boston, MA: Little, Brown, and Company, 1972), pp. 240–62.

16. See, for example, Lisa Schultz Bressman and Michael P. Vandenbergh, "Inside the Administrative State: A Critical Look at the Practice of Presidential Control," *Michigan Law Review* 105 (2006), pp. 47–99.

17. Michael Kagan, "Binding the Enforcers: The Administrative Law Struggle behind President Obama's Immigration Actions," *University of Richmond Law Review* 50 (2016), pp. 665–736.

18. See Joshua D. Clinton and David E. Lewis, "Expert Opinion, Agency Characteristics, and Agency Preferences," *Political Analysis* 16 (2008), pp. 3–20.

19. For classic treatments, see Michel Crozier, *The Bureaucratic Phenomenon* (University of Chicago Press, 1964); D. J. Hickson, C. R. Hinings, C. A. Lee, R. E. Schneck, and J. M. Pennings, "A Strategic Contingencies' Theory of Intraorganizational Power," *Administrative Science Quarterly* 16 (1971), pp. 216–29; Gerald R. Salancik and Jeffrey Pfeffer, "Who Gets Power—And How They Hold On To It: A Strategic Contingency Model of Power," *Organizational Dynamics* 5 (Winter, 1977), pp. 3–21; Rourke, "Agency Power"; Wilson, *Bureaucracy*.

20. See, for example, Daniel P. Carpenter, *The Forging of Bureaucratic Autonomy* (Princeton University Press, 2001).

21. Matthew Holden, "'Imperialism' in Bureaucracy," *American Political Science Review* 60 (1966), p. 944. See, also, Rourke, "Variations in Agency Power," p. 241.

22. For a description of the relationship between agencies, groups, and congressional committees, see J. L. Freeman, *The Political Process: Executive Bureau-Legislative Committee Relations* (New York: Random House, 1965); and Hugh Heclo, "Issue Networks and the Executive Establishment," in *The New American Political System*, edited by Anthony King (Washington, D.C.: American Enterprise Institute, 1978), pp. 262–87.

23. See, for example, William E. Kovacic, "The Institutions of Antitrust Law: How Structure Shapes Substance," *Michigan Law Review* 110 (2012), pp. 1019–44; and Anne Joseph O'Connell, "The Architecture of Smart Intelligence: Structuring and Overseeing Agencies in the Post-9/11 World," *California Law Review* 94 (2006), pp. 1655–744.

24. For an early formulation, see Long, "Power and Administration."

25. See, for example, Bressman and Vandenbergh, "Inside the Administrative State"; Jody Freeman and Jim Rossi, "Agency Coordination in Shared Regulatory Space," *Harvard Law Review* 125 (2012), pp. 1133–211.

26. For a full treatment, see Crozier, *The Bureaucratic Phenomenon*; Hickson and others, "A Strategic Contingencies' Theory of Intraorganizational

Power," p. 218; Salancik and Pfeffer, "Who Gets Power—And How They Hold On To It," p. 5.

27. For details of the 2007 survey, see Joshua D. Clinton, Anthony Bertelli, Christian Grose, David E. Lewis, and David C. Nixon, "Separated Powers in the United States: The Ideology of Agencies, Presidents and Congress," *American Journal of Political Science* 56 (2012), pp. 341–54. For the 2014 survey, see Mark D. Richardson, "Politicization and Expertise: Exit, Effort, and Investment," *Journal of Politics* (2019), forthcoming.

28. The survey sample was drawn from the *Federal Yellow Book*, and the survey was implemented by the Princeton Survey Research Center. The response rate was 24 percent, 18 percent for appointees and 25 percent for career executives. Of the 3,551 respondents, 586 answered via paper survey and the remainder took the online version.

29. The source for the agency list was David E. Lewis and Jennifer L. Selin, *Sourcebook of United States Executive Agencies* (Washington, D.C.: Administrative Conference of the United States, 2012).

30. Specifically, the survey was sent to all Senate-confirmed, other presidential appointees not requiring Senate confirmation, non-career SES, and Schedule C appointees in the instrumentalities of the United States government described in this section.

31. Among other career executives, the survey was sent to executives comparable to members of the Senior Executive Service (SES) in agencies without SES members, program and agency managers at the GS-14, GS-15 level with specific job functions as listed in the *Federal Yellow Book*.

32. This online and paper survey was sent to 7,448 career and appointed federal administrators and program managers. The overall response rate was 33 percent, and the sample was generally representative of the population of federal executives.

33. A respondent was shown either "Media" or "Contractors" with probability 0.5. "Media" or "Contractors" was listed last due to programming restrictions.

34. While both career executives and appointees report that the administration has more influence than Congress over policymaking in their agencies, for career executives the gap is smaller.

35. Another way of examining the figure 8-1 data is with the proportion responding *A good bit* or *A great deal*. The proportion of respondents answering this way are as follows: Political Appointees (80 percent); OMB (67 percent); Senior Civil Servants (65 percent); White House (67 percent); Congressional Committees (57 percent); Congressional Democrats (45 percent); Congressional Republicans (37 percent); Stakeholders (31 percent); Media (17 percent); Contractors (8 percent).

36. Because all executives deal with OMB and OPM, all respondents were asked to evaluate these agencies to make use of the scale comparable across respondents (Davis and Ripley, "The Bureau of the Budget and Executive Branch Agencies").

37. Refer to the online appendix to Richardson, Clinton, and Lewis, "Elite Perceptions of Agency Ideology and Workforce Skill" for details of how the list of agencies that respondents could evaluate was assembled.

38. We use a Bayesian multi-rater item response model with informed priors to estimate agency influence. The model allows each respondent to have a unique mapping from her perception of agency influence to her use of the scale from the survey. Because respondents who work with an agency should be best

able to evaluate its influence, we use the perceptions of respondents who work with each agency to construct the prior distribution for agency influence. This specification weights the perceptions of these individuals more heavily than the perceptions of other respondents. For a full description of the method, see Richardson, Clinton, and Lewis, "Elite Perceptions of Agency Ideology and Workforce Skill."

39. See www.mrichardson.info/data.

40. See Carpenter, *The Forging of Bureaucratic Autonomy*; Crozier *The Bureaucratic Phenomenon*; Hickson and others, "A Strategic Contingencies' Theory of Intraorganizational Power"; Salancik and Pfeffer "Who Gets Power—And How They Hold On To It"; Rourke, "Variations in Agency Power"; Wilson, *Bureaucracy*.

41. Rourke, "Variations in Agency Power," pp. 240–62.

42. Hickson and colleagues note that the parts of an organization that are more immediate, more pervasive, and that control the uncertainty of other units will tend to be more powerful. Hickson and others, "A Strategic Contingencies' Theory of Intraorganizational Power," p. 222.

43. Heclo details this argument in "Issue Networks and the Executive Establishment."

44. We included only those agencies for which we had ten respondents and thirty potential respondents in the survey.

45. Selin, "What Makes an Agency Independent?"

46. Source: Lewis and Selin, *Sourcebook of United States Executive Agencies*. Specifically, we use table 13 for OMB exemptions; table 14, column 7 to code independent funding sources; table 10, column 3 and table 6 to code for-cause protections; and table 8 to code party balancing. We coded Consumer Financial Protection Bureau (CFPB) as having independent funding and for-cause protections since it is separate from the Board of Governors of the Federal Reserve in our data.

47. See Carpenter, *The Forging of Bureaucratic Autonomy*; Sean Gailmard and John W. Patty, *Learning While Governing: Expertise and Accountability in the Executive Branch* (University of Chicago Press, 2013).

48. Richardson, Clinton, and Lewis, "Elite Perceptions of Agency Ideology and Workforce Skill."

49. The survey includes nine questions about the content of jobs. We focus here on the four most closely related to the work of OMB.

50. We include estimates of agency ideology (Mean -0.02, SD 1.02, Min -1.9, Max 1.9) and workforce skill (Mean 0.07, SD 0.81, Min -2, Max 1.8) from Richardson and others, "Elite Perceptions of Agency Ideology and Workforce Skill." We also include an indicator for whether the respondent works in an independent regulatory commission (0,1; 0.09). As above, we include a measure of respondent party identification (Mean 1.2, SD 1.5, Min 0, Max 4) and whether their job involves budget formulation/proposals (0,1; 0.72); developing notices of proposed rulemaking, summarizing related comments, writing final rules (0,1; 0.34); grants to state and local governments, other organizations, or individuals (0,1; 0.29); or procurement and contract management (0,1; 0.47).

51. We include both the natural log of the 2014 budget (Mean $756M; SD $2.7B) and the number of employees (Mean 30,011; SD 67,126).

52. In other analyses, agencies with larger numbers of discrete budget accounts reported more OMB influence, and agencies without their own lines in the budget reported less OMB influence.

53. Charles S. Clark, "OMB Reminds Agencies that It Vets Documents before Roll-Outs," *Government Executive*, February 27, 2019, govexec.com/management/2019/02/omb-reminds-agencies-it-vets-documents-roll-outs/155178/.

54. Patrick Bernhard, David E. Lewis, and Emily H. You, "President Trump as Manager: Reflections on the First Year," *Presidential Studies Quarterly* 48 (2018), pp. 480–501.

NINE

State of the Agency

Internal Developments at OMB

GEOVETTE E. WASHINGTON
THOMAS E. HITTER

This chapter offers a snapshot in time of the Office of Management and Budget (OMB). It examines how presidential use of OMB has evolved and increased such that OMB is now used to manage all aspects of agencies' activities. Related to this, Congress's views and expectations of the institution have changed as it also sees OMB as serving in this "manager" role. To provide this analysis, this chapter first offers a brief description of OMB's size and structure. After providing that context, the chapter then examines how administrations' use of OMB and Congress's expectations of the institution have evolved to shape OMB into its current role and function. In examining the more recent state, compared to where it once was, this chapter describes the reaction a hire from previous decades may have when examining the roles and responsibilities OMB personnel have today. The chapter concludes with a perspective on OMB's current resources and needs.

OMB'S INFRASTRUCTURE

Before examining OMB's evolving and increasing role in executive branch policymaking and execution, it is helpful to first explain OMB's size and structure. Most notably, it is important to note how the size of the institution is similar to its original composition from fifty years ago despite the agency's growth in power and influence, which will be described in later sections of this chapter.

In 1970, as part of President Nixon's reorganization plan, the agency's name was changed from the Bureau of the Budget to OMB.[1] At that time, the agency had over 500 full-time equivalent (FTE) employees, and it quickly increased to over 700 employees in the subsequent decade.[2] Since then, the number of FTEs has dropped and most recently has plateaued.[3] The staffing level is now similar to that of 1970. OMB reports that it had 466 FTEs in 2019 and estimated it would have 477 in FY 2020.[4]

Many aspects of OMB's current internal organization also existed when the agency was originally organized.[5] OMB is currently characterized as consisting of an "M side" (for management) and a "B side" (for budget), a description that has been applied to the agency historically.[6] Today, the M side consists mainly of the offices created by statute. These offices report to the deputy director for management (DDM) (a position created in the 1990 Chief Financial Officers [CFO] Act), who also serves as the federal government's chief performance officer.[7]

Congress has enacted legislation increasing the number of statutory offices within OMB that are focused on particular management areas. These offices have broad authority to develop and execute the executive branch's procurement, financial management, information technology, performance and personnel management, and information and regulatory policies. Below is a brief description of those offices:[8]

- In 1974, Congress created the Office of Federal Procurement Policy (OFPP) in OMB to shape the policies and practices federal agencies use to acquire the goods and services they need to carry out their responsibilities.[9]

- The Paperwork Reduction Act of 1980[10] established the Office of Information and Regulatory Affairs (OIRA) in OMB. This is the central authority for the review of executive branch regulations, approval of government information collections, establishment of government statistical practices, and coordination of federal privacy policy.[11]

- In 1990, Congress established OMB's Office of Federal Financial Management (OFFM) in the CFO act.[12] This office is responsible for the financial management policy of the federal government. Its responsibilities include implementing the financial management improvement priorities of the president, establishing government-wide financial management policies of executive agencies, and carrying out the financial management functions of the CFO act.[13]

- In the E-Government Act of 2002,[14] Congress established the Office of E-Government and Information Technology in OMB, which is headed by the federal government's chief information officer (CIO). This office is charged with developing and providing direction in the use of Internet-based technologies to make it easier for citizens and business to interact with the federal government.[15]

- Through the Government Performance and Results Act[16] (GPRA) and the GPRA Modernization act,[17] Congress has also charged OMB with overseeing agencies' performance, including their establishment of goals and reporting their successes or failures in meeting those goals.

The B side is divided into Resource Management Offices (RMOs), which were introduced in 1994 as part of an internal OMB reorganization.[18] These offices carry out OMB's responsibility for assisting the president in overseeing the preparation of the federal budget and supervising the administration of executive branch agencies.[19] The RMOs' responsibilities include assessing the effectiveness of agency programs, policies, and procedures; weighing competing funding demands within and among agencies; and helping work with agencies to set funding priorities.[20] Furthermore, once a budget is enacted, RMOs are responsible for the execution of federal budgetary policies and provide ongoing policy and management guidance to federal agencies.[21]

While the areas covered by specific RMOs and their names have changed slightly over several administrations, the RMOs have consistently been organized by subject matter.[22] The current RMOs are: Natural Resource Programs; Education, Income Maintenance, and Labor

Programs; Health Programs; General Government Programs; and National Security Programs.

The final category of units within OMB are the offices that support the activities of the M side and the B side. These support offices include the offices of General Counsel (OGC), Legislative Affairs (OLA), Communications, and Economic Policy (EP), as well as the Budget Review Division (BRD) and the Legislative Reference Division (LRD). OGC provides legal advice and counsel to OMB's components, including officials and staff. The activities of OLA include advising the OMB director and the organization on legislative issues and developments, managing correspondence with Congress, and disseminating budget materials to Congress.[23] EP is responsible for developing economic assumptions for the president's budget and assisting the RMOs in developing budget estimates, policy proposals, cost models, and other data analytics.[24] BRD plays a central role within the institution, with broad responsibility, including providing strategic and technical support in budget decisionmaking and negotiations.[25] Finally, LRD coordinates the articulation of the administration's position on legislation through the review and clearance of several types of materials.[26]

As discussed later in this chapter, over the last several decades, Congress has given OMB more authority, and administrations have called on OMB to be more involved in the management of the agencies. However, the current staffing levels and the current organizational structure of an M side and a B side largely reflect what was in place when the agency was originally organized under President Nixon's administration.[27] With this context in mind, after examining OMB's current role and responsibilities, the reaction of a hire from 1969, or even 1989, 1999, and 2009 would most likely be: How is it all done?

WHAT HAS CHANGED—OMB'S INCREASING ROLE IN MANAGING AGENCIES

OMB's power and authority in the executive branch's policymaking and execution have grown significantly over the past several administrations. This change is primarily the result of administrations using OMB as a tool to manage agencies more rigorously. Over time, this oversight of agencies has been broadened beyond simply managing the development of the agencies' budgets. OMB now has a more hands-on involvement with agencies, managing all aspects of agencies' operations, including personnel, grant making, acquisition of goods and services, regulations, and information technology (IT). Furthermore, Congress now sees OMB as a manager of agency policy execution. Consequently, Congress has codified new authorities in OMB or funded OMB to execute a more robust management role across the executive branch. Ironically, OMB's role in managing agencies is not limited to carrying out responsibilities found in the agency's M side.

Centralizing many of these authorities and duties in OMB has strengthened ties between the president and OMB, and increased OMB's influence in executive policymaking. This chapter concludes with a discussion of the unintended consequences of this evolution on the health of the institution and provides recommendations of specific actions to address the consequences of the size of the institution not keeping pace with the increase in responsibilities.

Presidential Use of OMB: Available Tools

Regardless of the administration, each president has relied on, or leveraged, OMB to manage agencies and implement the president's priorities.[28] OMB acts as the implementation and enforcement arm of presidential policy government-wide, through a variety of tools and processes.[29] This is a natural fit, as OMB has been the largest and most stable component of the White House across administrations.

These tools and processes include the management of the budget development and execution processes. Other publications provide details on how OMB can control agency policymaking through the president's budget process and through the responsibility of developing and executing the budget, noting how OMB is "in the stream of every policy decision made by the Federal government."[30]

OMB's management of agencies also includes the process to prepare, present, file, and publish executive orders and proclamations.[31] This process, which is governed by Executive Order 11030 and historically managed by OMB's OGC,[32] gives the OMB director the authority to approve proposed EOs and proclamations submitted by an originating federal agency before they are transmitted to the Attorney General for form and legality review and, eventually, to the president.[33]

OMB also controls the process by which agencies communicate their execution of presidential policy. Through Circular A-19, OMB manages the coordination and clearance of agency recommendations on proposed, pending, and enrolled legislation.[34] As stated in that circular, all executive branch agencies are subject to it (except for some limited exceptions) and OMB performs this function to:

(a) Assist the president in developing a position on legislation.
(b) Make known the administration's position on legislation for the guidance of the agencies and information of Congress.
(c) Assure appropriate consideration of the views of all affected agencies.
(d) Assist the president with respect to action on enrolled bills.[35]

Similarly, OMB runs the process to develop and clear Statements of Administrative Policy, agency testimony, and enrolled bills and signing statements.[36] By managing these processes, OMB can use these statements to communicate the president's and agencies' policies to the government as a whole and set forth policymakers' agendas.[37]

A significant responsibility given to OMB by presidential authority is the coordination and review of all significant federal regulations by executive agencies to ensure they reflect presidential priorities and that economic and other impacts are assessed as part of the regulatory decisionmaking process.[38] The authority to review agencies' draft, proposed, and final regulatory actions was provided by EO 12866, Regulatory Planning and Review, issued by President Clinton in 1993.[39] Presidents have continued to leverage OIRA's responsibility to manage the executive branch and to set policy. For instance, in 2017, President Trump issued EO 13771, Reducing Regulation and Controlling Regulatory Costs,[40] and EO 13777, Enforcing the Regulatory Reform Agenda.[41]

Finally, presidents have used the M side authorities given to OMB, increasing OMB's influence in policy development. The emphasis on the M side was previously explained in detail in this chapter and in other sources.[42] In addition to the statutory offices described, it is worth noting how presidents have used the President's Management Agenda (PMA) to set goals for the agency's performance generally. The Bush administration used a tool called the Program Assessment Rating Tool to assess and improve agencies' program performance[43] and President Obama's Evidence and Evaluation Agenda was created to better integrate evidence and rigorous evaluation in budget, management, operational, and policy decisions across the executive branch.[44] In practice, these management reforms and control over agencies' policymaking has been implemented in large part through OMB's budget process.⁴⁵

Presidential Use of OMB: Expanded Use of Available Tools

The current trend is for administrations to call on OMB to act as the "enforcement arm" of presidential policies more often. This is seen in situations where Congress has found it more difficult to legislate, as has occurred more regularly in recent years. In these situations, the administration has called on OMB to effectuate and enforce presidential policies through an expanded use of the tools and processes just mentioned. While there are several examples of this trend, this chapter highlights two that have received significant attention in recent years: (1) OMB's role in a government shutdown; and (2) OMB's role in the development of agency regulations.

A government shutdown serves as a stark example of OMB exercising its authority to fill a space created by a lack of congressional action. A government shutdown occurs when there is a lapse in appropriations, which happens when Congress has not appropriated funds to pay for an agency or program to operate, as required by the Constitution.⁴⁶ Historically, these shutdowns were rarely threatened and rarely occurred.⁴⁷ Now, the possibility of a shutdown exists each fiscal year, as Congress struggles to reach agreement on legislation to keep the government funded and open.

In these situations, agencies are required to "develop and maintain plans for an orderly shutdown" and submit those plans to OMB.⁴⁸ OMB's Circular A-11 details what those plans must include to be in compliance with the relevant authorities, including the Antideficiency Act (31 U.S.C. §§ 1341 *et seq*).⁴⁹ As further explained in Circular A-11, OMB's involvement in the development and execution of these shutdown plans is significant. Primarily through the program examiners in the RMOs, and with support from the attorneys in the OGC, OMB works with agencies in advance of making the plans public. Once a shutdown has occurred and the plans are public, OMB personnel continue to meet with agency personnel regularly to help those agencies implement those plans and to ensure the executive branch is acting in a coordinated manner. OMB is also often responsible for communicating updates on the White House's budget negotiations with Congress to end the shutdown. In fact, agencies cannot resume normal activities until OMB informs them that a budget deal has been reached, legislation has been enacted, and they are authorized to reopen.[50]

In practice, OMB does not merely receive the plans; OMB's role is to approve agencies' shutdown plans, ensuring they sufficiently explain the agencies' activities that will continue during the lapse in appropriations and the number of personnel expected to be on-board, as well as examining the legal basis for those determinations.[51] Given the level of discretion in the decisions that inform these plans, OMB's approval is, in essence, a policy decision, which has broad impacts across each agency, including its personnel (plans dictate who is considered "excepted"[52]) and its programs (plans dictate which programs must continue to operate and which must cease operations). Furthermore, given the frequency with which a government shutdown is threatened, the submission of these plans, and OMB's approval of them, must occur regularly. In fact, at a minimum, OMB requires agencies to submit updated plans every two years.[53] Consequently, the most recent administrations have leveraged OMB's approval of shutdown plans as another tool to manage agencies. OMB personnel are expected to have intimate knowledge of agency programs and their operations, which is an expertise administrations can now call on when making policy decisions regarding which programs and operations to prioritize.

Furthermore, as much of the guidance interpreting the legal standards governing the development of these plans comes from OMB memoranda, as well as legal opinions from the U.S. Department of Justice's Office of Legal Counsel,[54] administrations call on OMB to apply these standards in a manner consistent with their policy direction. This places OMB at the center of controversies regarding the policy decisions made during a shutdown.[55]

Another example of administrations calling for an increase in OMB's involvement is in the regulatory space. As mentioned, the past several administrations have used OIRA's authority to manage agencies. Having said that, starting with the Obama administration and continuing in the Trump administration, an effort has been made, or is being made, to expand OIRA's role significantly.

For instance, OIRA has taken a more active role in coordinating agency regulatory activity that impacts emerging industries or technologies. In the absence of congressional action that imposes rules on new industries or technologies, OIRA has issued guidance to agencies, establishing principles to be followed, to help agencies develop regulations that achieve the objectives of protecting safety, health, and the environment, while avoiding unjustifiably inhibiting innovation or stigmatizing new technologies.[56] An example of this type of guidance is the Obama administration's efforts to modernize the regulatory system for biotechnology products. In 2015, OIRA—in conjunction with the Office of Science and Technology Policy (OSTP), the United States Trade Representative (USTR), and the Council of Environmental Quality (CEQ)—issued a directive that established a process to coordinate the regulatory system for the products of biotechnology.[57] This process allowed OIRA (and the Executive Office of the President (EOP) as a whole) to ensure that the executive branch regulated in this area in a manner consistent with clear standards and administration priorities.[58] To coordinate this activity, the directive required: (1) the creation of an Emerging Technologies Interagency Policy Coordination Committee; (2) the relevant agencies to commission external, independent analysis of the future landscape of biotechnology products; (3) the relevant agencies to develop a budget plan to support this area; and (4) an annual report to be provided to the EOP.[59] These were the tools OIRA (and the EOP) used to coordinate agency regulatory activity.

A more recent example is the Trump administration's efforts to pull independent agencies under OIRA's purview. While prior administrations have contemplated requiring that independent regulatory agencies submit their proposed regulations to OIRA for review, those administrations declined to take action to do so.[60] The Trump administration took a more aggressive posture. This is seen in a couple of concrete actions taken in 2018. First, in April 2018, OIRA reached an agreement with the Department of the Treasury providing the terms under which OIRA will review tax regulatory actions.[61] This agreement changed the practice in place since the 1980s of exempting tax regulations from regulatory review under EO 12866. This change has allowed OIRA to apply its cost-benefit analysis to tax regulatory actions, thus providing OIRA an opportunity to shape policies implemented through taxation.[62]

Another recent example of OMB's expanding influence in policymaking is the use of the Unified Agenda of Regulatory and Deregulatory Actions as a tool to manage agency action. This agenda, which is published by OMB, is a government-wide publication of the rulemaking actions agencies expect to take in the coming months.[63] While the agenda helps agencies fulfill two transparency requirements (Section 602 of the Regulatory Flexibility Act, 5 U.S.C. § 602 and Section 4 of EO 12866), historically agencies have not been required to identify a proposed rule in the agenda before issuing it in the *Federal Register*. The Trump administration, however, changed this practice through executive order, turning the agenda into a tool OMB can use to monitor agency action. Specifically, EO 13771 states: "Unless otherwise required by law, no regulation shall be issued by an agency if it was not included on the most recent version or update of the published Unified Regulatory Agenda as required under Executive Order 12866, as amended, or any successor order, unless the issuance of such regulation was approved in advance in writing by the Director [of OMB]."[64]

OIRA's implementing guidance emphasizes the importance of the agenda as a tool to monitor an agency's compliance with EO 13771's "one-in two-out" requirement, stating specifically that an agency's agenda should reflect the deregulatory actions required by this executive order.[65] As an agency complies with "one-in two-out," they are forced to prioritize their policy goals. Thus, OIRA's implementation of the executive order, and its management of agencies through the agenda, serve as another example of how OMB's role in agency policymaking has increased.[66]

Therefore, this analysis of the recent trend finds that administrations are calling on OMB to act in a way that has expanded its traditional coordinating role. The agency is no longer limited to facilitating interagency discussions or government-wide response efforts. When examining this growth in responsibilities, an OMB employee hired in 1970 would most likely be struck by how the agency is now called on to actively set policy both across the executive branch and within an agency through a variety of tools and processes, including as part of planning for a lapse in appropriations or through a comprehensive regulatory review.

Congressional Recognition of OMB's Expanding Role

While administrations have emphasized the use of OMB as a tool to manage agencies, Congress has also recognized the benefits of OMB serving in this capacity.[67] Accordingly, they have codified new authorities in OMB and funded OMB to perform in this role. Related, in light of OMB's increased involvement and role in managing agencies, Congress has also held OMB accountable for the execution of agencies' programs.

Recently, Congress has expanded on OMB's existing authorities. For instance, Congress passed the Digital Accountability and Transparency

Act in 2014[68] with the intent to make information on federal expenditures more easily accessible and transparent. To achieve this goal, Congress called on OMB to work with the Department of Treasury to establish government-wide financial data standards for federal funds and entities receiving such funds and to make available a financial management status report and government-wide five-year financial management plan.[69] OMB took on this new responsibility, and OFFM implements those new tasks.

Another example is the 2014 enactment of the Federal Information Technology Acquisition Reform Act (FITARA).[70] Building on the authorities provided to OMB in the Clinger-Cohen Act of 1996[71] and the E-Government Act of 2002,[72] Congress authorized OMB to take a more active role in the management of IT across the government. This included requiring OMB to develop a plan for conducting a government-wide inventory of IT assets[73] and requiring the federal CIO to initiate certain directives, such as implementing the Federal Data Center Optimization Initiative, which sets priorities for data center closures and IT efficiency improvements across the executive branch.[74]

In addition to granting new authorities (or expanding on existing authorities), Congress has also funded OMB to perform an increasingly active role in an agency's policy development and even perform an operational role within agencies. As explained later, in these instances Congress has made it clear that it expects OMB to perform more oversight of agencies, including through creating policies, selecting projects for agencies to develop, and even executing specific projects.

OMB's Information and Technology Oversight and Reform (ITOR) fund serves as a good example of Congress's new expectations for OMB. Since FY 2012, Congress has provided OMB with ITOR funding to enable OMB to focus the federal government on strategically achieving more efficiency in and across its IT investments.[75] With ITOR funding, OMB, under the direction of the federal CIO, issues major technology policy and conducts oversight of agency implementation, focusing on streamlining and simplifying federal IT policy; modernizing out-of-date and inefficient technology; securing government systems and data; and improving the governance of IT projects and services.[76] To implement these tasks, OMB conducts direct oversight of agency programs and the performance of their initiatives, including assessing all aspects of IT's supporting functions.[77] This includes identifying underperforming and duplicative investments and taking corrective actions.[78] OMB is no longer merely monitoring agencies; it is actively setting agency priorities in this area.

Perhaps of even greater significance is the use of ITOR to support U.S. Digital Services (USDS) in OMB. In a break from a traditional OMB role, USDS performs an operational function, deploying teams to agencies to improve citizen-facing electronic services. For instance, USDS worked with the Centers for Medicare & Medicaid Services (CMS) to change the way Medicare pays doctors and clinicians, and worked with the Small Business Administration (SBA) to eliminate paper applications.[79] OMB has continued to focus its resources on expanding this operational function. OMB has highlighted that USDS has core federal agency teams (at the Departments of Veterans Affairs, Homeland Security, and Health and Human Services) and is seeing an increase in demand for engagements at other agencies, including the Office of Personnel Management, the Department of Justice, Department of Housing and Urban Development, and the Social Security Administration (SSA).[80] OMB has also noted that USDS expects an increase in demand in order to implement legislation, such as the 21st Century Integrated Digital Experience Act (Pub. L. No. 115-336).[81]

While IT does provide a clear example of this trend at OMB, the trend is not limited to that area. For instance, the emphasis on performing an operational role is seen in how OMB implements Cross-Agency Priority (CAP) goals. The GPRA Modernization Act of 2010[82] established the use of CAP goals to accelerate progress on a limited number of presidential priority areas where implementation requires active collaboration among multiple agencies.[83] Administrations have used the PMA, which is issued by OMB's DDM, to identify these CAP goals and report the administration's progress.[84] OMB identifies goal leaders and holds teams accountable for results.

Traditionally, there has been no established means for funding the execution of these cross-agency efforts; consequently, OMB's involvement was limited. More recently, Congress has provided funds and authority for the cross-agency implementation of CAP goals, strengthening OMB's management of this program and giving it a role in executing CAP goal programs.[85] Through the use of these funds OMB manages the execution of these priority goals directly, including for the purpose of hiring dedicated support for the administration of OMB's responsibilities in this area.[86] For example, OMB's budget requests seek funds to support the White House Leadership Development Program.[87] This program, administered by the Performance Improvement Council (PIC),[88] a body established to assist the director of OMB, selects fellows to work on these priority goals. By funding this program, Congress has given OMB (through PIC) a direct role in how agency programs are staffed, managed, and operationalized.

The responsibilities given to OMB in several other statutes demonstrate Congress's expectation that OMB serve in an expanded operational role. These include the Fixing America's Surface Transportation Act (FAST-41),[89] the Foundations for Evidence-Based Policymaking Act of 2018,[90] and the Middle Class Tax Relief and Job Creation Act, which established the First Responder Network Authority (FirstNet),[91] each highlighted here:

- The FAST-41 created the Federal Permitting Improvement Steering Council (FPISC) on which OMB serves as a member. OMB is directed to issue guidance to agencies, and also has an operational role to facilitate resolution of disputes over permitting timetables.[92] OMB now has staff dedicated to these new responsibilities.[93]

- The Foundations for Evidence-Based Policymaking Act of 2018 includes several new operational responsibilities for OMB, including establishing a unified evidence building plan for the executive branch, requiring OMB to establish an Advisory Committee on Data for Evidence Building, and creating the new position of Chief Data Officer, which participates in the Chief Data Officer Council, established within OMB.[94] Congress has funded, and OMB continues to request additional funding for, OMB to help "agencies develop new program designs and evaluation strategies to enable them to use and build evidence" to improve program outcomes.[95]

- Congress has required that OMB's director serve as a permanent member of the board governing FirstNet, an independent authority within the Department of Commerce, which is responsible for building and operating the national broadband network that equips first responders.[96] Through its position on the board, OMB has direct involvement in managing this entity.

It appears the administration and Congress will continue to build on authorities such as these and grow OMB's management responsibilities. In fact, in its fiscal year 2020 budget request, the administration asked Congress for funding to establish a new office that will provide government-wide strategic direction on federal human capital policy and coordinate personnel policies, regulations, and procedures for executive agencies.[97] The proposal argues that this office would ensure alignment of federal workforce planning and policies with other management activities, and would be modeled after other statutory offices in OMB.[98]

Finally, Congress' expectations for OMB are also evident in the type of oversight they are conducting over the agency. In recent years, Congress has asked OMB to participate in hearings and congressional briefings and to submit documents focused on OMB's management of another agency's budget execution. For instance, OMB was the target of several congressional investigations during President Obama's administration that focused on OMB's oversight and role in the Department of Energy's execution of its Loan Guarantee Program.[99]

By placing more management responsibilities in OMB, and by changing the type of responsibilities OMB must perform, Congress has enhanced the significance of OMB's role within the executive branch. Furthermore, the recent trend toward more of an operational role (in addition to the traditional policy development role) may require that OMB's recruitment efforts emphasize a skill set in its new hires that demonstrates a proficiency in a specific agency program or will allow those new hires to become experts in specific agency programs, rather than having only skill sets focused on a budget background or public policy development experience.

WHAT DOES OMB NEED?

The previous comments highlight how OMB has evolved to better implement congressional direction and serve each administration. Specifically, this evolution is seen in a number of activities, including how OMB has: (1) taken on a more active role in developing management-related policies; (2) developed an operational role to push forward presidential initiatives; (3) used a lack of congressional action as an opportunity to assert more control over agency action; and (4) expanded on its existing regulatory authorities to provide more comprehensive oversight and set policy across the executive branch. Yet, as mentioned at the start of this chapter, even with this increased authority, the institution's size and infrastructure have not evolved correspondingly.[100] Consequently, the health of the organization suffers.

There are a few potential reasons why the status quo has remained. The first potential reason is that, frankly, the institution moves fast, all the time. OMB is involved in virtually every aspect of the executive branch, so there is no cyclical downtime that the institution can anticipate and use toward self-reflection and planning. Indeed, even when the executive branch "shuts down," OMB is called on to manage the government's activities, programs, and personnel.

Second, the institution has numerous positions classified as (or filled by) a noncompetitive appointment (or political appointee). According to the 2016 Plum Book, in addition to the Office of the Director (which includes several positions, including the deputy director of management, chief of staff, and senior advisers), the leadership in each of the following offices is filled by political appointments: Legislative Affairs, General Counsel, Communications, National Security Programs, General Government Programs, Human Resource Programs, Office of Information and Regulatory Affairs, Health Division, Office of Federal Procurement Policy, Staff Offices, and Office of E-Government and Information Technology.[101] This structure is most likely a product of being a federal agency that sits within the EOP and being the largest component of the EOP. Political appointees by definition and design do not serve as long as career personnel. An unintended consequence of this structure is that the vast majority of the agency's leadership is at the agency only temporarily. While that leadership may hope the institution, and its personnel, are happy and functioning at full potential, they are generally unable to devote much of their limited time to tackle the long-term structural problems facing the institution. In fact, the political leadership is often not at OMB long enough to fully appreciate the institution's concerns and understand the long-term needs.

In light of this, OMB would benefit from two specific actions. First, the agency could use an official in a leadership position that must be filled by a career employee. This position would serve as a member of the senior leadership, reporting directly to the director, with a focus on the operational aspects of the agency and able to speak with authority on behalf of the career staff. The most efficient model would be to require that this official have sufficient expertise in the organization such that the official could serve as interim director in periods when the director position is vacated, creating continuity between different presidential appointments or other changes in leadership. This position would be able to devote time to addressing long-standing institutional issues and would be involved in all decisions that could impact agency resources.

While previous OMB directors have made some efforts to add high-level career personnel to its leadership team, the scope of the authority provided for the position was too limited. The position's responsibilities should not be limited, but instead should be viewed as capable of acting on behalf of the agency during periods in which the director's position is vacant, to allow the agency to make decisions and continue its policy work.[102] At the same time, this position should have oversight responsibilities for the agency's operational and financial procedures and practices, such as those related to human resources and its budget, to allow for operational continuity between director transitions. Similar to a company's chief operating officer, this career official would provide strategic direction for the growth of the agency and its employees.

For example, over the years, OMB has undertaken several initiatives to integrate its M side and B side. The goal is to have OMB speak with one voice when working with the agencies and to improve efficiency in OMB's annual review of agency programs and budgets. As explained in detail in other sources, OMB has tried several different approaches, from separating to combining the management and budget functions.[103] Despite these efforts, the problem persists, vacillating from an urgent problem to an underlying concern. An important reason the problem persists is that the agency leadership that has embarked on resolving it leaves before any real change can be institutionalized. Conversely, a career official would be able to spearhead any initiatives needed to tackle the long-standing question of the M side's relationship to the B side, as they would appreciate the issue and ensure solutions are fully implemented and their intent would be to remain at the institution for an extended time.

A career official who is a direct report to the director would also be a resource to address systemic morale issues. The morale at the institution tends to decline in periods of transition and in years impacted by government shutdowns.[104] Furthermore, the institution has struggled historically in helping its employees find work-life balance.[105] A career official could help to address these historical concerns at the institution. This official would also be able to analyze and address recurring or frequent scenarios or issues that continue to negatively impact personnel and would be in a position to work with others in leadership to create and institutionalize organizational change that would mitigate or remove those concerns.

The second action that could improve the health of the organization is devoting greater resources to the strategy or vision for the agency. While OMB sits within the EOP and is considered a component of the White House, it is also a federal agency.[106] Accordingly, it is often forgotten that OMB needs to devote resources to comply with requirements imposed on agencies by Congress and to respond to oversight initiated by congressional bodies. An initial reaction or suggestion may be to simply add more resources. Adding more people to the agency would allow OMB to better meet the increasing demands from administrations and Congress and execute its growing list of responsibilities, though simply adding more may come at a cost. There is significant benefit to the relatively small size of the agency. It has created a flatter organization, where information flows freely to and from decisionmakers. It is easy to find the expert on a particular area and have that person provide information to those making the policy decisions. This environment means program examiners (an entry level position) are often in meetings with the agency leadership rather than working through layers of hierarchy. To lose this type of collaboration may inhibit the ability of OMB to gather information and act on it quickly and decisively. It may also adversely impact recruitment, as OMB is currently able to advertise these opportunities to highly skilled examiners beginning their careers.

Instead, what may be more beneficial is to focus on the need for leaders devoted to establishing a strategy or vision for OMB, separate and apart from the EOP.[107] This is more pertinent now that the agency has taken on additional responsibilities from Congress with the establishment of management offices in OMB, and now that the agency frequently serves in an expanded operational role. While OMB is the "implementation and enforcement arm of Presidential policy government-wide,"[108] it is also now doing more to manage the federal agencies for the White House and Congress, and is even helping to execute programs at agencies. As these new responsibilities are added, the vision for the agency becomes less clear. To address this need, OMB should examine whether its support offices, including the Offices of Legislative Affairs and General Counsel, have the resources to advocate for the agency to external partners, as well as advise agency leadership in their interaction inside and outside the White House. These offices can help keep the agency focused on its mission while still effectively executing the responsibilities given to it by others.

This type of strategic planning will also help OMB navigate the inherent tension in trying to respond to the preferences and demands imposed by both the president and Congress. This tension exists as both branches of government may have, and often do have, conflicting interests, and there is little prospect of this tension diminishing. To influence how certain pieces of legislation are executed more effectively, administrations may often prefer for congressional mandates to be housed within OMB, its "enforcement arm," as this allows them to have greater control in how those mandates are interpreted and applied. If administrations wish for OMB to continue managing federal agencies, congressionally provided tools are valuable to have at its disposal. At the same time, Congress may be incentivized to continue to place the management of government-wide mandates in OMB, since having these in one central location makes it easier for Congress to conduct oversight on how those requirements are met. Consequently, OMB will most likely never be free of congressional mandates. Instead, the agency is left to navigate this tension. It must make case-by-case determinations of when it is acting on behalf of the president and when it is acting pursuant to a congressional mandate.

These determinations can have important consequences. For instance, when Congress requires OMB to gather information from federal agencies, is it required to gather information from itself? What if that information is directly relevant to presidential decisionmaking and responsive to requests made by the president? Answers to these questions are not clear. A clearer articulation of how the agency views its role and responsibilities, however, would help provide consistent answers to these tough and important questions. It would also allow the agency to identify when it is asked to do something it finds to be inconsistent with its mission or authority.

CONCLUSION

To develop a snapshot in time of OMB, this chapter began by first explaining how the agency has not changed significantly in size or organization over the past few administrations. It then explained the tools OMB uses to manage agencies as well as executive branch policy development and execution, followed by recent administrations' expanded use of those tools and Congress's view of OMB as having the authority to manage agencies. This change and growth in authority has happened because the agency continues to perform at a high level. At the same time, this contrast between what has not changed and what is now different at OMB appears to warrant a request for additional resources.[109] While additional resources are needed in general at the institution, the agency would be best served by applying these resources in ways that improve the well-being of the agency and its employees. Providing it with career leadership and stronger advocates will allow the agency to continue to deliver for each of its stakeholders in a way that also supports the health of the organization and those who serve within it.

To recognize the benefits these initiatives would provide will take time. That new structure would need to be created and given time to operationalize. There have also been efforts in the past to change OMB's culture that have failed to create the promised results, including moving career officials within the organization and adding resources, so skeptics would need to be convinced that these proposed initiatives are different and that anticipated changes are worth the effort. Despite those challenges, there will be opportunities to assess and potentially implement these proposals. OMB and its existing or proposed responsibilities continue to be examined by scholars,[110] nonprofit organizations,[111] government entities,[112] and even working groups within the organization,[113] each focused on addressing the challenges it faces. There is clearly a desire to improve OMB. In addition, the success of the federal government often depends on the success of OMB. With both presidents and Congresses relying on OMB to implement their agendas, there is a vested interest from decisionmakers across Washington, D.C., to make sure OMB works effectively and efficiently. The actions suggested here would be investments in OMB that would facilitate stronger partnerships with those policymakers.

Notes

1. OMB's predecessor was the Bureau of the Budget (or BOB), which was established within the Department of the Treasury pursuant to the Budget and Accounting Act of 1921, Pub. L. No. 67-13, 42 Stat. 20. See, for example, Jim Pfiffner, "The Budget Process from OMB's Perspective," in *Executive Policymaking: The Role of the OMB in the Presidency* (Brookings, 2020) (providing a historical prospective on OMB and the budget process); Larry Berman, *The Office of Management and Budget and the Presidency*, 1921–1979 (Princeton

University Press, 1979) (providing a comprehensive study of OMB up through the late 1970s).

2. (Name redacted) Analyst in Government Organization and Management, *Office of Management and Budget (OMB): A Brief Overview* (Congressional Research Service, March 31, 2006).

3. See Molly Reynolds, "OMB and the Budget: The View from Capitol Hill" in *Executive Policymaking: The Role of the OMB in the Presidency* (Brookings, 2020) (providing detail on OMB's staffing levels).

4. See Executive Office of the President, Fiscal Year 2021 Congressional Budget Submission at OMB-10-11.

5. There have been several efforts to review OMB's internal organization with varying degrees of success. See, for example, Office Memorandum No. 94-16 from Leon E. Panetta, Director, Office of Management and Budget, Executive Office of the President, and Alice M. Rivlin, Deputy Director, Office of Management and Budget, Executive Office of the President, to All OMB Staff, "Making OMB More Effective in Serving the Presidency: Changes in OMB as a Result of the OMB 2000 Review," March 1, 1994; see, also, Matthew Dickinson, "OMB 2000 at 25," in *Executive Policymaking: The Role of the OMB in the Presidency* (Brookings, 2020) (describing the review of OMB's effort in the 1990s).

6. See, for example, *Smoothing the Peaceful Transfer of Democratic Power, The Office of Management and Budget, an Insider's Guide Report 2017–22*, edited by Steve Redburn and Paul Posner (The White House Transition Project, Rice University's Baker Institute for Public Policy, Funded by the Moody Foundation, 2017), p. 14 (noting that after the 1994 reorganization effort, OMB staff referred less often to the two "sides," for several years, "but today the split is again recognized in common parlance within OMB").

7. See "Weekly Address: President Obama Discusses Efforts to Reform Spending, Government Waste; Names Chief Performance Officer and Chief Technology Officer" (White House, Office of the Press Secretary, April 18, 2009), https://obamawhitehouse.archives.gov/realitycheck/the-press-office/weekly-address-president-obama-discusses-efforts-reform-spending-government-waste-n (announcing first Chief Performance Officer).

8. Also of note is the Office of the Intellectual Property Enforcement Coordinator (IPEC), which was created in title III of the Prioritizing Resources and Organization for Intellectual Property Act of 2008 (P.L. 110-403), which required that the IPEC be a presidentially appointed, Senate-confirmed official who serves within the Executive Office of the President. IPEC was funded from FY 2010 through FY 2019 through OMB's appropriation and existed as part of the agency during that time period.

9. OFPP Act, Pub. L. No. 93-400, 88 Stat. 796.

10. As amended by the Paperwork Reduction Act of 1995, 44 U.S.C. §§ 3501 *et seq.*

11. See White House Office of Management and Budget, Information and Regulatory Affairs, www.whitehouse.gov/omb/information-regulatory-affairs/. While established by legislation, in terms of organizational and reporting structure, OIRA is often not considered an M side office within OMB. See, for example, White House, Office of Management and Budget, www.whitehouse.gov/omb/ (separating "Information and Regulatory Affairs" from "Management" offices in description of agency's organization).

12. Pub. L. No. 101-576, 104 Stat. 2838.

13. See White House, Office of Management and Budget, Office of Fed-

eral Financial Management, www.whitehouse.gov/omb/management/office-federal-financial-management/.

14. Pub. L. No. 107-347, 116 Stat. 2899.

15. See White House, Office of Management and Budget, Office of E-Government & Information Technology, www.whitehouse.gov/omb/management/egov/.

16. Pub. L. No. 103-62, 107 Stat. 285.

17. Pub. L. No. 111-352, 124 Stat. 3866.

18. See Eloise Pasachoff, "The President's Budget as a Source of Agency Policy Control," *Yale Law Journal* 125, (2016), pp. 2182, 2190 (providing a brief overview of the RMOs creation within OMB).

19. See President Barack Obama's White House, Office of Management and Budget, "The Mission and Structure of the Office of Management and Budget," https://obamawhitehouse.archives.gov/omb/organization_mission/.

20. Ibid.

21. Ibid.

22. Ibid.

23. Ibid.

24. Ibid.

25. Ibid.

26. Ibid.

27. See Reynolds, supra note 3 (providing detail on OMB's staffing levels).

28. See Matthew Dickinson and Andrew Rudalevige, "Presidents, Responsiveness, and Competence: Revisiting the 'Golden Age' at the Bureau of the Budget," *Political Science Quarterly* 119, no. 4 (2004–2005), pp. 633–54 (describing OMB's predecessor BOB and its relationship and responsiveness to the presidents and administrations of that era).

29. See President Barack Obama's White House, Office of Management and Budget, "The Mission and Structure of the Office of Management and Budget," https://obamawhitehouse.archives.gov/omb/organization_mission/.

30. Ibid.; see also, Pasachoff, supra note 18 (arguing that OMB's budget work serves as a regularized and pervasive form of agency control and quoting Paul O'Neill, former deputy director of OMB).

31. See Andrew Rudalevige, "Central Clearance of Legislation and Executive Orders," in *Executive Policymaking: The Role of the OMB in the Presidency* (Brookings, 2020) (providing detail on how the EO process developed and the purpose it serves).

32. See President Barack Obama's White House, Office of Management and Budget, "The Mission and Structure of the Office of Management and Budget," https://obamawhitehouse.archives.gov/omb/organization_mission/.

33. Executive Order No. 11050, 59 Fed. Reg. 7629 (Feb. 16, 1994). See, also, Andrew Rudalevige, "The Contemporary Presidency: Executive Orders and Presidential Unilateralism," *Presidential Studies Quarterly* 42, no. 1 (March 2012), pp. 138–60 (providing a historical perspective on the use of EOs).

34. See OMB Circular No. A-19 (Revised September 20, 1979).

35. Ibid.

36. Ibid.

37. Ibid.

38. See President Barack Obama's White House, Office of Management and Budget, "The Mission and Structure of the Office of Management and Budget," https://obamawhitehouse.archives.gov/omb/organization_mission/.

39. Executive Order No. 12866, 58 Fed. Reg. 51735 (October 4, 1993).

40. Executive Order No. 13771, 82 Fed. Reg. 9339 (February 3, 2017).
41. Executive Order No. 13777, 82 Fed. Reg. 12285 (March 1, 2017).
42. See, for example, Andrew Rudalevige, *The New Imperial Presidency: Renewing Presidential Power after Watergate* (University of Michigan Press, 2005).
43. See President George W. Bush White House, Office of Management and Budget, "Assessing Program Performance," https://georgewbush-whitehouse.archives.gov/omb/performance/.
44. See President Barack Obama White House, Office of Management and Budget, "Evidence and Evaluation," https://obamawhitehouse.archives.gov/omb/evidence.
45. See Pasachoff, supra note 18 (discussing the RMOs' ability to influence agencies' policy choice through management initiatives).
46. U.S. Const. Art. I, § 9, cl. 7.
47. Prior to 2012, the government shut down a total of thirty-three days (the longest of which was twenty-one days in 1995–1996). Since then, the government has shut down three times for a total of fifty-four days (the longest of which was thirty-five days that ended in January of 2019).
48. Executive Office of the President, Office of Management and Budget, Circular A-11, Preparation, Submission, and Execution of the Budget, Section 124.2.
49. Ibid.
50. Ibid.
51. Ibid.
52. Ibid. To work during a lapse in appropriations, agency personnel or an agency program is viewed as "excepted" from the Antideficiency Act and otherwise legally authorized to perform during that lapse.
53. Ibid.
54. See, for example, Sylvia M. Burwell, Director, Executive Office of the President, Office of Management and Budget, Memorandum M-13-22 for the Heads of Executive Departments and Agencies, "Planning for Agency Operations during a Potential Lapse in Appropriations," (September 17, 2013); and Mick Mulvaney, Director, Executive Office of the President, Office of Management and Budget, Memorandum M-18-05 for the Heads of Executive Departments and Agencies, "Planning for Agency Operations during a Potential Lapse in Appropriations," (January 19, 2018).
55. See, for example, Charles S. Clark, "OMB's Shutdown Improvising Draws Fire from Budget and Legal Experts," *Government Executive*, January 15, 2019, www.govexec.com/management/2019/01/ombs-shutdown-improvising-draws-fire-budget-and-legal-experts/154161/ (quoting former OMB official stating "OMB has pretty broad discretion in deeming certain people and certain activities essential").
56. See Memo for the Heads of Executive Departments and Agencies, "Principles for Regulation and Oversight of Emerging Technology" (March 11, 2011).
57. See Memo for Heads of Food and Drug Administration, Environmental Protection Agency, and Department of Agriculture, "Modernizing the Regulatory System for Biotechnology Products" (July 2, 2015).
58. See Robbie Barbero, James Kim, Ted Boling, and Julia Doherty, "Increasing the Transparency, Coordination, and Predictability of the Biotechnology Regulatory System," President Barack Obama White House Blog, January 4, 2017, https://obamawhitehouse.archives.gov/blog/2017/01/04/increasing-trans

parency-coordination-and-predictability-biotechnology-regulatory (providing a description of these implementation efforts).

59. Ibid.

60. See Susan E. Dudley, "Trump's Regulatory Czar Signals Readiness to Reign in Independent Agencies," *Forbes,* April 24, 2018, 8:20 AM (stating "while legal advisors to presidents from Ronald Reagan to Barack Obama have concluded that presidents have the constitutional authority to extend analytical and executive oversight requirements to independent agencies' regulations, presidents have declined to do so"), www.forbes.com/sites/susandudley/2018/04/24/trumps-regulatory-czar-signals-readiness-to-rein-in-independent-agencies/#3bb96c399f9c.

61. See Memorandum of Agreement, The Department of the Treasury and the Office of Management and Budget, Review of Tax Regulations under EO 12866 (April 11, 2018).

62. See, also, Executive Office of the President, Office of Management and Budget, *Fiscal Year 2020 Budget* (2019) (highlighting OMB's responsibility to review tax regulations as a new responsibility in its budget request to Congress).

63. See, for example, Executive Office of the President, Office of Information and Regulatory Affairs, Office of Management and Budget, "Spring 2019 Unified Agenda of Regulatory and Deregulatory Actions," www.reginfo.gov/public/do/eAgendaMain.

64. Executive Order No. 13771, 82 Fed. Reg. 9339 (Feb. 3, 2017), Section 3(c).

65. See Dominic J. Mancini, Acting Administrator, Office of Information and Regulatory Affairs, Executive Office of the President, Office of Management and Budget, Memorandum M-17-21, Guidance Implementing Executive Order 13771 (April 5, 2017).

66. See Executive Office of the President, Office of Management and Budget, *Fiscal Year 2020 Budget* (2019) (highlighting as a new responsibility OMB's charge to implement EO 13771 and EO 13777 and describing OMB as "key to process for determining regulatory cost allowances for each Federal agency"). See Potter, Central Clearance of Regulations, chapter 5 (providing a thorough analysis on OIRA's responsibilities and the growth of tasks delegated to it, from President Bush's EO giving OIRA new authority to review "significant" guidance documents issued by agencies to OIRA's responsibilities to monitor the implementation of President Trump's "1 in 2 out" EO).

67. See, for example, Executive Office of the President, Office of Management and Budget, *Fiscal Year 2020 Budget* (2019) (noting "OMB's responsibilities have increased with changes in administration priorities and policies as well as new legislative direction from Congress").

68. Pub. L. No. 113-101, 128 Stat. 1146.

69. Ibid.

70. National Defense Authorization Act for Fiscal Year 2015, Pub. L. No. 113-291, 128 Stat. 3292, Sec. 831, Title VIII, Subtitle D (2014).

71. 40 U.S.C. § 11314.

72. 44 U.S.C. § 3602.

73. See, for example, Shaun Donovan, Director, Executive Office of the President, Office of Management and Budget, Memorandum 15-14, Management and Oversight of Federal Information Technology (June 10, 2015).

74. See National Defense Authorization Act for Fiscal Year 2015, Pub. L. No. 113-291, 128 Stat. 3292, Sec. 831, Title VIII, Subtitle D (2014). This au-

thority was subsequently extended in the FITARA Enhancement Act of 2017. Pub. L. No. 115-88, 131, Stat. 1278.

75. See, for example, Executive Office of the President, Fiscal Year 2018 Congressional Budget Submission at ITOR-3.

76. Ibid.

77. Ibid.

78. Ibid.

79. USDS Fall 2017 Report to Congress, www.usds.gov/report-to-congress/2017/fall/.

80. Executive Office of the President, Fiscal Year 2021 Congressional Budget Submission at ITOR-6.

81. Executive Office of the President, Fiscal Year 2020 Congressional Budget Submission at ITOR-7.

82. Government Performance Results Act Modernization Act, Pub. L. 103-63.

83. See General Services Administration and the Office of Management and Budget, "Performance Framework," www.performance.gov/about/CAP_about.html.

84. See, for example, General Services Administration and the Office of Management and Budget, "President's Management Agenda," www.performance.gov/PMA/PMA.html.

85. See Executive Office of the President, Fiscal Year 2021 Congressional Budget Submission.

86. Ibid.

87. Ibid.

88. See Performance Improvement Council, "Our Mission," www.pic.gov/what-we-do/mission/ (which describes the mission and role of PIC).

89. Pub. L. No. 114-94.

90. Pub. L. No. 115-435.

91. Pub. L. No. 112-96, 126 Stat. 156 (codified at 47 U.S.C. § 1424).

92. See Federal Permitting Improvement Steering Council (FPISC) Agencies (Updated October 6, 2017), www.permits.performance.gov/about/federal-permitting-improvement-steering-council-fpisc-agencies.

93. Ibid.

94. See supra note 90. OMB's ongoing implementation efforts are seen in a variety of sources, including the Federal Data Strategy website, https://strategy.data.gov/.

95. See Executive Office of the President, Fiscal Year 2020 Congressional Budget Submission at OMB-9 and Executive Office of the President, Fiscal Year 2021 Congressional Budget Submission at OMB-11 (describing OMB's Data-Driven Innovation Fund).

96. See supra note 91 at Section 6204(b).

97. See Executive Office of the President, Fiscal Year 2020 Congressional Budget Submission at OMB-3. OMB made the same request for FY 2021. See Executive Office of the President, Fiscal Year 2021 Congressional Budget Submission at OMB-6.

98. Ibid.

99. For example, The Solyndra Failure, Committee on Energy and Commerce, U.S. House of Representatives, 112th Congress, August 2, 2012 (providing a summary of the House Committee's investigation into the Department of Energy's and OMB's work to review a loan application from the company Solyndra and the subsequent management of that loan guarantee in accordance

with the Energy Policy Act of 2005). See also House Committee on Oversight and Reform, 114th Congress Oversight Plan, https://oversight.house.gov/oversight-plan (providing the 114th U.S. House of Representative's Committee on Oversight and Reform's plan for oversight of the executive branch, which highlights examining compliance of OMB's directives in the area of cybersecurity and federal real property disposal).

100. See also Executive Office of the President, Fiscal Year 2020 Congressional Budget Submission at OMB-3 (stating "OMB's budget and staff have decreased" in recent years), and Executive Office of the President, Fiscal Year 2021 Congressional Budget Submission at OMB-3 (stating "OMB's current FTE levels are significantly less than they were just ten years ago, having dropped by more than 50 FTE—a reduction of approximately 10 percent—since FY 2010").

101. See U.S. Senate, Committee on Homeland Security and Governmental Affairs, Policy and Supporting Positions, 114th Congress, 2d Session, S.Prt. 114-26 (December 1, 2016).

102. Other federal agencies and offices with "political appointee" leadership may serve as an example of this model. For instance, an assistant attorney general is nominated by the president and confirmed by the Senate to be in charge of the U.S. Department of Justice's Office of Legal Counsel. In periods of transition between such appointments, a career deputy assistant attorney general has served as head of that office, including issuing OLC opinions. See, for example, Daniel L. Koffsky, deputy assistant attorney general, Office of Legal Counsel, "Application of the Anti-Nepotism Statute to a Presidential Appointment in the White House Office," in Opinions of the Office of Legal Counsel 41, January 20, 2017 (issuing opinion on the first day of a new administration, January 20, 2017, signed by a career deputy assistant attorney general).

103. See, for example, Dickinson, supra note 5.

104. See, for example, Partnership for Public Service, Best Places to Work, https://bestplacestowork.org/rankings/detail/BO00. OMB scored in the lowest quartile of small agencies in 2013, a year of significant transition in leadership, including an acting director and a confirmation of a new director, and a year in which the government shut down for sixteen days.

105. Ibid. (noting OMB continues to score below the median in employees' view of their work-life balance).

106. See A–Z Index of U.S. Government Departments and Agencies, www.usa.gov/federal-agencies.

107. See Martha Coven, "President and Presidency: White House and OMB Staff," in *Executive Policymaking: The Role of the OMB in the Presidency* (Brookings, 2020) (providing a more thorough discussion of the relationship between the White House and OMB).

108. See President Barack Obama's White House, Office of Management and Budget, "The Mission and Structure of the Office of Management and Budget," https://obamawhitehouse.archives.gov/omb/organization_mission/.

109. See Executive Office of the President, Office of Management and Budget, *Fiscal Year 2020 Budget* (2019) (making a request to Congress of an increase of $600,000 to OMB's budget).

110. See, for example, James P. Pfiffner, "OMB: Professionalization, Politicization, and the Presidency," in *Executive Leadership in Anglo-American Systems*, edited by Colin Campbell and Margaret J. Wyszomirski (University of Pittsburgh Press, 1991), pp. 195–218 (examining OMB's development).

111. See, for example, Andrew Feldman, *Strengthening Results-Focused Government: Strategies to Build on Bipartisan Progress in Evidence-Based*

Policy (Brookings, January 2017) (offering a proposal for government reform that highlights OMB's potential involvement).

112. See, for example, Government Accountability Office, "OMB Should Improve Guidelines and Working-Group Efforts to Support Agencies' Implementation of the Fraud Reduction and Data Analytics Act," December 4, 2018, www.gao.gov/products/GAO-19-34 (reviewing OMB's management efforts to reduce fraud in government programs).

113. See, for example, Dickinson, supra note 5 (examining OMB practices during the Clinton, Bush, Obama, and Trump Administrations).

TEN

Guarding the Emperor's New Clothes

OMB, the Presidency, and the "Problem" of Neutral Competence in the Era of Trump

MATTHEW J. DICKINSON

How does the Office of Management and Budget (OMB) serve a president's partisan goals without sacrificing its commitment to an ethos of neutral competence? That question received new scrutiny in light of revelations regarding the OMB's role in President Donald Trump's decision in June 2019 to withhold nearly $400 million appropriated in foreign aid to Ukraine. According to critics, Trump withheld the money, with the OMB's administrative assistance, to pressure that country's government to investigate the business dealings of the son of former Vice President Joe Biden, a key Trump rival in the 2020 presidential election. Trump's actions led the Democrat-controlled House to impeach him on charges of abuse of power and obstruction of Congress.[1] He was subsequently acquitted on both charges by the Republican majority in the Senate.[2]

The OMB's role in the Ukraine affair is not the first time the tension inherent in the agency's mission has been scrutinized. In a seminal 1975 article, Hugh Heclo made the most cogent defense of what he called neutral competence, and openly questioned whether OMB's longstanding commitment to this ethos was at risk.[3] By neutral competence, Heclo meant the OMB's ability to give "one's cooperation and best independent judgment of the issues to partisan bosses—and of being sufficiently uncommitted to be able to do so for a succession of partisan leaders."[4] That ethos, Heclo argued, depends on nurturing virtues—expertise, continuity, impartiality, and institutional memory—that have deep roots in the agency's prior existence as the Bureau of the Budget. "By giving a voice to those with a vested interest in the continuing good faith and credit of the government's own internal operations," Heclo wrote, neutral competence enabled the Bureau of the Budget (BOB) to serve not just presidents but the presidency as well.

Citing several contemporary developments, including the layering of additional political appointees and a more president-focused orientation, Heclo warned that the OMB was in danger of becoming identified as an overtly partisan institution. That would undercut the agency's reputation for neutral competence and its ability to speak authoritatively for the presidency as an institution without regard for partisan preferences.

Heclo traced the roots of the agency's growing politicization to changes emanating from President Nixon's 1970 reorganization of the BOB into the OMB. Because he was writing only five years after Nixon's actions, however, Heclo's assessment was necessarily preliminary, subject to further study of subsequent developments. Today, more than four decades later, and with the OMB at the center of an impeachment scandal, it seems appropriate to seek a more definitive answer. This chapter takes on that task, starting with the OMB's role in Trump's decision to withhold foreign aid.

According to the impeachment investigation, in July 2019, the OMB, responding to Trump's request, initially delayed releasing foreign assistance appropriated by Congress to Ukraine. Subsequently, the OMB extended that hold eight more times before the money was finally released in September. Defense department officials reportedly grew concerned that the appropriated money might not be spent by the end of the 2019 fiscal year, thus possibly violating the 1974 Impoundment Control Act (ICA), which placed restrictions on presidents' ability to withhold appropriated funds without Congress's approval.[5] Mark Sandy, a career OMB official, testified during impeachment hearings that two OMB careerists resigned in part due to concerns regarding the decision to withhold the aid, while other careerists deemed the withholding highly unusual. However, in a memorandum submitted to the Government Accountability Office (GAO), the OMB general counsel Mark R. Paoletta, a political appointee, defended withholding aid as a temporary move designed to give the OMB time to study whether the spending complied with U.S. policy.[6] That view was contested by the GAO, which ruled in January 2020 that the decision to withhold the aid was done to advance Trump's political agenda and thus violated the ICA.[7] The OMB political leadership pushed back against the GAO ruling, with Acting Director Russell Vought tweeting that "the adm[inistration] complied with the law at every step."[8]

At first glance, the controversy regarding the OMB's role in the actions leading to Trump's impeachment may appear to confirm Heclo's fears. Certainly, Trump, who ran successfully for president on a platform of "draining" the Washington, D.C., "swamp," and who spent his first three years breaking norms of presidential behavior, has left himself vulnerable to charges that he possesses little appreciation for the benefits of protecting the OMB's reputation as an independent guardian of the presidency. Consider, for example, his decision, announced by tweet on December 14, 2018, to appoint his OMB director Mick Mulvaney the "acting" White House chief of staff—but without relinquishing his director's hat.[9] Symbolically, at least, Mulvaney's twin roles suggest that Trump saw the two positions as interchangeable extensions of his personal partisan staff.[10]

However, the question regarding whether withholding aid to Ukraine violated the ICA, as the GAO contends, is not settled.[11] And Mulvaney's dual appointments may say more about Trump's idiosyncrasies, particularly his penchant for filling slots on an "acting" basis, than it does about his views regarding the relative roles of the OMB and White House staff. On the other hand, Mulvaney is now the fourth OMB director to become chief of staff (although the first to hold the two positions simultaneously), and all four instances occurred during the four most recent presidencies. This suggests there may be more fundamental factors driving Mulvaney's White House appointment than one president's personal quirks.[12]

Still, it is risky to generalize about the OMB based on the directors' role alone[13] to say nothing of a relatively unprecedented impeachment process. Neither tells us much about the role of careerists below the political layers and their commitment to neutral competence. Accordingly, this chapter digs deeper and across more years, drawing on interviews with nearly three dozen former and current OMB employees, including both careerists and political appointees as well as several former OMB directors.[14] Although not a statistically representative sample of OMB employees, collectively their work experience encompasses more than six decades of OMB history; the oldest started in the BOB under Eisenhower, and the youngest served during Obama's presidency.[15] They are well positioned, therefore, to assess Heclo's question, particularly for the period under focus here: from Nixon's 1970 reorganization through the first three years of Trump's presidency.

Have Heclo's fears been realized? Has the OMB become politicized at the expense of its commitment to neutral competence? If so, why? And should that cause concern?[16] Despite serving under different presidents and in different positions, respondents of all ranks voice almost universal agreement that the OMB should, and largely does, embody Heclo's ideal. Careerists and their immediate political bosses say they recognize what Heclo means by neutral competence, understand its importance, and in their time at the OMB worked assiduously to preserve it as the agency's primary operating principle. As one aide exclaimed in a remark that neatly summarized the prevailing sentiment of those interviewed: "I absolutely believe in neutral competence!"

Based on these interviews, it appears the agency's commitment to neutral competence, at least among careerists, remains strong, although this is not a universal sentiment. This ethos includes, when necessary, voicing opposition to the actions of political superiors. But this relative consensus regarding the continuing relevance of neutral competence as an operating ethos masks differences regarding the form in which that ethos has been sustained. The OMB's core skills, the interviews suggest, have shifted during the decades in response to presidents' changing political and administrative needs.[17] Stated perhaps too bluntly, some former OMB officials—but not all—believe the agency has become more capable of measuring whether government agencies are achieving the presidents' objectives but less able to explain how to do so.

In principle at least, shifting skill sets are consistent with Heclo's claim that neutral competence "envisions a continuous, uncommitted facility at the disposal of, and for the support of, *political leadership*" [emphasis added].[18] In practice, however, interviewees disagree regarding the relative merits of these changes and what, if anything, they say about the agency's commitment to Heclo's ideal. The differences are most evident when comparing the responses of those who worked in the OMB's managerial side, particularly those with experience predating the 1970 reorganization and the examiners specializing in program analysis from a budgetary perspective. Those in the managerial side decry what they see as the decline in the OMB's understanding of how government agencies work. The budget people, in contrast, applaud the OMB's increased capacity to measure what agencies accomplish and believe there has been little loss of managerial expertise.

Despite these differences, no one interviewed goes so far as to say the OMB has become too politicized. In their collective view, the shift in competencies—if in fact one sees a shift—does not entail a greater embrace of partisanship, nor a loss of neutral competence. By this measure, Heclo's fears have not been realized. However, his article remains an important warning flag. The perception of a shift in OMB's core competency across the decades highlights a critical point discussed by Heclo: "Lacking any outside clientele in Congress or interest groups, OMB can resist only through inactivity; its choice is to be of use to the President of the day or to atrophy."[19] To date, OMB has preferred to be of use. But that choice can, as Heclo foresaw, exact a price. If, as many of the interviews suggest, the OMB has shifted competencies to better assist presidents in exercising top-down managerial control, it is perhaps inevitable that outsiders will increasingly view it as a partisan presidential tool even if agency employees do not.

The rest of the chapter builds on these initial thoughts. The claims are necessarily preliminary, best seen as working hypotheses subject to additional study rather than conclusive results. Moreover, rather than a comprehensive history, the chapter focuses, instead, on a few major OMB organizational change points to illustrate the broader themes. These include Nixon's 1970 reorganization; the subsequent transformation, from a bottom-up to top-down approach, of the agency's budgeting functions; and an overview of developments on the management side, focusing in particular on the Clinton-era reintegration of the OMB's budgeting and management functions and Bush 43's development of agency performance measures. The concluding section returns to the question with which the chapter began: At what point does responsiveness to a president's immediate needs threaten OMB's commitment to neutral competence? Almost three years into Trump's presidency, and after a searing impeachment battle, it is a question whose answer seems more significant than ever.

CREATING THE OMB: RESPONSIVE OR NEUTRAL COMPETENCE?

In 1970, pursuant to reorganization authority granted him by Congress, President Nixon issued Reorganization Plan 2, transforming the BOB into OMB and, simultaneously, creating the White House Domestic Policy Council.[20] Nixon's plan was, in part, an effort to reinvigorate the agency's management functions, which critics argue had historically taken a back seat to the BOB's budgetary role. As Nixon explained in his reorganization statement, "The Domestic Council will be primarily concerned with what we do; the Office of Management and Budget will be primarily concerned with how we do it, and how well we do it."[21] In an era of divided government, growing policy complexity, rising budget deficits, and an increasingly powerful administrative state, Nixon evidently saw the OMB's ability to influence how government worked—and how well—as an increasingly important tool to achieve his policy objectives.

Nixon's reorganization, however, attracted criticism, and not just from political opponents. In his widely cited article written five years after the OMB was established, Heclo warned that the agency's managerial functions had not been strengthened, and in fact were in disarray. More important, he wrote that aspects of Nixon's reorganization, and its immediate aftermath, threatened the OMB's longstanding commitment to neutral competence.[22] As evidence, he cited several indicators of the OMB's politicization. These include Nixon's decision to elevate the OMB director to senior status in the White House staff and give him a West Wing office—a move that to some degree anticipates presidents' recent pattern of appointing OMB directors as chief of staff. Heclo also criticized the addition of a new layer of political appointees in the form of program associate directors. These positions, he argued, insulated the president and OMB political leadership from direct interaction with branch chiefs and examiners who possess the institutional memory regarding specific programs and agencies.

In addition, Heclo worried about the consequences of what he saw as a shift by OMB from "wholesaling" advice to the president toward "retailing" advice directly to outsiders, including Congress and the public, on the president's behalf. "The result," Heclo wrote, "was to identify OMB more as a member of the President's own political family and less as a broker supplying an independent analytic service to every

President."[23] In apparent confirmation of this perception, the Democrat-controlled Congress voted in 1973 to require Senate confirmation for OMB directors and their deputies.

BUDGETING: FROM BOTTOM-UP TO TOP-DOWN

Nixon's heavy-handed attempt to wrest greater control over government spending via impoundment contributed to this backlash and, in key respects, anticipates the controversy generated by Trump's withholding of Ukraine aid. Significantly, given its subsequent decline in prominence, the OMB's management wing opposed Nixon's impoundment strategy; as one former managerial aide recalled, he warned the Nixon White House against using impoundment to eliminate funding for the Office of Economic Opportunity, arguing instead that it was better to rely on existing reorganizational authority:

> Management strongly opposed the Nixon approach to closing down the anti-poverty agency . . . the agency would have gone out of existence under this reorganization but Nixon got impatient with all that sort of thing and so they—Paul O'Neill and the White House staff, unbeknownst to me—worked out a plan to kill it by simply impounding the funds. Starving it. I learned about it and I flew into [John] Ehrlichman's office and objected, I said 'this will infuriate the Congress, it'll almost certainly result in backlash from the Congress, and it's an overreach of presidential power and I think it's likely to result in Congressional restrictions.

As it turned out, the aide's warning proved prescient. In 1974, the Democrat majority passed the Congressional Budget and Impoundment act, revamping the budget process as well as creating two new congressional budget committees, limiting the president's impoundment power and creating the Congressional Budget Office (CBO) to serve as a counterpart to, and a check on, the OMB. In hindsight, the CBO's creation may have had a salutary impact on the OMB's budgetary role, not least because, as one staffer noted, it made the OMB's budget calculations "more honest," or, as another suggested, "less dishonest." But it also added to the perception that, on budget matters, the OMB was now speaking primarily for the president. As one aide told us: "The thing about the Congressional Budget Act is it not only made the Congress stronger in budgeting, with CBO and the Budget Committees, it made OMB and the Executive Office of the President stronger—because you now have these two centralized groups working with one another on the budget. So it's an interesting paradox."

In the following years, the factors driving Nixon's reorganization—and Heclo's reaction to it—grew more prominent. As measured by government outlays and pages in the *Federal Register* listed in figure 10-1, the scope of government activities expanded and policies became more complex even as the number of federal employees barely increased. That meant, in effect, that presidents were tasked with doing more with less.

FIGURE 10-1. **Relative Rate of Growth in Federal Outlays, Executive Branch Civilian Employment, and Number of Pages in the** *Federal Register,* **1940–2018 (Employment Figures through 2014)**

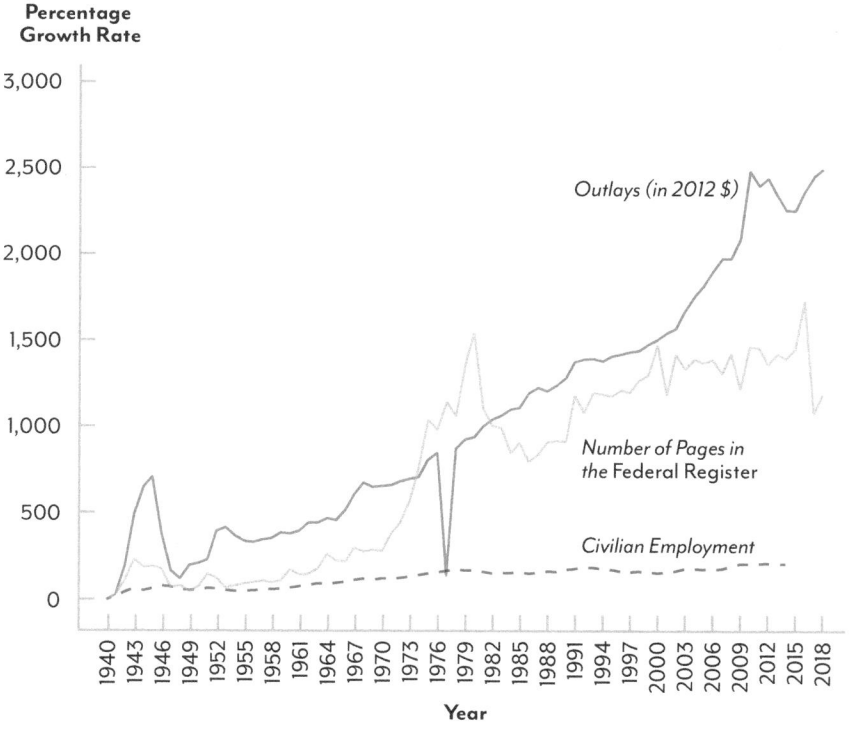

Sources: U.S. Office of Personnel Management, *Historical Federal Workforce Tables: Executive Branch Civilian Employment,* www.opm.gov; Office of Management & Budget, *Historical Tables: 1.3,* www.whitehouse.gov/omb/historical-tables/; government information, *Federal Register,* www.govinfo.gov/app/collection/fr.

Other developments—most notably party sorting, which created two ideologically polarized and electorally evenly-matched parties in Congress, as shown in figure 10-2, against the recurring backdrop of divided government—increased the likelihood of legislative gridlock and budgetary brinkmanship. As a result, presidents increasingly looked to the OMB for the tools to control what government did in their name.

The rise of persistent, large budget deficits, dating at least from Congress's 1981 enactment of Reagan's package of tax and spending cuts, accentuated this tendency. With Democrats and Republicans in Congress disagreeing on how to address structural deficits, presidents sought the means to exercise greater top-down control over aggregate spending. In an important way, as a former aide told us, structural budget deficits increased the OMB's leverage in the budgeting process:

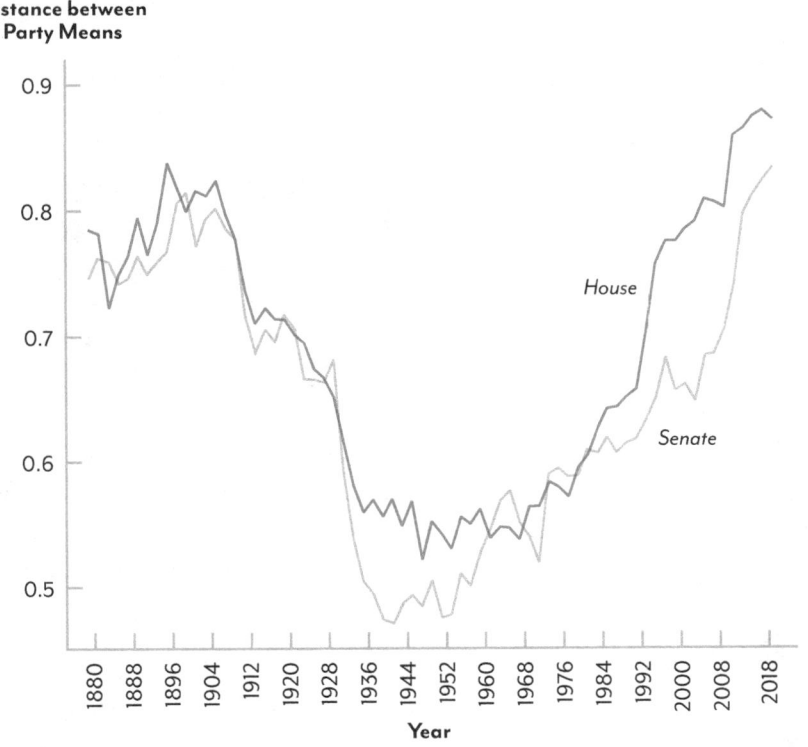

FIGURE 10-2. Party Polarization in Congress Based on DW-NOMINATE First Dimension Scores (1879–2018)

Source: Jeff Lewis, "Polarization in Congress," August 14, 2019, https://www.voteview.com/articles/party_polarization.

So in that sense OMB's always had a major role because it puts the budget together. . . . When we're in the situation we're in now, with such a huge deficit that we're trying to address, and they put restrictions on the agencies about what they can come in with, with their budgets, I think it gives OMB—this is sort of minutiae—it gives us more of a hammer, to say to the agencies, "no, you really can't do that." There's a lot less leeway for new ideas to come in that are going to cost money. And if they do come in with something like that, there's more leverage for us to be able to, at OMB, to say, "if you want to do that, and if you stick by the president's basic guidelines, you're going to have to come up with some other way to save money, so that it's at least neutral or comes in under your targets."

This effort to exercise top-down budgetary control manifested in several important ways. To begin with, the OMB's budgetary role expanded to encompass tracking budget requests from inception in the departments through the end of the congressional budget process. As one aide recalls:

It probably started with the passage of the Congressional Budget Act, which centralized authority for the budget process in the congressional leadership and in the Budget Committees, and as a natural consequence began to centralize—had the same effect on the executive branch, essentially, it began to move a lot of responsibilities for budgeting out of the agencies in the executive branch and into the executive office. I think that perhaps the first real strong move that was made in that direction was during the Reagan years, when OMB very suddenly began to track appropriations bills in great detail. Before those years, typically the Bureau of the Budget didn't . . . it did some of this, but it was a rather stark and dramatic change. And appropriations bills and actually other legislation were tracked at every single stage of the process and OMB began to analyze each stage and send up letters and position statements at each stage of the process to begin to influence the congressional agenda.

Some former aides, however, suggest the emphasis on top-down budgeting may have come at a substantive cost in OMB competence, not least because presidents sought to demonstrate their cost-cutting bona fides by holding down budget increases for the OMB even as it took on new responsibilities. As one aide told us:

It's impossible to understand OMB's history, I think, without understanding the reluctance of directors to grow OMB's budget in response to new missions. Because I think we've gotten every level of the organization to agree that this information explosion without any central data management capability is a problem. But the idea of standing up a new organization within OMB to manage that problem is something there's little receptivity to, for budgetary reasons.

Moreover, some of those interviewed suggest that by emphasizing the use of top-down aggregate spending controls to achieve budget targets, examiners had less incentive to understand the substance of what departments and agencies do. Even those who disagree that top-down budgeting came at the expense of managerial competence do acknowledge that, with budgets capped, examiners spent less time in the field. As one aide recalls, prior to the reorganization:

There was time for the budget people to get out in the field. And they had an opportunity to understand programs better from the perspective of their clients, that is the public, the local governments, and so on. The budget people today . . . they really don't have the opportunities to spend the time they used to have in thoroughly understanding, in seeing and watching, what's going on in the departments at various levels, not just at the top level.

A second former OMB aide concurs:

Over the years—I started in the Ford administration—over the years, the amount of time the examiners are spending in the agencies has dwindled, it's very small now, from my perspective anyway. . . . It's dwindled a lot, and part of it is because of the constant demands in today's internet/Twitter/what have you interchange that people want information, they want it right now, and it's difficult sometimes for the examiners to get away for the day to the agencies, let alone for a week or three days. And there are many more demands from the White House . . . And each year I could see that we were getting fewer and fewer dollars to be able to use for staff to go out in the field. And I think that's a bit of an effect on staff understanding.

The effort to estimate spending and revenue in the out years, as mandated by the 1974 congressional budget act as amended, contributed to the complexity and uncertainty of the budget process, as well as its politically contentious nature. As a former budget examiner noted:

> Projections are equally difficult for everybody. There was a study—people argued several years back whether OMB or CBO was doing a better job in its budget estimates, so someone actually did a study of both of their projections over the past several years. And the results were exactly as you would suspect. First, both agencies were wrong every year. [Laughter] Secondly, the error increased in the out-years. And third, if you averaged out their projections for the several years, they both came to about the same thing, averaged over the years. I mean, very good people in both agencies try very hard to project trillion-dollar budgets over ten years, affecting millions of people and billions of decisions—that isn't easy to do. No matter how well you do it, you're likely to be off by more or less some degree.

New process requirements imposed by Congress, such as the budget restrictions mandated by the 1990 Budget Enforcement act and enforced by the threat of sequestration, which imposed cuts if spending exceeded budget caps, also contributed to top-down budgeting while complicating forecasting. As one aide recalls, this encouraged the perception that OMB was pushing a partisan agenda on behalf of the president:

> When the Budget Enforcement Act was first debated and turned into law, way back in the 1980s . . . there was a big argument and debate about who was going to be the official scorekeeper of the deficit targets and legislation, and in the context of those negotiations—it may have been Darman, and Barry Anderson, then the assistant director—OMB was given the responsibility. In retrospect I think that was a mistake, because it put us right in the middle of the kind of thing that [redacted] is talking about, where Congress has a legislative agenda and they want to push that agenda and they don't want to be told they can't have the bill they want because OMB says it's horse-thus-and-thus. Now if you talk to the member of Congress who has that view, he will tell you that OMB is being "political." He will tell you that they're politicizing numbers.

Technological innovations, beginning with computers, followed by email and the Internet, also impacted the way OMB examiners did their job, by expanding their ability to both track budget requests from inception to completion and to estimate the impact of budget changes on various targets. One aide reacted to the rapid flow of information produced by new technology this way:

> We're creating a demand for enterprise-wide management of the federal government that would not have been reasonable previously. But when the Obama administration came in, and I know exactly one of the points they were saying this, they wanted with the Recovery Act to say, how is this—you need to track how this is going to be implemented, spent, where all of the money is going, who everybody [is that] gets it, what is happening, and you need to answer this question across the entire federal government. Right? And I do think that impact of technology—and I think this generation feels that they should probably be able to expect it. I think the next generation is going to find it totally unacceptable for that not to be the case.

The additional capability, however, did not lessen the difficulty of budgeting; indeed, it may have complicated the process. For example:

> I came to OMB—I was hired because I was presumed to have some technical competence, which shows you how busted the hiring process was [laughter]—in 1970, when we were automating the budget process. Later on we did a rolling budget system, in 1980. Clearly the mechanics of production have changed. But the net effect of that, as a technological sociologist, is—it's sort of like word processing, it isn't any easier to produce a document, you just do more iterations. Certainly . . . the mechanics of the process have been automated, which doesn't make it easier.

But the ease of internal communication brought by email and various devices did bring advantages. It allowed for more interaction, at the virtual level, between careerists and their superiors. As one analyst explained:

> Because we had email, and email in the Clinton administration, which tended to be a very collaborative group to begin with—these email chains would go on and on and on, and you'd have the deputy director or the deputy director for management . . . on the same chain with the youngest examiners, and you'd have the policy councils chiming in, and then it would spin out and go to an agency. And so you had

these sorts of brainstorming sessions going on in email, which gave everybody context for what are people thinking about, so you could understand, as an examiner, how to plug in and be relevant to the process. It gave everybody information, and then it became kind of a meritocracy—that if you had a really smart examiner, who's watching all this, who can synthesize it, and say, "oh, I know what to do with it," they could come back with proposals and ideas and be basically brought in to the circle.

Did the rise of top-down budgeting, and the growing importance of the budget more generally, increase the pressure to produce politically skewed budget numbers? Aides say this is not the case. As a former OMB director put it, "Their first loyalty is to doing a damned good job on the budget. Their first dedication is to making sure they are *credible* [emphasis added by author]."

However, former aides acknowledge that the greater ability to manipulate budget numbers afforded by technology makes it easier to respond to politicians' queries about the implication of changing budget assumptions. One aide put it this way:

Forecasting the economy is no precise science, as we learn all the time, but there's a lot of analytical information out there, and they're the ones who provide the basic framework for decision-making. Now, they can go to political people, and the political people can say, "you haven't quite given us all the options: we need one or two more options. Tell us what this would be." And that's what the career staff is there for. Not to gin up false assumptions but simply to provide the facts that support the assumptions.

A former director summarized: "It *is* about the budget, but the key to budgeting isn't numbers so much as *priorities* [emphasis added by author]." Presidents—not the OMB—set the priorities and related assumptions. But they increasingly expect the OMB to assist in enforcing them.

MANAGEMENT: FROM OUTSIDE-IN TO INSIDE-OUT

Despite Nixon's attempt to place the OMB's managerial functions on par with budgeting, the OMB aides interviewed generally agree this was unsuccessful. A major reason the effort failed, according to former staffers, is that in response to the movement toward top-down program-based budgeting and centralized control, it made less sense to think of management issues outside of the budget process. The risk, however, is that in trying to integrate the two, management becomes less of a priority, except as viewed through a budgetary lens, and managerial competence erodes. In the interviews, those with managerial experience believe this is precisely what occurred. The budget examiners, not surprisingly, strongly disagree.

The former management-based careerists point out that as budgeting expanded into a year-long process, from inception in the agencies through tracking in Congress, "downtime," formerly spent on managerial issues, disappeared. As one aide recalled, "Management took place when we weren't doing the budget, but now you're *always* doing the budget."

In part, the disagreement between the budget and management sides centers on the role played by the OMB's statutory management offices, which provide government-wide administrative support for procurement, technological development, and financial matters. These include:

- The Office of Federal Procurement Policy, established in 1974 by the Office of Federal Procurement Policy Act (88 Stat. 796)

- The Office of Information and Regulatory Affairs, established by the Paperwork Reduction Act of 1980 (94 Stat. 2812, later recodified as the Paperwork Reduction Act of 1995, 109 Stat. 163)[24]

- The Office of Federal Financial Management, established by the Chief Financial Officers (CFO) Act of 1990 (104 Stat. 2838)

- The Office of Electronic Government, or the E-Gov Office, created by the E-Government Act of 2002 (116 Stat. 2899)

While acknowledging the importance of these statutory offices, some former staffers took pains to distinguish the management services the offices provide from the expertise wielded by the managerial arm of the BOB.

To begin with, rather than utilize cross-agency coordination to implement best management practices, the statutory offices instead tend to operate in isolation, creating what one aide described as a "stove-pipe effect":

> First of all, the creation of all the statutory offices that are essentially management-side functions, which I think reflect the complexity of the world—issues are hard, you need strong expertise—and I think these offices were an attempt to make OMB as a bureaucracy more responsive to the president. I'm not sure they've necessarily succeeded in that, in that one of the issues is that you've essentially created a political layer of management experts who come in from the outside. Their functions are statutorily defined, and somewhat rigid, and the effect has been over time that there's some stove piping at OMB . . . We've now created these functions that are very structured and there are very few people in OMB, or the agencies, who are empowered to figure out how to make it all work and fit together.

More important, according to former staffers, these statutory offices are not advising presidents on issues of bureaucratic design and operations—expertise presidents need when attempting to reorganize or create government agencies to take on new functions, or to achieve efficiencies. One aide recalled: "There was a time when OMB's reputation, in the White House particularly, rested upon their capacity to come up with these good ideas. I remember, for example, Nixon or Johnson might say, 'I want to submit a piece of organizational legislation.' I ended up designing the organization. It might get modified by the Congress or whatever, but my staff was expected to have that kind of competence."

According to several former aides, this type of managerial expertise has atrophied—a point driven home when discussing efforts to create the Department of Homeland Security and to reorganize the intelligence agencies in the aftermath of the 9/11 terrorist attacks.

> *Aide #1:* "Now that [reorganization expertise] is missing and I guess the most dramatic example of that was the absence of OMB organizational expertise in designing the Department of Homeland Security.
>
> *Aide #2:* Equally important the national intelligence reorganization, which five years later is still demonstrably not working, as we predicted.

Aide #3: At the risk of being too glib I would argue that in—certainly in the case of Homeland Security—it was the absence of any expertise in the room that designed.
Aide #1: I agree with that. That used to be in OMB.

A fourth aide summarized the loss of this particular type of managerial expertise:

I'd point out that when I was in OMB '71 to '76 I tried to list all the organization initiatives with which I was involved—sixteen of them. I did about 2 or 3 of these things a year: creating new agencies, abolishing some old agencies, including the old Atomic Energy Commission, creation of EPA, and so on. It was a very active agenda of initiatives relating to proposals for reorganization.

I was expected to assist the White House, the President, in advancing legislative proposals; I was expected to know of any significant reorganization changes going on in the departments and agencies; I was expected to know all of the initiatives going on in Congress, and to decide whether they needed to be opposed or supported by the administration. All of that is—it just seems to me it's just disappeared.

If these former staffers are correct, that stand-alone managerial role is increasingly subservient to the budgeting process. Put in terms of Nixon's objectives in the 1970 reorganization, the OMB has become less concerned with how government agencies do things and much more focused on how well they do things, as measured by whether they are achieving particular outcomes. One former OMB aide explains the difference this way:

What people talk about in OMB today really deals with what is to be done. What is the program? What is the program objective? Management is much more how you get there. How you influence policy. And when we had a workshop several years ago on the Bush management agenda, and we had representatives from nine of the departments. . . . They were also unanimous in saying that OMB no longer has expertise, leadership, and neither do we in the departments, in how to get there. How to get from where we are to attain these objectives, these policy objectives.

How much of this loss of managerial expertise is linked to the lapse of presidents' reorganization authority after the Reagan presidency remains a matter of contention among former aides. According to one view, "Without the authority, there was little need for an OMB staff dedicated to reorganization authority. But in reality every administration since has challenged OMB to come up with restructuring proposals which we did." Others disagree, arguing that the erosion in managerial competence predates the lapse in reorganization authority.

CLINTON, OMB 2000, AND RMOs

In 1994, in recognition of this shift in competencies, the OMB reorganized its former budget divisions into Resource Management Offices while eliminating the managerial division. The reorganization grew out of an internal study the OMB conducted called "OMB 2000."[25] The study was prompted in part by the Clinton administration's National Performance Review (NPR), an effort begun in 1993 and inspired by the reinventing government movement to make government more results-oriented and less costly. Rather than entrust oversight of the NPR to the OMB's managerial division, however, Clinton asked Vice President Al Gore to, in effect, run the effort out of the vice president's office, staffed by non-OMB employees. Reacting in part to the fear that Gore's team might issue recommendations that cut into the OMB's mission, the agency decided to proactively conduct its own internal study.

The multi-volume internal report highlighted a number of issues, but perhaps the most significant centered on the uncertainty raised by OMB employees regarding the agency's management functions. As the report summarized, "Interviewees OMB-wide state that unlike most of parts of OMB . . . the M-side does not have clearly defined missions and ongoing transactions. . . . Many believe that OMB has never effectively defined what 'management' means, and what OMB's role in improving the management of federal programs should be."[26] But there was very little consensus expressed in the report regarding how to rectify this issue, with the management and budget sides starkly divided.

Ultimately, the decision was made to merge the management division with the budget examining divisions to form the RMOs. As one aide explained, the rise of program-driven, as opposed to object-based, budgeting made the need for a separate management division increasingly obsolete:

I think that the effect of program budgeting on the institution has been somewhat underestimated and that the change is one of the major reasons why OMB has now integrated management and budget. The comprehensive program-based framework has basically obviated the logic of separate management staff, and if you go back and look at the Bureau of the Budget when it was transferred to the Executive Office, and Harold Smith inherited these 40 or 50-so people who were doing object-based budgeting, there really wasn't the staff in 1940 to do much else than object-based budgeting; the original Bureau of the Budget staff that was in Treasury had a pretty broad mandate but they just weren't staffed to do a lot. And Harold, I think, was the one who looking at those staff thought it made more sense to divide the functions and have a group that wasn't so narrowly based as those 40 or 50 original staff that came to the Bureau of the Budget, and think more strategically and long term. That may have made sense when budgeting was object-based but in the evolution of program-based budgeting it's taken OMB I think nearly 40 years to get to that point. We can't be precise about that, but that's the underlying rationale for the Clinton-era reorganization: there's one basic comprehensive review of agency budgets that addresses both budget and management. . . . They're not just talking about administrative processes, they're talking about what works and what doesn't work.

Another aide concurs:

When the OMB was reorganized during the Clinton Administration and the management functions—a lot of the management functions—were integrated into the RMOs, the perspective that the RMOs have taken toward management, is not one of hands-on interference, but more an analytical type judgment about how well agency management is working in the field. So in a sense I think that perspective is now the right perspective within OMB, at least I view it that way. When OMB looks at how programs are doing in the field, they look at—much the way they look at budgets—they're looking at it as an analytical task, not as a management task. . . . I think that's what's sort of happened in OMB, setting aside the work of the statutory offices. And so the perspective on management has changed. I'm not sure presidential perspectives have changed. Presidents, I think, from the very start, when they think of management, what they mean is, "when I say, 'bunny,' I want you to hop!" [Laughter] and I think that's still what they want. That's what they're after.

Today, almost half of the OMB's 400-plus employees work in five RMOs, each under the direction of politically-appointed program associate directors (PADs).[27] The RMOs are segmented into separate divisions headed by deputy associate directors,[28] and the divisions split further into branches directed by branch chiefs and composed mostly of program examiners who exercise primary oversight of government agencies.[29]

The RMO structure is now more than two decades old. Its survival testifies to its utility as a budgetary-driven tool through which presidents can influence the entire policy process, from origin through implementation.[30] One aide summarized the underlying logic bluntly: "Every management issue is really a budgetary issue." Another puts it this way: "There was little question in my mind . . . that to make a difference, you had to be part of the budget process. And so the expertise needed to execute programs needed to exist in the RMOs."

But other former staffers, particularly those from the OMB's former management division, point out that although the RMO structure turned budget examiners into program examiners, it did not necessarily provide them with management expertise. As one aide remarks:

> The contrast is quite stark, because in the current model, each of the examiners in their branch is responsible for doing that. But they don't have, one, any kind of expertise or training or any of that in what performance improvement means. . . . They don't have any cross-agency perspective at all. . . . Working with multiple different agencies on like problems [they] could do best practice sharing and would have some expertise they could share across the agencies and help. The core of the central office management capability is often exactly in its coordination capability and look across multiple perspectives to be able to share, but what we've done under the model we're operating now is we've put all of our capacity within the silos, so you don't get any of that perspective.

Not surprisingly, some former budget examiners take issue with this characterization. They note that the RMOs incorporated managerial aides into the new organizational structure, and that the statutory management offices continued to operate independently. Moreover, they believe budget examiners have acquired managerial expertise over time.

BUSH 43 AND OBAMA: PMA, PART, AND EVIDENCE-BASED ANALYSIS

Despite reservations among some aides regarding the loss of managerial expertise, the emphasis on greater organizational integration of management and budgetary roles has persisted. During Clinton's second term, the country enjoyed a brief interregnum of budget surpluses, thanks to the "peace dividend" from ending the Cold War, the 1990 and 1993 budget agreements that raised taxes, and the additional revenue from strong economic growth. However, the Bush 43 tax cuts, an economic recession, and increased government spending after the 9/11 terrorist attacks and subsequent Iraq War brought budget deficits back. With deficits came a renewal of the budget battles that dominated the Clinton years, as a divided and deeply polarized Congress engaged with the president in repeated bouts of budgetary brinkmanship.

Not surprising given the legislative gridlock, presidents continued to seek administrative tools to control the budget process to achieve policy objectives. Beginning under Bush, this meant developing measurable program objectives and the means to hold agencies accountable for achieving them. That objective meshed well with the managerial focus of Bush's first OMB director Mitch Daniels, who came to government with extensive private sector experience.[31] In a 2002 interview, Daniels acknowledged that "OMB is not a deep repository of management expertise."[32]

In 2001, under Daniels' direction, the Bush administration began implementing the President's Management Agenda (PMA).[33] Its goal was to make government more "citizen-centered, market-based, and results-oriented." To do so, the OMB oversaw a series of performance reviews for government agencies, focusing on five areas: human capital, financial accountability, competitive outsourcing, e-government, and the integration of budget and performance.[34] To measure progress in each area, agencies were scored on a quarterly basis, using a red-yellow-green coding scheme, and the findings published on the OMB website.[35]

To more accurately measure program performance, in 2002, the OMB, working with private consultants, developed the Program Assessment Rating Tool (PART) program. Under PART, the OMB surveyed government agencies by asking a series of questions regarding each agency's program purpose and design, strategic planning, program management, and program results.[36] Based on the responses, the OMB then calculated a numerical score used to rate an agency's performance as either effective, adequate, or ineffective.[37] Over the course of Bush's presidency, more than 90 percent of government agencies were PART-ed before the process ended.

In interviews, former OMB aides familiar with the PMA and PART programs expressed mixed evaluations. On the one hand, several aides praised the programs for requiring agencies to meet with RMO staff at regular intervals, and to establish standards by which to measure their progress. The effort, as one former OMB aide told us, forced agencies to define program objectives and demonstrate that they were achieving them:

> I know when the Bush 43 administration started the scorecards and the red, green, yellow, I thought the agencies would just blow it off, based upon past experience with those types of issues. But, as hypercritical as I often would be of those types of processes, it did work, to a certain extent, in that—I think the key thing that the Bush 43 administration did was, many other management agendas I saw, going back to Carter, Reagan, etc., there'd be a flurry at the beginning of the administration, then it would drop off. There was no way for continuity. The quarterly meetings were a lot of continuity. I can remember with HHS, for about the first year, most of the meetings consisted of the agency people yelling at us, because they were extremely unhappy with what scorecard ratings they were getting. And those scorecards could not have been completed without working hand in hand with all the management staff that were involved, because they had a lot more expertise on those issues. And it was procurement, information technology, we worked with OPM on human capital and so forth. . . . At least when I left in 2008, there was a much greater meshing together of budget and management staff on those types of issues.

A second aide concurs:

> Because I think now that we don't have the President's Management Agenda that we had in Bush 43, my experience is that examiners in OMB, a lot of people very much miss it, because it was the closest thing that we had to that. And what the PMA did is it aligned ev-

erybody around a common set of expectations and a common set of issues, and the alignment was vertical in the sense that the President had blessed this framework and Clay Johnson and his predecessor Mark Everson were in charge of making sure that everybody across government understood it, and people were getting scored and getting red-yellow-greens—or in the PART, the program reviews, "results not demonstrated" or "adequate," or "moderate," or "effective." And with a singular focus that went vertically and it went horizontal and there were these quarterly meetings where the budget side of OMB and the management side came together with the deputy director of management and talked about where agencies were on these standards, and there was an attempt—and maybe they got it wrong in some places—but there was an attempt to set out very clear standards that applied to everybody, so that you could get kind of an objective view.

A third aide says, "I think many (not just me) would conclude that it was one of the most disciplined, cross-sectional, management oversight processes we've had in OMB. . . . and we've tried a number of them!"

But other aides are more critical, arguing that what was measured often bore little resemblance to what the agencies were trying to do. They suggest it is easier to impute partisan motives to the OMB's scoring when performance measures seem somewhat divorced from the agency's mission. One aide recalls:

A lot of us recommended, and were delighted to see, what Bush 43 did, by focusing a management agenda and having five things rather than 500. The problem is that they were almost all the wrong things. [Laughter] And that's the problem with central management. And if you look at the acquisitions, if you look at how you get to green, you outsourced. It was an ideological management agenda. If you look—to the extent that I have a specialization . . . I know a little bit about cybersecurity—almost all of the stuff that the agencies were being graded on in cybersecurity were the wrong things. So you could get to green and still be largely ineffective. So the Bush management agenda, while on the one hand it shows what you can get done if you exercise some focus, be careful what you wish for, because it's not obvious. And I think the Bush management agenda demonstrates the inherent weakness in having folks sitting ten blocks down that way come up with, to be very direct about it, stupid simplistic measures of what constitutes success. So absolutely, getting to green—in one sense the Bush management agenda is a wonderful example of how you can actually bring about change; the problem was, in the areas with which I have some familiarity, they were almost always wrong.

Another adds:

There were some really good things about that process and it forced action and coordinated discussion. It also revealed some—they had some weaknesses so that, by the end of the 8 years, there were a lot of career people who were really happy to throw it over the side. Some of the weaknesses were that it revealed—we were busy measuring like crazy, but OMB was not in a position to help agencies to find solutions to, we were not focusing on solutions, we were focusing on measuring and on standards but we didn't have the people who could tell the agencies how to improve their performance. So they were all going out and hiring consultants to bring in to meet the new test. It became a bit superficial in that there was so much incentive around getting a good score that there was—by the end of it, people were kind of hiding the ball in the agencies and not 'fessing up to the issues so that they could get their score.

Perhaps the most scathing critique of the OMB's managerial capacity came from an aide whose service predates the Nixon reorganization:

It is absolutely mind-boggling if you look at this organization that [the Obama] administration's faced with. It is absolutely shocking when you look at the confusion, the proliferation, the downright mess that we together with the states have made in trying to deal with the Gulf problems.[38] And there's no place in OMB to deal with that. No management capacity whatsoever. It is absolutely zilch. . . . We didn't have it for Katrina, and that was a terrible mess[39]; we didn't have it in postwar Iraq, after the military went in—the foreign assistance, we didn't have any capacity in OMB to help counter the godawful mistakes that were made. We just are suffering all kinds of problems both monetarily and in terms of program effectiveness for the demise of much of the management capacity that the Bureau of the Budget and Office of Management and Budget once had.

In 2009, Peter Orszag became Obama's first OMB director during the worst economic crisis since the Great Depression. According to sources close to him, he viewed the OMB staff as unable to respond to his requests with the alacrity and level of detail he needed. Consequently, many of the initial budget decisions leading to Obama's $800 billion economic recovery act were primarily generated by him and his immediate staff. Orszag's centralized control over the budget process, at least initially, may have contributed to the outside perception that the OMB was serving as a partisan tool of the president. Careerists, however, dispute this.

At the same time, the OMB also discontinued the PART process. Nonetheless, the pressures that led the Bush administration to develop performance measures continued, particularly in the aftermath of the economic crisis. Faced with steep deficits and a deeply divided Congress, the OMB during Obama's eight years was at the center of a succession of budget-related controversies. One senior OMB political aide described her experience under Obama this way: "Nearly every day was a fire drill."

Between drills, the OMB continued seeking ways to budget and manage more efficiently. This included encouraging the use of randomized control trials and other evidence-based initiatives to assess the effectiveness of government programs.[40] These efforts continue into the Trump administration.[41] Although space constraints prevent a detailed assessment, some former aides express skepticism regarding their long-term effectiveness. Lacking sustained political support, they say, the efforts can devolve into an exercise in box-checking. One aide captures the dynamic this way: "They had these huge convulsions of people in temporary organizations throwing papers around and making recommendations, all of which goes some place and then sort of peters out. And that is a political version of the trade-off between management reform as pursued by a substantial professional staff at OMB and management reform by political leadership."

Not surprisingly, several aides took issue with this characterization. There was greater consensus, however, in the belief that the OMB is suffering from a long-term failure to provide the resources in manpower and money commensurate with its increasing responsibilities. Instead, the recurring fiscal crises during the Obama era, culminating in sequestration in 2013, forced significant OMB layoffs, with demoralizing effects. "It was my saddest experience there," one aide with more than three decades experience recalled, noting that the cuts "damaged the place in a lasting sense." More than one former aide expressed concern that the agency was finding it increasingly difficult to hire and retain good people, although some attributed this to a broader climate of "government bashing" and a lack of promotion opportunities. Whatever the explanation, several aides described a decline in agency morale during Obama's presidency. Although no current OMB career officials were willing to speak about the OMB under Trump, it is hard to believe that the recent controversy regarding its role in withholding military aide to Ukraine has reversed that trend.

CONCLUSION: THE DECLINE OF NEUTRAL COMPETENCE?

Have Heclo's warnings come to fruition? There is general agreement among those interviewed that, consistent with Heclo's 1975 article, the Nixon reorganization marks an important turning point in the OMB's institutional development. In the words of one former OMB staffer:

> In the Nixon administrative reorganization of BOB to OMB a significant—I wouldn't call it the first step, but a major step towards shifting the perspective of the Executive Office—not just OMB, but the Executive Office—was away from this emphasis on president as clerk, and more towards an emphasis on influencing the political, policy, substantive agenda. I think that has taken another 30 years or so to come to maturation . . . I think that's matured in the Clinton administration and the president now has the tools to do the kind of things that presidents want to do.

The respondents differed, however, regarding the long-term impact of that reorganization on the ethos of neutral competence. One aide stated: "When I first came into OMB I was told by almost everybody, that the role of OMB was to be 'neutral competence.' And if somebody was going to speak frankly to the president, it may have to be OMB. And that OMB would deliberately put itself as an intervening analyst between the departments and agencies and the president and the White House. And I would say that the capacity for that kind of courage has declined."

Another aide, however, expressed a different perspective: "There's a lot of back and forth between the career staff and the policy staff over the particular issue, whatever it is, Medicare. Everybody says whatever their views are, the career staff says what objections there are. You must know of course that neither policy nor career staff in OMB are noted for their excessive humility!"

In part, the different perspectives reflect different work experiences. Interviewees consistently said their assessment of the agency's competence was shaped partly by where they worked and when. Through the decades, as the OMB's substantive strengths shifted in response to changing presidential priorities, resources and influence flowed accordingly, benefiting some employees at the expense of others. Inevitably, these changes color perceptions regarding the agency's practical commitment to neutral competence.

None of those interviewed, however, said the OMB has become a partisan agency. Instead, there was a prevailing belief that, among careerists at least, the commitment to the ethos of neutral competence remained strong. As one aide summarized, the current OMB is perhaps "less competent today than during the 'good old days' of BOB.... but I don't think we have lost our neutrality and our ability to speak truth to our political leaders." Nonetheless, one suspects that if Heclo were to revisit the OMB today, in the aftermath of the impeachment controversy, he might very well repeat his earlier warnings regarding a creeping politicization. The reason is that the OMB occupies a precarious position within the presidential establishment. To be relevant, it must serve successive presidents' interests, regardless of partisan affiliation. To be effective, it must do so without losing its independence and substantive competence. Ideally, it can be both responsive and "neutrally" competent at the same time. In practice, balancing those objectives is difficult. Moreover, outside perceptions may not match reality.

Based on the interviews, at least, OMB careerists strove to exemplify neutral competence during the post-Nixon reorganization era as strongly as they did during the BOB's "golden age" during the 1940s. What changed, however, is the context in which they operated. Presidential expectations became greater, time horizons for accomplishing them shorter, the political constraints more daunting, resources increasingly scarce, and—not least—the budgetary, regulatory, and management tasks even more complex. The OMB adapted as best it could to remain responsive to presidential needs.

Responsiveness, however, as Heclo warned almost five decades ago, poses a potential risk. The employees interviewed were clearly aware of the danger. In various ways, each stressed the need to be cognizant of politics while not acting politically. A senior political aide from the Obama era assessed the OMB careerists' approach this way: "They provide political history, which is different than politics."

Incoming administrations don't always grasp the difference—at least not initially. Sometimes it needs to be explained. As a former OMB director said, "[The OMB staff] are incredibly knowledgeable" but "it's the job of the Director to make sure the White House knows that." Most administrations, eventually, come to appreciate the OMB's role.

Is this the case for the Trump administration? Almost three years into his presidency, it is difficult to know just how much appreciation the political leadership has regarding the importance of neutral competence. At least superficially, the OMB's role in the Ukraine controversy and Mulvaney's joint appointment suggest perhaps not much. If so, it bears repeating why neutral competence is so crucial for presidents to succeed. In Heclo's words, it "consists of giving one's cooperation and best independent judgment of the issues to partisan bosses—and of being sufficiently uncommitted to be able to do so for a succession of partisan leaders. The independence entailed in neutral competence does not exist for its own sake; it exists precisely in order to serve the aims of elected partisan leadership."[42] That ethos can serve the Trump administration as effectively as it did previous presidencies.

A former aide with decades of OMB experience summarized the agency's role as follows: its job, he said, is to serve as "guardian of the 'Emperor's new clothes.'" Presidents are not emperors, of course (although some may aspire to be), but they are susceptible to convincing themselves that they are adequately attired for the prevailing political climate. It helps to have someone able and willing to tell them when this isn't the case. Whether presidents will listen is another matter.

Notes

Thanks to Eliza Van Voorhis for her research assistance, and for helpful comments on an earlier draft from David Haun and Kathleen Peroff and two anonymous reviewers. The views expressed here are my own, however, as are any errors.

1. On December 18, 2019, the House voted 230 to 197 to charge Trump with abuse of power and 229 to 198 to charge him with obstruction of Con-

gress. Both votes were largely split along party lines, with only two Democrats, Representatives Collin Peterson of Minnesota and Jeff Van Drew of New Jersey, voting with all Republicans against impeachment. Representative Jared Golden of Maine voted for one impeachment article. Democratic Representative Tulsi Gabbard of Hawaii, who at the time was running for the Democratic presidential nomination, voted present for both articles.

2. On February 5, 2020, the Senate voted to acquit Trump on both impeachment charges. The first article, abuse of power, was rejected 48 to 52, with Senator Mitt Romney the only Republican to break with his party to support conviction. The second article, obstruction of Congress, was defeated 47 to 53 on a straight party vote.

3. Hugh Heclo, "OMB and the Presidency: The Problem of 'Neutral Competence'," *The Public Interest* 38 (Winter 1975), pp. 80–98.

4. Heclo, "OMB and the Presidency," p. 81.

5. Ellen Mitchell, "Pentagon Officials were Confused, Concerned by Delay in Ukraine Aid Emails Show: Report," *The Hill*, February 5, 2020, https://thehill.com/policy/defense/481681-pentagon-officials-were-confused-concerned-by-delay-in-ukraine-aid-emails-show.

6. See the December 11, 2019, memorandum from Paoletta to GAO General Counsel Tom Armstrong, https://context-cdn.washingtonpost.com/notes/prod/default/documents/5dbd9f69-2537-4272-bd5d-60c94d3843b6/note/112b1caa-763c-4c4c-a5bb-0a04f7962d2c.pdf.

7. See Olivia Beavers and Rebecca Klar, "GAO Finds Trump Administration Broke Law by Withholding Ukraine Aid," *The Hill*, January 16, 2020, https://thehill.com/homenews/administration/478557-gao-finds-trump-administration-broke-law-by-withholding-aid-from.

8. See Vought's January 16, 2020, tweet, https://twitter.com/RussVought45/status/1217901188710051842.

9. See https://twitter.com/realDonaldTrump/status/1073703744766922754. To be sure, in a press release issued after Trump's tweet, Press Secretary Sarah Sanders clarified that although Mulvaney would retain his OMB's director's hat, Deputy OMB Director Russell Vought would assume day-to-day control of OMB operations. But the symbolism remains.

10. In March 2020, Mulvaney was replaced as chief of staff by former Congressman Mark Meadows.

11. See, for example, Charlie Dunlap "Why the GAO's Opinion of OMB's Withholding of Ukraine's Security Assistance is Problematic (Even If the Conclusion Is Right)," *LawFire*, January 18, 2020, https://sites.duke.edu/lawfire/2020/01/18/why-the-gaos-opinion-about-ombs-withholding-of-ukraine-security-assistance-is-problematic-even-if-the-conclusion-is-right/.

12. Previous OMB directors who gave up that post to become White House chief of staff include Leon Panetta under Bill Clinton; Josh Bolten under George W. Bush; and Jack Lew under Barack Obama.

13. As one former OMB careerist emailed to me, "I think the fact that four OMB directors ascended to COS [Chief of Staff] has more to do with the knowledge and experience that they gained from their OMB experience, than the President's views of OMB as an institution."

14. Although supplemented by archival documents and secondary sources, the interviews form the primary basis for the conclusions reported here. Note that many of the interviews were jointly conducted with Andrew Rudalevige, and several by him alone. The interpretations here, however, are solely my own.

15. Several current OMB employees were interviewed, but they did so with-

out agreeing to go on the record. In contrast, most of those serving under previous presidents did agree to allow their comments to be published, asking only that direct quotes be cleared with them before attribution. For the purposes of this chapter, however, I have chosen to maintain all respondents' anonymity.

16. Not all scholars share Heclo's defense of neutral competence. In his influential 1985 essay "The Politicized Presidency," Terry Moe critiqued the concept as a normative ideal that ignored the day-to-day realities that presidents confront. See Moe, "The Politicized Presidency," in *The New Direction in American Politics*, edited by John Chubb and Paul Peterson (Washington D.C.: Brookings, 1985).

17. For a similar argument based on archival research focused on an earlier era, see Matthew J. Dickinson and Andrew Rudalevige, "Presidents, Responsiveness, and Competence: Revisiting the 'Golden Age' at the Bureau of the Budget," *Political Science Quarterly* 119, no. 4 (Winter, 2004/2005), pp. 633–54.

18. Heclo, "OMB and the Presidency," p. 81.

19. Ibid., p. 88.

20. See EO 11541 (July 1, 1970), issued pursuant to Reorganization Plan 2 (1970). The relevant documents are contained in *Public Administration Review* 30, no. 6 (November–December 1970), pp. 611–19.

21. Reorganization Plan 2.

22. In his classic study of executive branch politics, *A Government of Strangers (Executive Politics in Washington)* (Washington, D.C.: Brookings, 1977), especially pp. 78–83, Heclo expands on this critique.

23. Ibid.

24. Although it has a statutory basis, OIRA does not really function as a management agency so much as it serves as a tool for controlling regulatory policy.

25. *OMB 2000 Project Team Finding* (draft) July 1993.

26. *OMB 2000 Project Team Finding*, p. 32.

27. The PADs are not Senate-confirmed appointments, however.

28. These are members of the Senior Executive Service.

29. Branch chief and examiners are career staff.

30. On the RMO's role as a presidential tool for policy control, see Eloise Pasachoff, "OMB's Resource Management Offices and Agency Policy Control," *The Regulatory Review* (September 6, 2016).

31. One aide described Daniels as the most "management-oriented" director he had served under.

32. Timothy B. Clark, "OMB May Add Asset Management to Its Reform Agenda," *Government Executive*, July 24, 2002.

33. The President's Management Agenda (Fiscal Year 2002), https://georgewbush-whitehouse.archives.gov/omb/budget/fy2002/mgmt.pdf.

34. During the PMA's implementation, Bush would sometimes surprise department heads by pulling out a scorecard to discuss the department's management progress.

35. See OMB document "Agency Scorecards," https://georgewbush-whitehouse.archives.gov/omb/budintegration/scorecards/agency_scorecards.html.

36. See the OMB's description of the program, https://georgewbush-whitehouse.archives.gov/omb/expectmore/part.html.

37. If evaluators could not come to a judgment, they could render a "results not demonstrated" verdict, although this was interpreted by some as a negative finding.

38. The aide is referencing the Obama administration's struggles to respond to the 2010 Deepwater Horizon oil spill in the Gulf of Mexico.

39. In 2005, the Bush administration received heavy criticism for its response to the impact of Hurricane Katrina in the Gulf region.

40. Peter Orszag, "Building Rigorous Evidence to Drive Policy," OMB blog, June 8, 2009. See also the OBM document "Evidence and Evaluation," https://obamawhitehouse.archives.gov/omb/evidence.

41. See OMB Acting Director Vought's memo to agency and department heads regarding implementation of the 2019 "Evidence Act," www.whitehouse.gov/wp-content/uploads/2019/07/M-19-23.pdf.

42. Heclo, p. 81.

ELEVEN

Conclusion

OMB and Presidential Transitions: Building a More Effective Government through a Transformed Office of Management and Budget

KRISTINE SIMMONS
PETER KAMOCSAI

The Office of Management and Budget (OMB), more than any other institution in the federal arena, represents the best bridge for turning White House priorities into reality by providing coordination, oversight, and assistance to agencies across the government.

Over the years, OMB has been extraordinarily adept performing its primary function—producing the president's budget. It also has been good at issuing guidance and direction, but less successful in following through to ensure its directives have been obeyed and that the priorities and goals outlined in the president's budget have been met.

Part of the problem lies in OMB's own organizational structure and processes. First, OMB is often trapped in its own silos. Fragmentation among its components—especially budget, management, regulation, information, procurement, and technology—hurts its ability to coordinate government-wide activities. Second, OMB is rewarded for challenging agency proposals and operations. Its historical mission has been to protect the president from ideas that do not fit administration priorities and from spending that would bust the budget. However, this focus too often has made OMB into what some refer to as "the Agency of No" instead of an engine to drive the government toward success. Third, OMB frequently finds itself caught up in relatively low-priority issues. This limits its ability to build a more effective government.

Besides its budget responsibilities, OMB can and should be doing more as a facilitator, a collaborator, and a convener to embed greater use of evidence-based decisionmaking at the agencies to reduce barriers to innovation and spur experimentation with new ideas for better governance and to enable greater interagency and intergovernmental coordination. OMB also must do more to link management challenges with budgetary decisions to make sure agencies connect spending plans with the ability to get results. Taking on a more significant role in these areas may require more resources, and it will mean reordering priorities, making internal staffing changes, and altering how work gets done without undermining critical budget functions.

TOP INTERNAL CHALLENGES

To make OMB a more effective instrument for program and policy implementation, a number of internal organizational issues must be addressed.

One central problem is that, in seeking to reduce the fragmentation of government, OMB's own staffing patterns sometimes increase it. Its management and budget branches too often have failed to connect. There are many cross-cutting implementation issues for which the budget staff has more capacity than the management staff. Fundamentally, both OMB branches often lack the expertise needed to address implementation issues. As long as management and budget components work on separate tracks, as long as OMB's staff capacity is not aligned with its mission and mandate, and as long as its leadership fails to take aggressive steps to resolve the agency's own fragmentation, OMB will not be able to effectively serve the president.

Based on interviews with more than seventy experts, including those who have served at OMB and at other federal agencies in political and career capacities, there are a number of options for internal reform. In a number of instances, interviews were conducted on a background basis and quotes used from those interviews were kept anonymous throughout this chapter.

REASSESS THE AGENCY'S STRUCTURE, PROCESSES, AND STAFF

Too many of OMB's exceptionally talented staff are spending time on activities with low returns. Investing more staff time in high-value activities, focusing less on the preparation of the budget and more on the results the budget produces, could transform both OMB and the federal government's outcomes.

Restructure budget reviews. OMB could avoid duplicating the budget reviews performed by analysts in the agencies and concentrate efforts on areas where it has greater experience or a big-picture perspective rather than second-guessing knowledgeable agency staff. OMB staff freed from areas in which they do not have a comparative advantage could be reallocated to higher-value-added work. This could include helping agencies develop solid implementation plans and coordinating with other agencies or outside stakeholders, a process that could strengthen the proposals and increase their chances of winning congressional approval.

Redefine OMB's work products. OMB could change its focus from producing the president's budget to producing results flowing from the budget. A very large share of OMB's staff time is devoted each year to producing the budget and its supporting documents. Highly skilled staff members spend vast amounts of energy producing voluminous documents, many of which are never used. In other cases, staff create detailed backup materials, even for what many OMB staffers call "fake mandatories"—proposals for mandatory programs that have no chance of passage. As one interviewee argued, "If you could shift all that OMB staff time toward a more productive emphasis on implementation, the country would be better off, and I'm doubtful anyone in the White House or anyone else would notice."

Moreover, one interviewee said OMB has a whole division of very talented budgetary experts who produce technical volumes full of tables that have a very limited readership. These documents help provide a valuable perspective on the federal government's complicated enterprise, and they provide a measure of transparency. However, another interviewee noted, "I don't think these volumes have ever been audited for usefulness—imagine what folks of such talent could do if working to make government programs more effective."

"The real challenge here is rethinking what belongs in a budget," explained Robert Gordon, who served as acting deputy director of OMB during the Obama administration. "That's a complicated task that needs buy-in from both parties in Congress. Until this happens, OMB staff will have less time than they should to focus on implementation."

OMB has not considered, in a very long time, what the budget documents should look like and how it should conduct its budget and management reviews. In fact, many of OMB's major budget review processes are idle, waiting for a return to the old budget processes that focused on annual budget submissions and congressional appropriations on a regular, predictable cycle. Those days are unlikely to return. Even if they do, the old OMB processes will prove a poor fit for the federal government's increasingly complex strategies and tools. Only a fundamental transformation of OMB will help it serve the purposes for which it was created—in an environment its creators could not have imagined.

Reallocate employees among the divisions. The number of employees in each OMB branch has not been reviewed comprehensively for several years, nor has there been an evaluation of whether the branches should be reorganized.

Reconsider how the divisions work. The director could focus OMB's processes on issues that cut across multiple related agencies. For example, the Income Maintenance Branch examines income support programs in the departments of Health and Human Services, Agriculture, and the Treasury, as well as the Social Security Administration. Because the government's biggest challenges do not fit neatly into program- or agency-based silos, OMB could expand this model to other branches and charge them with integrating budget, policy, and implementation analysis to achieve important policy objectives.

Increase OMB's staff. Over the years, OMB's responsibilities have increased, but the staffing has trended downward over time. Additionally, OMB's inflation-adjusted budget has been stagnant since the 1970s. Many of those interviewed made strong arguments about the need to increase OMB's staffing. There's little doubt that, because of OMB's ability to leverage action across the government, small investments in added staffing could produce outsized impact.

Seek employees with experience outside OMB. Many current OMB analysts have worked only inside the agency. Many experts interviewed pointed out that this circumstance reinforces a culture that sees relationships with agency employees as one of "us" versus "them." Employing more analysts with experience outside OMB could bring a broader perspective to the issues, open the staff to new views, and stimulate more effective problem-solving.

Several of those interviewed said OMB could require its employees to have experience elsewhere in government or in another sector before they join the Senior Executive Service (SES), or give added weight to candidates who do. The Department of Defense and the intelligence community have implemented similar policies to encourage diversity of experience for SES candidates. As part of this initiative, OMB could develop a rotation program for high-performing GS-15 staff to rotate to other agencies.

Manage existing talent. There is broad consensus that OMB needs to invest much more in professional staff development, especially in creating strong managers and supervisors. Many managers have been promoted to supervisory positions because they are "super analysts," but do not have strong management skills.

"No good manager or leader at OMB will ever be recognized for being a good manager," one OMB official said. OMB needs to do more to ensure its managers are prepared to lead. OMB should strive to provide management training to help those individuals make the transition from staff to management, according to former OMB officials.

Manage firefighting. Many current and former OMB employees reported they often found themselves thrown unexpectedly into high-priority demands from the White House. Such requests create a difficult dilemma. On one hand, the most important part of OMB's mission is supporting the president, so if the president and the president's staff urgently need help, OMB's employees want to provide it. In fact, OMB never wants to be in the position of not responding to the president's pressing needs. OMB, after all, is the principal repository for the deepest expertise in the Executive Office of the President.

On the other hand, OMB staffers suggested that the pace of such requests is increasing, and the urgent ones make it hard to deal with other important elements of their jobs. At worst, too many of these requests force OMB to be reactive rather than able to provide the objective analysis that represents its strongest suit, which, in the process, dilutes the work product.

Interviewees suggested three ways in which these "firefighting" requests could be handled:

- *Screening:* A former high-ranking official in OMB said one of the director's top jobs is to protect the staff: to filter out low-priority requests from the White House and to focus on requests for high-priority issues. Only the director can do that well, the official suggested.

- *SWAT teams:* OMB's director could create a small SWAT team of first-tier management consultants to provide quick response to big challenges; to organize the agency's ongoing response; and to convene experts, both from within and outside of government, for longer-term issues.

- *Data service:* The OMB director could create a small executive secretariat to field lower-tier—but still urgent—information requests from the West Wing. Because such requests are always important and are unlikely to decrease, OMB's director should proactively craft a strategy to deal with them responsively without the staff becoming overwhelmed. OMB also should find a way to filter requests coming from other sources that sap the time of agency employees, including requests from Congress, the OMB communications office, the Government Accountability Office, and elsewhere.

CONCLUSION

The mission of OMB is to serve the nation's chief executive in implementing and supporting the administration's budget, policy, management, regulatory, and legislative objectives. To do so more effectively, OMB must modernize and reorganize its own processes. That will mean reordering some priorities, making internal staffing changes, and altering how work gets done without undermining the critical budget functions. This will require addressing the fragmentation in its own divisions to focus more on getting effective results from policy decisions, and by melting the barriers that too often separate OMB's actions into distinct, unconnected management and budget silos. Taking fundamental steps to strengthen the organization and augment its role will make a big dif-

A CONCLUDING NOTE ON OMB AND PRESIDENTIAL TRANSITIONS

When the Presidential Transition Act of 1963 (Public Law 88-277) was enacted, it was noted in the legislation that "it is the intent of the Congress that appropriate actions be authorized and taken to avoid or minimize any disruption" during a transition in the faithful execution of laws and the conduct of government business. As Congress has amended this law in the years since and presidents have augmented the law via executive order, the role of the Office of Management and Budget has become more prominent in the presidential transition process.[1]

OMB and Presidential Transition Law

With the enactment of the Presidential Transition Act, government institutions began to assume a more formal role in the transition between administrations. The law provided government support services to a president-elect and vice president-elect, including office space and equipment, and services to former presidents and former vice presidents.

Subsequent legislation authorized orientation activities for new senior presidential appointees, including interchange between appointees and OMB staff.[2] In 2010, Congress passed the Pre-Election Presidential Transition Act to provide resources for major party presidential candidates following the party conventions.[3] Moving the date at which government support is available encouraged presidential candidates to begin planning for a transition before the election, a reflection of concerns that transitions may occur in a dangerous national security environment and incoming administrations should prepare accordingly.

The 2010 legislation authorized, but did not require, the creation of two transition coordinating councils. One of these councils was to include high-level officials of the executive branch, including the director of OMB and other presidential appointees. The second council was designated as an Agency Transition Directors Council, to include career employees designated to lead transition efforts within executive departments or agencies. Congress enacted legislation in March 2016 to require the establishment of these councils, clarify their respective membership and purpose, and designate OMB's deputy director for management as the cochair of the Agency Transition Director's Council.[4] The 2016 law also authorized training and orientation activities for individuals appointed to senior positions in a president's second term and provided that available training funds could be used throughout an administration, not only at the beginning of a presidential term of office.

OMB and the Transition to a New President

The effectiveness of OMB career staff in helping a newly elected president in the post-election period depends on the level of cooperation, transparency, and information offered by the incumbent administration.

Following the 2008 presidential election, President George W. Bush made a public statement committing to a smooth transfer of power to President-elect Barack Obama, which he viewed as imperative given that the United States was at war. Obama and White House Chief of Staff Denis McDonough built on this example during the 2016–2017 election cycle, and the outgoing administration took both external and internal actions to facilitate a smooth handoff.

An executive order signed by Obama in May 2016 established that it is "the policy of the United States to undertake all reasonable efforts to ensure that Presidential transitions are well-coordinated and effective, without regard to party affiliation."[5] The Executive Order (EO) formalized the establishment and functions of the aforementioned transition councils; informally, OMB became a central driver of government-wide transition planning while simultaneously managing OMB's internal transition efforts and preparing to onboard the next administration's OMB leadership team.

Prior to the 2016 presidential election, staff members from the Partnership for Public Service interviewed individuals who have held career and politically appointed positions in government and identified a number of important steps OMB can take to support an effective transition for a newly elected president. These activities and recommendations are enabled and enhanced when the outgoing chief executive is supportive.

OMB career staff should assist the president-elect's transition team and prepare an "Introduction to OMB" for all political appointees. The career OMB staff should be prepared to help the president-elect's transition team understand the processes, deadlines, challenges, and opportunities they will face in seeking to push through the administration's policy and budget priorities, and how they might navigate the system to best achieve their goals. This could include ways to sequence the policy agenda and craft the messaging, advocacy, and legal components necessary to get policy priorities adopted.

The OMB staff should be prepared to flag problems that might hinder program and policy implementation, and highlight opportunities to leverage existing processes to achieve goals. Appointees new to federal service seldom have a working understanding of OMB and the outsize influence it exerts over their agencies. One outgoing Cabinet secretary even described OMB as being so mysterious and omnipotent that it was like "God on Earth."[6] The briefings should include an introduction to the regulatory process, specific deadlines for the preparation of the new administration's first budget, and an overview of the performance review process required by the Government Performance and Results Modernization Act. The briefings should be substantive and provide appointees with an understanding of the quality of support OMB career staff can offer and the benefits of early collaboration on policy initiatives and implementation challenges.

Help organize a retreat for the president, vice president, and senior White House staff with Cabinet members and their deputies on governing and decisionmaking. The White House should hold a retreat for Cabinet members and their deputies in the first month or two of the new administration to brief them on a range of issues, including the role of OMB and the budget process. The retreat should include sessions on understanding the president's budget as a statement of policy; where and when Cabinet secretaries can have an impact on the budget; and how departments can coordinate with the White House and OMB on budget, policy, management, and implementation issues.

Begin work on the president's budget request during the transition. By law, the president's first budget must be submitted just two weeks after the inauguration. New presidents typically do not meet this deadline and instead submit a broad outline of budget priorities in March. To meet even this timeline, work on the budget must start well before the inauguration.

After the election, officials from the incoming administration should provide as much direction as possible to OMB so the customary first part of the new budget, a broad outline of budget priorities, can be issued by March. In addition, the new administration should seek permission to have a few OMB staff assigned to transition headquarters to facilitate the budget preparation process. The new administration may find the Government Performance and Results Modernization Act a useful tool for signaling and organizing its priorities, since it provides a strategic plan and the metrics to use in judging its success. The incoming administration also should conduct an immediate assessment of OMB's own budget to determine if specific functions need increased staff to meet their responsibilities.

Use OMB staff to develop a coordinated legislative, management, and regulatory agenda in concert with the new budget. Simultaneous with the development of the new fiscal year budget, the administration also will be developing legislative, regulatory, and management agendas. Rather than crafting these agendas in isolation, the new administration should develop a coordinated, integrated strategy and use the expertise of OMB staff to assist in this effort. This can ensure that the administration is speaking with one voice to the rest of the executive branch, to Congress, and to citizens. It can also reduce the chance that one element of the strategy can create impediments to others.

Appoint OMB leaders quickly and engage OMB career staff in substantive conversations. The president-elect should announce the nominees for top OMB positions well before Inauguration Day, and work with Congress to win quick Senate confirmation. These positions should include, at a minimum, the director, deputy director, deputy director for management, and the administrator for the Office of Information and Regulatory Affairs. The OMB director should promptly appoint all program associate directors.

The director, deputy directors, and politically appointed associate directors should be viewed as a team whose knowledge and experience complement each other. They also should include and work closely with top OMB career staff in their deliberations. OMB staff should provide insights to help the new administration get things done. This includes providing the easiest possible path for new initiatives and alternatives for ideas that could prove difficult to implement.

Previous senior OMB leaders, including former directors, encouraged new administrations to use OMB's staff to develop policy and budget proposals and cautioned that failure to tap career OMB expertise could set back the new administration's initiatives.

Meet with leaders from the White House to explain OMB's role in supporting the policy councils. OMB's political leaders should connect early with White House and policy council staff. The White House functions best when OMB, the president's personal staff, and the policy councils all work as a team to implement the administration's agenda.

Former OMB officials said in interviews that OMB and the policy councils have at times viewed each other as adversaries, competing for influence and the president's attention. They also noted that policy discussions in the councils often fail to connect with OMB's management concerns. Both problems can undermine the president's effectiveness, lead to mixed messages for agencies about the president's priorities, and frustrate advancement of the new president's agenda.

OMB can support the councils by identifying where resources are currently available to advance the new president's priorities; highlighting gaps that need to be filled through presidential and congressional action; identifying where information and expertise exist within federal agencies to solve problems; exploring regulatory changes that might be needed to implement the president's policies; helping policy staff negotiate the legal and regulatory requirements of new policy ideas; and eliminating administrative barriers that impede achieving the president's goals.

OMB and a Second-Term Transition

A president's second term is often approached as a continuation of the first term rather than an opportunity to renew, refresh, and reprioritize. But the reelection of a president is a significant turning point for every administration. A transition from a first to a second term usually results in significant changes in the Cabinet and other leadership positions while offering an opportunity to pursue new policies, accomplish second-term campaign promises, and improve government performance.

Presidents seeking a second term rarely use the months leading up to and following their reelection to absorb lessons from the first four years and plan for changes and adjustments. For the most part, incumbents have not considered that a transition is occurring when they are reelected because they already run the government and have people and policies in place.

As a result, they have missed the opportunity to engage in a thorough evaluation of their governance and to establish plans to improve policymaking, program effectiveness, and management practices. Using the second term well, and leaving a lasting legacy for the president, requires serious planning and preparation.

As is true with first-term presidents, the policy agenda stems in large measure from promises made on the campaign trail. This may include building on the success of the first-term agenda with more ambitious goals, or with entirely new ideas and fresh thinking. Legislative achievements from the first term (or lack thereof), congressional relationships, national needs, the political environment, and the vision of the president's long-term legacy will all impact how a second-term administration sets and sequences its policy agenda.

The OMB director is a critical actor in helping drive an administration's agenda forward, and if history is an accurate indication, a second-term president will need to select a new individual to lead OMB. The last four two-term presidents have all experienced a change in OMB leadership from their first to their second term. In many cases, the OMB director was asked to accept another challenging assignment in the second term. For example, George W. Bush tapped OMB Director Joshua Bolten to serve as White House chief of staff, and President Obama nominated OMB Director Sylvia Mathews Burwell for secretary of the Department of Health and Human Services.

In interviews, several former top White House officials said that neither Bush nor Obama engaged in organized transition planning during their successful bids for a second term. In hindsight, the former officials said, it would have been useful if they had a team of trusted aides inside the White House working with political leaders at the agencies to lay the groundwork. This would have increased their ability to implement the major policy promises made during the presidential campaign, identify and plan for other strategic second-term priorities, make informed decisions on presidential personnel, and strengthen the management of government to ensure policies could be implemented effectively.

OMB can add exceptional value for an incumbent who seeks to actively engage in second-term planning. Depending on the process chosen by the incumbent, OMB can help the White House and political leaders at the agencies assess what programs and initiatives have worked during the first term and what needs to be fixed or dropped. Agency political appointees are well positioned to highlight important initiatives that should continue and be strengthened in a second term, offer new ideas that could be incorporated with OMB's assistance, and determine both the resources needed to achieve the various goals and the risks that must be managed.

In the past, presidents elected to a second term have not engaged in robust planning for the next four years or fully utilized the expertise of OMB early in the process. The time between reelection and Inauguration Day offers a chance for a recalibration and a new start for a second four-year term. OMB can play an important role in this effort.

Notes

These recommendations are updated from the Partnership for Public Service's 2016 report "From Decisions To Results: Building a More Effective Government through a Transformed Office of Management and Budget" (October 2016), pp. 1–42, https://ourpublicservice.org/publications/from-decisions-to-results.

1. See Clinton OE 13176 of November 27, 2000, Facilitation of a Presidential Transition; Bush EO 13476 of October 9, 2008, Facilitation of a Presidential Transition; and Obama EO 13727 of May 6, 2016, Facilitation of a Presidential Transition.
2. Presidential Transition Act of 2000, P.L. 106-293.
3. Pre-Election Presidential Transition Act of 2010, P.L. 111-283.
4. Edward "Ted" Kaufman and Michael Leavitt Presidential Transitions Improvements Act of 2015, P.L. 114-136.
5. EO 13727 of May 6, 2016: Facilitation of a Presidential Transition.
6. Ian Kullgren, "Vilsack Discusses 'God on Earth'," *Politico*, December 8, 2016, www.politico.com/tipsheets/morning-agriculture/2016/12/vilsack-discusses-god-on-earth-217775.

Appendix

BOB/OMB Directors
1921–2020

Russell Vought*	2019–
Mick Mulvaney*	2017–2020
Shaun Donovan	2014–2017
Sylvia M. Burwell	2013–2014
Jefferey Zients (Acting)	2012–2013
Jacob J. Lew	2010–2012
Jeffrey Zients (Acting)	2010
Peter R. Orszag	2009–2010
Jim Nussle	2007–2009
Robert J. Portman	2006–2007
Joshua B. Bolten	2003–2006
Mitchell E. Daniels Jr.	2001–2003
Jacob J. Lew	1998–2001
Franklin D. Raines	1996–1998
Alice M. Rivlin	1994–1996
Leon E. Panetta	1993–1994
Richard G. Darman	1989–1993
Joseph R. Wright Jr.	1988–1989
James C. Miller III	1985–1988

---

*Mulvaney was named acting White House chief of staff as of January 1, 2019, while still nominally continuing as OMB director; Deputy Director Russell Vought began serving as acting OMB director as of that date. After Mulvaney left both his White House and OMB posts in March 2020, President Trump announced his intention to formally nominate Vought as director, and Senate confirmation followed on July 21, 2020.

David A. Stockman	1981–1985
James T. McIntyre Jr.	1977–1981
Thomas Bertram Lance	1977
James T. Lynn	1975–1977
Roy L. Ash	1973–1975
Caspar W. Weinberger	1972–1973
George P. Shultz	1970–1972
Robert P. Mayo	1969–1970
Charles J. Zwick	1968–1969
Charles L. Schultze	1965–1968
Kermit Gordon	1962–1965
David E. Bell	1961–1962
Maurice H. Stans	1958–1961
Percival F. Brundage	1956–1958
Rowland R. Hughes	1954–1956
Joseph M. Dodge	1953–1954
Frederick J. Lawton	1950–1953
Frank Pace	1949–1950
James E. Webb	1946–1949
Harold D. Smith	1939–1946
Daniel W. Bell	1934–1939
Lewis W. Douglas	1933–1934
J. Clawson Roop	1929–1933
Herbert M. Lord	1922–1929
Charles G. Dawes	1921–1922

For OMB's current organizational chart, see the *U.S. Government Manual* (www.usgovernmentmanual.gov). Also see useful charts tracing OMB's changing organizational structure from 1921 to the late 1970s in Larry Berman, *The Office of Management and Budget and the Presidency, 1921–1979* (Princeton University Press, 1979), Appendix Two. The direct link to the manual's OMB listing is www.usgovernmentmanual.gov/Agency.aspx?EntityId=8tCwuc2dRmg=&ParentEId=p0fnvDxExmY=&EType=/sbLHImeIYk=. The OMB organization chart may be found at www.usgovernmentmanual.gov/ReadLibraryItem.ashx?SFN=DjwsLvg6HT/zFuXGHf1j1w==&SF=PAmu4nDRyaoCugTKvsXyXx/6G6ZqqOY-1fk7ZHZboqk4=.

Contributors

Meena Bose is executive dean for Public Policy and Public Service Programs, Peter S. Kalikow School of Government, Public Policy and International Affairs, and director of the Peter S. Kalikow Center for the Study of the American Presidency at Hofstra University. She is the author of *Shaping and Signaling Presidential Policy: The National Security Decision Making of Eisenhower and Kennedy* (Texas A&M University Press, 1998), and the editor of several volumes in presidential studies. She is a co-author of the *American Government: Institutions and Policies* textbook (17th edition, forthcoming 2021) and of *The Paradoxes of the American Presidency* textbook (5th edition, Oxford University Press, 2018). Dr. Bose taught for six years at the United States Military Academy at West Point, where she also served as director of American Politics in 2006. She serves on the editorial board of *Political Science Quarterly* and is a member of the Council on Foreign Relations.

Martha B. Coven is lecturer and John L. Weinberg/Goldman Sachs & Co. Visiting Professor at Princeton University's Woodrow Wilson School of Public & International Affairs. Her professional experience includes more than twenty years working on federal policy in the executive branch, legislative branch, and nonprofit sector. She served in the Obama administration as a special assistant to the president at the Domestic Policy Council and as program associate director for Education, Income Maintenance, and Labor at OMB. Coven holds a B.A. in economics and a J.D. from Yale University.

Matthew J. Dickinson is professor of political science at Middlebury College. His blog on presidential power can be found at http://blogs.middlebury.edu/presidentialpower. He is author of *Bitter Harvest: FDR, Presidential Power, and the Growth of the Presidential Branch* (1999), coeditor of *Guardian of the Presidency: The Legacy of Richard E. Neustadt*, and has published numerous articles on the presidency, Congress, and the executive branch. His current book manuscript, titled *Clerk or Leader? The President and the White House Staff: People, Positions and Processes, 1945–2020*, examines the growth of presidential staff in the post–World War II era.

Thomas E. Hitter is assistant vice chancellor for Policy Development and Management at the University of Pittsburgh. Prior to joining the university, Hitter served as associate general counsel in the OMB at the White House. Earlier in his career, Hitter served as an attorney in the U.S. Department of Justice and clerked for an administrative law judge in the U.S. Department of Labor. He graduated from Binghamton University and from George Mason University School of Law.

Peter Kamocsai is research and analysis manager at the Partnership for Public Service. He leads the partnership's research portfolio on technology, including the potential of artificial intelligence to improve government, technology's role in delivering federal agency missions, and hiring and recruiting technology experts into government. He holds a B.A. in international studies from the Corvinus University of Budapest, Hungary, and an M.P.A. from the George Washington University.

Jacob J. Lew is partner at Lindsay Goldberg LLC and a visiting professor of international and public affairs at Columbia University's School of International and Public Affairs. He served as secretary of the Treasury in the Obama administration from 2013 to 2017. Before that position, he served as President Obama's White House chief of staff from 2012 to 2013. From 2010 to 2012, he served in the Obama administration as director of OMB, a position he also held in President Clinton's Cabinet from 1998 to 2001. His long government service also includes service as deputy secretary of state; OMB deputy director; and special assistant to the president, as well as a top aide to Speaker of the House Thomas P. O'Neill Jr. In the private sector, he has served as managing director and chief operating officer for two different Citigroup business units as well as executive vice president and chief operating officer of New York University.

David E. Lewis is the William R. Kenan Jr. Professor in the Department of Political Science at Vanderbilt University. He is the author of two books and numerous articles on American politics, public administration, and management. His research has been featured in outlets such as the *Harvard Business Review*, *New York Times*, and *Washington Post*. Before joining Vanderbilt's Department of Political Science, he was an assistant professor of politics and public affairs at Princeton University and assistant professor of government at the College of William & Mary. He serves on the editorial boards of *Presidential Studies Quarterly* and *Public Administration*. He is a member of the National Academy of Public Administration.

Eloise Pasachoff is the Agnes N. Williams Research Professor and associate dean at the Georgetown University Law Center. Her scholarship has won national awards in administrative law and education law. She has also won Georgetown Law's teaching award. A former middle school and high school teacher, she began her legal career clerking for Justice Sotomayor on the United States Supreme Court, Chief Judge Katzmann in the Second Circuit Court of Appeals, and Judge Rakoff in the Southern District of New York. She earned her J.D. from Harvard Law School and an M.P.A. from Harvard's Kennedy School of Government.

James P. Pfiffner is university professor in the Schar School of Policy and Government at George Mason University. He has taught at the University of California, Riverside and Cal State Fullerton and worked in the office of the director of the U.S. Office of Personnel Management. In 2007, he was S. T. Lee Professorial Fellow at the Institute for Advanced Study at the University of London. He is the author or editor of sixteen books, including *Power Play: The Bush Administration and the Constitution* (Brookings, 2008) and *Torture as Public Policy* (Paradigm Publishers, 2010).

Rachel Augustine Potter is assistant professor of politics at the University of Virginia. She is the author of *Bending the Rules: Procedural Politick-*

ing in the Bureaucracy (University of Chicago Press, 2019), as well as numerous journal articles on regulatory politics, the bureaucracy, and the separation of powers. From 2005 to 2007, she was a desk officer at the Office of Information and Regulatory Affairs in the Office of Management and Budget. She holds degrees from Boston College, the University of Southern California, and the University of Michigan.

Molly E. Reynolds is a senior fellow in governance studies at The Brookings Institution. She studies Congress, with an emphasis on how congressional rules and procedures affect domestic policy outcomes. She is the author of *Exceptions to the Rule: The Politics of Filibuster Limitations in the U.S. Senate* (Brookings 2017), which explores the creation, use, and consequences of the budget reconciliation process and other procedures that prevent filibusters in the U.S. Senate. Reynolds received her Ph.D. in political science and public policy from the University of Michigan and her A.B. in government from Smith College.

Mark D. Richardson is assistant professor in the Department of Government at Georgetown University. His research has been published in *The Journal of Politics* and the *Journal of Public Policy* and covered by the *Washington Post*, the *Federal Times*, and the *Political Research Digest* podcast. Previously, he was an assistant professor of political science at James Madison University. He also spent six years as a bank regulator in the Federal Reserve System and at the Tennessee Department of Financial Institutions.

Eric Rosenthal is a graduate student at Cornell University in the department of Statistics and Data Science. He graduated from Williams College with a degree in statistics and political science.

Andrew Rudalevige is Thomas Brackett Reed Professor and chair of the Department of Government at Bowdoin College. His scholarship includes *Managing the President's Program*, which won the national Neustadt prize; *The New Imperial Presidency: Renewing Presidential Power after Watergate*; the coauthored textbook *The Politics of the Presidency*; and the forthcoming *Executive Orders and the Executive Branch*. Rudalevige writes frequently on executive power, the administrative presidency, and national politics, including as a masthead contributor to the *Wash-*

ington Post's "The Monkey Cage" blog; he is the creator of "Founding Principles," a series of videos on American government available from PBS LearningMedia.

Kristine Simmons is vice president for government affairs at the Partnership for Public Service, a nonpartisan, nonprofit organization dedicated to making the federal government more effective for the American people. She leads the partnership's work on Capitol Hill and serves as a member of the senior leadership team and the Center for Presidential Transition. Prior to joining the partnership, she served as a special assistant for domestic policy to President George W. Bush and handled issues pertaining to government reform and management. Earlier in her career, she was the staff director of the U.S. Senate Subcommittee on Oversight of Government Management and the chairman's primary adviser on government management, government organization, and the federal workforce. She also served as a professional staff member for the U.S. Senate Committee on Governmental Affairs and the U.S. House of Representatives Committee on Government Reform and Oversight.

Geovette E. Washington served as general counsel and senior policy advisor for the Office of Management and Budget at the White House from 2013 to 2015. She currently serves as senior vice chancellor and chief legal officer at the University of Pittsburgh, a position she has held since August 2015. She joined OMB after serving as deputy general counsel at the U.S. Department of Commerce from 2010 to 2013. Prior to that, she spent fourteen years in the District of Columbia litigation firm of Baach Robinson and Lewis PLLC (now Lewis Baach Kaufman Middlemiss PLLC). She received her undergraduate degree from Wesleyan College in Macon, Georgia, and her law degree from the Duke University School of Law.

ADDITIONAL SYMPOSIUM PARTICIPANTS

Boris Bershteyn is a partner at Skadden, Arps, Slate, Meagher & Flom, LLP. Bershteyn previously served as the acting administrator of the Office of Information and Regulatory Affairs at the Office of Management and Budget from 2012 to 2013, as the general counsel of the Office of Management and Budget from 2011 to 2012, and as the deputy general counsel of OMB from 2009 to 2010. Between his tours at OMB, he served as special assistant to the president and associate White House counsel, with responsibility for legal issues in regulatory, economic, health, and environmental policy. Before joining the Obama administration, he was a litigator at Skadden and at Wachtell, Lipton, Rosen and Katz in New York. He also served as a law clerk to Justice David H. Souter of the U.S. Supreme Court and Judge José A. Cabranes of the U.S. Court of Appeals for the Second Circuit. He holds a B.A. in economics and political science from Stanford University and a J.D. from Yale Law School.

Kathleen Peroff served five U.S. presidents during her twenty-nine-year career with the Office of Management and Budget. She last held the position of deputy associate director of the National Security Division, where she led several teams responsible for the budget development and fiscal policy review of the Department of Defense, Department of Veterans Affairs, Intelligence agencies, and the National Nuclear Security Agency. In this capacity, she oversaw the analysis of over one-half of the U.S. federal discretionary budget. A recognized expert in the field of national security budgetary and fiscal policy, her opinions were sought out by the most senior policy officials within the West Wing. Peroff recommended and shaped critical national security budget and fiscal policy issues following the attacks of September 11, 2001, and during the implementation of sequestration reductions. Earlier in her OMB career, she oversaw a variety of domestic agencies, including those having energy, space, science, and housing missions. As a member of the senior executive service, Kathleen Peroff received four Presidential Rank Awards—a recognition bestowed annually to only the highest performing career officials in the executive branch. She is president of Peroff and Associates, and an elected fellow of the National Academy of Public Administration. Prior to her federal experience, she was a professor at the University of Maryland, College Park. She has a Ph.D. from the University of Wisconsin.

Kathryn Stack is CEO of KB Stack Consulting. She had a distinguished career in the federal government, including twenty-seven years at the White House OMB, where she served under five presidents. Under the Barack Obama and George W. Bush administrations, she helped federal agencies design innovative grant-making models that allocate funding based on evidence and evaluation. While at OMB, she oversaw budget, policy, legislation, regulations, and management issues for the Departments of Education and Labor, the Social Security Administration, the Corporation for National and Community Services, and major human services programs including Head Start, Temporary Assistance for Needy Families, child welfare, and food and nutrition assistance. She co-led a review of science and mathematics education programs across fourteen federal agencies, which spurred development and adoption of common evidence guidelines for evaluating a broad range of other programs. In addition, she devised strategies for sharing data—while preserving privacy protections—across federal agencies. After retiring from the federal government in 2015, Stack served for several years as vice president at the Laura and John Arnold Foundation where she focused on building federal, state, and local government capacity to link data and evaluate programs and launched projects to identify the most effective strategies for treating opioid addiction. She is now an independent consultant working with partners in federal, state, and local government and in the academic, nonprofit, and philanthropic communities that collaborate to improve the impact of social programs using evidence and innovation. Stack is a graduate of Cornell University and a fellow of the National Academy of Public Administration.

Index

Across-the-board cuts, 49–53
Administration for Children and Families (ACF), 189
Affordable Care Act (ACA, 2010), 31, 61–62, 125
Afghanistan War, 26
Agency budget requests, 72
Agency guidance documents, 157–59, 162–63
Agency Transition Director's Council, 271–72
Agriculture Department, U.S., 88
American Recovery and Reinvestment Act (ARRA, 2009), 24, 245
Anderson, Barry, 20
Antideficiency Act (1884), 30–31, 73–74, 82–86, 89–90
Apportionment of appropriated funds, 73–76
Appropriations bills: continuing resolutions and, 22, 30–32, 81; for defense spending, 26; OMB tracking of, 56–57, 126, 242; president's budget request and, 44; Reagan and defense spending, 18; regular order and, 29; sequestration and, 51–52
Appropriations Clause, 83
Armstrong, Thomas, 75

Backdoor spending, 15
Bailey Task Force on Intergovernmental Program Coordination, 54

Balanced Budget and Emergency Deficit Control Act (Gramm-Rudman-Hollings, 1985), 21, 49–51
BCA (Budget Control Act, 2011), 25, 53
BEA (Budget Enforcement Act, 1990), 21–22, 24, 51–52, 244
Benefit-cost analyses, 152, 154–57, 215
Biden, Joe, 233
Biotechnology regulations, 215
BOB. *See* Bureau of the Budget
Boehner, John, 25
Bolten, Joshua, 276
Border wall with Mexico, 31, 72, 80–81, 104, 112
Bose, Meena, 1
Bottom-up budgeting, 14–15
Bowles, Erskine, 133–34
Bowsher v. Synar (1986), 50, 54
Brat, Dave, 61
Brownlow Committee, 117
Brundage, Percival, 133
Budget and Accounting Act (1921), 12–13, 70, 120
Budget Bureau, 120
Budget Control Act (BCA, 2011), 25, 53
Budget Data Request, 112
Budget deficits. *See* Deficits
Budget Enforcement Act (BEA, 1990), 21–22, 24, 51–52, 244
Budget estimates, 19, 27, 51, 59–60, 244, 246

Budget gimmicks, 20–21
Bureau of the Budget (BOB): budgetary process regular order, 14–16; establishment of, 12–13, 118; Great Depression and WWII, 14; New Deal spending and, 13; president's program and, 120–24; reorganization to OMB, 16, 54–55, 208, 238. *See now* Office of Management and Budget
Burwell, Sylvia Mathews, 276
Bush, George H. W., 21–22, 157–58
Bush, George W.: agency guidance documents and, 157–58; budget priorities of, 23–24, 253; executive order process and, 130; Great Recession and, 24; legislative draft bills of, 125; OIRA and agency proposal reviews, 148; OIRA staff and, 162; OMB influence and, 196–97; PART for OMB performance review, 212, 253–56; second-term transition and, 276; transfer of power to Obama, 272

Cameron, Charles, 127
Canes-Wrone, Brandice, 44
CAP (Cross-Agency Priority) goals, 218
CARES (Coronavirus Aid, Relief, and Economic Security Act, 2020), 35
Carter, Jimmy, 18, 131
Cassidy, Bill, 53
CBA. *See* Congressional Budget and Impoundment Control Act
CBO. *See* Congressional Budget Office
CBP (Customs and Border Protection), 178–79
Centers for Disease Control and Prevention (CDC), 72
Central clearance, 4–5, 117–43; bureaucratic management and, 135–38; current procedures for, 124–27; executive orders and, 127–35; history of, 120–24; president's program, management of, 119–27
CEQ (Council of Environmental Quality), 215
Cheney, Dick, 23, 136–37
Chief Financial Officers Act (1990), 208–09, 247
Circular A-4, 156–57, 165
Circular A-11, 72, 213
Circular A-19, 123–24, 211–12
Citizenship and Immigration Services, 88
Classical budgeting, 14–15
Clendenin, Barry, 136
Climate change, 72
Clinger-Cohen Act (1996), 217
Clinton, Bill: budget priorities of, 22–23; executive orders and, 133, 135, 212; government shutdowns and, 31, 60, 84; OIRA and agency proposal reviews, 147–48, 151; OMB and CBO conflict, 60–61; RMOs and reorganization of OMB, 250–53
Clinton v. City of New York (1998), 76
Code of Federal Regulations, 160–61
Coercive deficiencies, 12–13
Coglianese, Cary, 160
Concurrent resolutions, 17–18, 58
Congress: 1920s budgets and, 12–13; appropriations bills, 29; budget committees, 3, 17, 58–59, 239–40; confirmation requirements for OMB directors, 2, 17, 54, 239; debt limits and, 31–32; executive branch reorganization, limits on, 87; executive budgets, policing of, 89–91; expectations of OMB, 207, 211, 216–20; increase in number of OMB offices, 208–09; influence in agency decision-making, 183; political polarization and partisanship of, 2, 241; presidential power, constraints on, 17, 74; president's program and, 119, 125–27; reconciliation bills, 17–18; transfer and reprogramming of funds, 79. *See also* Congressional budget process; Government shutdowns; *specific legislation*
Congressional Budget and Impoundment Control Act (CBA, 1974): budgetary control and, 242–44; budget committees created by, 3, 17; executive budget and, 70;

needed amendments to, 90; OMB relationship with Congress and, 57–59; OMB role in fulfillment of requirements, 107; on policy impoundments, 76–78; role of, 2, 239; submission deadline for president's budget, 107, 111; Ukraine, withholding appropriated funds from, 234–35; violations of, 64, 78

Congressional Budget Office (CBO): conflict with OMB, 59–62; establishment and role of, 3, 58–59, 239–40; mandatory spending projections, 32–33; on Trump and national debt, 27

Congressional budget process, 3–4, 41–68; budgetary information, politics of, 57–62; classical budgeting and, 14–15; Congressional Budget and Impoundment Control Act and, 17; efforts to control OMB and, 54–57; hearings, 45–46; OMB as enforcer of congressional choices, 49–54; partisanship and, 63–64; president's budget request and, 42–49; Reagan's budget priorities and, 20

Congressional Research Service (CRS), 27, 58, 87

Congressional Review Act (CRA, 1996), 159

Consumer Financial Protection Bureau, 74

Continuing resolutions (CRs), 22, 30–32, 81

Contract for America, 22

Cook, Ian, 44

Cooper, Charles, 134

Coronavirus Aid, Relief, and Economic Security Act (CARES, 2020), 35

Corporation for National and Community Service, 188

Council of Environmental Quality (CEQ), 215

Coven, Martha B., 4, 101

COVID-19 pandemic, 34–35

CRA (Congressional Review Act, 1996), 159

Crisis response, 112–13

Cross-Agency Priority (CAP) goals, 218

CRS (Congressional Research Service), 27, 58, 87

Cruz, Ted, 62

Customs and Border Protection (CBP), 178–79

DACA (Deferred Action for Childhood Arrivals) program, 178

Daniels, Mitch, 253

Darman, Richard, 21, 135–36

Data calls, 112

Dawes, Charles, 13, 120–21

DDM (deputy director for management), 208, 218, 271–72

Dean, John, 134

Debt. *See* National debt

Debt ceiling, 25, 30–32

Debt-to-GDP ratio: Bush (G. H. W.) and, 21; Bush (G. W.) and, 21, 23; COVID-19 pandemic and, 35; Great Recession and, 16; Obama and, 24–25; OMB control and, 11, 34; Reagan and, 19; Trump and, 27; uncontrollables and defense spending, 33

Defense spending: border wall with Mexico, 81; in Carter vs. Reagan budgets, 18–19; as discretionary spending, 33; exclusion from sequestration, 26; president's budget request and, 44; in Trump budgets, 73

Deferral of funds, 76–78

Deferred Action for Childhood Arrivals (DACA) program, 178

Deficits: in 1920s, 12; Bush, (G. W.) and, 21–22, 253; Clinton and, 22–23, 60; COVID-19 pandemic and, 35; discretionary spending and, 30, 33; Great Recession and, 16, 23–25; Obama and, 23–25, 257; OMB's impact on budget totals and, 11; partisan politics and, 241; Reagan and, 18–21, 49; reduction of, 18–19, 26–28, 49–52; top-down budgeting and, 15, 34; Trump and, 26–27, 72–73; WWII and, 14

Deputy director for management (DDM), 208, 218, 271–72

Dickinson, Matthew J., 6–7, 233
Digital Accountability and Transparency Act (2014), 216–17
Directors of OMB: career employees vs. political appointees as, 221–22; divisions, reconsideration of, 268; dual appointments, 28, 200, 235; list, 279–80; presidential control of policy through, 16–18; presidential transitions and, 274, 276; role of, 2, 109; Senate confirmation of, 2, 17, 54, 239; senior status of, 238
Dole, Robert, 22
Donovan, Shaun, 48
Douglas, Lewis, 13
Dudley, Patrick, 156
Duffey, Michael, 64

Earmarking, 29
Education Department, 88, 155
E-Government Act (2002), 209, 217, 247
Ehrlichman, John, 239
Eisenhower, Dwight, 14, 119
Eizenstat, Stuart, 131
Employment Act (1946), 122
Employment and Training Administration (ETA), 188
Entitlement programs: Clinton and spending cuts, 22; health costs and demographic shifts, 3, 15, 27, 32; mandatory spending and, 32–33; Obama and Grand Bargain, 25; OMB's impact on budget totals and, 11; partisan politics and, 28
Environmental Protection Agency (EPA), 88, 133–34, 155–56
EOP. *See* Executive Office of the President
Evidence and Evaluation Agenda, 212
Executive branch reorganization, 86–88
Executive budget, 3, 11–40; in 1920s, 12–13; balancing, 12; budgetary process regular order, 14–16, 29–30; Congress and constraints on presidential power, 17–18; congressional budget process and, 42–49; continuing resolutions, shutdowns, and debt ceiling, 30–32; deadline for submission, 107, 111; establishment of OMB and, 16–17; Great Depression and WWII, 13–14; mandatory spending and, 32–33; OMB role in, 3–4, 70–71; presidential transitions and, 273–74; presidential use of OMB tools for, 211–16. *See also specific presidents*
Executive Office of the President (EOP), 4, 101–16; agency experts and, 105; case studies, 110–13; crisis response, 112–13; establishment of, 14, 102; issues, identification of, 105–06; OMB role in, 102–06, 178; presidential transitions and, 271–77; president's agenda and, 103–04; staff perception of OMB, 106–10; State of the Union Address, preparation of, 111–12. *See also* Office of Management and Budget
Executive orders, 127–35, 165, 211
Executive Order 6247, 128
Executive Order 7298, 128–29
Executive Order 8248, 14, 121, 128
Executive Order 11030, 129, 135, 211
Executive Order 11058, 136
Executive Order 12291, 147, 150
Executive Order 12866, 147–48, 151–52, 158–59, 161, 212, 215–16
Executive Order 13045, 133
Executive Order 13422, 158
Executive Order 13771, 148, 212, 216
Executive Order 13777, 212
Executive Order 13880, 131

FAST-41 (Fixing America's Surface Transportation Act, 2015), 219
Federal agencies: in 1920s, 12–13; agency budget requests, 72; competition for influence in decision making of, 181–83; congressional hearings and, 45; guidance documents for, 157–59, 162–63; ideologies of, 178–79, 190, 194, 197, 199; interagency processes, 184–87; neutral competence vs. ideologies of, 178–79; OMB influence in, 187–97; presidential management and, 177–78; Trump's relationship with, 175. *See also specific agencies*

Federal Data Center Optimization Initiative, 217
Federal employees: on changes in influence of OMB, 196–97; government shutdowns and, 22, 30–31, 83–84; on interagency power and influence, 184–87; number of, 177; on OMB areas of influence, 187–96; on OMB competition for influence, 181–83; summary of OMB influence, 197–200. See also Office of Management and Budget staff
Federal Information Technology Acquisition Reform Act (FITARA, 2014), 217
Federal Labor Relations Authority, 88
Federal Permitting Improvement Steering Council (FPISC), 219
Federal Reserve, 189
Federal Trade Commission (FTC), 189
Fenno, Richard, 15
Filibuster, 29
First Responder Network Authority (FirstNet), 219
Fixing America's Surface Transportation Act (FAST-41, 2015), 219
Focke, Arthur, 129–30
Food and Drug Administration, 156, 157, 196
Forecasting and projections, 19, 27, 51, 59–60, 244, 246
Foundations for Evidence-Based Policymaking Act (2018), 219
FPISC (Federal Permitting Improvement Steering Council), 219
FTC (Federal Trade Commission), 189

General Accounting Office, 13
Gordon, Robert, 268
Gore, Al, 250
Government Accountability Office (GAO): executive apportionment of appropriations oversight, 74–76; government shutdowns and, 84–85; on Mexican border wall funding, 81–82; on OMB withholding funds from Ukraine, 64, 75–76, 235; on policy impoundments, 77; on Trump's deficit spending and national debt, 27

Government Performance and Results Act (GPRA, 1993), 56, 209
Government Performance and Results Modernization Act (2010), 209, 218, 273–74
Government shutdowns: Clinton and, 22–23, 60, 84; Congress and, 84, 90; continuing resolutions and, 22, 30–32, 81; federal employees and, 22, 30–31, 83–84; OMB and, 31, 82–86, 213–14; Trump and, 31, 82–86
Graham, John, 158
Graham, Lindsey, 137
Gramm, Phil, 49
Gramm-Rudman-Hollings Act (1985), 21, 49–51
Grand Bargain, 25
Great Depression, 14
Great Recession (2008–2009), 16, 23–25
Great Society, 15
Gross domestic product (GDP). See Debt-to-GDP ratio
Guidance documents, 157–59, 162–63
Gulick, Luther, 122

Hahn, Robert, 156
Haldeman, H. R., 130
Hanson, Peter, 29
Health and Human Services Department (HHS), 72, 155–56, 254
Heclo, Hugh, 7, 233–34, 237–38, 260
Heinzerling, Lisa, 146
Hensarling, Jeb, 53
Hitter, Thomas E., 6, 207
Holden, Matthew, 179
Hollings, Fritz, 49
Homeland Security Department, 82, 178, 248–49
Howell, William, 44
Hurricane Sandy (2012), 112–13

Immigration and Customs Enforcement (ICE), 80, 82, 178–79
Immigration policies, 80, 89, 178
Impoundment of funds, 76–78
Income Maintenance Branch, 268
Independent commissions, 183
Information and Technology Oversight and Reform, 217–18

Information requests, 124, 270
INS v. Chadha (1983), 79–80, 87
Intellectual Property Enforcement Coordinator, 28
Interior Department, 88, 189
Internal developments at OMB, 6, 207–32; agency management role, 210–20; future needs of OMB, 220–24; infrastructure, 208–10; presidential use of OMB tools for executive budget, 211–16
Interviews with government experts: on high priority White House demands, 269–70; on OMB internal challenges, 266; on OMB work products, 267–68; on outside experience of staff, 269; on policy councils, 275; on second-term transitions, 276
Interviews with OMB aides: on budgeting, 239–46; on management, 247–50; on neutral competence, 258–60; on PMA, PART, and evidence-based analysis, 253–58; on RMOs, 250–53
Iraq War, 26

Johnson, Bruce, 126
Johnson, Clay, 255
Johnson, Lyndon, 15, 119
Joint Select Committee on Deficit Reduction (Super Committee), 25
Joint Study Committee on Budget Control (JSC), 58
Jones, Roger, 122–24
Judicial branch, 88–89
Justice Department, 127, 134, 189

Kamocsai, Peter, 265
Katzen, Sally, 158
Kennedy, John F., 15, 129, 131–32
Kernell, Samuel, 126
Keynesian-inspired fiscal policy, 15
Krause, George, 43–44

"Let's Move!" initiative, 104
Lew, Jack, 31–32
Lew, Jacob J., 1
Lewis, David E., 6, 44, 175
Line Item Veto Act (1996), 76

Management role of OMB, 6, 175–206; agency resistance of OMB, 178–81; areas of influence, 187–96; changes in influence, 196–97; competition for influence, 181–83; increase in, 210–20; interagency power and influence, 184–87; management offices, 247–48; neutral competence and, 247–50; presidential management and, 177–78, 212–13; Resource Management Offices, 209–10, 213, 250–53; summary of influence, 197–200. *See also specific management offices*
Management training, 269
Mandatory spending, 3, 15, 32–33, 51
Mansfield, Mike, 119
Martin, Bernard, 124–26, 137
Mayer, Kenneth, 127
McDonough, Denis, 272
McKinley, William, 119
McNamara, Robert, 136
Media: on OIRA, 145–46; on president's budget request, 43, 46–48
Medicare. *See* Entitlement programs
Mexico, border wall with, 31, 72, 80–81, 104, 112
Middle Class Tax Relief and Job Creation Act (2012), 219
Moe, Terry, 151
Morgan, Iwan, 19–20
Mulvaney, Mick: on deficits, 27; executive branch reorganization and, 86, 88; on Mexico border wall, 104; OMB directives from, 72; as White House chief of staff and OMB director, 235
Murphy, Charles, 119

National Commission on Fiscal Responsibility and Reform (Simpson-Bowles), 25
National Credit Union Administration (NCUA), 189
National debt: in 1920s, 12–13; Bush (G. H. W.) and, 21; Bush (G. W.) and, 23–24; CBO projections of, 27; Clinton and, 22–23; COVID-19 pandemic and, 35; Gramm-Rudman-Hollings Act to

reduce, 21; Great Recession and, 16, 24–25; lack of concern for, 26–27, 34; mandatory spending on interest for, 32–33; Obama and, 24–25; OMB's impact on budget totals and, 11; Reagan and, 18–21; statutory limit on, 31–32; Trump and, 26–27. *See also* Debt-to-GDP ratio

National Emergencies Act (1976), 81

National intelligence reorganization, 248

National Performance Review (NPR), 24, 250

National Security Council (NSC), 102, 186

Natural disasters, 112–13

NCUA (National Credit Union Administration), 189

Neustadt, Richard, 119, 123, 137

Neutral competence, 6–7, 233–63; budgeting and, 239–46; central clearance and, 137; decline of, 258–60; establishment of OMB and, 238–39; ideologies of federal agencies vs., 178–79; management and, 247–50; PMA, PART, and evidence-based analysis, 253–58; RMOs and, 250–53

New Deal, 13–14

New Frontier, 15

Nixon, Richard: apportionment of appropriations, 74; budget priorities of, 57–58; executive order process and, 130; executive power and, 16–18; impoundment strategy, 239; reorganization of BOB to OMB, 16, 54, 208, 238

No Child Left Behind Act (2001), 125

Noe, Paul, 158

Nolan, Beth, 134

NPR (National Performance Review), 24, 250

NSC (National Security Council), 102, 186

Obama, Barack: agency guidance documents and, 158; biotechnology regulations, 215; budget priorities of, 24–26; childhood obesity initiative, 104; Evidence and Evaluation Agenda, 212; final budget request, Congress and, 48–49; Great Recession and, 24–25; immigration policies, 178; legislative draft bills of, 125; OIRA and agency proposal reviews, 148; OMB influence and, 196–97; PART for OMB performance review, 256–57; regulatory lookbacks and, 160; second-term transition and, 276; Sequestration Transparency Act, 52–53; Social Cost of Carbon and, 165; transfer and reprogramming of funds, 79; transfer of power from Bush, 272

Obama, Michelle, 104

OBRA (Omnibus Budget and Reconciliation Act, 1993), 22

OCO (Overseas Contingency Operations), 26

Office of E-Government and Information Technology, 28, 209

Office of Federal Financial Management (OFFM), 28, 209, 217, 247

Office of Federal Procurement Policy (OFPP), 28, 54, 208, 247

Office of Federal Procurement Policy Act (1974), 247

Office of General Council (OGC), 211, 213

Office of Information and Regulatory Affairs (OIRA), 5, 145–71; administrator role, 109; contrasting successes and failures, 164–66; establishment of, 28, 247; evaluation of performance, 149–50; failures of, 154–63; guidance documents and, 157–59; history of, 147–48; media on, 145–46; overview, 208–09; regulatory activity of, 214–16; regulatory lookbacks and, 160–61; RIAs and, 154–57; staff capacity and, 161–63; successes of, 150–54

Office of Legal Counsel (OLC), 83, 85, 134, 186, 214

Office of Management and Budget (OMB), 1–8; apportionment of appropriations, 73–74; budget process and, 3–4, 70–71; congressional budget decisions, enforcement of, 49–54; congressional efforts to control, 54–57; establishment of,

Office of Management and Budget (OMB) (*cont.*)
16, 54–55, 86, 208, 238; government shutdowns and, 31, 82–86; infrastructure, 208–10; management duties, 5–7, 86–88; negative reputation of, 108; OMB 2000 internal study, 250; overview of responsibilities, 1–2, 71; partisan politics and, 63–64; politics of budgetary information and, 57–62; presidential transitions and, 271–77; president's budget request to Congress and, 42–49; Regulatory Impact Analyses, 5, 147–48, 154–57; role in Executive Office of the President, 102–10. *See also* Central clearance; Internal developments at OMB; Management role of OMB; Neutral competence; Recommendations for OMB

Office of Management and Budget staff: agency experts and, 105; appointees and career staff, trust among, 4; overview, 28; program associate directors (PADs), 17, 105, 108–09, 238; recommendations for, 221–24, 268–69; role of, 102–06; Senate confirmation requirements for, 2, 55–56; size of, 2, 15–16, 28, 55, 71, 102, 208; White House staff and, 106–10. *See also* Directors of OMB; Internal developments at OMB; Interviews with OMB aides

Office of Personnel Management (OPM), 186, 196–97, 201

Office of Science and Technology Policy (OSTP), 215

Office of the Secretary of Defense, 186

OGC (Office of General Council), 211, 213

OIRA. *See* Office of Information and Regulatory Affairs

OLC (Office of Legal Counsel), 83, 85, 134, 186, 214

OMB. *See* Office of Management and Budget

OMB 2000 internal study, 250

Omnibus Budget and Reconciliation Act (OBRA, 1993), 22

Omnibus legislation, 29, 30

O'Neill, Paul, 107, 239

OPM (Office of Personnel Management), 186, 196–97, 201

Orszag, Peter, 257

OSTP (Office of Science and Technology Policy), 215

Overseas Contingency Operations (OCO), 26

PADs (program associate directors), 17, 105, 108–09, 238

Pandemic (COVID-19), 34–35

Paoletta, Mark R., 75–76, 78, 85, 235

Paperwork Reduction Act (1980), 147, 150, 161, 208, 247

PART (Program Assessment Rating Tool), 24, 28, 55, 212, 253–58

Partnership for Public Service, 7, 272

Pasachoff, Eloise, 4, 69

Pay-as-you-go (PAYGO) procedures, 21–22, 24, 51–53

Penner, Rudy, 35

Performance Improvement Council (PIC), 219

Perkins, Frances, 117, 122

Peroff, Kathleen, 34

Pfiffner, James P., 3, 11

PMA (President's Management Agenda), 71, 212–13, 218, 253–58

Policy Agendas Project, 45–46

Policy councils, 104, 109, 112, 275

Political appointees: dual appointments, 200, 235; influence on agency decisions, 182, 197; presidential transitions and, 274; reorganization of OMB and, 238; temporary nature of, 221; of Trump, 201

Political polarization and partisanship: budget process and, 2, 3, 11; congressional budget process and, 63–64; continuing resolutions, reliance on, 30; entitlement programs and, 28; government shutdowns and, 84; OMB and CBO conflict, 60–62; party sorting of

Congress, 241; president's budget and, 28–29, 42
Potter, Rachel Augustine, 5, 145
Powell, Colin, 136
The Power of the Purse (Fenno), 15
PPA (program, project, and activity) reports, 52–53
Pre-Election Presidential Transition Act (2010), 271
Presidential Transition Act (1963), 271
Presidential transitions, 271–77. *See also specific presidents*
President's Committee on Administrative Management, 13
President's Management Agenda (PMA), 71, 212–13, 218, 253–58
Professional staff development, 269, 272
Program, project, and activity (PPA) reports, 52–53
Program Assessment Rating Tool (PART), 24, 28, 55, 212, 253–58
Program associate directors (PADs), 17, 105, 108–09, 238
Program examiners, 105
Projections. *See* Forecasting and projections

Rao, Neomi, 152
Reagan, Ronald: agency guidance documents and, 157–58; budget deficits and taxation, 18–21, 241; budget priorities of, 18–21, 49–50; legislative draft bills of, 126; OIRA and agency proposal reviews, 147; OMB and CBO conflict, 59–60
Reciprocal Trade Act (1934), 124
Recommendations for OMB, 265–77; budget review restructuring, 267; divisions, reconsideration of, 268; employee reallocation, 268; internal OMB challenges, 266; OMB staff and, 268–69; presidential transitions and, 271–77; work products, redefinition of, 267–68
Reconciliation bills, 17–18, 22
Reed, Mac, 136
Regular order, 14–16, 29–30
Regulatory Flexibility Act (1980), 215–16

Regulatory Impact Analyses (RIAs), 5, 147–48, 154–57
Regulatory lookbacks, 160–61
Regulatory review. *See* Office of Information and Regulatory Affairs
Rehnquist, William, 134
Reorganization Act (1939), 13–14
Reprogramming of funds, 78–82, 88–90
Rescission of funds, 76–78
Resource Management Offices (RMOs), 209–10, 213, 250–53
Retrospective reviews, 160–61
Reynolds, Molly E., 3, 41
Richardson, Mark D., 6, 175
Rivlin, Alice, 57–59
Roosevelt, Franklin: central clearance and, 117–19, 121; establishment of BOB, 128; Executive Office of the President, establishment of, 102; on executive orders, 128–29; spending increases and, 13–14
Rosenthal, Eric, 6, 175
Rourke, Francis, 186
Rubin, Irene, 23
Rudalevige, Andrew, 5, 117
Rudman, Warren, 49

Sandy, Mark, 234
SAPs (Statements of Administration Policy), 126–27, 212
SCC (Social Cost of Carbon), 165
Schick, Allen, 58, 60
Schultz, George, 17
Second-term presidential transitions, 275–76
Sequestration, 25–26, 49–53, 258
Sequestration Transparency Act (2012), 52–53
Shapiro, Stuart, 146
Shelby, Richard, 64
Simmons, Kristine, 265
Smith, Harold D., 14, 118, 121–22, 135, 251
Social Cost of Carbon (SCC), 165
Social Security. *See* Entitlement programs
Space Force, 72–73
Spending caps, 21–22, 26, 51–53, 63
Staats, Elmer, 123
Staff of OMB. *See* Office of Management and Budget staff

State Department, 44, 82
Statements of Administration Policy (SAPs), 126–27, 212
State of the Union addresses, 111–12
"Status of Administration Legislative Proposals," 125–26
Statutory Pay-As-You-Go Act (2010), 51–52
Steelman, John, 122
Stefan, Melanie, 149
Stockman, David, 16, 18–20, 126
Sunstein, Cass, 145
Supreme Court, U.S.: on Congress and execution of laws, 50, 53–54; on Line Item Veto Act, 76; on transfer and reprogramming of funds, 79–80, 89; on travel ban of Trump, 89
Survey of federal employees: on changes in influence of OMB, 196–97; on interagency power and influence, 184–87; on OMB areas of influence, 187–96; on OMB competition for influence, 181–83; summary of OMB influence, 197–200
Synar, Mike, 50

TARP (Troubled Assets Relief Program), 24
Taxation: Bush (G. H. W.) and, 21–22; Bush (G. W.) and, 23, 253; COVID-19 pandemic and, 35; Great Recession and, 24–25; Obama and, 24–25; political polarization and, 28; Reagan and, 18–21, 241; Trump and, 26–27, 215
Tax Cuts and Jobs Act (TCJA, 2017), 26–27, 125
Technological innovations, 244–46
Toomey, Pat, 53
Top-down budgeting, 15, 20, 24, 34
Transfers of funds, 78–82, 88–90
Transparency: agency guidance documents and, 159; budget documents for, 267; consequences of funding decisions and, 4; Digital Accountability and Transparency Act, 216–17; of OIRA, 152–54; omnibus legislation and, 29–30; regulatory lookbacks and, 160; RIAs and, 155; rulemaking actions, publication of, 215–16; Sequestration Transparency Act, 52–53
Transportation Department, 155–56
Travel ban, 89, 137
Treasury Department, 32, 189, 215, 217
Treasury Forfeiture Fund, 81
Troubled Assets Relief Program (TARP), 24
Truman, Harry, 14, 119, 122–23
Trump, Donald, 4, 69–98; agency guidance documents and, 159, 162–63; apportionment of appropriated funds, 73–76; budget execution, 73–86; budget preparation, 71–73; budget priorities, 26–27, 72–73; congressional policing of executive budget, 89–90; on deregulation, 160; executive branch reorganization, 86–88; executive orders and, 131, 212; government shutdowns and, 31, 82–86; immigration policies, 80, 89, 137, 178–79; impeachment of, 63–64, 75, 233–34; law, politics, and accountability, 88–91; management agenda, 86–88; Mexico, border wall with, 31, 72, 80–81, 104, 112; neutral competence of OMB and, 260; OIRA and, 148, 162, 215; OMB and CBO conflict, 61–62; political appointees of, 200–01, 235; presidential program of, 127; relationship with departments and agencies, 175, 200, 235; rescission, deferral, and impoundment of funds, 76–78; Social Cost of Carbon and, 165; transfer and reprogramming of funds, 78–82; travel ban, 89, 137; Ukraine funding and, 63–64, 74–76, 78, 233–35; Unified Agenda of Regulatory and Deregulatory Actions and, 215–16
Trump v. Hawaii (2018), 89
21st Century Integrated Digital Experience Act (2018), 218

Ukraine, 63–64, 74–76, 78, 233–35
Uncontrollables, 3, 15, 32–33

Unemployment, 34–35
Unified Agenda of Regulatory and Deregulatory Actions, 215–16
United States Agency for International Development (USAID), 196
United States Trade Representative (USTR), 215
U.S. Digital Services (USDS), 218

Vaeth, Matt, 126
Value of a statistical life (VSL), 155–56
Veto bargaining, 127
Vought, Russell, 64, 235

Washington, Geovette E., 6, 207
Wayne, Stephen, 120
Webb, James, 14, 122
Weinberg, Jeffrey, 119, 125
White, Joseph, 44
White House Domestic Policy Council, 109, 133, 238
White House Leadership Development Program, 219
Wildavsky, Aaron, 14
World War I, 31
World War II, 14

Yates, Sally, 134